ECONOMIC ISSUES, PROBLEMS AND PERSPECTIVES

EXCHANGE RATES IN DEVELOPED AND EMERGING MARKETS

PRACTICES, CHALLENGES AND ECONOMIC IMPLICATIONS

ECONOMIC ISSUES, PROBLEMS AND PERSPECTIVES

Additional books in this series can be found on Nova's website under the Series tab.

Additional e-books in this series can be found on Nova's website under the e-book tab.

GLOBAL ECONOMIC STUDIES

Additional books in this series can be found on Nova's website under the Series tab.

Additional e-books in this series can be found on Nova's website under the e-book tab.

ECONOMIC ISSUES, PROBLEMS AND PERSPECTIVES

EXCHANGE RATES IN DEVELOPED AND EMERGING MARKETS

PRACTICES, CHALLENGES AND ECONOMIC IMPLICATIONS

MOHSEN BAHMANI-OSKOOEE
EDITOR

nova publishers
New York

Library of Congress Cataloging-in-Publication Data

Exchange rates in developed and emerging markets : practices, challenges and economic implications / editor, Mohsen Bahmani-Oskooee.
pages cm
Includes index.
ISBN 978-1-62808-164-0 (hardcover)
1. Foreign exchange rates--Developing countries. 2. Foreign exchange--Developing countries. 3. Foreign exchange market--Developing countries. I. Bahmani-Oskooee, Mohsen.
HG3877.E934 2013
332.4'56091724--dc23

2013020310

Published by Nova Science Publishers, Inc. † New York

CONTENTS

In: Exchange Rates in Developed and Emerging Markets
Editor: Mohsen Bahmani-Oskooee
ISBN: 978-1-62808-164-0

Chapter 1

EXCHANGE RATE VOLATILITY AND THE DEMAND FOR MONEY IN CHINA

***Mohsen Bahmani-Oskooee*[1*], *Sahar Bahmani*[2] *and Dan Xi*[3]**

[1]University Distinguished Professor and Patricia and Harvey Wilmeth Professor of Economics, Department of Economics, Center for Research on International Economics, University of Wisconsin-Milwaukee, Milwaukee, WI, US

[2]Economics, University of Wisconsin-Parkside, Kenosha, WI, US

[3]Economics, School of Finance, University of International Business and Economics, Beijing, China

ABSTRACT

China is said to manipulate its currency in order to gain international competitiveness. Since depreciation of the yuan implies appreciation of foreign currencies such as the U.S. dollar, Chinese who hold foreign currencies will experience an increase in domestic currency value of their assets abroad. If they perceive this as an increase in their wealth, they could stimulate their spending at home by demanding more money. Exchange rate volatility or uncertainty may break this link. Thus, in this chapter we propose to estimate the demand for money in China by including the exchange rate and a measure of its volatility in the money demand specification in China.

I. INTRODUCTION

Since introduction of economic reforms in 1978, Chinese economy has been growing steadily and Chinese people have been enjoying increased standard of living. As income grows, so does saving part of which is invested abroad in foreign assets. These assets that are considered to be part of people's wealth could fluctuate in value when the yuan-dollar exchange rate changes. If such changes are volatile, exchange rate uncertainty could change people's desire to hold more or less of domestic currency. Thus, the main purpose of this

* E-mail: bahmani@uwm.edu

chapter is to test and determine whether exchange rate uncertainty has any effect on the demand for money in China. The plan of this chapter is as follows. In Section II we review relevant studies related to the demand for money in China. In Section II we introduce our model and explain estimation method. We then present the empirical results in Section III. Section IV concludes. Data definition and sources are provided in an Appendix.

II. The Literature

One implication of the Quantity Theory of Money is that if an increase in money supply is to be transmitted to an increase in output or prices, the velocity of money should be stable. Therefore, establishing stability of the velocity is important for the effectiveness of the monetary policy. Alternatively, since velocity is proxied by the linear combination of money, price level, and real income, testing stability of the velocity of money is reduced to testing the stability of the linear combination of money, price level and real output or income. The theory that links these variables together is the demand for money function. Thus, the task is reduced to testing the stability of the demand for money by using different measures of monetary aggregates or by introducing a new determinant of the demand for money.

Due to extensive research related to the demand for money, every country seems to have its own literature and China is no exception. Early studies used standard estimation methods to estimate the demand for money in China (e.g., Feltenstein and Farhadian, 1987; Chan et al. 1991; Ma, 1993; and Yi, 1993). Since introduction of the cointegration and error-correction modeling techniques, almost all studies have engaged in cointegration analysis and have tried to establish the stability of the demand for money in China. Example of studies in this later group includes Hafer and Kutan (1994), Huang (1994), Qin (1994), Huang (2000), Bahmani-Oskooee and Wang (2007), Lee and Chien (2008), and Baharumshah, Mohd and Masih (2009). Most of these studies have concluded that the M2 monetary aggregate is cointegrated with income, price level, interest rate, and the exchange rate.

One recent study has deviated from all others by including a measure of economic uncertainty as well as a measure of monetary uncertainty. Bahmani-Oskooee *et al.* (2012) argued that since China has become more market-oriented, it faces possibility of business cycles which introduce economic uncertainty. The idea was originally applied to the U.S. demand for money by Choi and Oh (2003) who found that output uncertainty as a measure of economic uncertainty has negative effect and monetary uncertainty has positive effect on the money demand in the U.S. Unlike Choi and Oh (2003), Bahmani-Oskooee *et al.* (2012) distinguished the short-run effects from the long-run effects and found that in China both measures of uncertainty have only short-run effects.

Pressure by the U.S. on China to allow its currency to appreciate introduces another channel of uncertainty to Chinese in allocating their money holding toward foreign assets. While Mundell (1963) introduced the intuition behind including the exchange rate itself in the demand for money so that we can account for currency substitution, Mcgibany and Nourzad (1995) argued and empirically demonstrated including a measure of exchange rate uncertainty in the demand for money specification in the U.S. They argued that erratic exchange rates can cause uncertainty in the foreign exchange market. This could induce domestic investors to lean towards safer foreign assets and thus, hold less of domestic money. Indeed, the U.S. data supported the negative impact of exchange rate uncertainty on the demand for real M2 monetary aggregate. So did the Iranian data when Bahmani and Bahmani-Oskooee (2012) tested such hypothesis by drawing data from Iran during post-revolutionary period.

III. The Money Demand Model and the Method

As mentioned in the introductory section, the purpose of this chapter is to establish weather exchange rate uncertainty has any effect on the demand for money in China. As such we adopt the following specification from the literature:

$$LnM_t = a + bLnY_t + cLnr_t + eLnEX_t + fLnVEX_t + \varepsilon_t \tag{1}$$

In (1) it is assumed that the demand for real cash balances (M) depends positively on a scale variable, income denoted by y and negatively on the opportunity cost of holding money, the interest rate, r. Thus, the expected signs of an estimate of b and c are positive and negative respectively. To account for currency substitution, it is also assumed that the nominal exchange rate, EX is another determinant. The historical background in including the exchange rate in the money demand function goes back to Mundell (1963) who argued that the demand for money could depend on the exchange rate in addition to income and interest rate. Subsequent studies in the literature have provided theoretical arguments to Mundell (1963) and provided empirical support. The intuition is that an increase in the value of foreign currency in terms of domestic currency (i.e., a devaluation or depreciation of domestic currency) raises domestic currency value of foreign assets held by domestic residents. This could be perceived as an increase in wealth, thus an increase in domestic spending and consequently an increase in demand for money. On the other hand, if a devaluation or depreciation triggers expectation of further devaluation, domestic residents may increase holding of their foreign assets. Hence, they may hold less of domestic money. For that reason an estimate of e could be positive or negative.[1] Finally, a measure of exchange rate volatility VEX is included to determine whether exchange rate volatility has any negative or positive effect on the demand for money in China. Based on the arguments provided in the introductory section, an estimate of *f* could be negative or positive.

Estimate of equation (1) by any method could only yield the long-run effects of exogenous variables on the demand for money. In order to distinguish the short-run effects from the long-run effects, we express (1) in an error-correction modeling format as in equation (2).

Error-correction model outlined by (2) follows the bounds testing approach of Pesaran *et al.* (2001). It is similar to Engle and Granger (1987) approach with a difference that the lagged error-correction terms is replaced by a linear combination of lagged level variables. This could easily be seen by lagging all variables in equation (1) by one period and solving it for ε_{t-1}. In such setting, once equation (2) is estimated the short-run effects are inferred by the

[1] For more on these arguments see Arango and Nadiri (1981) and Bahmani-Oskooee and Pourheydarian (1990).

estimate of coefficients attached to first-differenced variables and the long-run effects are inferred by the estimates of $\rho_1 - \rho_4$ which are normalized on ρ_0.[2]

$$\Delta LnM_t = \alpha + \sum_{i=1}^{n1} \beta_i \Delta LnM_{t-i} + \sum_{i=0}^{n2} \delta_i \Delta LnY_{t-i} + \sum_{i=0}^{n3} \gamma_i Lnr_t + \sum_{i=0}^{n4} \eta_i \Delta LnEX_{t-i} + \sum_{i=0}^{n5} \lambda_i \Delta LnVEX_{t-i} + \rho_0 LnM_{t-1} + \rho_1 LnY_{t-1} + \rho_2 Lnr_{t-1} + \rho_3 LnEX_{t-1} + \rho_4 LnVEX_{t-1} + \mu_t \quad (2)$$

However, for the long-run coefficient estimates not to be spurious, Pesaran *et al.* (2001) recommend establishing joint significance of lagged level variables by using the standard F test with new critical values that they supply.

Since the critical values incorporate integrating properties of all variables, there is no need for pre unit root testing. For cointegration, calculated F statistic must be greater than the upper bound critical value.[3]

IV. The Results

In this section we estimate error-correction model (2) using quarterly data over the period 1983I – 2010 II from China. While exact definition of each variable and sources of the data are provided in an appendix, it should be mentioned that the volatility of the nominal exchange rate is based on GARCH method.[4] GARCH assumes that nominal exchange rate, EX, is a random variable which is drawn from a conditional density function $f(EX_t | EX_{t-1})$. The forecast of EX and its variance are assumed not to be constant and depend on the past information.

In a simple GARCH model we assume EX follows a first order auto-regressive process, i.e. $EX_t = \alpha_0 + \alpha_1 EX_{t-1} + \varepsilon_t$, where ε_t is white noise with $E(\varepsilon) = 0$ and $V(\varepsilon) = h^2$. The conditional mean of EX_t is $\alpha_0 + \alpha_1 EX_{t-1}$ while the unconditional mean is zero. To forecast the variance of EX, we need to estimate the conditional variance of ε_t. The following theoretical specification of a GARCH model is therefore adopted:

$$EX_t = \alpha_0 + \alpha_1 EX_{t-1} + \varepsilon_t \quad (3)$$

$$\varepsilon_t | I_{t-1} \sim N(0, h_t^2) \quad (4)$$

$$V(X_t | I_{t-1}) = V(\varepsilon_t | I_{t-1}) = h_t^2 \quad (5)$$

$$h_t^2 = \beta_0 + \beta_1 \varepsilon_{t-1}^2 + \beta_2 \varepsilon_{t-2}^2 + \ldots + \beta_q \varepsilon_{t-q}^2 + \varphi_1 h^2_{t-1} + \varphi_2 h^2_{t-2} + \ldots + \varphi_p h^2_{t-p} \quad (6)$$

---

[2]For more details of normalization, see Bahmani-Oskooee and Tanku (2008).
[3] Note that the main assumption here is that variables in the model are either I(0) or I(1) or combination of the two.
[4] This section closely follows Bahmani-Oskooee et al. (2010).

where I_{t-1} includes all available information and h_t^2 is the conditional variance. The GARCH (p,q) model outlined by equation 6 is used to generate predicted value of h_t^2 as a measure of volatility of EX.

However, in estimating (6) we must first establish that the ARCH effect exits. The ARCH effect states that the variance of the current error term is a function of the variance of error term in the past. Thus, equation (3) is estimated first and residuals are used to estimate the following ARCH(q) equation:

$$\varepsilon_t^2 = a_0 + a_1 \varepsilon_{t-1}^2 + a_2 \varepsilon_{t-2}^2 + \ldots + a_q \varepsilon_{t-q}^2 \quad (7)$$

A few significant a's will support the ARCH effect. Once ARCH is established, equations (3) and (6) are estimated simultaneously. The order of GARCH is determined by significance of β's and φ's in (6). In most instances a GARCH (1,1) specification is sufficient which is what we follow in this chapter. The results are as follows:[5]

$$\ln EX_t = 0.002901 + 1.059203 \ln EX_{t-1} - 0.097258 EX_{t-2} + \varepsilon_t$$
$$(0.35) \qquad (15.89) \qquad (1.42)$$

$$\hat{\varepsilon}_t^2 = 0.002485 - 0.014850\, \hat{\varepsilon}_{t-1}^2$$
$$(17.20) \qquad (2.61)$$

$$\hat{h}_t^2 = 0.001838 - 0.026188\, \hat{\varepsilon}_{t-1}^2 + 0.577163\, \hat{h}_{t-1}^2$$
$$(0.42) \qquad (0.46) \qquad (0.57)$$

Once the predicted value of h_t^2 as a measure of VEX is generated, we estimate our error-correction model (2). Since data are quarterly, we impose a maximum of six lags on each first-differenced variable and use Akaike's Information Criterion to select the optimum model. The results are reported in Table 1.

From the short-run coefficient estimates reported in Panel A, there is at least one significant coefficient for interest rate, the exchange rate, and the volatility of the exchange rate, implying that all three variables have short-run effect on the demand for money inn China.

More importantly, exchange rate uncertainty seems to have short-run effects but not long-run effects. From the long-run coefficient estimates reported in panel B, only income carries its expected positive sign and significant coefficient. Therefore, in China the transaction demand for money seems to play a major role in the long run. Estimated income elasticity is higher than one, indicating 1% economic growth requires more than 1% increase in money supply to meet the demand for money, signifying some diseconomies of scale and rigidities in the Chinese economy. The long-run estimates, however, are valid only if we establish cointegration among the variables.

[5] Note that the EX variable was de-trended first. Numbers inside the parentheses are the z-ratios.

Table 1. Full-Information Estimate of Equation(2)

Panel A: Short-Run Coefficient Estimates

	Lag Order			
	0	1	2	3
Δ Ln M	-	0.0051 (0.06)	-0.4918 (5.97)	
Δ Ln Y	-0.0076 (0.25)			
ΔLn r	-0.0647 (1.77)	-0.0916 (2.50)	-0.0671 (1.79)	
Δ Ln EX	-0.0708 (1.01)	-0.2423 (2.20)		
Δ Ln VEX	0.0369 (2.20)			

Panel B: Long-Run Coefficient Estimates

Constant	*Ln Y*	*Ln r*	*Ln EX*	*Ln VEX*
5.2627 (1.72)	1.4119 (4.53)	-0.16893 (0.86)	0.041338 (0.07)	0.70254 (1.10)

Panel C: Diagnostic Statistics

F	ECM_{t-1}	*LM*	*RESET*	*Adj.* R^2
3.20	-0.05 (1.38)	13.02	10.40	0.39

Notes:

[a.] Number inside parentheses are absolute value of t-ratios.

[b.] The upper bound critical value of the F statistic at the usual 5% level of significance is 3.61 This comes from Pesaran *et al.* (2001, Table CI-Case III, p. 300).

[c.] LM is the Lagrange multiplier test for serial correlation. It has a χ^2 distribution with 4 degrees of freedom. The critical value at the 5% level of significance is 9.48.

[d.] RESET is Ramsey's specification test. It has a χ^2 distribution with only one degree of freedom. The critical value at the 5% level of significance is 3.84.

The diagnostic statistics are reported in Panel C. The calculated F statistic is not higher than its critical value but very close. Therefore, the significant income elasticity combined with the F test could support the transaction demand for money in the long run. In order to infer the rate at which variables are adjusting to their long-run values, we use the long-run normalized coefficient estimates and calculated the error term using equation (1). We then replaced the linear combination of the lagged level variables in (2) by this calculated lagged error term labeled as ECM_{t-1} and estimate equation (2) one more time after imposing the same optimum lags reported in Table 1. A significantly negative coefficient will reflect adjustment toward long run equilibrium. As can be seen, while the estimated coefficient is negative, it is not significant reflecting very slow adjustment. Even if the estimated coefficient was significant, still 5% of the adjustment takes place in a quarter.

A few other diagnostic statistics are also reported in Panel C. The Lagrange Multiplier (LM) statistic which is distributed as χ^2 with four degrees of freedom is used to test for serial correlation. Our calculated LM statistic is greater than its critical value of 9.48 implying presence of serial correlation. Ramsey's RESET statistic is also reported to test for functional misspecification. It is distributed as χ^2 with only one degree of freedom. Given its critical value of 3.84, this staticstic is highly significant, signifying a misspecified model. Finally, to establish the stability of all coefficient estimates (short run as well as long run) following the literature we apply the well-known CUSUM or CUSUMSQ tests proposed by Brown, Durbin and Evans (1975) to the residuals of the optimum error-correction model. A common practice is to rely upon graphical presentation of these tests as in Figure 1. All coefficients seem to be stable since plot of the two statistics are within critical boundaries represented by straight lines.

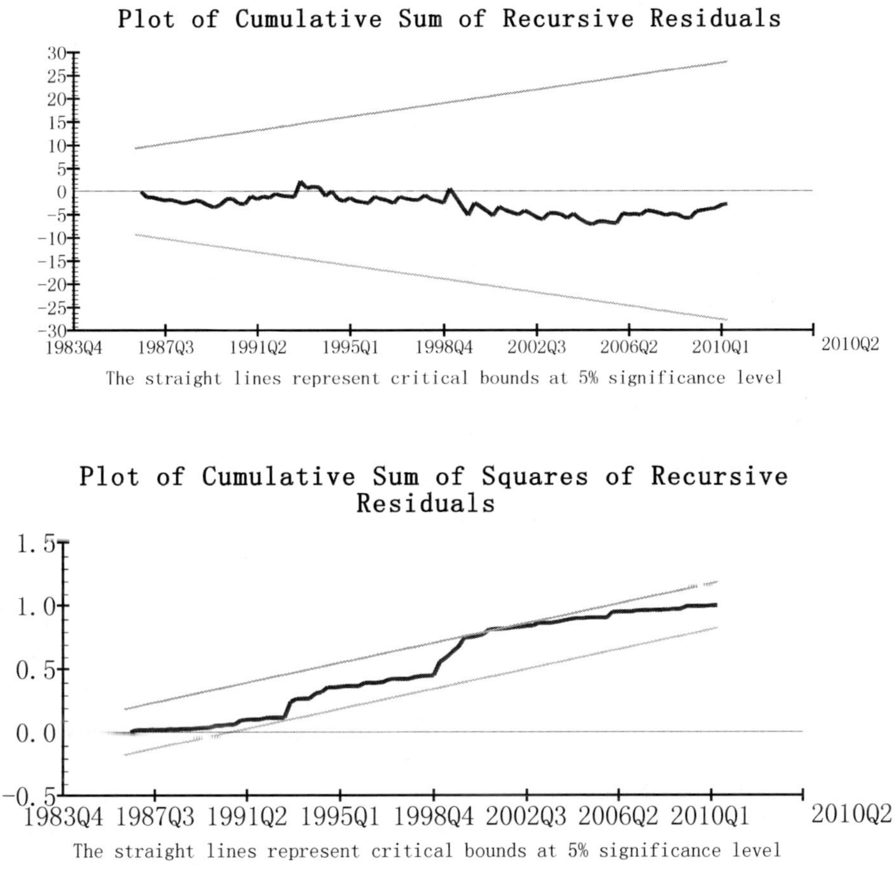

Figure 1. Graphical Presentation of the CUSUM and CUSUMSQ Tests.

SUMMARY AND CONCLUSION

To account for currency substitution, it is a common practice to include the exchange rate in the demand for money. The idea goes back to the Nobel Lauriat, Robert Mundell (1963) who only conjectured this idea. Subsequent studies argued theoretically and demonstrated empirically that when domestic currency depreciates or foreign currency appreciates, the domestic currency value of foreign assets held by domestic residents rises.

If this is perceived as an increase in wealth, then the demand for domestic money could increase. On the other hand, if domestic residents expect further appreciation of foreign currency, they could speculate and hold more of foreign currency or less of domestic currency. Abnormal fluctuation in the exchange rate itself could introduce uncertainty and could have direct impact on the demand for money.

In this chapter we include a measure of exchange rate uncertainty in the specification of the demand for money in China in addition to the exchange rate itself. Of course, income and interest rate are also included to account for transaction and precautionary purpose of cash balances. The model is estimated using quarterly data over the period 1983Q1-2010Q2. The results indicate that exchange rate volatility in China has only short-run effects on the demand for money.

APPENDIX

Data Definition and Sources

All data are quarterly over the period 1983Q1-2010Q2 and they come from the following sources:

- International Financial Statistics of IMF.
- Chinese Statistical Yearbook.

M2 = Money supply measured by real M2. Quasi money is added to M1 to get nominal M2. Since CPI is the only price index available, nominal M2 is deflated by CPI to get the real M2. All variables come from source a. Note that the CPI data was not available for the whole period from source a. Indeed for the period 1983Q1-1989Q4 it comes from Yi (1993).

Y: Quarterly Real GDP. It is defined as Nominal GDP divided by CPI. Nominal Chinese quarterly GDP data are not available from IFS until Q1of 1999. In the absence of quarterly data for the period1983-1998, we generated quarterly figures from annual figures using the method by Bahmani-Oskooee (1998, p. 142). Data come from sources a and b.

r = interest rate defined as deposit rate, source a.

EX = Index of nominal effective exchange rate, source a. A decline reflects a depreciation of Chinese yuan.

VEX = Volatility measure of the nominal effective exchange rate.

REFERENCES

Arango, Sebastian, and M. Ishag Nadiri, (1981). "Demand for Money in Open economies," *Journal of Monetary Economics*, 7, pp. 69-83.

Baharumshah, A. Z., S. H. Mohd, and A. M. M. Masih, (2009), "The Stability of Money Demand in China: Evidence from the ARDL Model", *Economic Systems,* Vol. 33, pp.231-244.

Bahmani, S. and M. Bahmani-Oskooee (2012), "Exchange Rate Volatility and the demand for Money in Iran", *International Journal of Monetary and Financial Economics,* Vol. 5, No. 3 (2012), pp. 268-276.

Bahmani-Oskooee, M. (1998). "Are Devaluations Contractionary in LDCs?", *Journal of Economic Development*, Vol. 23, pp. 131-144.

Bahmani-Oskooee, Mohsen and Mohammad Pourheydarian, (1990). "Exchange Rate Sensitivity of the Demand for Money and Effectiveness of Fiscal and Monetary Policies," *Applied Economics*, 22 pp. pp. 1377-1384.

Bahmani-Oskooee, M. and Y. Wang, (2007), "How Stable is the Demand for Money in China?", *Journal of Economic development*, Vol.32(1), pp. 21-33.

Bahmani-Oskooee, M. and A. Tanku, (2008). "Black Market Exchange Rate vs. Official Rate in Testing the PPP: Which Rate Fosters the Adjustment Process", *Economics Letters,* Vol. 99, pp. 40-43

Bahmani-Oskooee, M., Z. Ardalani, and M. Bolhassani, (2010). "Exchange-Rate Volatility and U.S. Commodity Trade with the Rest of the World", *International Review of Applied Economics,* Vol. 24, pp. 511-532.

Bahmani-Oskooee, M., Y. Wang, and D. Xi (2012), "Economic Uncertainty, Monetary Uncertainty and the Demand for Money in China", *The Chinese Economy*, Vol. 45, pp. 26-37.

Chan, M. L., W. Cheng, and R. Deaves, (1991), "Money Demand in China Revisited: Some New Empirical Evidence", *Journal of Asian Economics*, Vol. 2(1), pp. 137-44.

Choi, W. G., and S. Oh, (2003), A Demand Function with Output Uncertainty, Monetary Uncertainty, and Financial Innovations", *Journal of Money, Credit, and Banking,* Vol. 35(5), pp. 685 709.

Feltenstein, A. and Z. Farhadian, (1987), "Fiscal Policy, Monetary Targets, and the Price Level in a Centrally Planned Economy: an Application to the Case of China", *Journal of Money, Credit and Banking*, Vol. 19, pp. 137-56.

Hafer, R.W. and A. M. Kutan, (1994), "Economic Reform and Long Run Money Demand in China: Implications for Monetary Policy", *Southern Economic Journal*, Vol. 60(4), pp. 936-945.

Huang, G. (1994), "Money Demand in China in the Reform Period: an Error Correction Model", *Applied Economics*, Vol. 29, pp. 713-719.

Huang, C. (2000), "Economic Reform and the Stability of Long-run Demand for Money in China: Some Results from Co-integration Tests", The Chinese Economy under Transition, pp.276-296.

Lee, C. and M. Chien, (2008), "Stability of Money Demand Function Revisited in China", *Applied Economics,* Vol. 40, pp. 3185-3197.

Qin, D. (1994), "Money Demand in China: the Effect of Economic Reform", *Journal of Asian Economics*, Vol. 5, pp. 253-271.

Ma, G. (1993), "Macroeconomic Disequilibrium, Structural Changes, and the Household Savings and Money Demand in China", *Journal of Development Economics,* Vol. 41(1), pp. 115-136.

Mcgibany, J. and F. Nourzad, (1995), "Exchange rate Volatility and the Demand for Money in the U.S.", *International Review of Economics and Finance*, Vol. 4, pp. 411-425.

Mundell, A. Robert, "Capital Mobility and Stabilization Policy under Fixed and Flexible Exchange Rates," *Canadian Journal of Economics and Political Science*, Vol. 29 (November 1963), 475-485.

Pesaran, M. H., Y. Shin, and R. J. Smith., "Bounds Testing Approaches to the Analysis of Level Relationships", *Journal of Applied Econometrics.* Vol. 16 (2001), pp.289 -326.

Yi, G. (1993), "Towards Estimating the Demand for Money in China", *Economics of Planning*, Vol. 26(3), pp. 243-70.

In: Exchange Rates in Developed and Emerging Markets ISBN: 978-1-62808-164-0
Editor: Mohsen Bahmani-Oskooee

Chapter 2

EXCHANGE RATE DYNAMICS, SPECULATION AND LOCALIZATION OF MONETARY POLICY

Gregory Gagnon*
Department of Economics University of Toronto Mississauga,
Mississauga, Ontario, Canada

Abstract

This paper constructs a monetary model of the exchange rate with a speculative bubble using the methods of evolutionary finance and stochastic differential equations. The exchange rate can be decomposed into a continuous time fundamental exchange rate determined by monetary policy and a continuous time bubble that jumps only at integer times. The exchange rate and bubble form a coupled stochastic system. Coupling occurs because the bubble affects monetary policy and monetary policy affects speculation. If monetary policy possesses a form of local attraction and the central bank sets monetary policy to propagate higher bubbles locally, then the exchange rate exhibits bifurcation. The exchange rate also remains trapped in a bounded region, providing an explanation for the empirical observation that exchange rates can move in distinct trading ranges. If speculation is high in comparison to money growth, currency crises result.

Keywords: Evolutionary Finance, Speculative Bubble, Bifurcation, Currency Crisis

1. Introduction

In models of evolutionary finance, investors switch between being speculators and fundamentalists at discrete times based on the past behaviour of the asset price. Fundamentalists examine economic variables and calculate a rational asset price. Speculators extrapolate market trends and de-emphasize economic fundamentals. Their actions create deviations from the fundamental price referred to as bubbles. The aim of evolutionary finance is to analyze the dynamics of bubbles through theorems and computer simulations. Complex

*E-mail address: gregory.gagnon@utoronto.ca

dynamics for bubbles are known to result from switching between fundamentalist and speculative behaviour, cf. Brock and Hommes (1997, 1998), Follmer, Horst and Kirman (2005), Brock, Hommes and Wagener (2005) and Lux and Schornstein (2005).

One typical phenomenon in the evolutionary finance literature is bifurcation of the bubbles, cf. Brock and Hommes (1997,1998). However, the mathematical structures describing evolution of the bubble in Brock and Hommes (1997,1998) are deterministic. Consequently, their bifurcation results do not apply in stochastic economies. Bifurcation analysis in stochastic economies is still in its infancy but constitutes an important issue. The reason is that statistical tests of financial data suggest that asset prices are stochastic rather than chaotic cf. Brock, Hsieh and LeBaron (1991). If asset prices are random rather than deterministic, bifurcation analysis of nonrandom financial markets is of limited use in understanding asset price instability.

The purpose of this paper is to extend the stochastic foreign exchange market with evolutionary dynamics presented in Gagnon (2012) and to analyze the bifurcation of prices. It constructs a discrete time stochastic process for the bubble and continuous time processes for monetary policy and the exchange rate. The motivation for discrete and continuous time trading is that many foreign exchange traders are professionals who trade continuously, whereas many less sophisticated traders who might be speculators change their portfolios less frequently. The model also develops stochastic versions of Brock-Hommes bubbles. Monetary policy is a forward stochastic differential equation whose drift and diffusion coefficients depend on the speculative bubble. It has sometimes been observed that currency crises trigger interest rate changes by central banks. Allowing monetary policy to depend on the bubble formalizes the intuition that policy is sometimes determined by exchange rate speculation. Moreover, both fundamentalists and speculators must form expectations about central bank policy. Consequently, the model also allows the bubble to be affected by monetary policy.

The exchange rate without speculation is referred to as the fundamental exchange rate. It depends on monetary policy via a backward stochastic integral equation. The exchange rate in the market is the fundamental exchange rate plus the bubble. Thus, the model is a variant of the monetary model of the exchange rate which couples monetary policy, the bubble and exchange rate. The monetary model has been controversial since Meese and Rogoff (1983) demonstrated that random walk forecasts of the exchange rate outperformed forecasts based on macroeconomic fundamentals. However, a number of studies have pointed to a resurgence of the monetary model, cf. Rapach and Wohar (2002), Mark and Sol (2001), Clarida, Sarno, Taylor and Valente (2003), Abhyankar, Sarno and Valente (2005). Therefore, it is natural to consider the monetary model with a speculative bubble. It is possible that the empirical failure of the monetary model stems from a failure to account for the kind of speculaton arising in evolutionary finance.

It is assumed that the central bank is interested in propagating higher bubbles. While this might seem counter-intuitive since the usual view is that policymakers strive to stabilize the economy, there are instances where central banks have encouraged speculation. During the 1930's central banks engaged in competitive depreciations to stimulate exports. Monetary policy in the United States under Bretton Woods encouraged speculation against the dollar. More recently, the United States entered into international agreements such as the Plaza Accord to depreciate the dollar. In the post-financial crisis of 2008 environment, depreciation of the U.S. dollar has been crucial in preventing a recurrence of recession. Encouraging depreciation of the domestic currency can result in an export stimulus and this can be regarded as the motive for stimulating bubbles.

However, there should be a bound on the amount of speculation the central bank will encourage. For this reason, it is assumed that monetary policy exhibits a form of local attraction. The paper proves that if the drift and volatility of the money supply exhibit a form of local attraction then the exchange rate exhibits bifurcation. The local attraction means that there are certain open sets where the drift and volatility fluctuate. Beyond these sets there are bounded regions where the drift and volatility are zero. Eventually the drift and volatility become non-zero once again. The pockets of zero money growth are interpreted as reluctance to change policy beyond certain localized bounds. Such behaviour may represent an upper bound on the amount of depreciation to be tolerated. If monetary policy begins in one of these pockets surrounded by the zero money growth regions, the money supply remains trapped in a bounded region. If the regions are disjoint there is a type of exchange rate bifurcation. The exchange rate also remains trapped in a bounded region, providing an explanation for the empirical observation that exchange rates can move in distinct trading ranges.

The principle difference with the results in Gagnon (2012) is that monetary policy in that paper was assumed to counteract bubbles, not encourage them. Neither did policy experience localization in the earlier study. Moreover, this paper proves that if speculation is high in comparison to money growth, currency crises result. The currency crisis manifests itself as unbounded bubbles and is absent from Gagnon (2012). The paper is organized as follows. Section 2 extends the Brock and Hommes (1997,1998) model. Section 3 presents the exchange rate dynamics and section 4 concludes.

2. The Stochastic Foreign Exchange Market

All action happens on complete probability space $(\Omega, \mathcal{F}, P)$ with a right-continuous filtration $(\mathcal{F}_t, t \in R^+)$ such that $\mathcal{F}_0$ contains all P null sets. Random variables are defined on Ω and are $\mathcal{F}$-measurable. If a process is adapted it is with respect to $(\mathcal{F}_t, t \in R^+)$. In particular, we let $(W_t, t \geq 0)$ be a one dimensional standard Brownian motion relative to $(\mathcal{F}_t, t \in R^+)$.

The situation being modelled is a foreign exchange market where some investors switch between being speculators and fundamentalists at discrete times. Fundamentalists focus on monetary policies to determine the exchange rate whereas speculators extrapolate trends. Throughout the paper the terms speculator, noise trader and chartist are used synonomously. In addition, there is a core group of traders who are always fundamentalists and they trade in continuous time. Consequently, the fundamental price of the currency which is referred to as the fundamental exchange rate, is a continuous time stochastic process. The investors who change their type trade only at integer times. They constitute a critical mass of the market and can affect the exchange rate. Their trades generate a deviation from the fundamental price called the bubble. It is denoted by w_n at time n and is constant on $[n, n+1)$ where $n \geq 0$ is an integer. Of course the fundamental exchange rate fluctuates on the interval $[n, n+1)$. This assumption captures the situation that some agents may only alter their portfolios infrequently. To this end, consider the following coupled discrete-continuous time dynamical system where the discrete dynamics are defined for $n \in Z^+$ and the continuous dynamics are defined for $t \in R^+$.

$$w_n = R_{n-1}^{-1} q_{2,n-1} g_n w_{n-1}, n \geq 0, \quad (w_{-1}, w_{-2}, w_{-3}) = \text{initial condition} \quad (2.1)$$

$$q_{1,n} = Z_n^{-1} \exp(\beta(\frac{1}{s\gamma^2} R_{n-1} w_{n-1})(R_{n-1} w_{n-1} - w_n) - C), \quad n \geq -1 \quad (2.2)$$

$$q_{2,n} = Z_n^{-1} \exp(\beta(\frac{1}{s\gamma^2}(w_n - R_{n-1} w_{n-1})(g_{n-1} w_{n-2} - R_{n-1} w_{n-1}))), n \geq -1, (2.3)$$

$$Z_n = \exp(\beta(\frac{1}{s\gamma^2} R_{n-1} w_{n-1})(R_{n-1} w_{n-1} - w_n) - C) +$$

$$\exp(\beta(\frac{1}{s\gamma^2}(w_n - R_{n-1} w_{n-1})(g_{n-1} w_{n-2} - R_{n-1} w_{n-1}))) \quad (2.4)$$

$$g_n = g + f(k_{n-1}^{\mu}), \quad n \geq 1, \quad g_0 = g_{-1} = g_{-2} = g > 0 \quad (2.5)$$

$$k_t^{\mu} = k_0^{\mu} + \int_0^t b(s, \mu_s, k_s^{\mu})\, ds + \int_0^t \sigma(s, \mu_s, k_s^{\mu})\, dW_s, \quad t \in R^+ \quad (2.6)$$

$$R_n = 1 + r + b(n, \mu_n, k_n^{\mu}) \quad n \geq 0; R_{-1} = R_{-2} = 1 + r \quad (2.7)$$

$$x_t^{\mu} = \alpha^{-1} \int_t^{\infty} \exp(\frac{t-s}{\alpha}) E(k_s^{\mu} | \mathcal{F}_t)\, ds, \quad t \in R^+ \quad (2.8)$$

$$y_t^{\mu} = x_t^{\mu} + w_n, \quad t \in R^+, n \leq t < n+1, n \geq 0 \quad (2.9)$$

In (2.1)-(2.9) β, γ, g, C, r and s are positive parameters from the Brock-Hommes system and f is a bounded, continuous function. Their precise role in the model is detailed below. The process $\mu \equiv (\mu_s, s \geq 0)$ is the set of tuples describing the time evolution of speculation. It is defined by $\mu_s = (w_s, m_s)$ where $w_s = w_n, m_s = m_n = q_{2,n}$ for $s \in [n, n+1)$ and integers $n \geq 0$. The $q_{i,n}, i = 1,2$ are the probabilities of being a fundamental investor and speculator respectively at integer times $n \geq -1$. In a strict sense the process $(w_n, n \geq 0)$ is the bubble. However, for convenience μ_s is referred to as the bubble at time s. The initial conditions in (2.1), w_{-1}, w_{-2}, w_{-3}, are initial conditions for the bubble and are required to generate the bubble at $t = 0$. Direct inspection of (2.2)-(2.5) reveals that the bubbles at times $-1, -2$ and -3 are the only variables required to generate w_0. The initial bubbles may be random variables that are $\mathcal{F}_0$ measurable or real numbers.

The process $(x_t^{\mu}, t \geq 0)$ is the fundamental exchange rate. It is defined as the natural logarithm of the domestic price of one unit of foreign currency; hence x_t^{μ} can be positive or negative. For expositional purposes it is easier to refer to x_t^{μ} as the exchange rate instead of the logarithm of the exchange rate. It is the exchange rate yielded by the monetary model. This model rests on long run structural relations such as interest parity and emphasizes foreign and domestic money supplies as well as incomes as the determinants of exchange rates. These variables are combined into a stochastic process denoted by $(k_t^{\mu}, t \geq 0)$; k_0^{μ} is the initial condition which can depend on μ_0. The parameter α is a constant from the economic model that ensures the integral in (2.8) exists, cf. Flood and Garber (1983). For simplicity $(k_t^\mu, t \geq 0)$ is referred to as the money supply process and is assumed to be determined by the domestic central bank. Once the process $(w_t, t \geq 0)$ is added to the fundamental exchange rate we obtain the process $(y_t^\mu, t \geq 0)$, the observed exchange rate in the market.

The bubble is modelled as an additive deviation from the logarithm of the exchange rate. Another method is to specify a Brock-Hommes bubble as an additive deviation from the exchange rate instead of its natural logarithm. In this case, it is necessary to use a linear stochastic differential equation for the money supply to ensure the exchange rate is positive. Using the logarithm of the exchange rate as the relevant price allows a general stochastic differential equation to be used in the money supply equation. Since the purpose of any paper dealing with noise trader impact on prices is to capture the deviation from the relevant market price, our specification is a rational one.

Theorem 2.1: Let b be bounded, nonegative and continuous on $R^+ \times R^3$ and σ be continuous on $R^+ \times R^3$. Suppose b, σ satisfy assumption 3.1 of section 3 and that the initial vector of bubbles is bounded on Ω. Let $k_0^\mu \in L^4(\Omega, \mathcal{F}_0, P)$. Then $(x_t^\mu, t \geq 0)$ is continuous in probability. Consequently, $(y_t^\mu, t \geq 0)$ has endogenous jumps at integer times.

Continuity in probability means that for each $t \in R^+$ and each $\delta > 0, \lim_{s \to t} P(|x_s^\mu - x_t^\mu| > \delta) = 0$. The result is weaker than Gagnon (2012) where the sample paths are continuous a.e., however, the previous paper treats the case where σ depends only on t rather than on the bubble and money supply. When σ depends on the money supply and bubble it is not possible to establish the sample path bounds in Gagnon (2012) and those bounds are key to proving sample path continuity. However, using more general functions in the drift and diffusion coefficient will give policy localization substance. This is treated in section 3; in fact theorem 2.1 will be proved in section 3. Note that the terms diffusion coefficient and volatility are used interchangeably. Similarly, the notion of w_n giving an endogenous jump at time n is weaker than Gagnon (2012) since it occurs in probability rather than along almost all sample paths. Nevertheless, a model with endogenous jumps is interesting. Usually, financial models use additive Poisson processes to capture market jumps and these processes are invariably exogenous.

The stochastic differential equation (SDE) defined by (2.6) differs from those often considered in the literature since the process $(\mu_s, s \geq 0)$ in the drift and diffusion comes from a discrete time process which is itself linked to past values of the SDE. Consequently, equation (2.6) is not a stochastic delay differential equation of the class analyzed in Mohammed and Scheutzow (1997). The interpretation of the equation is that the central bank considers speculation when it sets monetary policy. Conditions for the existence and uniqueness of this class of equations are discussed in section 3. It is clear that when $k_t^\mu = k_0^\mu + \int_0^t b(s, \mu_s, k_s^\mu)\, ds + \int_0^t \sigma(s, \mu_s, k_s^\mu)\, dW_s$ then $x_t^\mu = k_t^\mu + \alpha^{-1} \int_t^\infty \exp(\frac{t-s}{\alpha}) E(\int_t^s b(u, \mu_u, k_u^\mu)\, du | \mathcal{F}_t)\, ds$. Since the interval $[t, \infty)$ occurs in the integration, equation (2.8) is an infinite horizon backward stochastic equation. However, the money supply-exchange rate system is different from the forward-backward systems in the probability literature cf. Antonelli (1993), Peng and Shi (2002) and Hu and Yong (2000).

Equations (2.1)-(2.5) define the dynamics of the bubble. These equations are derived in a manner analagous to Brock-Hommes (1997,1998). One main difference comes from the fact that with interest parity the interest rate depends on expected depreciation and varies over time; Brock and Hommes assumed the interest rate was constant. In our model the foreign interest rate is constant and is denoted by r. Following Ikeda and Shibata (1995) expected depreciation at time n is $b(n,\mu_n,k_n^\mu)$. According to interest parity, the total return for lending at time n is $R_n = 1+r+b(n,\mu_n,k_n^\mu)$.

As in Brock-Hommes (1997,1998), the bubble evolves in discrete time and depends on the percentages of agents who are fundamentalists and speculators. These agents constitute a large enough segment of the market to create a deviation from x_t^μ. The agents who change type are "bounded rational" in the sense that they solve a sequence of one period mean-variance optimization problems rather than a lifetime optimization problem. Their bounded rationality is also reflected in their belief that γ^2, the conditional variance of excess returns, is constant. This essential structure yielding equations (2.1)-(2.5) is detailed below.

In our model the bounded rational agents allocate their wealth to either money or the risk free domestic bond. The money in the portfolio can be foreign or domestic currency. To have a close connection with Brock-Hommes structures assume that foreign currency is held by agents as an asset and that domestic currency is used for transactions purposes. Wealth is measured in domestic currency; A_n denotes wealth at time n. At time $n+1$ the agent will have wealth A_{n+1} given by $A_{n+1} = R_nA_n + (y_{n+1}^\mu + d_{n+1} - R_n y_n^\mu)h_n$ where $R_n = 1+r+b(n,\mu_n,k_n^\mu)$, $d_{n+1} = y_{n+1}^\mu r$ and h_n is the number of foreign currency units purchased at time n. The wealth equation requires explanation. Clearly, $y_n^\mu h_n$ is the amount of domestic currency invested in foreign exchange. Every domestic bond earns a return equal to R_n. Bond holdings measured in domestic currency are $A_n - y_n^\mu h_n$; the total bond return is $R_n(A_n - h_n y_n^\mu)$. Since the foreign interest rate is r, the wealth generated by every unit of foreign currency when measured in domestic currency is $y_{n+1}^\mu(1+r)$. Adding up the terms yields total wealth at $n+1$.

Speculators and fundamentalists are distinguished by the expectation of the exchange rate in the next period. Fundamentalists use conditional expectations i.e. rational expectations. At time n, their predictor of the exchange rate at $n+1$ is $E(y_{n+1}^\mu|\mathcal{F}_n)$. Speculators have expectations $E_n(y_{n+1}^\mu) \equiv E(y_{n+1}^\mu|\mathcal{F}_n) + g_n(y_{n-1}^\mu - x_{n-1}^\mu)$. The term $g_n(y_{n-1}^\mu - x_{n-1}^\mu)$ allows the bubble at $n-1$ to affect the predicted exchange rate at $n+1$. In effect, the parameter $g>0$ in (2.5) reflects a core tendency to extrapolate trends. The term $f(k_{n-1}^\mu)$ in g_n allows changes in the money supply to affect trend chasing. For example, if f is nonnegative and monotone increasing, raising the money supply increases the tendency to chase trends. This is plausible behaviour since higher money growth induces higher depreciation. Knowing this, noise traders would have a more definite trend to extrapolate.

At each nonnegative integer time n, every agent in the group which changes type decides whether to be a speculator or fundamentalist. The decision is based on the profitability of each trading type in the previous period. The parameter β measures the intensity to switch predictors. It is assumed that the conditional expectation forecast is available at constant cost $C \geq 0$. Clearly, C is the cost of becoming an informed trader. To formalize these notions let fundamentalists be type one traders and speculators be type two traders. Time n fundamentalist expectations of the exchange rate at $n+1$ are denoted by $E_{1n}(y_{n+1}^\mu) = E(y_{n+1}^\mu|\mathcal{F}_n)$ and speculators' expectations are $E_{2n}(y_{n+1}^\mu) \equiv E_n(y_{n+1}^\mu) = E(y_{n+1}^\mu \mathcal{F}_n) + g_n(y_{n-1}^\mu - x_{n-1}^\mu)$. Moreover, all these agents are bounded rational. Bounded rationality is reflected in the expectations of speculators since they extrapolate trends. It is also reflected in the assumption that both trading types assume constant conditional variance of excess returns over time and that they solve a sequence of one period mean-variance maximization problems. Whether speculators or fundamentalists, these agents are essentially short term investors.

Assumption 2.1: Let $V_{jn}(y^{\mu}_{n+1}+d_{n+1}-R_n y^{\mu}_n)$ be the conditional variance of excess returns, $y^{\mu}_{n+1}+d_{n+1}-R_n y^{\mu}_n$, for trader type j at time n. Then $V_{jn}(y^{\mu}_{n+1}+d_{n+1}-R_n y^{\mu}_n)=\gamma^2 \quad \forall j=1,2,n\in Z_+$.

Assumption 2.2: Each trading type is a mean-variance maximizer and solves the problem $max_{h_n} E_{jn}A_{n+1}-\frac{s}{2}V_{jn}(A_{n+1})$. The parameter s is risk aversion and $E_{jn}A_{n+1}, V_{jn}(A_{n+1})$ are the conditional mean and variance of A_{n+1} for trader type j at time n respectively.

The optimization problem in assumption (2.2) is well defined since A_{n+1} depends on holdings of foreign currency h_n and can be solved with calculus. Equilibrium holdings are $h_n = s^{-1}\gamma^{-2}E_{jn}(y^{\mu}_{n+1}+d_{n+1}-R_n y^{\mu}_n)$. Let $q_{j,n-1}$ be the percentage of trader type j at the beginning of time n. Imposing market clearing implies $\sum_{j=1}^{2} q_{j,n-1}E_{jn}(y^{\mu}_{n+1}+d_{n+1}-R_n y^{\mu}_n)=0$. If there are only rational agents this condition collapses to $R_n x^{\mu}_n = E(y^{\mu}_{n+1}|\mathcal{F}_n)+E(d_{n+1}|\mathcal{F}_n)$ since they assume there is no bubble. With speculators market clearing implies

$$R_n y^{\mu}_n = q_{1,n-1}(E(y^{\mu}_{n+1}|\mathcal{F}_n)+E(d_{n+1}|\mathcal{F}_n))+$$
$$q_{2,n-1}(E(y^{\mu}_{n+1}|\mathcal{F}_n)+E(d_{n+1}|\mathcal{F}_n)+g_n(y^{\mu}_{n-1}-x^{\mu}_{n-1})) \quad (2.10)$$

In writing the market clearing condition we assume linearity of noise trader expectations. Specifically, $E_{2n}(y^{\mu}_{n+1}+d_{n+1}-R_n y^{\mu}_n)=E_n(y^{\mu}_{n+1})+E(d_{n+1}|\mathcal{F}_n)-R_n y^{\mu}_n$. By assumption agents use rational expectations for interest returns but not the exchange rate. This specification preserves an essential feature of the Brock-Hommes equations. Furthermore, this assumption represents bounded rationality in that investors use different expectations for interest returns and exchange rate capital gains.

Combining market clearing with only rational agents and market clearing with both types of agents yields $R_n(y^{\mu}_n-x^{\mu}_n)=q_{2,n-1}g_n(y^{\mu}_{n-1}-x^{\mu}_{n-1})$. Of course, this becomes equation (2.1) if we insist that loans made at the beginning of time n command interest rate R_{n-1}. In this case R_{n-1} would replace R_n in the optimization problem. Again, this delay in updating the interest rate is a manifestation of bounded rationality and maintains a closer connection with the original Brock-Hommes structures. Since Brock and Hommes (1998) take the percentages of trader types at n to be their values at the end of $n-1$, it is consistent to apply this convention to the interest rate as well. The theorems in section 3 are unchanged if R_n replaces R_{n-1} in (2.1). Immediately after the markets clear, $q_{1,n}$ and $q_{2,n}$ become the new percentages of trader types and enter the market clearing problem at $n+1$.

Equations (2.2)-(2.4) complete the model since they specify a dynamical system for the percentages of trader types as in Brock and Hommes (1998). For instance, in (2.2) the probability of being a fundamentalist at the beginning of $n+1$ is linked to $(s^{-1}\gamma^{-2}R_{n-1}w_{n-1})(R_{n-1}w_{n-1}-w_n)-C$. The cost of the fundamental predictor as well as the extra interest return, $R_{n-1}w_{n-1}-w_n$, determine the probability of being a fundamentalist. Similarly, excess returns and the lagged bubbles at $n-1$ as well as $n-2$ affect the probability of noise trading at the beginning of $n+1$.

Assumption 2.3: The function $f: R\rightarrow R$ in (2.5) is nonnegative, increasing, bounded and continuous. The function $b: R^+\times R^3\rightarrow R$ in (2.6) is nonnegative, bounded and continuous and $\sigma: R^+\times R^3\rightarrow R$ in (2.6) is continuous.

There are two issues that must be addressed. First, the money supply and bubble in our model are defined for $t \geq 0$ whereas the Brock-Hommes (1998) bubble is defined $\forall n \in Z$, the set of integers. To start the model at time zero take (w_{-1}, w_{-2}, w_{-3}) as given and set $R_{-1} = R_{-2} = R \equiv 1 + r$; also set $g_{-1} = g_{-2} = g$. Assume that the bubble evolves up to time zero via the original Brock-Hommes equations and via our modified ones for all $t \geq 0$. This evolution holds whether $w_i, i = -1, -2, -3$ are random or deterministic. In this framework, lagged money supplies only affect the bubble for $t \geq 1$. In fact, the ability of the money supply to affect the bubble is one of our key modifications of the Brock-Hommes framework. Another important modification is that the switching probabilities $q_{i,n}, i = 1, 2$ are eventually random since the money supply is random even when the initial bubbles are deterministic. Second, there is an issue of terminology. Specifically, the process for the bubble and percentages of noise traders $((w_s, m_s), s \geq 0)$ which solve (2.1)-(2.5) is called a Brock-Hommes equilibrium. Theorem 2.2, the key result of Brock and Hommes (1997,1998), is critical in acting as a springboard for thinking about bifurcation of the exchange rate. In theorem 2.2 the equilibrium is the sequence of tuples of the bubble and differences in the percentages of fundamentalists and noise traders arising from the Brock-Hommes system.

Theorem 2.2:

1) Let $C \geq 0$ and let $0 < g < R$, then the fundamental state $E_1 = (0, \tanh(-\beta C/2)) \equiv (0, m^e)$ is globally stable.

2) If $g > 2R$ and $C \geq 0$ there are two non-fundamental steady states, E_2 and E_3. E_1 is a steady state but is unstable for $g > 2R$. The non-fundamental steady states are defined by $E_2 = (a^*, m^*)$ and $E_3 = (-a^*, m^*)$ where a^* is the positive solution of $\tanh(\beta/2(1/s\gamma^2(g - 1)(R-1)(a^*)^2 - C) = m^*$ and $m^* = 1 - 2R/g$.

3) For $R < g < 2R$ and $C > 0$, there exists β', β^* satisfying $0 < \beta' < \beta^*$ such that for $\beta < \beta'$, E_1 is stable. For $\beta = \beta'$ a pitchfork bifurcation occurs creating the non-fundamental steady states E_2 and E_3. If $\beta' < \beta < \beta^*$ the fundamental steady state is unstable and the non-fundamental states are stable. For $\beta > \beta^*$ all steady states are unstable. At β^* a Hopf bifurcation of the steady states occurs. Periodic solutions fluctuate around one of two invariant circles, one above and one below the fundamental steady state.

4) For $R < g < 2R$ and $m^* > m^e$, E_1, E_2 and E_3 are steady states and E_1 is unstable. If $m^* < m^e$ then E_1 is the unique stable steady state.

Assume $b, f \geq 0$ then $g_n \geq 0 \quad \forall n$ and equation (2.1) implies that the sign of the bubble at n is the same as the sign of the bubble at $n-1$. Hence, the sign of the bubble at all times is the same as the sign of the bubble at $t = 0$. Since the bubble at $t = 0$ is generated by the original Brock-Hommes equations, theorem 2.2 identifies initial conditions for the bubble from which the stochastic bubbles evolve. For example, if $g > 2R$ there are three fixed point bubbles in the deterministic model: one is positive, one negative and the other is zero. Taking w^i as the deterministic bubble corresponding to E_i and using this in each coordinate of the vector of initial conditions generates three random bubbles $(w_t^i, t \geq 0), i = 1, 2, 3$ satisfying $w_t^3 < w_t^1 < w_t^2 \quad \forall t$ and $w_0^i = w^i$ for all i. Moreover, if a bubble $(w_t^{3,*}, t \geq 0)$ is started from a negative initial condition different from that in E_3 and another bubble $(w_t^{2,*}, t \geq 0)$ is started from a positive condition different from that in E_2, then $w_t^{3,*} < w_t^{2,*} \quad \forall t$. However, there would be no comparison with the known dynamics of the Brock-Hommes model. Hence, bubbles with Brock-Hommes initial conditions act as a benchmark for the analysis.

3. Exchange Rate Bifurcation and Currency Crises

The exchange rate at time t corresponding to $(k_s^\mu, s \geq 0)$ is denoted by x_t^μ. Constants are denoted by C, K or L and may vary from line to line. For any dimension $d, |\cdot|$ will denote the Euclidean norm on R^d. Let $\mathcal{M}(R^2)$ denote the space of $(\mathcal{F}_t)_{t\geq 0}$ progressively measurable processes, μ, taking values in R^2 such that $\forall T < \infty \quad \sup_{t\in[0,T]} E|\mu_t|^2 < \infty$. For any topological space $Y, \mathcal{B}(Y)$ denotes the Borel sets of Y and $(W_t, t \geq 0)$ is a d-dimensional Brownian motion. Throughtout, if $U \subset R^n$ the closure of U is denoted $\bar{U}$.

Definition 3.1: Let $b : R^+ \times R^2 \times R^d \to R^d$ and σ be a $d \times d$ matrix with components $\sigma_{i,j} : R^+ \times R^2 \times R^d \to R$. Let the components of $b(s,z,x)$, and $\sigma(s,z,x)$ restricted to $[0,t] \times R^2 \times R^d$ be measurable relative to $\mathcal{B}([0,t]) \times \mathcal{B}(R^2) \times \mathcal{B}(R^d)$ and $\mathcal{B}(R)$ for any t. For $\mu \in \mathcal{M}(R^2)$ let $|\sigma(s,\mu_s,x)|^2 = \sum_{i,j} \sigma_{i,j}^2(s,\mu_s,x)$. Then a solution to the stochastic differential equation $dk_t^\mu = b(t,\mu_t,k_t^\mu)\, dt + \sigma(t,\mu_t,k_t^\mu)\, dW_t$ with initial condition k_0^μ is a continuous, $(\mathcal{F}_t, t \geq 0)$ adapted process such that for each $T > 0$:

1) $E\int_0^T |b(s,\mu_s,k_s^\mu)|^2\, ds + E\int_0^T |\sigma(s,\mu_s,k_s^\mu)|^2\, ds < \infty$

2) $k_t^\mu = k_0^\mu + \int_0^t b(s,\mu_s,k_s^\mu)\, ds + \int_0^t \sigma(s,\mu_s,k_s^\mu)\, dW_s$ almost everywhere $\forall t \in [0,T]$. This means $k_t^i = k_0^{\mu,i} + \int_0^t b_i(s,\mu_s,k_s^\mu)\, ds + \sum_{j=1}^d \int_0^t \sigma_{i,j}(s,\mu_s,k_s^\mu)\, dW_s^j$ for all $i = 1,\ldots,d$. We assume $k_0^{\mu,i} \in L^2(\Omega, \mathcal{F}_0, P) \quad \forall i$. For the economic model in section 2 we take $d = 1$.

Assumption 3.1: The functions b and σ are jointly measurable. Also there is a constant $K > 0$ such that for $z, v \in R^2, s \in R^+$ and $x, y \in R^d$

1) $|b(s,z,x) - b(s,v,y)| + |\sigma(s,z,x) - \sigma(s,v,y)| \leq K(|x-y| + |z-v|)$

2) $|b(s,z,x)| + |\sigma(s,z,x)| \leq K(1 + |x| + |z|)$

Theorem 3.1: Let μ be a Brock-Hommes equilibrium generated by the model in section 2. Then $\mu \in \mathcal{M}(R^2)$ and there exists a unique solution to the SDE in definition 3.1 corresponding to μ.

A Brock-Hommes equilibrium lies in $\mathcal{M}(R^2)$ by construction and depends on lagged values of the SDE. Consequently, it is necessary to prove simultaneous existence and uniqueness of $((\mu_t, k_t^\mu), t \geq 0)$. This is the substance of theorem 3.1 which is proved in Gagnon (2012). Frequently, the superscript μ is deleted for convenience but it is understood that the money supply depends on the bubble. For the theorems in this section we often take k_0^μ to be a number rather than a random variable. If k_0^μ is random then at the very least we assume $k_0^\mu \in L^4(\Omega, \mathcal{F}_0, P)$. Also, the bubbles generated from the fixed points in the Brock-Hommes model receive a special notation; specifically, the bubble from equilibrium E_i is denoted μ^i. Thus, $(\mu_t^i, t \geq 0) \quad i = 1,2,3$ is generated from the zero, positive and negative bubbles respectively.

Since lagged money supplies only affect the bubble for $t \geq 1$ the bubble at $t = 0$ depends on the triple $\mu_0^* = (\mu_{-1}, \mu_{-2}, \mu_{-3})$; μ_0^* is referred to as initial conditions for the bubble. Generally, at time $n \geq 1$ the bubble w_n depends on $q_{2,n-1}$, which itself depends on $(w_{n-1}, w_{n-2}, w_{n-3})$, the bubbles at times $n-1, n-2$ and $n-3$, as well as k_{n-2} and k_{n-3} via the terms R_{n-2} and g_{n-2}. Thus, we can think of the vector $\mu_n^* = (\mu_{n-1}, \mu_{n-2}, \mu_{n-3})$ together with k_{n-1}, k_{n-2} and k_{n-3} via the terms $q_{2,n-1}$ and g_n, as generating the bubble at $t = n$. Consequently, we can think of μ_n as being generated by μ_n^* and $k_n^* = (k_{n-1}, k_{n-2}, k_{n-3})$. Also, since $q_{2,n-1}$ depends on μ_n^*, k_{n-2} and k_{n-3}, it is convenient to think of $q_{2,n-1}$ as a function of (μ_n^*, k_n^*). Thus, we can think of w_n and $q_{2,n-1}$ as functions of $(\mu_n^*, k_n^*) \in R^6$; sometimes we are more specific and think of $q_{2,n-1}$ as a function of $(\mu_n^*, k_{n-2}, k_{n-3}) \in R^5$. This becomes very important in proving theorem 2.1. Also, in the proofs of the following lemmas and theorems it is often convenient to ignore the percent of noise traders in μ_s and take $\mu_s = w_s$. This is rational since lagged bubbles and money supplies generate everything; lagged noise trader percents are not necessary to generate the bubbles.

In an additional point concerning the bubble, note that the proof of theorem 3.1 in Gagnon (2012) assumes initial conditions for the bubble are deterministic. However, the proof is also applicable for a bubble μ which evolves randomly via the Brock-Hommes equations from $\mathcal{F}_0$ measurable random variables μ_i for $i = -1, -2, -3$ provided $\sup_{\omega \in \Omega} |\mu_0^*(\omega)| < \infty$ where $\mu_0^*(\omega) = (\mu_{-1}(\omega), \mu_{-2}(\omega), \mu_{-3}(\omega))$. In the proof of theorem 3.1 the initial bubbles are implicitly assumed to be deterministic since initial bubbles from the Brock-Hommes model are non-random. Henceforth, it is assumed that either the initial bubbles are deterministic or $\sup_{\omega \in \Omega} |\mu_0^*(\omega)| < \infty$. Moreover, we can generate the bubbles for $t \geq 1$ given either k_0 and μ_0^* or k_0 and μ_0 since μ_0 has $q_{2,0}$ as a component and lagged money supplies only affect the bubble for times $t \geq 1$. Theorem 2.1 rests on several moment inequalities linked to the bubbles which are introduced now.

Lemma 3.1: Let $k_0^\mu \in L^4(\Omega, \mathcal{F}_0, P)$. There exists a constant $L > 0$, a nonnegative polynomial $p(t)$ that increases in t and a continuous, positive, increasing function $a(t)$ such that for each $t > 0$

$$(1) \quad E|k_t^\mu|^2 \leq L\exp(Lt)(E|k_0^\mu|^2 + p(t) \sup_{s \in [0,t]} E|\mu_s|^2 + p(t))$$

$$(2) \quad E \sup_{s \in [0,t]} |k_s^\mu|^2 \leq a(t)(E|k_0^\mu|^2 + \sup_{s \in [0,t]} E|\mu_s|^2 + 1)$$

Proof: First it is established that if $k_0 \in L^p(\Omega, \mathcal{F}, P)$ for some $p > 2$ and $T > 0$ there is a finite constant $J_p(T)$ such that $E|k_t|^p \leq J_p(T)$ for $0 \leq t \leq T$. Since f is bounded and continuous, bubbles are bounded on bounded intervals meaning that for any $T > 0$ there is a $B(T) \in (0, \infty)$ such that $\sup_{w \in \Omega} |\mu_t(w)| \leq B(T)$ when $t \leq T$. Let $\tau_n = \inf\{t \in [0,T] : |k_t| > n\}$ for $n \geq 1$. There is a constant $C > 0$ varying from line to line and depending on T such that for $t \leq T$

$$|k_{t\wedge\tau_n}|^p \leq C(|k_0|^p + t^{p-1} \int_0^{t\wedge\tau_n} |b(u, \mu_u, k_u)|^p \, du + |\int_0^{t\wedge\tau_n} \sigma(u, \mu_u, k_u) \, dW_u|^p)$$

Thus,

$$E|k_{t\wedge\tau_n}|^p \leq C(E|k_0|^p + t^{p-1} E \int_0^{t\wedge\tau_n} |b(u, \mu_u, k_u)|^p \, du +$$

$$E(\int_0^{t\wedge\tau_n} \sigma^2(u, \mu_u, k_u) \, du)^{\frac{p}{2}}) \leq C(E|k_0|^p + t^p + t^{\frac{p}{2}-1} E \int_0^t 1 + |\mu_u|^p + |k_{u\wedge\tau_n}|^p \, du) \leq$$

$$C(E|k_0|^p + t^p + t^{\frac{p}{2}} + t^{\frac{p}{2}} \sup_{s \in [0,t]} E|\mu_s|^p + \int_0^t E|k_{u\wedge\tau_n}|^p \, du)$$

Gronwall's inequality implies

$$E|k_{t\wedge\tau_n}|^p \leq J_p(T) = C\exp(CT)(E|k_0|^p + T^p + T^{\frac{p}{2}} + T^{\frac{p}{2}}B(T)^p)$$

when $t \leq T$. Applying Fatou's lemma yields $E|k_t|^p \leq J_p(T) \quad \forall t \leq T$.

By Ito's lemma

$$|k_t|^2 = k_0^2 + 2\int_0^t k_s b(s,\mu_s,k_s)\, ds + 2\int_0^t k_s\sigma(s,\mu_s,k_s)\, dW_s +$$

$$\int_0^t \sigma^2(s,\mu_s,k_s)\, ds$$

Since $E|k_s|^4 \leq J_4(t)$ when $s \leq t$ we have $E\int_0^t k_s^2\sigma^2(s,\mu_s,k_s)\; ds < \infty$ and hence $E\int_0^t k_s\sigma(s,\mu_s,k_s)\; dW_s = 0$. Thus, applying Young's inequality and boundedness of b to the first integral and the linear growth conditions to the second integral, yields a constant $C > 0$ varying from line to line such that

$$Ek_t^2 = Ek_0^2 + 2E\int_0^t k_s b(s,\mu_s,k_s)\, ds + E\int_0^t \sigma^2(s,\mu_s,k_s)\, ds \leq$$

$$Ek_0^2 + CE\int_0^t 1 + |k_s|^2\, ds + CE\int_0^t 1 + |\mu_s|^2 + |k_s|^2\, ds \leq$$

$$Ek_0^2 + C(t + t\sup_{s\in[0,t]} E|\mu_s|^2) + C\int_0^t E|k_s|^2\, ds$$

Gronwall's inequality gives

$$E|k_t|^2 \leq Ek_0^2 + Ct(1 + \sup_{s\in[0,t]} E|\mu_s|^2) +$$

$$C\int_0^t \exp(C(t-s))(Ek_0^2 + Cs(1 + \sup_{u\in[0,s]} E|\mu_u|^2))\, ds \leq$$

$$Ek_0^2 + Ct(1 + \sup_{s\in[0,t]} E|\mu_s|^2) +$$

$$C\int_0^t \exp(C(t-s))(Ek_0^2 + Ct(1 + \sup_{u\in[0,t]} E|\mu_u|^2))\, ds \leq$$

$$\exp(Ct)(Ek_0^2 + Ct(1 + \sup_{u\in[0,t]} E|\mu_u|^2)) \leq C\exp(Ct)(Ek_0^2 + t(1 + \sup_{u\in[0,t]} E|\mu_u|^2))$$

provided we choose an appropriate $C > 1$. Thus, take $p(t) = t$ and the first inequality is established. For the second inequality observe there is a constant $C > 0$ varying from line to line satisfying

$$\sup_{s\in[0,t]} |k_s|^2 \leq C|k_0|^2 + Ct\int_0^t |b(v,\mu_v,k_v)|^2\, dv + C\sup_{s\in[0,t]} |\int_0^s \sigma(v,\mu_v,k_v)\, dW_v|^2$$

$$\leq C|k_0|^2 + Ct\int_0^t 1+|\mu_v|^2+|k_v|^2 dv + C\sup_{s\in[0,t]}|\int_0^s \sigma(v,\mu_v,k_v)\,dW_v|^2$$

Applying Doob's inequality gives

$$E\sup_{s\in[0,t]}|k_s|^2 \leq CEk_0^2 + CtE\int_0^t 1+|\mu_v|^2+|k_v|^2 dv + CE\int_0^t \sigma^2(v,\mu_v,k_v)\,dv$$

$$\leq CEk_0^2 + C(t+1)E\int_0^t 1+|\mu_v|^2\,dv + C(t+1)\int_0^t E|k_v|^2 dv \leq$$

$$CEk_0^2 + C(t+1)(t+t\sup_{s\in[0,t]}E|\mu_s|^2) + C(t+1)\int_0^t E|k_v|^2 dv$$

Since $E|k_v|^2 \leq L\exp(Lv)(E|k_0|^2 + v\sup_{s\in[0,v]}E|\mu_s|^2 + v)$ we have

$$\int_0^t E|k_v|^2 dv \leq \int_0^t L\exp(Lv)(E|k_0|^2 + v\sup_{s\in[0,v]}E|\mu_s|^2 + v)\,dv \leq$$

$$\exp(Lt)E|k_0|^2 + t\exp(Lt)\sup_{s\in[0,t]}E|\mu_s|^2 + t\exp(Lt). \quad \text{Hence}$$

$$E\sup_{s\in[0,t]}|k_s|^2 \leq (C+C(t+1)\exp(Lt))Ek_0^2 + C(t+1)((t+t\exp(Lt))\sup_{s\in[0,t]}E|\mu_s|^2)$$

$$+C(t+1)(t+t\exp(Lt))$$

Take $a(t) = \max(C+C(t+1)\exp(Lt), C(t+1)(t+t\exp(Lt)))$. q.e.d.

Lemma 3.2: Let $k_0^1, k_0^2 \in L^4(\Omega, \mathcal{F}_0, P)$ be initial money supplies and μ_0^1, μ_0^2 initial bubbles. Let $(\mu_t^1, t\geq 0), (k_t^1, t\geq 0)$ and $(\mu_t^2, t\geq 0), (k_t^2, t\geq 0)$ be the bubbles and money supplies generated by k_0^1, μ_0^1 and k_0^2, μ_0^2 respectively. Then there exists a constant $L>0$, a nonnegative polynomial $p(t)$ that increases in t and a continuous, positive, increasing function $a(t)$ such that $\forall t\geq 0$

$$(1)\quad E|k_t^1-k_t^2|^2 \leq L\exp(Lt)(E|k_0^1-k_0^2|^2 + p(t)\sup_{s\in[0,t]}E|\mu_s^1-\mu_s^2|^2)$$

$$(2)\quad E\sup_{s\in[0,t]}|k_s^1-k_s^2|^2 \leq a(t)(E|k_0^1-k_0^2|^2 + \sup_{s\in[0,t]}E|\mu_s^1-\mu_s^2|^2)$$

Proof: Let $C>0$ be a constant which varies from line to line. Clearly,

$$k_t^2-k_t^1 = k_0^2-k_0^1 + \int_0^t b(s,\mu_s^2,k_s^2)-b(s,\mu_s^1,k_s^1)\,ds + \int_0^t \sigma(s,\mu_s^2,k_s^2)-\sigma(s,\mu_s^1,k_s^1)\,dW_s$$

By Ito's lemma

$$|k_t^2-k_t^1|^2 = |k_0^2-k_0^1|^2 + 2\int_0^t (k_s^2-k_s^1)(b(s,\mu_s^2,k_s^2)-b(s,\mu_s^1,k_s^1))\,ds+$$

$$2\int_0^t (k_s^2-k_s^1)(\sigma(s,\mu_s^2,k_s^2)-\sigma(s,\mu_s^1,k_s^1))\,dW_s+$$

$$\int_0^t (\sigma(s,\mu_s^2,k_s^2)-\sigma(s,\mu_s^1,k_s^1))^2\,ds$$

Using the Lipschitz conditions and Young's inequality there is a constant $C>0$ such that

$$|k_t^2-k_t^1|^2 \le C|k_0^2-k_0^1|^2 + C\int_0^t |\mu_s^2-\mu_s^1|^2+|k_s^2-k_s^1|^2 ds +$$

$$2\int_0^t (k_s^2-k_s^1)(\sigma(s,\mu_s^2,k_s^2)-\sigma(s,\mu_s^1,k_s^1))\,dW_s + C\int_0^t (\sigma(s,\mu_s^2,k_s^2)-\sigma(s,\mu_s^1,k_s^1))^2\,ds$$

Since $E\int_0^t(|k_s^2-k_s^1||\sigma(s,\mu_s^2,k_s^2)-\sigma(s,\mu_s^1,k_s^1)|)^2\,ds \le CE\int_0^t |\mu_s^2-\mu_s^1|^4+|k_s^2-k_s^1|^4\,ds < \infty$, $E\int_0^t(k_s^2-k_s^1)(\sigma(s,\mu_s^2,k_s^2)-\sigma(s,\mu_s^1,k_s^1))\,dW_s = 0$. Hence,

$$E|k_t^2-k_t^1|^2 \le CE|k_0^2-k_0^1|^2 + CE\int_0^t |\mu_s^1-\mu_s^2|^2+|k_s^2-k_s^1|^2\,ds \le$$

$$CE|k_0^2-k_0^1|^2 + Ct\sup_{s\in[0,t]} E|\mu_s^1-\mu_s^2|^2 + C\int_0^t E|k_s^2-k_s^1|^2\,ds$$

Applying Gronwall's inequality yields

$$E|k_t^2-k_t^1|^2 \le C\exp(Ct)(E|k_0^2-k_0^1|^2 + t\sup_{s\in[0,t]} E|\mu_s^1-\mu_s^2|^2)$$

Thus, we can take $p(t)=t$ establishing the first inequality. For the second inequality observe that for some constant $C>0$ varying from line to line

$$\sup_{s\in[0,t]} |k_s^2-k_s^1|^2 \le C|k_0^2-k_0^1|^2 + Ct\int_0^t |b(v,\mu_v^2,k_v^2)-b(v,\mu_v^1,k_v^1)|^2\,dv +$$

$$C\sup_{s\in[0,t]} |\int_0^s \sigma(v,\mu_v^2,k_v^2)-\sigma(v,\mu_v^1,k_v^1)\,dW_v|^2 \le C|k_0^2-k_0^1|^2 +$$

$$Ct\int_0^t |\mu_v^2-\mu_v^1|^2+|k_v^2-k_v^1|^2 dv + C\sup_{s\in[0,t]} |\int_0^s \sigma(v,\mu_v^2,k_v^2)-\sigma(v,\mu_v^1,k_v^1)\,dW_v|^2$$

Applying Doob's inequality gives

$$E\sup_{s\in[0,t]} |k_s^2-k_s^1|^2 \le CE|k_0^2-k_0^1|^2 + CtE\int_0^t |\mu_v^2-\mu_v^1|^2\,dv +$$

$$Ct\int_0^t E|k_v^2-k_v^1|^2 dv + CE\int_0^t (\sigma(v,\mu_v^2,k_v^2)-\sigma(v,\mu_v^1,k_v^1))^2\,dv \le$$

$$CE|k_0^2-k_0^1|^2 + C(t^2+t)\sup_{s\in[0,t]} E|\mu_s^2-\mu_s^1|^2 + C(t+1)\int_0^t E|k_v^2-k_v^1|^2 dv \quad (3.1)$$

By inequality (1) we have

$$E|k_v^1-k_v^2|^2 \le L\exp(Lv)(E|k_0^1-k_0^2|^2 + v\sup_{s\in[0,v]} E|\mu_s^1-\mu_s^2|^2)$$

Integrating this inequality with respect to v and substituting the resulting inequality for $\int_0^t E|k_v^2 - k_v^1|^2 dv$ into inequality (3.1) yields

$$E \sup_{s\in[0,t]} |k_s^2 - k_s^1|^2 \le CE|k_0^2 - k_0^1|^2 + C(t^2+t) \sup_{s\in[0,t]} E|\mu_s^2 - \mu_s^1|^2 +$$

$$C(t+1)\int_0^t L\exp(Lv)(E|k_0^1 - k_0^2|^2 + v \sup_{s\in[0,v]} E|\mu_s^1 - \mu_s^2|^2)\,dv \le$$

$$(C + C(t+1)\exp(Lt))E|k_0^2 - k_0^1|^2 + C(t^2+t) \sup_{s\in[0,t]} E|\mu_s^2 - \mu_s^1|^2 +$$

$$C(t+1)\int_0^t L\exp(Lv)t \sup_{s\in[0,t]} E|\mu_s^2 - \mu_s^1|^2\,dv$$

$$\le (C + C(t+1)\exp(Lt))E|k_0^2 - k_0^1|^2 + (C(t^2+t) + C(t+1)t\exp(Lt)) \sup_{s\in[0,t]} E|\mu_s^2 - \mu_s^1|^2$$

Take $a(t) = \max(C(t^2+t) + C(t+1)t\exp(Lt), C + C(t+1)\exp(Lt))$ to establish the second inequality. q.e.d.

Lemma 3.3 (Continuity Lemma): Let μ_0^* and ν_0^* be vectors of initial bubbles and $k_0^\mu, k_0^\nu \in L^4$ be initial conditions. Let $(k_t^\mu, t \ge 0)$ and $(k_t^\nu, t \ge 0)$ be the money supplies they generate. Let $\sup_{w\in\Omega}|k_0^\mu(w)|, \sup_{w\in\Omega}|k_0^\nu(w)| \le M < \infty$ and $\sup_{w\in\Omega}|\mu_0^*(w)|, \sup_{w\in\Omega}|\nu_0^*(w)| \le M < \infty$. Given $\varepsilon, \gamma, T > 0$ there exists a $\delta = \delta(T, \varepsilon, \gamma)$ such that if both $\sup_{w\in\Omega}|k_0^\mu(w) - k_0^\nu(w)| < \delta$ and $\sup_{w\in\Omega}|\mu_0^*(w) - \nu_0^*(w)| < \delta$ then

1. $P(\sup_{t\in[0,T]}|k_t^\mu - k_t^\nu| > \gamma) < \varepsilon$
2. for $t \in [0,T], P(|\mu_t - \nu_t| > \gamma) < \varepsilon$
3. $E\sup_{t\in[0,T]}|k_t^\mu - k_t^\nu|^2 < \varepsilon$

Moreover if $\sup_{w\in\Omega}|\mu_0^*(w)|, \sup_{w\in\Omega}|\nu_0^*(w)| \le M$ and $E|k_0^\mu|^2, E|k_0^\nu|^2 \le M$ then given $\varepsilon, \gamma, T > 0$ there exists a $\delta = \delta(T, \varepsilon, \gamma)$ such that if $E|k_0^\mu - k_0^\nu|^2 < \delta$ and $\sup_{w\in\Omega}|\mu_0^*(w) - \nu_0^*(w)| < \delta$, then inequalities (1)-(3) continue to hold.

Proof: First we treat the case of $\sup_{w\in\Omega}|k_0^\mu(w)|, \sup_{w\in\Omega}|k_0^\nu(w)| \le M$ and then we deal with the case of $E|k_0^\mu|^2, E|k_0^\nu|^2 \le M$ where $M < \infty$.

For $n \ge 0$ the probabilities $q_{1,n}$ and $q_{2,n}$ as well as the bubble are defined by functions on R^6 since they depend on three dimensional vectors of lagged bubbles and money supplies. For $n = 0$ the switching probabilities are actually functions on R^3 since the lagged money supplies are not involved. The functions are continous in the vector of lagged bubbles and money supplies. Hence, they are uniformly continuous on bounded sets. Moreover, the bubble at $t = 0$ is a continous function of the vector of lagged bubbles since lagged money supplies only affect the bubble for $t \ge 1$. Since the bubble at $t = 1$ is a continous function of the bubble at $t = 0$, lagged bubbles and the initial money supply, it is a continuous function of the vector of initial bubbles and the initial money supply. Since $\sup_{w\in\Omega}|k_0^\mu(w)|, \sup_{w\in\Omega}|k_0^\nu(w)| \le M$ and $\sup_{w\in\Omega}|\mu_0^*(w)|, \sup_{w\in\Omega}|\nu_0^*(w)| \le M$, uniform continuity of the functions defining the bubble at $t = 1$ on $[-M,M]^4$ means that for any given $\varepsilon > 0$ $\exists$ a $\delta > 0$ such that $|k_0^\mu(w) - k_0^\nu(w)| < \delta$ and $|\mu_0^*(w) - \nu_0^*(w)| < \delta$ implies $|\mu_1(w) - \nu_1(w)| < \varepsilon \quad \forall w \in \Omega$. Together with lemma 3.2, this implies that given $\varepsilon > 0$ there exists a $\delta > 0$ such that $|k_0^\mu(w) - k_0^\nu(w)| < \delta$ and $|\mu_0^*(w) - \nu_0^*(w)| < \delta \quad \forall w \in \Omega$ ensures that

$$E \sup_{s\in[0,1]} |k_s^\mu - k_s^\nu|^2 \leq a(1)(E|k_0^\mu - k_0^\nu|^2 + \sup_{s\in[0,1]} E|\mu_s - \nu_s|^2) < \varepsilon \quad (3.2)$$

Applying the methods in the proof of lemma 3.2, we can establish that whenever $s < t$ the continuous function $a(\cdot)$ in that lemma satisfies

$$E \sup_{u\in[s,t]} |k_u^\mu - k_u^\nu|^2 \leq a(t)(E|k_s^\mu - k_s^\nu|^2 + \sup_{u\in[s,t]} E|\mu_u - \nu_u|^2)$$

Taking $s = n$ and $t = n+1$ this becomes

$$E \sup_{u\in[n,n+1]} |k_u^\mu - k_u^\nu|^2 \leq a(n+1)(E|k_n^\mu - k_n^\nu|^2 + \sup_{u\in[n,n+1]} E|\mu_u - \nu_u|^2)$$

Provided the inequality in the statement of lemma 3.3 holds for positive integers it holds for all T since for $T < n$, $P(\sup_{t\in[0,T]} |k_t^\mu - k_t^\nu| > \gamma) \leq P(\sup_{t\in[0,n]} |k_t^\mu - k_t^\nu| > \gamma)$ and $E\sup_{t\in[0,T]} |k_t^\mu - k_t^\nu|^2 \leq E\sup_{t\in[0,n]} |k_t^\mu - k_t^\nu|^2$. Thus, lemma 3.3 can proved by induction. To employ induction, assume that for any $\varepsilon, \gamma > 0 \quad \exists$ a $\delta > 0$ such that if $|k_0^\mu(w) - k_0^\nu(w)| < \delta$ and $|\mu_0^*(w) - \nu_0^*(w)| < \delta \quad \forall w \in \Omega$ then inequalities (1)-(3) in the statement of the theorem hold for some n. Then for given $\varepsilon, \gamma > 0$ and appropriate $\delta > 0$ bounding initial conditions we have

a. $P(\sup_{t\in[0,n]} |k_t^\mu - k_t^\nu| > \gamma) < \varepsilon$
b. $E\sup_{t\in[0,n]} |k_t^\mu - k_t^\nu|^2 < \varepsilon$ as well as
c. $P(|\mu_{n+1}^* - \nu_{n+1}^*| > \gamma) < \varepsilon$ Recall $\mu_{n+1}^*(w) = (\mu_n(w), \mu_{n-1}(w), \mu_{n-2}(w))$ for any bubble

μ and $w \in \Omega$. Notice that inequality (c) follows if inequality (2) in the statement of the theorem is true. By assuming (1)-(3) hold for some n the three inequalities (a)-(c) must be true. Note that inequalities (a)-(c) clearly hold for $n = 1$ since the argument presented above ensures $|\mu_1(w) - \nu_1(w)| < \varepsilon \quad \forall w \in \Omega$ and lemma 3.2 bounds $P(\sup_{t\in[0,1]} |k_t^\mu - k_t^\nu| > \gamma)$ and $E\sup_{t\in[0,1]} |k_t^\mu - k_t^\nu|^2$ as seen in inequality (3.2).

For the inductive step, observe that since f is bounded and $b \geq 0, |w_n| \leq (g + \sup_{y\in R} |f(y)|)^n |w_0| \quad \forall n \geq 1$. Consequently, if $|w_0|$ is bounded on Ω by the constant $M > 0$ there is a constant $B > 1$ such that $|w_n| \leq B^n M$ for all $n \geq 1$. Letting $(w_n^1, n \geq 0)$ and $(w_n^2, n \geq 0)$ be the bubbles corresponding to μ and ν respectively, it is clear that $|w_j^1|, |w_j^2| \leq B^j M$ for some $M > 0$ and all j such that $1 \leq j \leq n+1$. By lemma 3.1, if $\sup_{w\in\Omega} |\mu_0^*(w)| \leq M, \sup_{w\in\Omega} |k_0^\mu(w)| \leq M$ where $M < \infty$ and $n, m \in N$ then

$$P(\sup_{t\in[0,n]} |k_t^\mu| > m) \leq m^{-2} E \sup_{t\in[0,n]} |k_t^\mu|^2 \leq$$

$$m^{-2} a(n)(E|k_0^\mu|^2 + \sup_{s\in[0,n]} E|\mu_s|^2 + 1) \leq m^{-2} a(n)(M^2 + (B^n M)^2 + 1) \quad (3.3)$$

Clearly, the right hand side of (3.3) can be made less than $\frac{\varepsilon}{4}$ provided m is appropriately chosen. Thus, there is an integer $m > 0$ such that $P(\sup_{t\in[0,n]} |k_t^\mu| > m) < \frac{\varepsilon}{4}$ and $P(\sup_{t\in[0,n]} |k_t^\nu| > m) < \frac{\varepsilon}{4}$. Again, viewing the transition probabilities as functions on R^6 it is clear that $\mu_{n+1}(w)$ depends on $(k_n^\mu(w), k_{n-1}^\mu(w), k_{n-2}^\mu(w), \mu_n(w), \mu_{n-1}(w), \mu_{n-2}(w))$ and that $\nu_{n+1}(w)$ depends on $(k_n^\nu(w), k_{n-1}^\nu(w), k_{n-2}^\nu(w), \nu_n(w), \nu_{n-1}(w), \nu_{n-2}(w))$. Clearly, both $(\mu_n(w), \mu_{n-1}(w), \mu_{n-2}(w))$ and $(\nu_n(w), \nu_{n-1}(w), \nu_{n-2}(w))$ are in a bounded set. If $\sup_{t\in[0,n]} |k_t^\mu(w)|, \sup_{t\in[0,n]} |k_t^\nu(w)| \le m$, given $\eta > 0$ we can choose $\gamma > 0$ such that $\sup_{t\in[0,n]} |k_t^\mu(w) - k_t^\nu(w)| \le \gamma, |\mu_{n+1}^*(w) - \nu_{n+1}^*(w)| \le \gamma$ ensures $|\mu_{n+1}(w) - \nu_{n+1}(w)| < \eta$. Choose δ such that if $|k_0^\mu(w) - k_0^\nu(w)| < \delta$ and $|\mu_0^*(w) - \nu_0^*(w)| < \delta \quad \forall w \in \Omega$ then $P(\sup_{t\in[0,n]} |k_t^\mu - k_t^\nu| > \gamma) < \frac{\varepsilon}{4}, E\sup_{t\in[0,n]} |k_t^\mu - k_t^\nu|^2 < \varepsilon$ as well as $P(|\mu_{n+1}^* - \nu_{n+1}^*| > \gamma) < \frac{\varepsilon}{4}$. Define the measurable set A by

$$A = \{w : \sup_{t\in[0,n]} |k_t^\mu(w)| \le m, \sup_{t\in[0,n]} |k_t^\nu(w)| \le m, |\mu_{n+1}^*(w) - \nu_{n+1}^*(w)| \le \gamma,$$

$$\sup_{t\in[0,n]} |k_t^\mu(w) - k_t^\nu(w)| \le \gamma\}, \quad \text{then} \quad P(A^C) < \varepsilon$$

Clearly, $A \subset \{|\mu_{n+1} - \nu_{n+1}| < \eta\}$ implying $P(|\mu_{n+1} - \nu_{n+1}| \ge \eta) \le P(A^C) < \varepsilon$ proving $|\mu_{n+1} - \nu_{n+1}|$ can be made arbitrarily small with high probability provided δ is appropriately chosen. Furthermore, define $B_n = \{|\mu_n - \nu_n| \le \gamma\}$; then $P(B_n^C) \le P(|\mu_{n+1}^* - \nu_{n+1}^*| > \gamma) < \frac{\varepsilon}{4}$. Thus, for the δ bounding initial conditions used to ensure $P(A^C) < \varepsilon$ where the set A is defined above, we have

$$E \sup_{u\in[n,n+1]} |k_u^\mu - k_u^\nu|^2 \le a(n+1)(E|k_n^\mu - k_n^\nu|^2 + \sup_{u\in[n,n+1]} E|\mu_u - \nu_u|^2) \le$$

$$a(n+1)(\varepsilon + \int_A |\mu_{n+1} - \nu_{n+1}|^2\, dP + \int_{A^C} |\mu_{n+1} - \nu_{n+1}|^2\, dP +$$

$$\int_{B_n} |\mu_n - \nu_n|^2\, dP + \int_{B_n^C} |\mu_n - \nu_n|^2\, dP) \le$$

$$a(n+1)(\varepsilon + \eta^2 + \gamma^2 + 4(B^n M)^2 \frac{\varepsilon}{4} + 4(B^{n+1} M)^2 \varepsilon) \quad (3.4)$$

Clearly, the right hand side of (3.4) can be made arbitrarily small. Thus, given any $\varepsilon, \gamma > 0$ for appropriate δ we have

$$P(\sup_{u\in[n,n+1]} |k_u^\mu - k_u^\nu| > \gamma) < \varepsilon \quad \text{and} \quad E \sup_{u\in[n,n+1]} |k_u^\mu - k_u^\nu|^2 < \varepsilon$$

Suppose $\sup_{w\in\Omega} |k_0^\mu(w) - k_0^\nu(w)| < \delta_1$ and $\sup_{w\in\Omega} |\mu_0^*(w) - \nu_0^*(w)| < \delta_1$ ensures $P(\sup_{u\in[0,n]} |k_u^\mu - k_u^\nu| > \frac{\gamma}{2}) < \frac{\varepsilon}{2}$ and $E\sup_{u\in[0,n]} |k_u^\mu - k_u^\nu|^2 < \frac{\varepsilon}{4}$. Suppose $\sup_{w\in\Omega} |k_0^\mu(w) - k_0^\nu(w)| < \delta_2$ and $\sup_{w\in\Omega} |\mu_0^*(w) - \nu_0^*(w)| < \delta_2$ ensures $P(\sup_{u\in[n,n+1]} |k_u^\mu - k_u^\nu| > \frac{\gamma}{2}) < \frac{\varepsilon}{2}$ and $E\sup_{u\in[n,n+1]} |k_u^\mu - k_u^\nu|^2 < \frac{\varepsilon}{4}$. Observe $\sup_{u\in[0,n+1]} |k_u^\mu - k_u^\nu| \le \sup_{u\in[0,n]} |k_u^\mu - k_u^\nu| + \sup_{u\in[n,n+1]} |k_u^\mu - k_u^\nu|$. Then for $\sup_{w\in\Omega} |k_0^\mu(w) - k_0^\nu(w)| < \delta$ as well as $\sup_{w\in\Omega} |\mu_0^*(w) - \nu_0^*(w)| < \delta$ where $\delta = min(\delta_1, \delta_2)$ we have

$$P(\sup_{u\in[0,n+1]} |k_u^\mu - k_u^\nu| > \gamma) \le$$

$$P(\sup_{u\in[0,n]} |k_u^\mu - k_u^\nu| > \frac{\gamma}{2}) + P(\sup_{u\in[n,n+1]} |k_u^\mu - k_u^\nu| > \frac{\gamma}{2}) < \varepsilon$$

Moreover,

$$E \sup_{u\in[0,n+1]} |k_u^\mu - k_u^\nu|^2 \le 2E \sup_{u\in[0,n]} |k_u^\mu - k_u^\nu|^2 + 2E \sup_{u\in[n,n+1]} |k_u^\mu - k_u^\nu|^2 < \varepsilon$$

If δ and the bounds in the set A defined above are chosen correctly $P(|\mu_{n+1} - \nu_{n+1}| \leq \gamma) \geq P(A) > 1 - \varepsilon$ implying $P(|\mu_{n+1} - \nu_{n+1}| > \gamma) < \varepsilon$ for any given γ. Hence, using similar arguments as above, there exists $\delta > 0$ such that $\sup_{w\in\Omega} |k_0^\mu(w) - k_0^\nu(w)| < \delta$ and $\sup_{w\in\Omega} |\mu_0^*(w) - \nu_0^*(w)| < \delta$ ensures that $P(|\mu_j - \nu_j| > \gamma) < \varepsilon$ for $j = 1, \ldots, n+1$, $E\sup_{u\in[0,n+1]} |k_u^\mu - k_u^\nu|^2 < \varepsilon$ and $P(\sup_{u\in[0,n+1]} |k_u^\mu - k_u^\nu| > \gamma) < \varepsilon$. This completes the inductive step.

If instead $E|k_0^\mu|^2, E|k_0^\nu|^2 \leq M$ and $\sup_{w\in\Omega} |\mu_0^*(w)|, \sup_{w\in\Omega} |\nu_0^*(w)| \leq M$ then we proceed inductively as above. Since the proof is similar only the initial step is presented. Given $\varepsilon > 0$ choose $n > 0$ such that $M/n^2 < \frac{\varepsilon}{3}$; then $P(|k_0^\mu| > n), P(|k_0^\nu| > n) < \frac{\varepsilon}{3}$. By continuity of the functions defining the bubble at $t = 1$ on $[-n,n] \times [-M,M]^3$, there is a $\gamma > 0$ such that $|k_0^\mu(w)| \leq n$, $|k_0^\nu(w)| \leq n$, $|k_0^\mu(w) - k_0^\nu(w)| < \gamma$ and $|\mu_0^*(w) - \nu_0^*(w)| < \gamma$ implies $|\mu_1(w) - \nu_1(w)| < \varepsilon$. Now, $P(|k_0^\mu - k_0^\nu| \geq \gamma) \leq \gamma^{-2} E|k_0^\mu - k_0^\nu|^2 < \frac{\varepsilon}{3}$ provided $E|k_0^\mu - k_0^\nu|^2 < \delta$ for small enough δ. Thus, for small enough δ we have $P(\{|k_0^\mu| \leq n\} \bigcap \{|k_0^\nu| \leq n\} \bigcap \{|k_0^\mu - k_0^\nu| < \gamma\}) > 1 - \varepsilon$. Let $A = \{|k_0^\mu| \leq n\} \bigcap \{|k_0^\nu| \leq n\} \bigcap \{|k_0^\mu - k_0^\nu| < \gamma\}$. Using boundedness of bubbles gives a constant $B > 0$ such that if $\sup_{w\in\Omega} |\mu_0^*(w) - \nu_0^*(w)| < \rho$ where $\rho = min(\gamma, \delta)$ we have

$$E \sup_{s\in[0,1]} |k_s^\mu - k_s^\nu|^2 \leq a(1)(E|k_0^\mu - k_0^\nu|^2 + \sup_{s\in[0,1]} E|\mu_s - \nu_s|^2) \leq$$

$$a(1)(\delta + \rho^2 + \int_A |\mu_1 - \nu_1|^2 \, dP + \int_{A^C} |\mu_1 - \nu_1|^2 \, dP) \leq$$

$$a(1)(\delta + \rho^2 + \varepsilon^2 + 4B^2\varepsilon)$$

which can be made arbitrarily small by a suitable choice of ε and δ. The rest of the proof is the same as the first case for which bounds are placed on $|k_0^\mu(w) - k_0^\nu(w)| \quad \forall w \in \Omega$. q.e.d.

Proof of Theorem 2.1: For expositional convenience the superscript μ on the exchange rate and money supply is deleted and it is assumed that $\alpha = 1$ in equation (2.8). We will prove left continuiity at a fixed t since the case of right continuity is similar. Throughout the proof assume $|b| \leq M < \infty$ and $s < t$. Clearly, $x_t - x_s =$

$$\int_t^\infty \exp(t-u)E(k_u|\mathcal{F}_t) - \exp(s-u)E(k_u|\mathcal{F}_s) \, du - \int_s^t \exp(s-u)E(k_u|\mathcal{F}_s) \, du$$

The proof works by breaking this expression into a number of random integrals. Some integrals converge to zero a.e. as $s \to t$ from below; others converge to zero in probability as $s \to t$ from below. As in Gagnon (2012) it can be shown that

$$|\int_s^t \exp(s-u)E(k_u|\mathcal{F}_s) \, du| \leq |k_s|(t-s) + M(t-s)^2$$

Thus, $\lim_{s\to t^-} \int_s^t \exp(s-u)E(k_u|\mathcal{F}_s) \, du = 0$. Consequently, we can focus on $\int_t^\infty \exp(t-u)E(k_u|\mathcal{F}_t) - \exp(s-u)E(k_u|\mathcal{F}_s) \, du$.

Clearly,

$$\int_t^\infty \exp(t-u)E(k_u|\mathcal{F}_t) - \exp(s-u)E(k_u|\mathcal{F}_s) \, du =$$

$$\int_t^\infty \exp(t-u)(E(k_u|\mathcal{F}_t) - E(k_u|\mathcal{F}_s)) \, du +$$

$$\int_t^\infty (\exp(t-u) - \exp(s-u))E(k_u|\mathcal{F}_s)\,du$$

Using the inequalities in Gagnon (2012) it can be established that a.e.

$$\lim_{s\to t^-} \int_t^\infty (\exp(t-u) - \exp(s-u))E(k_u|\mathcal{F}_s)\,du = 0$$

Thus we can focus on $\int_t^\infty \exp(t-u)(E(k_u|\mathcal{F}_t) - E(k_u|\mathcal{F}_s))\,du$. Again as in Gagnon (2012), given $\varepsilon > 0$ there exists a $T > t$ such that $\forall s \le t$ we have $|\int_T^\infty \exp(t-u)E(k_u|\mathcal{F}_s)\,du| < \varepsilon$ and $|\int_T^\infty \exp(t-u)E(k_u|\mathcal{F}_t)\,du| < \varepsilon$. Thus, given $\varepsilon > 0$ there exists a $\delta > 0$ such that for suitable T with $t < T$ and $s < t, |t-s| < \delta$ we have

$$|x_t - x_s| < |\int_t^T \exp(t-u)(E(k_u|\mathcal{F}_t) - E(k_u|\mathcal{F}_s))\,du| + \varepsilon$$

Thus, $P(|x_t - x_s| > \delta) \le P(|\int_t^T \exp(t-u)(E(k_u|\mathcal{F}_t) - E(k_u|\mathcal{F}_s))\,du| > \delta - \varepsilon)$ for $\varepsilon < \delta$ and so it suffices to prove for any $\delta > 0$

$$\lim_{s\to t^-} P(|\int_t^T \exp(t-u)(E(k_u|\mathcal{F}_t) - E(k_u|\mathcal{F}_s))\,du| > \delta) = 0$$

To proceed with the proof it is critical to find expressions for $E(k_u|\mathcal{F}_t)$ and $E(k_u|\mathcal{F}_s)$ for $u > t$ which can be easily manipulated. To this end, let $\mu_t^* = (\mu_{[t]-1}, \mu_{[t]-2}, \mu_{[t]-3})$ and $k_t^* = (k_t, k_{[t]}, k_{[t]-1}, k_{[t]-2}, k_{[t]-3})$ where $[\cdot]$ is the greatest integer function. The motivation for these definitions is that we can let the bubble and money supply evolve randomly from time t taking $k_t^*(w)$ and $\mu_t^*(w)$ as initial data for fixed $w \in \Omega$. Since bubbles evolve from money supplies at previous integer times and k_t affects the money supply at integer times $n > t$, k_t^* defined above must include k_t and $k_{[t]}$ if it is going to represent initial data. In the discussion following theorem 3.1 we defined $k_n^* = (k_{n-1}, k_{n-2}, k_{n-3})$ for integers $n \ge 1$; note $k_{-2} = k_{-1} = k_0$. It is trusted that no confusion results from the identical notation for the more general object defined here. Fix $x \in R^5, y \in R^3$ and let $(\xi_{t,x,y}(u), u \ge t)$ be the process solving

$$\xi_{t,x,y}(u) = x_1 + \int_t^u b(v, \mu_v, \xi_{t,x,y}(v))\,dv + \int_t^u \sigma(v, \mu_v, \xi_{t,x,y}(v))\,dW_v$$

where the bubble in this SDE is generated on $[[t], \infty)$ by (x_3, x_4, x_5) and (y_1, y_2, y_3). By this we mean the bubble at $[t]$, denoted $\mu_{[t]}$, is generated by taking y_1, y_2, y_3 as the bubbles at $[t]-1, [t]-2, [t]-3$ respectively and (x_3, x_4, x_5) as the money supplies at $[t]-1, [t]-2, [t]-3$ respectively in (2.1)-(2.5). The variable x_2 is the money supply at $[t]$ and enters the calculation of $\mu_{[t]+1}$. The bubble continues to evolve on (t, ∞) via (2.1)-(2.5) using $(\xi_{t,x,y}(u), u \ge t)$ as the money supply. As in Gagnon (2012), $k_u(w) = \xi_{t,k_t^*(w),\mu_t^*(w)}(u)(w)$ for $u \ge t$ and $k_u(w) = \xi_{s,k_s^*(w),\mu_s^*(w)}(u)(w)$ when $u \ge s$ for a.a. $w \in \Omega$. Note that in the paper there is no expositional distinction between the bubble and the tuple of the bubble and percent of noise traders. For this reason (y_1, y_2, y_3) is referred to as a vector in R^3 instead of R^6. If $b(s, \cdot, k)$ depends only on w_s instead of μ_s, there is a clear cut case for ignoring noise trader percentages in the definition of the Brock-Hommes equilibrium and instead defining a Brock-Hommes equilibrium as the process of bubbles $(w_s, s \ge 0)$. In any case, only lagged bubbles and lagged money supplies are required to generate the next bubble; lagged trader percentages are irrelevant and thus we let $(y_1, y_2, y_3) \in R^3$.

For some integer n, $n < t \leq n+1$ and we may assume $n < s \leq n+1$ as well. If $n < t < n+1$ we can take $s \in (n, n+1)$ and then $\mu_t^* = \mu_s^*$. If $t = n+1$ the initial entry of μ_t^* is μ_n. Let $\mu_s^*(t)$ be the vector of lagged bubbles at $t = n+1$ generated from μ_s^* and k_s^*; then clearly μ_t^* equals $\mu_s^*(t)$. Let $(\mu_u^1, u \geq t)$ be the bubble proccess for times $u \geq t$ associated to $(\xi_{t,k_t^*(w),\mu_t^*(w)}(u), u \geq t)$. It is generated by μ_t^* and k_t^*. Let $(\mu_u^2, u \geq t)$ denote the bubble process for $u \geq t$ associated to $(\xi_{s,k_s^*(w),\mu_s^*(w)}(u), u \geq t)$. It is generated by $\xi_{s,k_s^*(w),\mu_s^*(w)}(t), k_s^*$ and $\mu_s^*(t)$. Moreover, $\mu_{n+1}^1 = \mu_{n+1}^2$ since the bubble at $n+1$ is generated by variables realized before $n+1$; at $n+1$ the money supply $(\xi_{s,k_s^*(w),\mu_s^*(w)}(u), u \geq t)$ has yet to affect $(\mu_u^2, u \geq t)$ and thus μ_{n+1}^2 is determined by the same variables that determine μ_{n+1}^1. Thereafter the bubbles fluctuate because of differences in $(\xi_{s,k_s^*(w),\mu_s^*(w)}(u), u \geq t)$ and $(\xi_{t,k_t^*(w),\mu_t^*(w)}(u), u \geq t)$.

Lemma 3.3 can be established for SDE beginning at any time $s > 0$. Due to continuity of bubbles in initial money supplies and initial bubbles which is used to prove lemma 3.3, bounds on differences in the bubbles $(\mu_u^1, u \geq t)$ and $(\mu_u^2, u \geq t)$ depend exclusively on the difference between $\xi_{s,k_s^*(w),\mu_s^*(w)}(t)$ and k_t since $\mu_t^* = \mu_s^*(t)$. To be precise, we will apply the continuity lemma for a fixed $w \in \Omega$ over $[t, T]$. We treat $k_s^*(w)$, $k_t^*(w), \mu_s^*(w)$ and $\mu_t^*(w)$ as deterministic initial conditions and use these to generate $\mu_s^*(t)$ as well as $\xi_{s,k_s^*(w),\mu_s^*(w)}(t)$. The initial conditions at t in the application of lemma 3.3 are $\mu_s^*(t) = \mu_t^*, k_t$ and $\xi_{s,k_s^*(w),\mu_s^*(w)}(t)$. Then we derive bounds on the random evolution of $\xi_{t,k_t^*(w),\mu_t^*(w)}(u)(z)$ and $\xi_{s,k_s^*(w),\mu_s^*(w)}(u)(z)$ for $u \geq t$ and $z \in \Omega$. Notice that if $t \in (n, n+1)$ the bubbles $(\mu_u^1, u \geq t)$ and $(\mu_u^2, u \geq t)$ still evolve from μ_t^*, $\xi_{s,k_s^*(w),\mu_s^*(w)}(t)$ and k_t^*. Bounds on differences in μ_u^1 and μ_u^2 for $u > t$ still depend on differences in $\xi_{s,k_s^*(w),\mu_s^*(w)}(t)$ and k_t. The reason this representation simplifies the analytics whether $t < n+1$ or $t = n+1$ is that the conditional expectations $E(k_u|\mathcal{F}_t)$ and $E(k_u|\mathcal{F}_s)$ can be expressed as integrals of $\xi_{t,k_t^*(w),\mu_t^*(w)}(u)(z)$ and $\xi_{s,k_s^*(w),\mu_s^*(w)}(u)(z)$ respectively. Specifically, for almost all $w \in \Omega$

$$E(k_u|\mathcal{F}_t)(w) = \int_\Omega \xi_{t,k_t^*(w),\mu_t^*(w)}(u)(z)\, dP(z) \quad \forall u > t \quad \text{and}$$

$$E(k_u|\mathcal{F}_s)(w) = \int_\Omega \xi_{s,k_s^*(w),\mu_s^*(w)}(u)(z)\, dP(z) \quad \forall u > s$$

When convenient the notation $w \in \Omega$ in these expressions is surpressed. Lemma 3.2 can be proved for SDE beginning at any time $s > 0$ without any change in the constant L or the polynomial p. Since for $u > t$ we have $\xi_{s,k_s^*,\mu_s^*}(u) = \xi_{s,k_s^*,\mu_s^*}(t) + \int_t^u b(v, \mu_v^2, \xi_{s,k_s^*,\mu_s^*}(v))\; dv + \int_t^u \sigma(v, \mu_v^2, \xi_{s,k_s^*,\mu_s^*}(v))\; dW_v$ and $\xi_{t,k_t^*,\mu_t^*}(u) = k_t + \int_t^u b(v, \mu_v^1, \xi_{t,k_t^*,\mu_t^*}(v))\; dv + \int_t^u \sigma(v, \mu_v^1, \xi_{t,k_t^*,\mu_t^*}(v))\; dW_v$, applying lemma 3.2 for $t \leq u \leq T$ yields $\int_\Omega |\xi_{t,k_t^*,\mu_t^*}(u)(z) - \xi_{s,k_s^*,\mu_s^*}(u)(z)|^2\, dP(z)$

$$\leq L\exp(LT)\Big(\int_\Omega |\xi_{s,k_s^*(w),\mu_s^*(w)}(t)(z) - k_t|^2\, dP(z) +$$

$$p(T) \sup_{t \leq v \leq T} \int_\Omega |\mu_v^1(z) - \mu_v^2(z)|^2\, dP(z)\Big)$$

Returning to the essential argument in the proof, it is necessary to show that $\lim_{s \to t^-} P(|\int_t^T \exp(t-u)(E(k_u|\mathcal{F}_t) - E(k_u|\mathcal{F}_s))\, du| > \delta) = 0$. Clearly,

$$E|\int_t^T \exp(t-u)(E(k_u|\mathcal{F}_t) - E(k_u|\mathcal{F}_s))\, du| \leq$$

$$E\int_t^T \exp(t-u)|E(k_u|\mathcal{F}_t)-E(k_u|\mathcal{F}_s)|\,du$$

$$\leq \int_t^T \exp(t-u)E\int_\Omega |\xi_{t,k_t^*,\mu_t^*}(u)(z)-\xi_{s,k_s^*,\mu_s^*}(u)(z)|\,dP(z)\,du$$

Since

$$P(|\int_t^T \exp(t-u)(E(k_u|\mathcal{F}_t)-E(k_u|\mathcal{F}_s))\,du|>\delta)\leq$$

$$\delta^{-1}E|\int_t^T \exp(t-u)(E(k_u|\mathcal{F}_t)-E(k_u|\mathcal{F}_s))\,du|$$

we need only show

$$\lim_{s\to t^-}\int_t^T \exp(t-u)E\int_\Omega |\xi_{t,k_t^*,\mu_t^*}(u)(z)-\xi_{s,k_s^*,\mu_s^*}(u)(z)|\,dP(z)\,du=0$$

To this end we apply the continuous parameter version of the Dominated Convergence Theorem. The first step is to show that for $u\in[t,T]$

$$\lim_{s\to t^-}\int_\Omega |\xi_{t,k_t^*,\mu_t^*}(u)(z)-\xi_{s,k_s^*,\mu_s^*}(u)(z)|\,dP(z)=0$$

Since

$$\int_\Omega |\xi_{t,k_t^*,\mu_t^*}(u)(z)-\xi_{s,k_s^*,\mu_s^*}(u)(z)|\,dP(z)\leq \int_\Omega |\xi_{t,k_t^*,\mu_t^*}(u)(z)-\xi_{s,k_s^*,\mu_s^*}(u)(z)|^2\,dP(z)^{\frac{1}{2}}$$

it suffices to show $\lim_{s\to t^-}\int_\Omega |\xi_{t,k_t^*,\mu_t^*}(u)(z)-\xi_{s,k_s^*,\mu_s^*}(u)(z)|^2\,dP(z)=0$. Using the fact that μ_0^* is bounded on Ω yields that μ_s^* and μ_t^* are bounded on Ω. It can be shown that the bubbles $(\mu_u^1,u\geq t)$ and $(\mu_u^2,u\geq s)$ are uniformly bounded on Ω over finite intervals containing s; in fact the bound depends only on the upper bound of the interval and not on s. Thus, by lemma 3.1, there is a constant $C>0$ such that

$$\int_\Omega |\xi_{s,k_s^*(w),\mu_s^*(w)}(t)(z)|^2\,dP(z)\leq L\exp(Lt)(|k_s(w)|^2+C)$$

Since $k_u(w)$ is bounded on finite intervals a.e. when viewed as a function of u, $L\exp(Lt)(|k_s(w)|^2+C)\leq M(w)$ for $s\leq t$ where $M(w)$ is a finite constant depending on w. Hence, the integrability conditions in lemma 3.3 are satisfied for any $s\leq t$. By lemma 3.3, if $\lim_{s\to t^-}\int_\Omega |\xi_{s,k_s^*(w),\mu_s^*(w)}(t)(z)-k_t|^2\,dP(z)=0$ and $u\in[t,T]$, we can choose $\varepsilon,\gamma>0$ arbitrarily small and define the set A_u by $A_u=\{z\in\Omega:|\mu_u^1(z)-\mu_u^2(z)|\leq\gamma\}$ and be assured that $P(A_u^C)<\varepsilon$ provided s is close to t. Then because bubbles are bounded on $[t,T]$ by a constant $M>0$ we have $\int_\Omega |\mu_u^1(z)-\mu_u^2(z)|^2\,dP(z)=$

$$\int_{A_u}|\mu_u^1(z)-\mu_u^2(z)|^2\,dP(z)+\int_{A_u^C}|\mu_u^1(z)-\mu_u^2(z)|^2\,dP(z)\leq\gamma^2+4M^2\varepsilon$$

implying $\sup_{t\leq u\leq T}\int_\Omega |\mu_u^1(z)-\mu_u^2(z)|^2\,dP(z)\leq\gamma^2+4M^2\varepsilon$.

Thus, for suitable $\delta>0$ and $s<t$ where $|t-s|<\delta$ there is a constant $K>0$ such that when $u\in[t,T]$

$$\int_\Omega |\xi_{t,k_t^*(w),\mu_t^*(w)}(u)(z)-\xi_{s,k_s^*(w),\mu_s^*(w)}(u)(z)|^2\,dP(z)\le L\exp(LT)$$
$$(\int_\Omega |\xi_{s,k_s^*(w),\mu_s^*(w)}(t)(z)-k_t|^2\,dP(z)+p(T)\sup_{t\le v\le T}\int_\Omega |\mu_v^1(z)-\mu_v^2(z)|^2\,dP(z))$$
$$\le K(\int_\Omega |\xi_{s,k_s^*(w),\mu_s^*(w)}(t)(z)-k_t|^2\,dP(z)+\gamma^2+M^2\varepsilon)<K(\varepsilon+\gamma^2+M^2\varepsilon)$$

implying $\lim_{s\to t^-}\int_\Omega |\xi_{t,k_t^*,\mu_t^*}(u)(z)-\xi_{s,k_s^*,\mu_s^*}(u)(z)|^2\,dP(z)=0$ for $u\in[t,T]$ as asserted above.

To establish $\lim_{s\to t^-}\int_\Omega |\xi_{s,k_s^*(w),\mu_s^*(w)}(t)(z)-k_t|^2\,dP(z)=0$ observe that for some $K>0$

$$\int_\Omega |\xi_{s,k_s^*(w),\mu_s^*(w)}(t)(z)-k_t|^2\,dP(z)\le$$
$$K(\int_\Omega |\xi_{s,k_s^*(w),\mu_s^*(w)}(t)(z)-k_s|^2\,dP(z)+|k_s-k_t|^2) \quad (3.5)$$

By continuity, $\lim_{s\to t^-}|k_s(w)-k_t(w)|^2=0$ so we need only prove

$$\lim_{s\to t^-}\int_\Omega |\xi_{s,k_s^*(w),\mu_s^*(w)}(t)(z)-k_s|^2\,dP(z)=0$$

Since

$$\xi_{s,k_s^*,\mu_s^*}(t)=k_s+\int_s^t b(v,\mu_v^2,\xi_{s,k_s^*,\mu_s^*}(v))\,dv+\int_s^t \sigma(v,\mu_v^2,\xi_{s,k_s^*,\mu_s^*}(v))\,dW_v$$

we have $\int_\Omega |\xi_{s,k_s^*,\mu_s^*}(t)-k_s|^2\,dP(z)\le C\int_s^t(\int_\Omega |\xi_{s,k_s^*,\mu_s^*}(u)(z)|^2\,dP(z)+1)\,du$ for a suitable constant $C>0$ since bubbles are bounded on bounded intervals. However, by lemma 3.1 and boundedness of bubbles on bounded intervals, for $u\subset[s,t]$ there is a constant $D>0$ such that

$$\int_\Omega |\xi_{s,k_s^*(w),\mu_s^*(w)}(u)(z)|^2\,dP(z)\le L\exp(Lt)(|k_s(w)|^2+D)\le$$
$$L\exp(Lt)(\sup_{v\in[0,T]}|k_v(w)|^2+D)$$

Thus, there is a constant $K>0$ such that for $u\in[s,t]$ we have

$$\int_\Omega |\xi_{s,k_s^*(w),\mu_s^*(w)}(u)(z)|^2\,dP(z)\le K(\sup_{v\in[0,T]}|k_v(w)|^2+1)\quad \text{implying that}$$

$$\int_\Omega |\xi_{s,k_s^*,\mu_s^*}(t)-k_s|^2\,dP(z)\le C(t-s)(K\sup_{v\in[0,T]}|k_v(w)|^2+K+1)\quad (3.6)$$

This proves $\lim_{s\to t^-}\int_\Omega |\xi_{s,k_s^*(w),\mu_s^*(w)}(t)(z)-k_t|^2\,dP(z)=0$.

Clearly, $\int_\Omega |\xi_{t,k_t^*(w),\mu_t^*(w)}(u)(z)-\xi_{s,k_s^*(w),\mu_s^*(w)}(u)(z)|^2\,dP(z)$ can be regarded as a function of $w\in\Omega$ and $K(\sup_{v\in[0,T]}|k_v(w)|^2+1)\in L^1(\Omega,\mathcal{F},P)$ for any $K>0$. By lemma 3.2 and inequalities (3.5) and (3.6), for $u\in[t,T]$ and a suitable constant $K>0$

$$\int_\Omega |\xi_{t,k_t^*(w),\mu_t^*(w)}(u)(z)-\xi_{s,k_s^*(w),\mu_s^*(w)}(u)(z)|^2\,dP(z)\le K(\sup_{v\in[0,T]}|k_v(w)|^2+1)\in L^1$$

Hence, for $u \in [t,T]$

$$\int_\Omega |\xi_{t,k_t^*,\mu_t^*}(u)(z) - \xi_{s,k_s^*,\mu_s^*}(u)(z)|\, dP(z) \le \int_\Omega |\xi_{t,k_t^*,\mu_t^*}(u)(z) - \xi_{s,k_s^*,\mu_s^*}(u)(z)|^2\, dP(z)^{\frac{1}{2}}$$

$$\le (K \sup_{v\in[0,T]} |k_v(w)|^2 + K)^{\frac{1}{2}} \in L^2 \subset L^1$$

Applying the continuous parameter version of the Dominated Convergence Theorem yields $\lim_{s\to t^-} E\int_\Omega |\xi_{t,k_t^*,\mu_t^*}(u)(z) - \xi_{s,k_s^*,\mu_s^*}(u)(z)|\, dP(z) = 0$ for any $u \in [t,T]$. Since

$$E\int_\Omega |\xi_{t,k_t^*,\mu_t^*}(u)(z) - \xi_{s,k_s^*,\mu_s^*}(u)(z)|\, dP(z) \le E(K \sup_{v\in[0,T]} |k_v(w)|^2 + K)^{\frac{1}{2}}$$

and $E(K\sup_{v\in[0,T]} |k_v(w)|^2 + K)^{\frac{1}{2}} = C$ can be regarded as a constant function of $u \in [t,T]$, we have $\exp(t-u)E\int_\Omega |\xi_{t,k_t^*,\mu_t^*}(u)(z) - \xi_{s,k_s^*,\mu_s^*}(u)(z)|\, dP(z) \le C\exp(t-u) \in L^1([t,T])$. Consequently, we can apply the continuous parameter version of the Dominated Convergence Theorem on $[t,T]$ to yield

$$\lim_{s\to t^-} \int_t^T \exp(t-u)E\int_\Omega |\xi_{t,k_t^*,\mu_t^*}(u)(z) - \xi_{s,k_s^*,\mu_s^*}(u)(z)|\, dP(z)\, du = 0$$

We have shown that $\forall\delta > 0 \quad \lim_{s\to t^-} P(|x_s - x_t| > \delta) = 0$. Similar arguments establish $\lim_{s\to t^+} P(|x_s - x_t| > \delta) = 0$. q.e.d.

One of the main innovations in the proof of exchange rate continuity in probability when compared to the continuity of exchange rate sample paths in Gagnon (2012), is that critical bounds can only be placed on expectations instead of individual sample paths. Establishing critical inequalities on a sample path basis is clearly stronger than establishing bounds on expectations. Once again, the complication comes from allowing σ to depend on bubbles and money supplies instead of just time. This generalization of σ makes it impossible to establish the sample path bounds in Gagnon (2012). Nevertheless, the portrait which emerges is one of a financial market with endogenous, rather than exogenous, jumps. Now, we turn to the assumptions driving the exchange rate bifurcation. Recall that if $V \subset R^n$ then $\bar{V}$ denotes the closure of V.

Assumption 3.2: Let $\mu = ((w_s^1, m_s^1), s \ge 0)$ and $\nu = ((w_s^2, m_s^2), s \ge 0) \in \mathcal{M}(R^2)$ be Brock-Hommes equilibria satisfying $\mu_0 \ne \nu_0$. Then $k_0^\mu \ne k_0^\nu$ a.e. In particular, if $w_0^1 < w_0^2$ then $k_0^\mu < k_0^\nu$ a.e. Moreover, if μ, ν are generated from deterministic Brock-Hommes bubbles, k_0^μ and k_0^ν are deterministic.

Assumption 3.3: Let $\mu^i, i = 1,2,3$ represent the bubbles generated by the fixed points of the deterministic Brock-Hommes model. Let k_0^i be the initial money supply associated to μ^i. For each i there exists an open set U_i of k_0^i such that for some bounded open set V_i with $\bar{U}_i \subset V_i$ we have $b(s,z,x) = \sigma(s,z,x) = 0 \quad \forall (s,z,x) \in R^+ \times R^2 \times V_i - U_i$.

Assumption 3.4: Suppose the sets $\bar{V}_i$ in assumption 3.3 are disjoint, $i = 1,2,3$. Let $\mu^i = ((w_s^i, m_s^i), s \ge 0) \in \mathcal{M}(R^2), i = 1,2,3$ be the bubbles generated by the fixed points of the deterministic Brock-Hommes model. Let $(k_s^i, s \ge 0)$ be the money supply generated by $\mu^i, i = 1,2,3$. Then a.e.:

1) $b(s,\mu_s^3,k) \le b(s,\mu_s^1,k) \le b(s,\mu_s^2,k) \quad \forall (s,k) \in R^+ \times R$
2) $\sigma(s,\mu_s^2,v) \le \sigma(s,\mu_s^1,k) \le \sigma(s,\mu_s^2,k) \quad \forall s \in R^+, k \in \bar{V}_1, v \in \bar{V}_2$
3) $\sigma(s,\mu_s^1,k) \le \sigma(s,\mu_s^3,v) \le \sigma(s,\mu_s^1,v) \quad \forall s \in R^+, k \in \bar{V}_1, v \in \bar{V}_3$
4) $b(s,\mu_s^1,k) \le b(s,\mu_s^2,v)$ when $v \in \bar{V}_2, k \in \bar{V}_1 \quad \forall s \in R^+$
5) $b(s,\mu_s^3,v) \le b(s,\mu_s^1,k)$ when $v \in \bar{V}_3, k \in \bar{V}_1 \quad \forall s \in R^+$

The meaning of assumptions 3.2-3.4 is that the central bank distinguishes between different bubbles when it sets money growth. Condition (1) of assumption 3.4 states that policy responds to the higher bubble with higher money growth. Assumption 3.2 is similar in spirit since the bank sets a higher initial money supply for the higher bubble state. The motivation is that if the central bank observes a higher bubble it might decide to encourage it via higher money growth. If the function f in (2.5) is monotone increasing, the higher money supply will increase the chance that trend chasing g_n is high. This can perpetuate the bubble and result in greater depreciation. The background motivation is that depreciation will provide the economy with an export stimulus. While the export impact is not specifically in the model, it does form an adequate motivation for policy which can be made explicit in the coefficients of the stochastic differential equation governing money growth. To see that a policy which propagates bubbles with the aim of encouraging depreciation is plausible, we point to certain key episodes. For instance, the 1930's witnessed a period of competitive depreciations by central banks trying to counter the depression with export lead growth. Furthermore, the Plaza Accord represented an attempt by central banks to depreciate the U.S. dollar and improve the U.S. current account. Central banks intended that U.S. interest rate reductions coupled with interest rate increases in Europe and Japan, would depreciate the dollar. They must have anticipated that such policy changes would intensify speculation against the dollar.

Assumption 3.3 will result in the money supply corresponding to μ^i being confined to the set V_i; for convenience we say it is confined to the compact set $\bar{V}_i$. The interpretation is that the central bank is reluctant to implement money growth outside certain bounded neighbourhoods of the initial conditions. Monetary policy is in effect localized to certain regions. This might also be interpreted as monetary targeting. Provided the function f in the trend chasing equation is increasing, a further interpretation is that the central bank does not allow unrestrained encouragement of bubbles as it depreciates its currency. Condition 1 of assumption 3.4 states that the central bank does respond to a higher bubble with higher money growth. Thus, it does act to encourage bubbles. However, the encouragement is held within well prescribed limits. The sets $V_i - U_i$ act as barriers to unrestrained money growth and depreciation. Again, this is a rational assumption since even when a central bank seeks an export stimulus there are limits to the amount of inflation it is willing tolerate. Specifically, in proving theorem 3.3 we show that the money supply in $\bar{V}_2$ is higher than the money supply in $\bar{V}_1$; generally, the money supply in $\bar{V}_i$ is higher than the money supply in $\bar{V}_j$ for all $j < i$.

Conditions (2) and (3) of assumption 3.4 are necessary to prove theorem 3.3, the comparison theorem. They place restrictions on the diffusion coefficients in the sets which trap the money supplies. For example, condition (2) states that the bank implements lower volatility for the higher bubble provided the money supply remains in $\bar{V}_2$. The volatility used in the comparison corresponds to the lower bubble and money supply in $\bar{V}_1$. If the money supply in the higher bubble state is in $\bar{V}_1$, then volatility rises. The meaning of the condition is that the bank implements lower volatility with the higher money supply, but that if the money supply is lower it allows greater volatility. Since the bank acts to perpetuate a bubble it seems reasonable that it might allow smaller fluxes around the higher money growth rate. Otherwise it would create both high money growth and high volatility; their product could be unacceptably high inflation. For money supplies in $\bar{V}_1$, the higher bubble encourages the central bank to raise volatility. Again, there is a reasonable interpretation. Since the bank encourages speculation, it couples a lower money growth rate with greater volatility. Greater volatility around the low money growth rate will give some added depreciation and induce more speculation.

While these assumptions might appear stylized it is worth noting that no one really understands the internal dynamics governing central bank monetary policy. It has sometimes been observed that forecasting interest rates is difficult because of the personalities of members of the Federal Reserve Open Market Committee. It is worth exploring what certain policy structures will imply for the exchange rate even if they are not currently being implemented. The conclusions of theoretical models thereby act as a framework for understanding exchange rate dynamics if these policies are implemented. However, it is not inconceivable that central banks do construct monetary policy with some localization. For instance, localization requires that money growth vanish outside some bounded sets. It is known that there can be long term patterns in monetary policy. For example, prior to the subprime mortgage crisis central banks followed a low interest rate policy. This suggests that money growth would be confined to a certain set to maintain the interest rate target. Furthermore, central banks have been known to practice monetary targeting. Again, this suggests that the money supply would be confined to a certain set. Theorem 3.2 shows that localization implies exactly this kind of restriction in the money supply. This result is known to probabilists, but not economists, so its proof is included for completeness.

Theorem 3.2: Let $\mu^i, i = 1,2,3$ represent the bubbles generated by the fixed points of the deterministic Brock-Hommes model and $(k_t^i, t \geq 0)$ the corresponding money supplies. Then $k_t^i \in \bar{V}_i$ a.e. for all $t \geq 0$ simultaneously for all $i = 1,2,3$. This means there are measurable sets A_i with $P(A_i) = 1 \quad \forall i = 1,2,3$ such that $w \in A_i$ implies $k_t^i(w) \in \bar{V}_i \quad \forall t \geq 0$.

Proof: For concreteness take $i = 1$. Let $\tau = \inf\{t \geq 0 : k_t^1 \notin V_1\}$. For $t < \tau$ clearly $k_t^1 \in V_1$. On the set where $(k_t^1, t \geq 0)$ is continuous, we prove that $\tau = \infty$ a.e. If $\tau < \infty$ then there exists $s \geq \tau$ with $k_s^1 \notin V_1$. The process begins at $k_0^1 \in U_1$. By continuity of the sample paths the process must exit U_1 at a finite time before it exits V_1. Let $\tau_1 = \inf\{t \geq 0 : k_t^1 \notin U_1\}$; clearly $k_{\tau_1}^1 \in \bar{U}_1$. By continuity there must be some $t \in (\tau_1, \tau)$ such that $k_t^1 \in V_1 - \bar{U}_1$.

Let $\tau_2 = \sup\{s \in [\tau_1, t] : k_s^1 \in \bar{U}_1\}$. Clearly, since $V_1 - \bar{U}_1$ is open there exists δ with $\tau_1 < \delta < t$ and $k_s^1 \in V_1 - \bar{U}_1 \quad \forall s \in (\delta, t]$. Thus, $t > \tau_2$ and hence $k_t^1 = k_{\tau_2}^1 + \int_{\tau_2}^t b(s, \mu_s^1, k_s^1)\, ds + \int_{\tau_2}^t \sigma(s, \mu_s^1, k_s^1)\, dW_s$. However, for $s \in (\tau_2, t]$ we have $k_s^1 \in V_1 - U_1$ because $s \leq t < \tau$ implies $k_s^1 \in V_1$ and $s > \tau_2$ implies $k_s^1 \notin \bar{U}_1$. Thus, $b(s, \mu_s^1, k_s^1) = \sigma(s, \mu_s^1, k_s^1) = 0 \quad \forall s \in (\tau_2, t]$ and this implies $\int_{\tau_2}^t b(s, \mu_s^1, k_s^1)\, ds = \int_{\tau_2}^t \sigma(s, \mu_s^1, k_s^1)\, dW_s = 0$. Clearly, $k_t^1 = k_{\tau_2}^1$ and $k_{\tau_2}^1 \in \bar{U}_1$, implying a contradiction. q.e.d.

Theorem 3.3: Let $\mu^i, i = 1,2,3$ represent the bubbles generated by the fixed points of the deterministic Brock-Hommes model. Let $(k_t^i, t \geq 0)$ be the money supply associated to $\mu^i, i = 1,2,3$. Thus, $\mu^i = ((w_t^i, m_t^i), t \geq 0)$ where $w_t^3 < w_t^1 < w_t^2 \quad \forall t$. Let y_t^i and x_t^i denote the exchange rate at t and the fundamental exchange rate at t corresponding to $\mu^i, i = 1,2,3$ respectively. Then $y_t^3 < y_t^1 < y_t^2$ a.e. and $x_t^3 < x_t^1 < x_t^2$ a.e. for all t simultaneously.

Proof: The result will be proved for μ^1 and μ^2 since the proof for μ^3 and μ^1 is analagous. First, it is shown that $k_t^2 > k_t^1$ a.e. The semimartingale $(k_t^1 - k_t^2, t \geq 0)$ satisfies

$$k_t^1 - k_t^2 = k_0^1 - k_0^2 + \int_0^t b(s,\mu_s^1,k_s^1) - b(s,\mu_s^2,k_s^2)\, ds + \int_0^t \sigma(s,\mu_s^1,k_s^1) - \sigma(s,\mu_s^2,k_s^2)\, dW_s$$

The function $h(x) = (x^+)^2$ is in $C^2(R - \{0\}, R)$ where $x^+ = max(0,x)$. We may apply Ito's lemma using h and the semimartingale $(k_t^1 - k_t^2, t \geq 0)$ because $\bar{V}_1 \bigcap \bar{V}_2 = \emptyset$ implies $P(k_t^1 - k_t^2 \neq 0 \quad \forall t \geq 0) = 1$. Thus,

$$((k_t^1 - k_t^2)^+)^2 = 2\int_0^t 1_{\{k_s^1 > k_s^2\}}(k_s^1 - k_s^2)(b(s,\mu_s^1,k_s^1) - b(s,\mu_s^2,k_s^2))\, ds +$$

$$2\int_0^t 1_{\{k_s^1 > k_s^2\}}(k_s^1 - k_s^2)(\sigma(s,\mu_s^1,k_s^1) - \sigma(s,\mu_s^2,k_s^2))\, dW_s +$$

$$\int_0^t 1_{\{k_s^1 > k_s^2\}}(\sigma(s,\mu_s^1,k_s^1) - \sigma(s,\mu_s^2,k_s^2))^2\, ds$$

Taking expectations yields

$$E((k_t^1 - k_t^2)^+)^2 = 2E\int_0^t 1_{\{k_s^1 > k_s^2\}}(k_s^1 - k_s^2)(b(s,\mu_s^1,k_s^1) - b(s,\mu_s^2,k_s^2))\, ds +$$

$$E\int_0^t 1_{\{k_s^1 > k_s^2\}}(\sigma(s,\mu_s^1,k_s^1) - \sigma(s,\mu_s^2,k_s^2))^2\, ds$$

Clearly, $1_{\{k_s^1 > k_s^2\}}(k_s^1 - k_s^2)(b(s,\mu_s^1,k_s^1) - b(s,\mu_s^2,k_s^2)) =$

$$1_{\{k_s^1 > k_s^2\}}(k_s^1 - k_s^2)^+(b(s,\mu_s^1,k_s^1) - b(s,\mu_s^2,k_s^2)) \leq$$

$$1_{\{k_s^1 > k_s^2\}}(k_s^1 - k_s^2)^+(b(s,\mu_s^2,k_s^1) - b(s,\mu_s^2,k_s^2)) \leq K((k_s^1 - k_s^2)^+)^2$$

where K is the constant in the Lipschitz conditions of assumption 3.1.

Since $k_t^2 \in \bar{V}_2$ and $k_t^1 \in \bar{V}_1$ we have $0 \leq \sigma(s,\mu_s^1,k_s^1) - \sigma(s,\mu_s^2,k_s^2) \leq \sigma(s,\mu_s^2,k_s^1) - \sigma(s,\mu_s^2,k_s^2)$. Thus, $1_{\{k_s^1 > k_s^2\}}(\sigma(s,\mu_s^1,k_s^1) - \sigma(s,\mu_s^2,k_s^2))^2 \leq K^2((k_s^1 - k_s^2)^+)^2$ and hence $E((k_t^1 - k_t^2)^+)^2 \leq (2K + K^2)\int_0^t E((k_s^1 - k_s^2)^+)^2\, ds$. Gronwall's inequality implies $(k_t^1 - k_t^2)^+ = 0$ a.e. implying $k_t^1 \leq k_t^2$. By continuity $k_t^1 \leq k_t^2$ a.e. for all t simultaneously. Since $\bar{V}_1 \bigcap \bar{V}_2 = \emptyset, \quad k_t^1 \neq k_t^2$ implying $k_t^1 < k_t^2$ a.e. for all t simultaneously.

For simplicity assume $\alpha = 1$, then

$$\int_t^\infty \exp(t-s) E(\int_t^s b(u,\mu_u^1,k_u^1)\, du | \mathcal{F}_t)\, ds \leq$$

$$\int_t^\infty \exp(t-s) E(\int_t^s b(u,\mu_u^2,k_u^2)\, du | \mathcal{F}_t)\, ds$$

Hence

$$x_t^2 = k_t^2 + \int_t^\infty \exp(t-s) E(\int_t^s b(u,\mu_u^2,k_u^2)\, du | \mathcal{F}_t)\, ds >$$

$$k_t^1 + \int_t^\infty \exp(t-s)E(\int_t^s b(u,\mu_u^1,k_u^1)\, du|\mathcal{F}_t)\, ds = x_t^1$$

Adding w_t^1 to both sides and observing that $w_t^1 < w_t^2$ yields $y_t^2 > y_t^1$ q.e.d.

Bifurcation refers to a change in the structure of the equilibrium in a dynamical system as critical parameters are varied. In the case of the deterministic Brock-Hommes model small changes in either g or β produce multiple fixed point bubbles. This translates into random bubbles which are positive, negative or zero. Each bubble produces a distinct exchange rate. For example, when changes in core trend chasing force g above $2R$ then x_t^2 as well as x_t^3 join x_t^1 as interesting exchange rates. Therefore, small changes in the propensity to chase trends or switch predictors creates quanitatively different exchange rate paths. The form of bifurcation contemplated in theorem 3.3 might be called pathwise bifurcation since fluxes in critical parameters affects random paths with probability one.

Theorem 3.3 clearly demonstrates a form of exchange rate instability. Fluxes in g or β result in distinct bubbles and distinct exchange rates. Policy localization and the tendency to encourage positive bubbles generate multiple possible equilibrium exchange rates. Moreover, it is not necessary that policy localization occurs for all times to generate the fluctuation. If localization occurs up to a random time τ and then the central bank follows a different policy for times $t > \tau$, theorem 3.3 will still hold for $t < \tau$ provided the policy for $t > \tau$ is unanticipated by investors. One of the major differences with Gagnon (2012) is that the inequalities presented here apply to both the fundamental and actual exchange rates. In Gagnon (2012), it is assumed that the central bank tries to counter speculation and inequalities are presented only for fundamental exchange rates.

The inequalities in theorem 3.3 are not the only form of bifurcation observed in stochastic models cf. Arnold (1998), Berglund and Gentz (2002) and Chiarella, He and Zheng (2011). Since Berglund and Gentz (2002) analyze the sample paths of a stochastic equation their analysis is closest in spirit to the analysis of the stochastic Brock-Hommes system. Berglund and Gentz (2002) analyze fluxes in the sample paths of a stochastic differential equation where the drift has a bifurcation parameter. The deterministic differential equation defined by the drift exhibits pitchfork bifurcation. They demonstrate that if the bifurcation parameter varies slowly the stochastic counterpart of the deterministic system exhibits delayed bifurcation. This means the stochastic sample paths stay within a neighbourhood of the origin for a significant period of time even after the origin has ceased to be a stable equilibrium point. Once again, the parallel is that our paper analyzes variations in the sample paths of a stochastic dynamical system.

It is clear that the system defined by (2.1)-(2.9) is a general dynamical system. Its behavior depends on the parameters of the classical Brock-Hommes system as well as the drift and volatility of the money supply. Assumptions on the drift, volatility and parameters are necessary to be precise about the qualitative behavior of the system. Of course, this is hardly a new concept in either the probability or dynamical systems literature. However, it is worth noting that the results here describe one interesting set of dynamics and there might be considerable variation in dynamics depending on how the central bank chooses to behave. Often, researchers use a control theoretic framework to describe central bank policy. The bank chooses policy controls to minimize a loss function cf. Mundaca and Oksendal (1998), Zampolli (2006). While perfectly valid, this approach does not provide in depth analysis of what a central bank might have latitude to accomplish. Part of the motivation in examining the dynamics presented here is to analyze exactly this kind of issue. In this case, the tendency to encourage depreciation and policy localization generates a kind of exchange rate instability. The next assumption gives a sharper result on the exchange rate sample paths.

Assumption 3.5: $\bar{V}_i \subset [a_i, b_i]$ where $-\infty < a_i < b_i < \infty, i = 1,2,3$. Furthermore, $b_3 < a_1 < b_1 < a_2$.

Theorem 3.4: Let $\mu^i, i = 1,2,3$ represent the bubbles generated by the fixed points of the deterministic Brock-Hommes model. Let $(k_t^i, t \geq 0)$ be the money supply associated to $\mu^i, i = 1,2,3$. Then $x_t^i \in [a_i, b_i], i = 1,2,3$ where $(x_t^i, t \geq 0)$ is the fundamental exchange rate corresponding to μ^i.

Proof: For convenience take $\alpha = 1$ in (2.8). Since $a_i \leq k_t^i \leq b_i \quad \forall t \geq 0$, $a_i \leq E(k_s^i|\mathcal{F}_t) \leq b_i \quad \forall s \geq t$. Thus, $a_i \exp(t-s) \leq \exp(t-s)E(k_s^i|\mathcal{F}_t) \leq b_i \exp(t-s)$. Integrating both inequalities with respect to s and observing $\int_t^\infty \exp(t-s)\, ds = 1$ yields $a_i \leq \int_t^\infty \exp(t-s)E(k_s^i|\mathcal{F}_t)\, ds \leq b_i$. q.e.d.

Essentially, theorem 3.4 is a trapping result for exchange rates and is the mirror image of policy localization which traps money supplies. Theorem 3.4 follows from assumption 3.5. While exchange rate bifurcation follows from assumptions 3.3 and 3.4, the fact that exchange rates are only continuous in probability makes it difficult to make precise sample path comparisons for x_t^i and x_t^j over bounded intervals when $i \neq j$. Theorem 3.4 gives a sharp sample path result since it traps exchange rates in certain sets for all t simultaneously. It represents an interesting result in that one conventional method of trapping exchange rates is to assume that at some time the central bank fixes the exchange rate. One policy option for fixing rates is to assume the central bank freezes the money supply at a particular level. Clearly, this is a restrictive policy assumption. One appealing feature of localization is that the money supply continues to fluctuate randomly at all times. At the same time the random process does not become unbounded, reflecting a commitment to monetary targeting. While localization does not fix the exchange rate, it leaves the currency trapped in bounded regions. More to the point, exchange rates often move in distinct trading ranges for some periods of time. This might even be regarded as a stylized fact. However, there does not seem to be a theoretical model to explain this phenomenon. Trapping of the fundamental exchange rates does not immediately mean that the observed exchange rates $(y_t^i, t \geq 0)$ become trapped in distinct ranges as the next result demonstrates.

Definition 3.2: Suppose $\{f_n\}_{n=1}^\infty$ is a sequence of functions such that $f_n : \Omega \to R$ for an arbitrary set Ω. We say $\liminf_{n\to\infty} f_n(w) > v$ uniformly if there exists a $\delta > 0$ and an integer $n \geq 1$ such that for all $w \in \Omega$ we have $\inf_{k\geq n} f_k(w) > v + \delta$.

Clearly, $\liminf_{n\to\infty} f_n(w) > v$ uniformly if $\inf_{k\geq n} f_k(w)$ converges uniformly on Ω to $\sup_{n\geq 1} \inf_{k\geq n} f_k(w)$ and there exists a $\delta > 0$ such that $\sup_{n\geq 1} \inf_{k\geq n} f_k(w) > v + \delta$ for every $w \in \Omega$. The criteria in definition 3.2 gives a lower bound on the growth of the sequence of functions $\{f_n\}_{n=1}^\infty$. The application of the notion in definition 3.2 comes from considering the switching probability $q_{2,n}$ as a function on $\bar{V}_i^2 \times R^3$ which we denote by $q_{2,n}(k_1, k_2, w_1, w_2, w_3)$ where $\bar{V}_i^2 = \bar{V}_i \times \bar{V}_i$. We are going to assume that $\liminf_{n\to\infty} q_{2,n}(k_1, k_2, w_1, w_2, w_3) \frac{g+f(k_1)}{1+r+b(n,k_1)} > 1$ uniformly. This criteria ensures that bubbles explode as theorem 3.5 demonstrates.

Theorem 3.5: Suppose $b, f \geq 0$ and that $b(s,z,k) = b(s,k)$ for all $(s,z,k) \in R^+ \times R^3$. Consider the switching probability $q_{2,n}$ as a function on $\bar{V}_i^2 \times R^3$. Denote it by $q_{2,n}(k_1,k_2,w_1,w_2,w_3)$ for $(k_1,k_2,w_1,w_2,w_3) \in \bar{V}_i^2 \times R^3$. For some region $\bar{V}_i$ where $i = 2$ or $i = 3$ assume that uniformly on $\bar{V}_i^2 \times R^3$

$$\liminf_{n\to\infty} q_{2,n}(k_1,k_2,w_1,w_2,w_3)\frac{g+f(k_1)}{1+r+b(n,k_1)} > 1$$

Then if $w_0 \neq 0$ we have $\lim_{n\to\infty} |w_n| = \infty$.

Proof: For some $\delta > 0$ and $n \geq 1$, $\inf_{m\geq n} q_{2,m}(k_1,k_2,w_1,w_2,w_3)\frac{g+f(k_1)}{1+r+b(m,k_1)} > 1+\delta$ for all $(k_1,k_2,w_1,w_2,w_3) \in \bar{V}_i^2 \times R^3$. Thus, $\forall m \geq n$

$$q_{2,m}(k_1,k_2,w_1,w_2,w_3)\frac{g+f(k_1)}{1+r+b(m,k_1)} > 1+\delta$$

for all $(k_1,k_2,w_1,w_2,w_3) \in \bar{V}_i^2 \times R^3$. Since k_t^i is trapped in $\bar{V}_i$, $\forall m \geq 1$ we have

$$|w_{n+m}| = R_{n+m-1}^{-1} q_{2,n+m-1} g_{m+n} |w_{n+m-1}| \geq (1+\delta)^m |w_n| \to \infty \quad \text{as} \quad m \to \infty$$

since $w_0 \neq 0$ implies $w_n \neq 0 \quad \forall n$. q.e.d.

The essential idea is that if trend chasing as reflected by the function f, is high relative to money growth as reflected by the function b, we might find $\liminf_{n\to\infty} q_{2,n}(k_1,k_2,w_1,w_2,w_3)\frac{g+f(k_1)}{1+r+b(n,k_1)} > 1$ uniformly. In this case the strength of trend chasing causes bubbles to exceed all bounds; as a result y_t^i becomes unbounded. In effect, a currency crisis develops. If $w_0 > 0$ there is unbounded depreciation; if $w_0 < 0$ there is unbounded appreciation. This is particularly interesting since the central bank bounds money growth and fundamental exchange rates. The criteria in theorem 3.5 suggests that even in the presence of responsible monetary policies trend chasing by speculators can produce currency crises. Notice that this phenomenon is absent from Brock-Hommes (1997,1998). It also expands on Gagnon (2012) which presents conditions for the nonexistence of fixed point bubbles in the random Brock-Hommes model detailed in equations (2.1)-(2.9). One of the major Brock-Hommes (1997,1998) contributions demonstrates persistence of bubbles, however, they do not suggest that speculative crises can result from trend chasing.

4. Conclusion

The paper analyzes exchange rate dynamics in an evolutionary finance framework under the assumption that monetary policy experiences local attraction. The local attraction traps the money supply in a bounded set and happens even though the central bank has a policy of perpetuating higher bubbles. Precise criteria for bifurcation, trapping of exchange rates and currency crises are presented. Future research could investigate fluctuations of this system with stochastic differential equations driven by more complex assumptions on the drift and volatility. For instance, actual monetary policy is probably generated by fluctuations in financial markets, the real economy and inflation. Monetary policy that targets several variables could generate more intricate dynamics. Further research on the potential of the model to produce currency crises is also essential.

Acknowledgment

Many thanks are due to my mother, Linda Gagnon, for her constant encouragement.

References

Abhyankar, A., Sarno, L. and Valente, G. (2005). Exchange rates and fundamentals: evidence on the economic value of predictability. Journal of International Economics 66, 325-348.

Antonelli, F. (1993). Backward-forward stochastic differential equations. Annals of Applied Probability 3, 777-793.

Arnold, L. (1998). Random Dynamical Systems. Springer, New York.

Berglund, N. and Gentz, B. (2002). Pathwise description of dynamic pitchfork bifurcations with additive noise. Probability Theory and Related Fields 122, 341-388.

Brock, W. and Hommes, C. (1998). Heterogeneous beliefs and routes to chaos in a simple asset pricing model. Journal of Economic Dynamics and Control 22, 1235-1274.

Brock, W. and Hommes, C. (1997). Models of complexity in economics and finance. In: Hanzon, B., Heij, C., Praagman, C., Schumacher, J.M. (eds.) System Dynamics in Economic and Financial Models, pp. 3-34. Wiley, New York.

Brock, W., Hommes, C. and Wagener, F. (2005). Evolutionary dynamics in markets with many trading types. Journal of Mathematical Economics 41, 7-42.

Brock, W., Hsieh, D. and LeBaron, B. (1991). Nonlinear Dynamics, Chaos and Instability: Statistical Theory and Economic Evidence. MIT Press, Cambridge MA.

Chiarella, C., He, X.Z. and Zheng, M. (2011). The analysis of the effect of noise in a heterogeneous agent financial market model. Journal of Economic Dynamics and Control 35, 148-162.

Clarida, R.H., Sarno, L., Taylor, M.P. and Valente, G. (2003). The out of sample success of term structure models as exchange rate predictors. Journal of International Economics 60, 61-83.

Flood, R. and Garber, P. (1983). A model of stochastic process switching. Econometrica 51, 537-551.

Follmer, H., Horst, U. and Kirman, A. (2005). Equilibria in financial markets with heterogeneous agents: a probabilistic perspective. Journal of Mathematical Economics 41, 123-155.

Gagnon, G. (2004). Exchange rate fluctuations in an economy with noise traders. Journal of Macroeconomics 26, 45-63.

Gagnon, G. (2012). Exchange Rate Bifurcation in a Stochastic Evolutionary Finance Model. Decisions in Economics and Finance 35, 29-58.

Hu, Y. and Yong, J. (2000). Forward-backward stochastic differential equations with nonsmooth coefficients. Stochastic Processes and Applications 87, 93-106.

Ikeda, S. and Shibata, A. (1995). Fundamentals, uncertainty, bubbles and exchange rate dynamics. Journal of International Economics 38, 199-223.

Kabanov, Y. and Pergamenshchikov, S. (2003). Two Scale Stochastic Systems. Springer, New York, New York.

Lux, T. and Schornstein, S. (2005). Genetic learning as an explanation of stylized facts of foreign exchange markets. Journal of Mathematical Economics 41, 169-196.

Mark, N.C. and Sol, D. (2001). Nominal exchange rates and monetary fundamentals: evidence from a small post Bretton Woods sample. Journal of International Economics 53, 29-52.

Meese, R.A. and Rogoff, K. (1983). Empirical exchange rate models of the seventies: do they fit out of sample? Journal of International Economics 14, 3-24.

Mundaca, G. and Oksendal, B. (1998). Optimal stochastic intervention control with application to the exchange rate. Journal of Mathematical Economics 29, 225-243.

Mohammed, S-E A. and Scheutzow, M. (1997). Lyapunov exponents of linear stochastic functional differential equations. Part 2. Examples and case studies. Annals of Probability 25, 1210-1240.

Peng, S. and Shi, Y. (2000). Infinite horizon forward-backward stochastic differential equations. Stochastic Processes and Applications 85, 75-92.

Rapach, D. and Wohar, M. (2002). Testing the monetary model of exchange rate determination: new evidence from a century of data. Journal of International Economics 58, 359-385.

Zampolli, F. (2006). Optimal monetary policy in a regime-switching economy: the response to abrupt shifts in exchange rate dynamics. Journal of Economic Dynamics and Control 30, 1527-1567.

In: Exchange Rates in Developed and Emerging Markets ISBN: 978-1-62808-164-0
Editor: Mohsen Bahmani-Oskooee

Chapter 3

WHICH KOREAN INDUSTRY WILL BENEFIT FROM THE WEAKENING WON?

Mohsen Bahmani-Oskooee** and Ruixin Zhang
Center for Research on International Economics and Department of Economics
University of Wisconsin-Milwaukee, Milwaukee, WI

ABSTRACT

Since 1960, the index of nominal effective exchange rate of the Korean won has dropped from 2114 to 80, a depreciation by almost 2700%. Since depreciation makes exports cheaper in foreign currency and imports expensive in domestic currency, Korean trade balance is expected to improve. However, not all industries that engage in trade are affected equally. Indeed, due to different price elasticities associated with different commodities, different industries react to currency depreciation differently. The S-Curve hypothesis is a concept that could be used to identify industries that will benefit from depreciation of the won. In this chapter we test the S-Curve hypothesis for almost 150 industries that are engaged in exporting and importing to the rest of the world in Korea. The main goal is to identify industries that benefit from won depreciation.

JEL Classification*:* F31

Keywords: S-Curve, industry data, the U.S., Korea

INTRODUCTION

Since 1960 the average value of the Korean won measured by the index of effective exchange rate has dropped from 2114 to 80, a depreciation of almost 2700%. Concentrating on the current float, the index has dropped from 402 in 1971 to 80 in 2011, a depreciation of 500%. Figure 1 shows the plot of nominal effective exchange rate of Korean won.

* Corresponding Author: Email: bahmani@uwm.edu, Phone: (414) 229-4334, Fax: (414) 229-2438.

However, since depreciation is inflationary, domestic prices do rise over time and we may lose part of the competitiveness due to increased prices. Adjusting the nominal effective exchange rate by changes in average price level in Korea and by changes in price level of all Korean trading partners yields the real effective exchange rate. Thus, if Korea is to gain competitiveness, nominal depreciation must lead to real depreciation. Figure 2 shows the path of real effective exchange rate of Korean won. Clearly, the won has depreciated over the study period in real term as well.

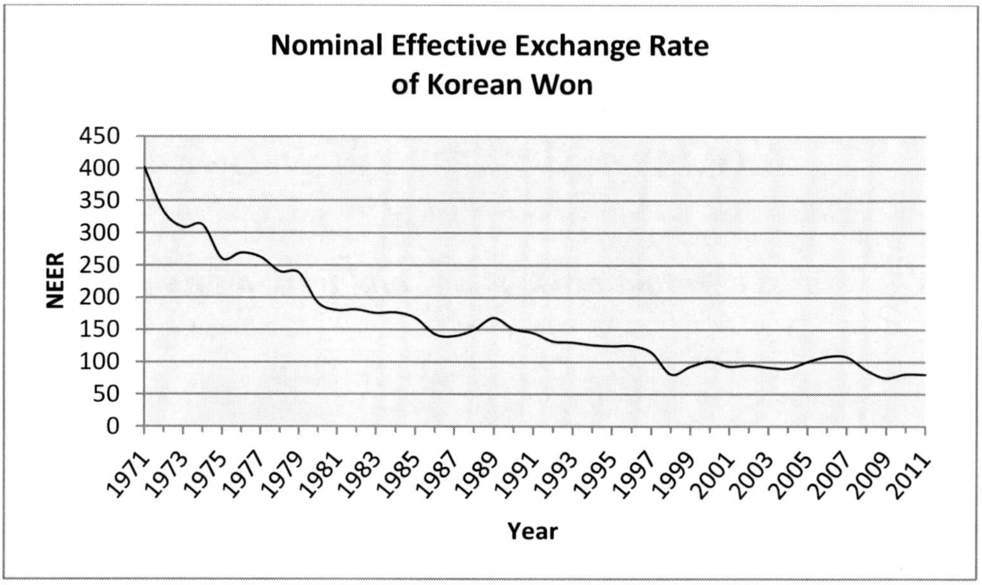

Figure 1. The Nominal Effective Exchange Rate (NEER) of Korean Won.

Obviously not all Korean exporting industries will benefit equally from depreciation of the won. The literature introduces two methods of assessing the effects of currency depreciation on the trade balance of each industry. The J-Curve approach and the S-Curve approach. While the J-Curve approach relies upon a reduced form model and engages in regression analysis between the trade balance and the real exchange rate, the S-Curve approach concentrates on cross-correlation concept between the trade balance and the real exchange rate.

Previous research that dealt with the Korean trade balance relied upon the J-Curve approach and regression analysis. Bahmani-Oskooee (1985, 1989) who introduced a method of testing the J-Curve phenomenon, used quarterly data from four countries of Greece, India, Korea, and Thailand. He found neither short-run effects nor any long-run effects of depreciation of the won on Korean trade balance. The results were the same for Korea when Bahmani-Oskooee and Malixi (1992) tested the J-Curve effect for more developing countries using expanded data set. Finally, similar conclusion was reached by Hsing and Savvides (1996) and Hsing (2005).

We suspect that the above studies suffer from aggregation bias. Most likely significant relation between the trade balance of some industries and the real exchange rate could be offset by insignificant relationship between the same two variables yielding insignificant outcome. To justify our suspicion we disaggregate the trade data between Korea and the world by industry and consider the experiences of 150 industries that trade between Korea and the world. We find that more than 1/3rd of the industries benefit from real depreciation of the won. To that end we introduce the method in Section II and the results in Section III. Finally, a summary is provided in Section IV.[6]

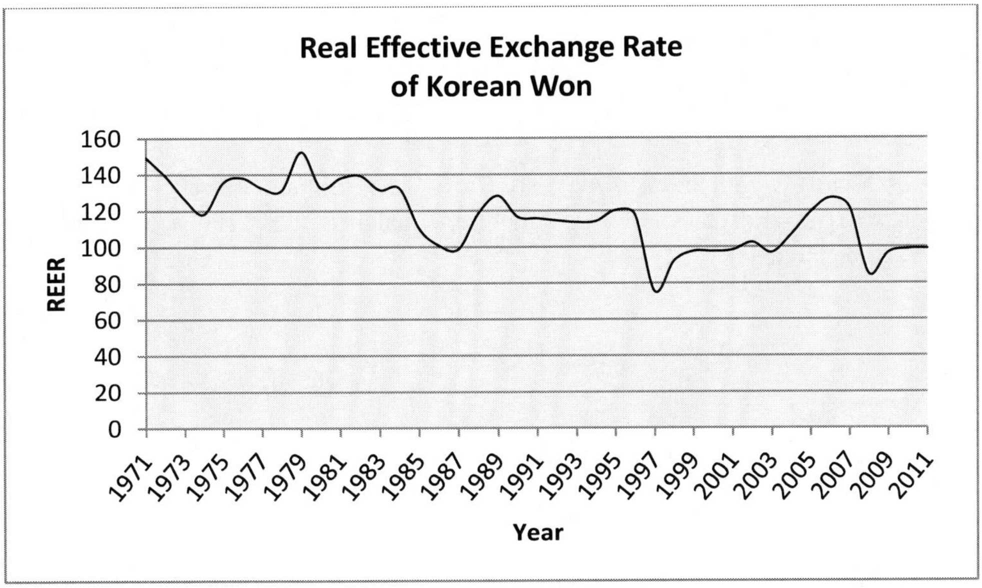

Figure 2. The Nominal Effective Exchange Rate (REER) of Korean Won.

I. THE METHOD

Our approach of identifying industries that will benefit from a real depreciation of the won is based on the concept and construction of the S-Curve. The concept originally was introduced by Backus *et al.* (1994) and postulates that due to adjustment lags, currency depreciation improves the trade balance only in the future. Thus, cross-correlation between current exchange rate and the future values of the trade balance should be positive. It also postulates that the same cross-correlation between current exchange rate and past values of the trade balance should be negative. Since plot of number of lags and leads and corresponding correlation coefficients resemble the letter "S", it is labeled the "S-Curve".[7'8.]

In constructing the S-Curve or calculating the cross-correlation coefficient we first must define the trade balance and the exchange rate in a manner that an increase in the exchange rate leads to an increase in the trade balance so that the contemporaneous correlation is positive. As such and following previous studies on this subject matter, we define the trade

[6] Several other studies have disaggregated Korean trade by trading partners rather than by commodities and have found some support for depreciation or devaluation to be successful. Examples are Wilson (2001), Lal and Lowinger (2002), and Bahmani-Oskooee and Ratha (2004).

[7] It must be mentioned that Backus *et al.* (1994) tested the S-Curve for 11 industrial countries; Senhadji (1998) for developing countries, and Parikh and Shibatha (2004) for many more developing countries. They all used aggregate trade flows between one country and rest of the world. Bahmani-Oskooee and Ratha (2007a), however, tested the curve between the U.S. and her major trading partners using bilateral trade flows.

[8] For a recent review of the J- and S-curves see Bahmani-Oskooee and Hegerty (2010).

balance of industry i as $TB_i = \frac{(X_i - M_i)}{GDP_{KOR}}$ where X_i is the Korean exports by industry i to the rest of the world; M_i is the Korean imports by the same industry from the rest of the world, and GDP_{KOR} is the Korean Gross Domestic Product. All variables are measured in nominal U.S. dollars so that the ratio could measure the trade balance in terms of domestic output. Next we define the measure of exchange rate to be the real effective exchange rate (REER). By construction a decline in REER reflects a real depreciation of the won. However, for contemporaneous correlation to be positive, we use inverse of the REER which we denote by IREER.[9]

Next following Bahmani-Oskooee and Ratha (2007b) and others we define Cross-Correlation Coefficient (COR) between the trade balance (TB) and the inverse of real effective exchange rate (IREER) as:

$$COR = \frac{\sum (IREER_t - \overline{IREER})(TB_{t+k} - \overline{TB})}{\sqrt{\sum (IREE_t - \overline{IREER})^2 (TB_{t+k} - \overline{TB})^2}} \tag{1}$$

where $\overline{IREER}$ *and* $\overline{TB}$ are the mean of all observation used in calculating COR. By allowing k to be zero, we calculate COR_0 which is a measure of contemporaneous correlation coefficient. If k takes a value of +1, then we calculate COR_1. Similarly, COR_2 for k=2; COR_3 for K =3, etc. are calculated. Following the same approach we allow k to take negative values and calculate COR_{-1}, COR_{-2}, etc. Plot of calculated CORs against k produces the S-Curve.[10]

II. The Results

Annual data over the period 1971-2011 are used to carry out the empirical exercise. To confirm previous studies that used aggregate trade data between one country and rest of the world, we first produce the S-Curve using aggregate trade flows. As shown in figure 3, the S-Curve is supported using aggregate trade data. To identify industries that contribute to this pattern and therefore, will benefit from real depreciation of the won, we disaggregate Korean trade flows with the rest of the world by industry and produce the S-Curve for 150 industries.

Due to the volume of the results, we first summarize the results in Table 1 by indicating which industry conforms to S-Curve patter. In this table, in order to see if size of an industry

---

9 It should also be mentioned that the industry level trade data come from World Bank's WITS system (The World Bank in turn receives the data from United Nations COMTRADE data base). Korean nominal GDP in dollar comes from the IFS of IMF and the real and nominal effective exchange rate comes from the Bank for International Settlements web site: http://www.bis.org/statistics/eer/index.htm

10 Note that in order to avoid spurious correlation, following previous studies we use Hodrick-Prescott filter to decompose each variable to its trend value and deviation from the trend. It is the deviation from the trends that is commonly used in constructing the correlation coefficients.

matters we also report the size of each industry over a few years which is measured by the ratio of exports plus imports of each industry to total exports plus imports of Korea.

Table 1. Industries Studied and Their Trade Shares (5-digit levels)

Code	Product Name	2008	2009	2010	2011	Suppor
1	Live animals	0.00004	0.00004	0.00004	0.00005	Yes
11	Meat, fresh, chilled or frozen	0.00240	0.00249	0.00236	0.00323	
13	Meat in airtight containers, n.e.s	0.00015	0.00014	0.00014	0.00018	
25	Eggs	0.00001	0.00001	0.00001	0.00001	
31	Fish, fresh & simply preserved	0.00427	0.00514	0.00470	0.00483	Yes
32	Fish, in airtight containers, n.e.s	0.00053	0.00062	0.00055	0.00058	Yes
42	Rice	0.00023	0.00038	0.00029	0.00041	Yes
45	Cereals, unmilled excl. wheat, rice	0.00002	0.00003	0.00002	0.00003	Yes
47	Meal & flour of cereals	0.00001	0.00001	0.00001	0.00001	Yes
48	Cereal preps & preps of flour of fr	0.00084	0.00094	0.00082	0.00087	Yes
51	Fruit, fresh, and nuts excl. Oil nuts	0.00083	0.00102	0.00101	0.00100	
52	Dried fruit including artificially	0.00003	0.00002	0.00003	0.00002	Yes
53	Fruit, preserved and fruit	0.00053	0.00055	0.00051	0.00054	Yes
54	Vegetables, roots & tubers	0.00075	0.00078	0.00079	0.00078	Yes
55	Vegetables, roots & tubers	0.00044	0.00048	0.00047	0.00043	Yes
61	Sugar and honey	0.00106	0.00146	0.00157	0.00160	
62	Sugar confectionery, sugar preps.	0.00019	0.00021	0.00019	0.00020	
71	Coffee	0.00053	0.00066	0.00064	0.00089	
74	Tea and mate	0.00001	0.00001	0.00001	0.00001	
75	Spices	0.00007	0.00007	0.00008	0.00010	
81	Feed. Stuff for animals	0.00262	0.00266	0.00227	0.00205	
99	Food preparations, n.e.s.	0.00152	0.00189	0.00184	0.00196	Yes
111	Non alcoholic beverages, n.e.s.	0.00017	0.00022	0.00023	0.00028	Yes
112	Alcoholic beverages	0.00086	0.00091	0.00084	0.00080	
121	Tobacco, unmanufactured	0.00027	0.00037	0.00028	0.00020	Yes
122	Tobacco manufactures	0.00064	0.00084	0.00076	0.00064	
211	Hides & skins, excluding fur skins	0.00048	0.00044	0.00046	0.00045	
221	Oil seeds, oil nuts and oil kernels	0.00117	0.00116	0.00089	0.00086	
231	Crude rubber incl. synthetic	0.00416	0.00378	0.00477	0.00621	
242	Wood in the rough or roughly	0.00098	0.00091	0.00082	0.00074	
243	Wood, shaped or simply worked	0.00045	0.00054	0.00051	0.00053	Yes
261	Silk	0.00003	0.00003	0.00003	0.00003	
262	Wool and other animal hair	0.00023	0.00025	0.00026	0.00029	
263	Cotton	0.00042	0.00045	0.00048	0.00082	
266	Synthetic and regenerated	0.00144	0.00147	0.00153	0.00161	
267	Waste materials from textile fabric	0.00031	0.00038	0.00030	0.00033	

Table 1. (Continued)

Code	Product Name	2008	2009	2010	2011	Suppor
273	Stone, sand and gravel	0.00017	0.00014	0.00015	0.00014	Yes
276	Other crude minerals	0.00075	0.00086	0.00085	0.00081	
282	Iron and steel scrap	0.00593	0.00444	0.00503	0.00523	
283	Ores & concentrates of non ferrous	0.00820	0.00804	0.00892	0.00968	
284	Non ferrous metal scrap	0.00334	0.00229	0.00285	0.00332	
291	Crude animal materials, n.e.s.	0.00019	0.00019	0.00023	0.00035	
292	Crude vegetable materials, n.e.s.	0.00072	0.00093	0.00086	0.00080	Yes
332	Petroleum products	0.06439	0.05239	0.05561	0.06901	
411	Animal oils and fats	0.00015	0.00015	0.00011	0.00012	
421	Fixed vegetable oils, soft	0.00061	0.00054	0.00051	0.00061	
422	Other fixed vegetable oils	0.00051	0.00050	0.00047	0.00056	Yes
512	Organic chemicals	0.03090	0.03170	0.03212	0.03440	
513	Inorganic chemicals elements,	0.00575	0.00528	0.00575	0.00659	Yes
514	Other inorganic chemicals	0.00204	0.00203	0.00224	0.00228	
521	Crude chemicals from coal,	0.00287	0.00274	0.00261	0.00291	
531	Synthetic organic dyestuffs, natural	0.00094	0.00111	0.00113	0.00101	
532	Dyeing & tanning extracts	0.00007	0.00008	0.00007	0.00006	
533	Pigments, paints, varnishes	0.00257	0.00285	0.00273	0.00272	
541	Medicinal & pharmaceutical	0.00521	0.00681	0.00582	0.00524	Yes
551	Essential oils, perfume and flavors	0.00020	0.00023	0.00021	0.00019	
553	Perfumery, cosmetics, dentifrices,	0.00155	0.00199	0.00215	0.00197	
554	Soaps, cleansing & polishing	0.00087	0.00102	0.00095	0.00098	
561	Fertilizers manufactured	0.00178	0.00120	0.00101	0.00115	
571	Explosives and pyrotechnic	0.00007	0.00012	0.00018	0.00018	
581	Plastic materials, regenerated.	0.02814	0.03248	0.03314	0.03111	
599	Chemical materials and products	0.01068	0.01159	0.01183	0.01116	
611	Leather	0.00142	0.00142	0.00135	0.00123	
612	Manufacturers of leather	0.00064	0.00059	0.00053	0.00048	Yes
613	Fur skins, tanned or dressed	0.00005	0.00007	0.00010	0.00013	Yes
621	Materials of rubber	0.00047	0.00057	0.00060	0.00060	
629	Articles of rubber, n.e.s.	0.00476	0.00516	0.00515	0.00535	Yes
631	Veneers, plywood boards & other	0.00117	0.00113	0.00095	0.00085	
632	Wood manufactures, n.e.s.	0.00033	0.00035	0.00033	0.00030	
633	Cork manufactures	0.00000	0.00000	0.00000	0.00000	Yes
641	Paper and paperboard	0.00393	0.00412	0.00389	0.00363	Yes
642	Articles of paper, pulp, paperboard	0.00091	0.00102	0.00102	0.00091	Yes
651	Textile yarn and thread	0.00368	0.00401	0.00441	0.00415	
652	Cotton fabrics, woven excluding	0.00100	0.00106	0.00102	0.00093	
653	Text fabrics woven excluding	0.00815	0.00908	0.00836	0.00808	Yes
654	Tulle, lace, embroidery, ribbons, t	0.00058	0.00062	0.00056	0.00045	Yes

Table 1. (Continued)

Code	Product Name	2008	2009	2010	2011	Suppor
655	Special textile fabrics and related	0.00250	0.00265	0.00248	0.00225	
656	Made up articles, wholly or chiefly	0.00085	0.00100	0.00083	0.00076	Yes
657	Floor coverings, tapestries, etc.	0.00016	0.00016	0.00013	0.00013	Yes
661	Lime, cement & fabric building	0.00147	0.00157	0.00134	0.00119	
662	Clay and refractory construction	0.00071	0.00075	0.00059	0.00054	Yes
663	Mineral manufactures, n.e.s.	0.00148	0.00148	0.00151	0.00145	Yes
664	Glass	0.00297	0.00354	0.00358	0.00331	Yes
665	Glassware	0.00059	0.00067	0.00066	0.00064	
666	Pottery	0.00015	0.00014	0.00014	0.00014	Yes
667	Pearls and precious and semi	0.00015	0.00014	0.00025	0.00033	
671	Pig iron, spiegeleisen, sponge iron	0.00511	0.00310	0.00397	0.00369	Yes
672	Ingots & other primary forms of	0.01917	0.01412	0.01616	0.01411	
673	Iron and steel bars, rods, angles,	0.00944	0.00593	0.00637	0.00657	
674	Universals, plates and sheets of	0.02590	0.02112	0.01981	0.02127	
676	Rails & track construction	0.00016	0.00024	0.00012	0.00007	
677	Iron and steel wire, excluding wire	0.00134	0.00118	0.00135	0.00133	
678	Tubes, pipes and fittings of iron ore	0.00726	0.00534	0.00530	0.00637	
679	Iron steel castings forgings	0.00066	0.00061	0.00060	0.00047	Yes
681	Silver and platinum group metals	0.00244	0.00192	0.00222	0.00364	
682	Copper	0.00981	0.00928	0.00973	0.00898	
683	Nickel	0.00117	0.00112	0.00128	0.00113	
684	Aluminum	0.00714	0.00594	0.00640	0.00614	
685	Lead	0.00046	0.00082	0.00069	0.00080	
686	Zinc	0.00114	0.00112	0.00117	0.00123	
687	Tin	0.00043	0.00036	0.00043	0.00044	
689	Miscellaneous ferrous base metals	0.00185	0.00142	0.00153	0.00196	Yes
691	Finished structural parts	0.00307	0.00647	0.00368	0.00433	
692	Metal containers for storage and	0.00168	0.00215	0.00136	0.00146	
693	Wire products	0.00121	0.00110	0.00100	0.00108	Yes
694	Nails, screws, nuts, bolts, rivets	0.00092	0.00089	0.00090	0.00096	Yes
695	Tools for use in the hand or in	0.00210	0.00219	0.00215	0.00220	
696	Cutlery	0.00025	0.00028	0.00026	0.00024	Yes
697	Household equipment of base	0.00056	0.00062	0.00059	0.00055	Yes
698	Manufactures of metal, n.e.s.	0.00521	0.00600	0.00533	0.00500	
711	Power generating machinery	0.01100	0.01403	0.01213	0.01274	
712	Agricultural machinery and	0.00092	0.00101	0.00085	0.00083	
714	Office machines	0.02587	0.02559	0.02645	0.01891	Yes
715	Metalworking machinery	0.00453	0.00463	0.00398	0.00407	
717	Textile and leather machinery	0.00278	0.00328	0.00345	0.00315	
718	Machines for special industries	0.00992	0.00786	0.01030	0.01091	

Table 1. (Continued)

Code	Product Name	2008	2009	2010	2011	Suppor
719	Machinery and appliances, non	0.04961	0.05183	0.05587	0.05103	
722	Electric power machinery and	0.02183	0.02592	0.02529	0.02409	
723	Equipment for distributing	0.00568	0.00577	0.00568	0.00568	
724	Telecommunications apparatus	0.06036	0.06519	0.05120	0.04505	Yes
725	Domestic electrical equipment	0.00444	0.00491	0.00449	0.00398	Yes
726	Electrical apparatus for medical	0.00164	0.00170	0.00175	0.00153	Yes
729	Other electrical machinery and	0.08750	0.09933	0.10407	0.09293	
731	Railway vehicles	0.00082	0.00076	0.00095	0.00099	
732	Road motor vehicles	0.06384	0.06026	0.06811	0.06997	
733	Road vehicles other than motor	0.00046	0.00048	0.00045	0.00040	Yes
734	Aircraft	0.00300	0.00330	0.00454	0.00432	
735	Ships and boats	0.05187	0.06637	0.05647	0.05260	
812	Sanitary, plumbing, heating & light	0.00067	0.00079	0.00079	0.00108	
821	Furniture	0.00249	0.00256	0.00250	0.00236	Yes
831	Travel goods, handbags and similar	0.00110	0.00132	0.00141	0.00161	Yes
841	Clothing except fur clothing	0.00693	0.00694	0.00673	0.00728	Yes
842	Fur clothing	0.00008	0.00009	0.00012	0.00013	
851	Footwear	0.00118	0.00135	0.00143	0.00156	Yes
861	Scientific, medical, optical,	0.04378	0.05426	0.05480	0.04545	
862	Photographic and cinematographic	0.00141	0.00159	0.00154	0.00147	
863	Developed cinematographic film	0.00010	0.00009	0.00007	0.00005	
864	Watches and clocks	0.00044	0.00051	0.00053	0.00056	Yes
891	Musical instruments, sound	0.00792	0.00802	0.00767	0.00613	Yes
892	Printed matter	0.00181	0.00212	0.00220	0.00187	
893	Articles of artificial plastic mate	0.00337	0.00387	0.00376	0.00369	Yes
894	Perambulators ,toys, games and	0.00196	0.00231	0.00192	0.00164	Yes
895	Office and stationery supplies,	0.00047	0.00050	0.00048	0.00042	Yes
896	Works of art, collectors pieces	0.00175	0.00074	0.00036	0.00031	Yes
897	Jewellery and gold/silver smiths	0.00079	0.00094	0.00072	0.00072	Yes
899	Manufactured articles, n.e.s.	0.00155	0.00177	0.00166	0.00162	
941	Animals, n.e.s. including zoo	0.00002	0.00002	0.00002	0.00002	Yes
951	Firearms of war and ammunition	0.00085	0.00069	0.00071	0.00047	

Note: n.e.s.= not elsewhere specified.

As can be seen from Table 1 the S-Curve pattern is supported in almost 1/3rd of industries and almost all these industries are small. Only one large industry, i.e., industry coded 724 (Telecommunications apparatus with 4.5% market share) is among these industries which conform to the S-Curve. Thus, it appears that the nine other large industries will not benefit from currency depreciation. These nine large industries are industries coded 332 (Petroleum products with 6.9% market share); 512 (Organic chemicals with 3.5% market share); 581

(Plastic materials, regenerated, with 3.1% market share); 719 (Machinery and appliances, non electric, with 5.1% market share); 722 (Electric power machinery and switch with 2.4% market share); 724 (Telecommunication apparatus with 4.5% market share); 729 (Other electrical machinery and apparatus with 9.29% market share); 732 (Road motor vehicles with 7% market share); 735 (Ships and boats with 5.3% market share); and 861 (Scientific, medical, and optical measures with 4.54% market share). For brevity of presentation we only report the S-Curves in Figure 3 for industries that support the S-Curve.[11]

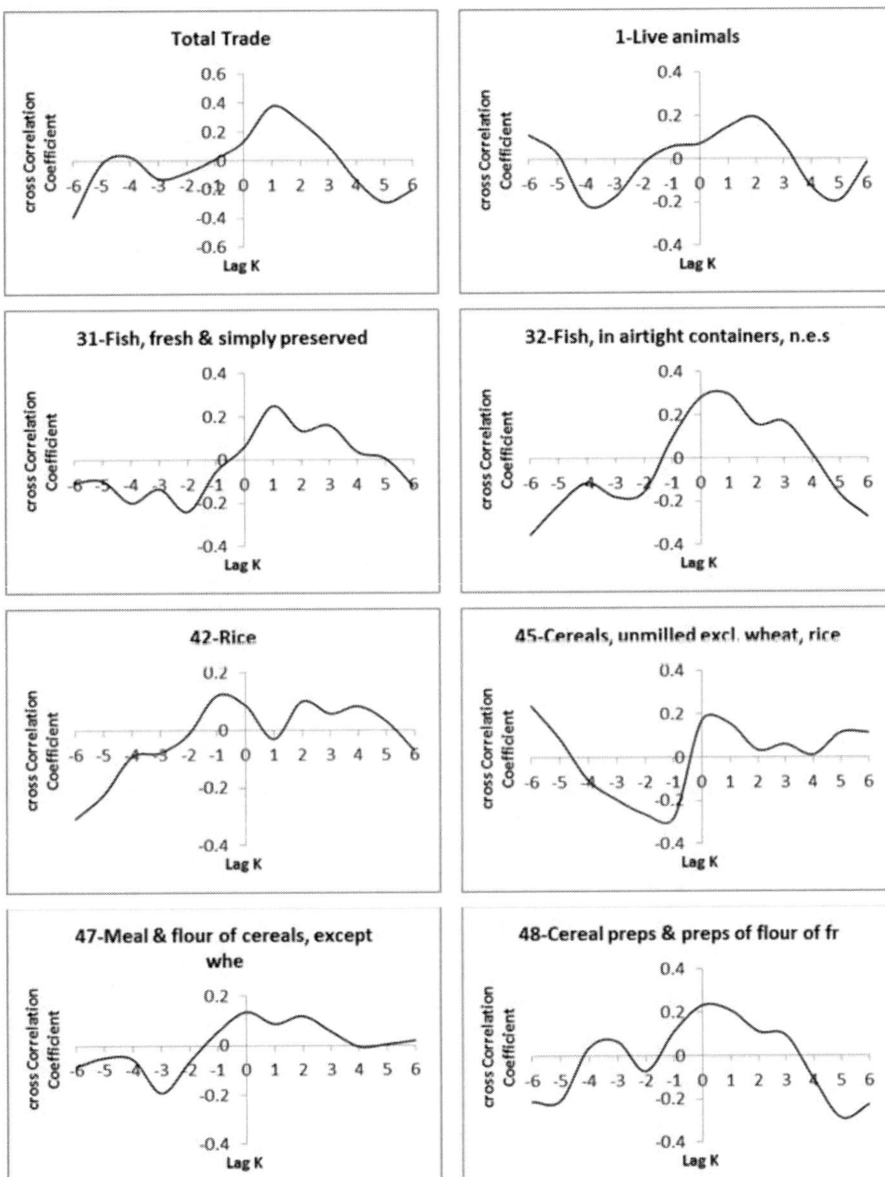

Figure 3. S-Curves in Industries that Support the Pattern.

[11] As can be seen most of the curves do not go through the original implying presence of Harberger-Larsen-Metzler (HLM) effect.

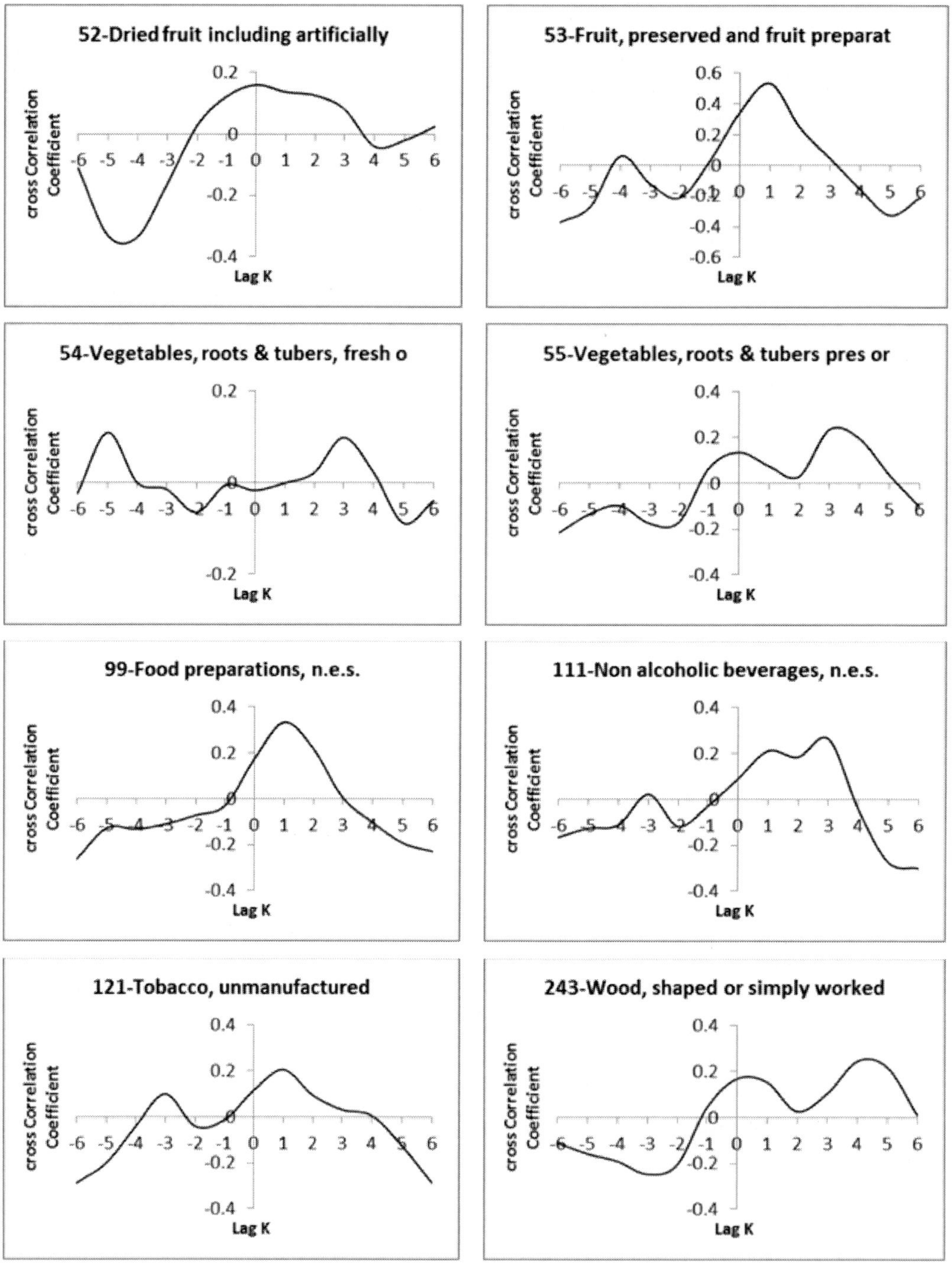

Figure 3. S-Curves in Industries that Support the Pattern (Continued).

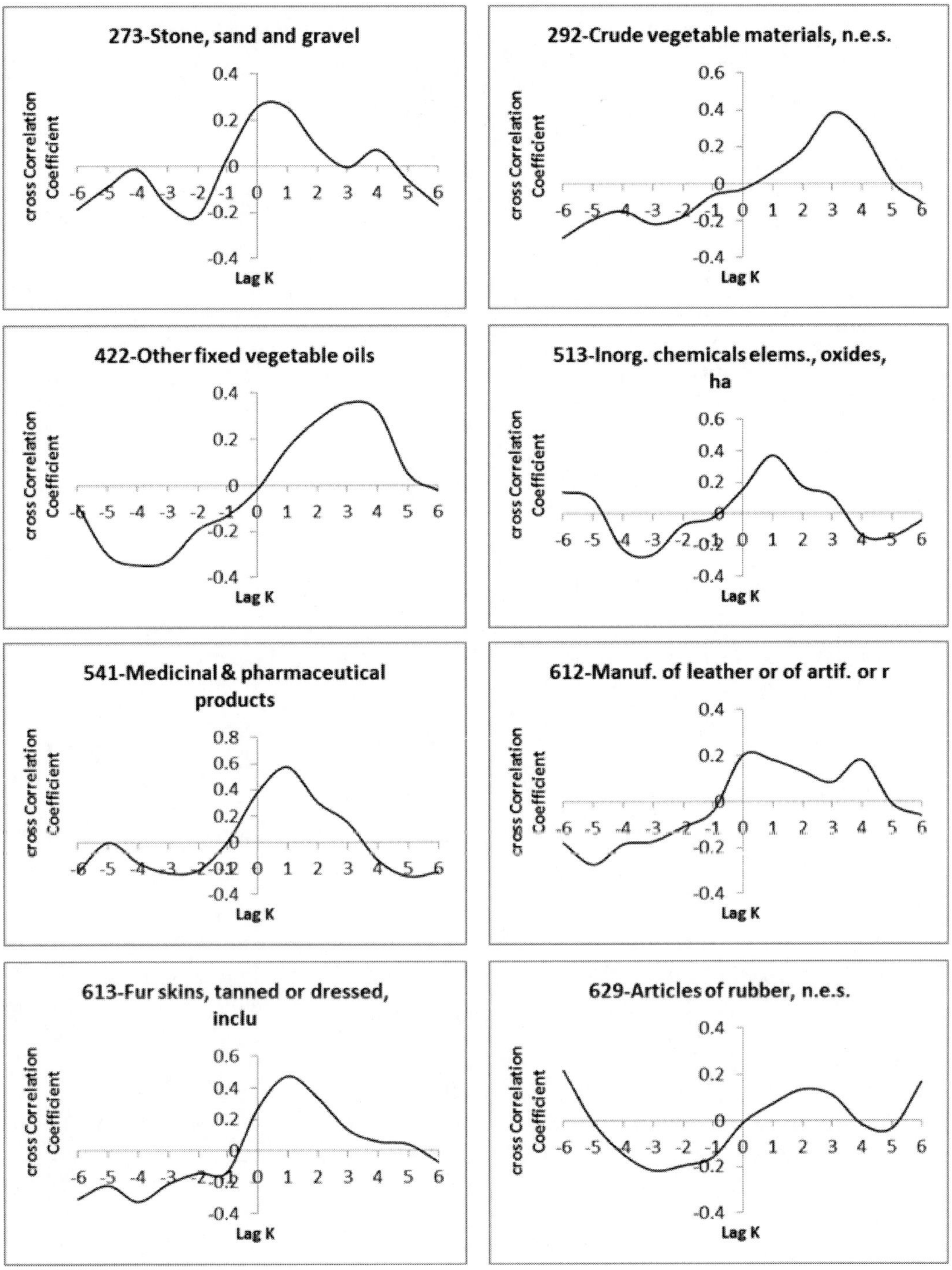

Figure 3. S-Curves in Industries that Support the Pattern (Continued).

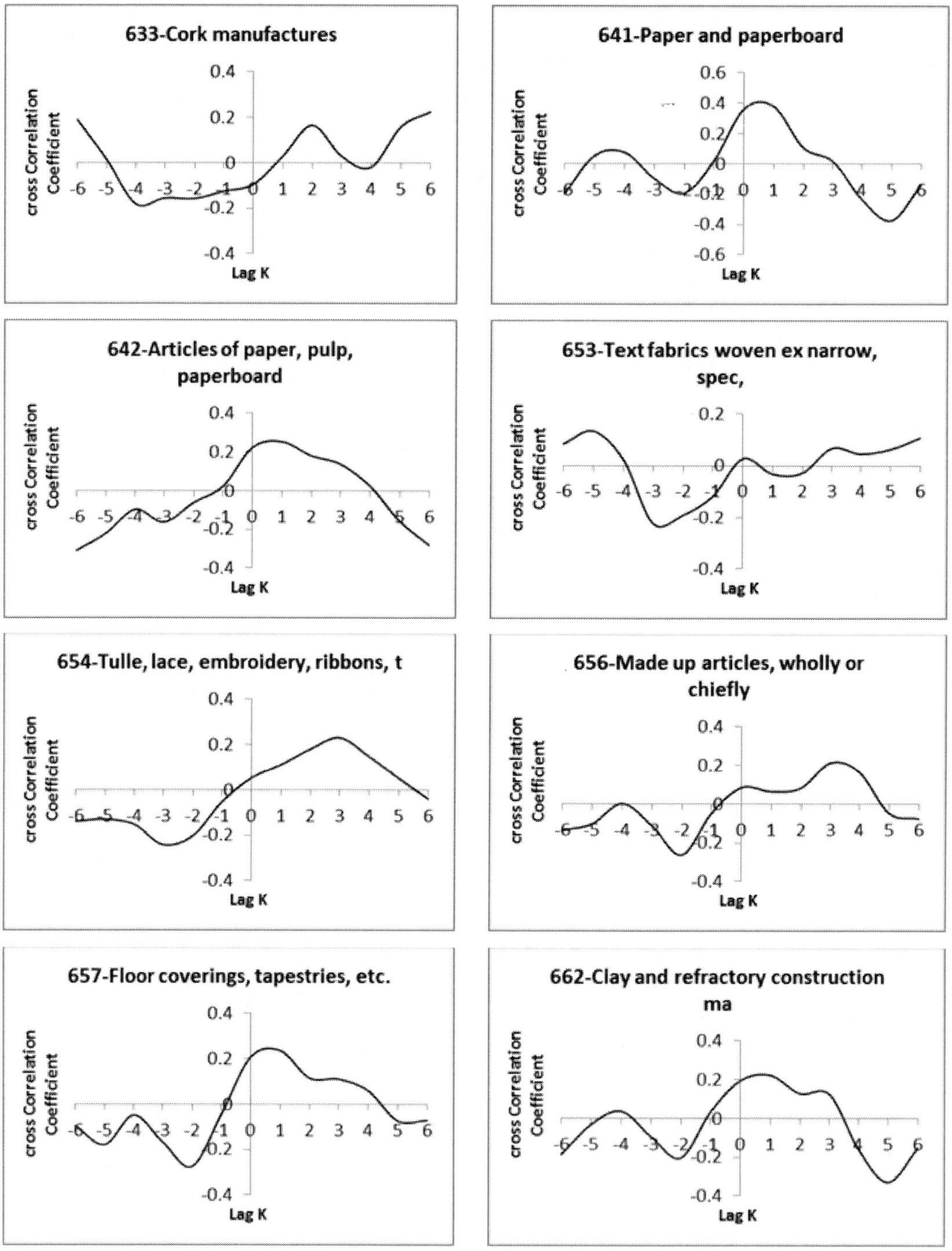

Figure 3. S-Curves in Industries that Support the Pattern (Continued).

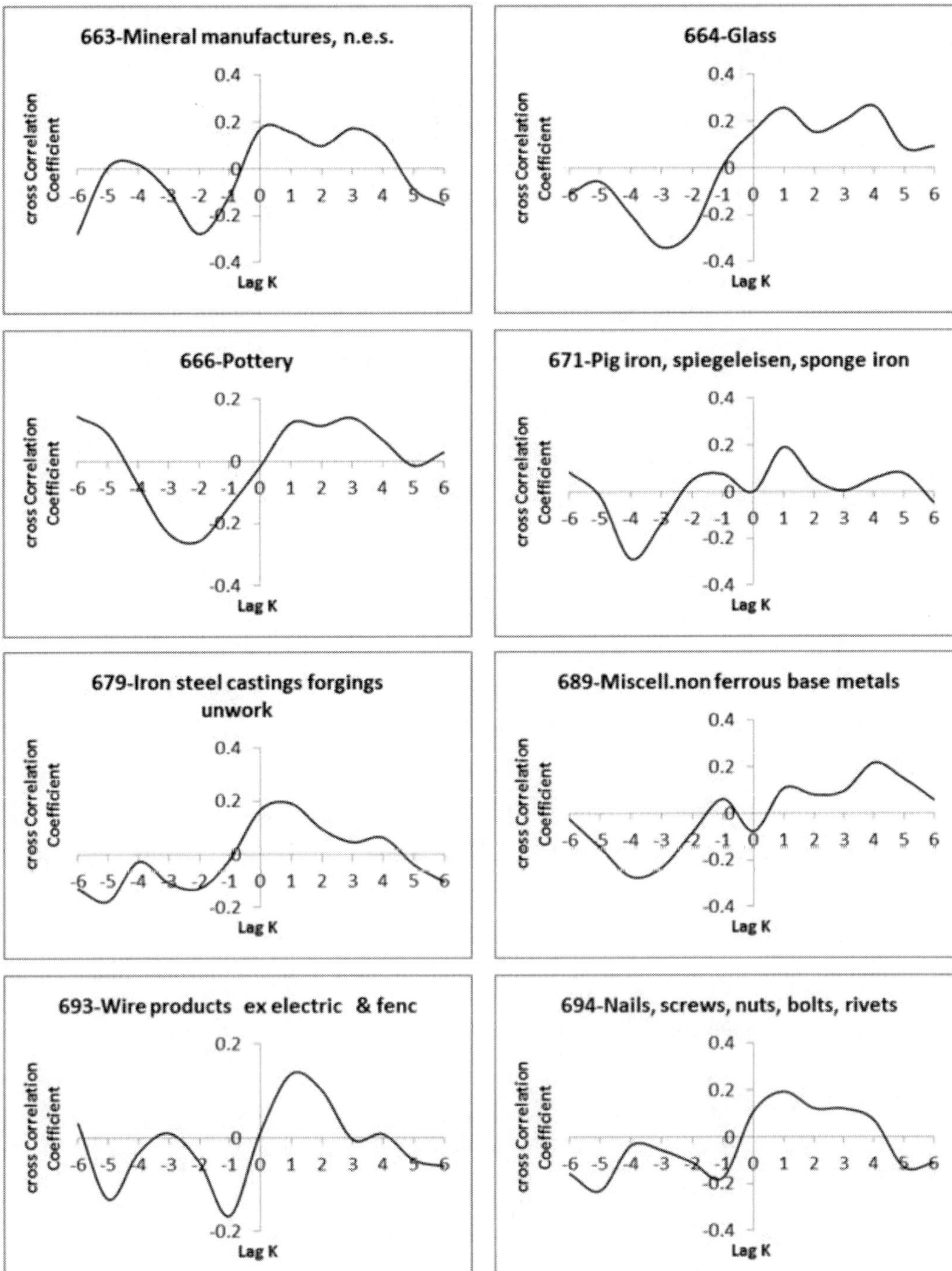

Figure 3. S-Curves in Industries that Support the Pattern (Continued).

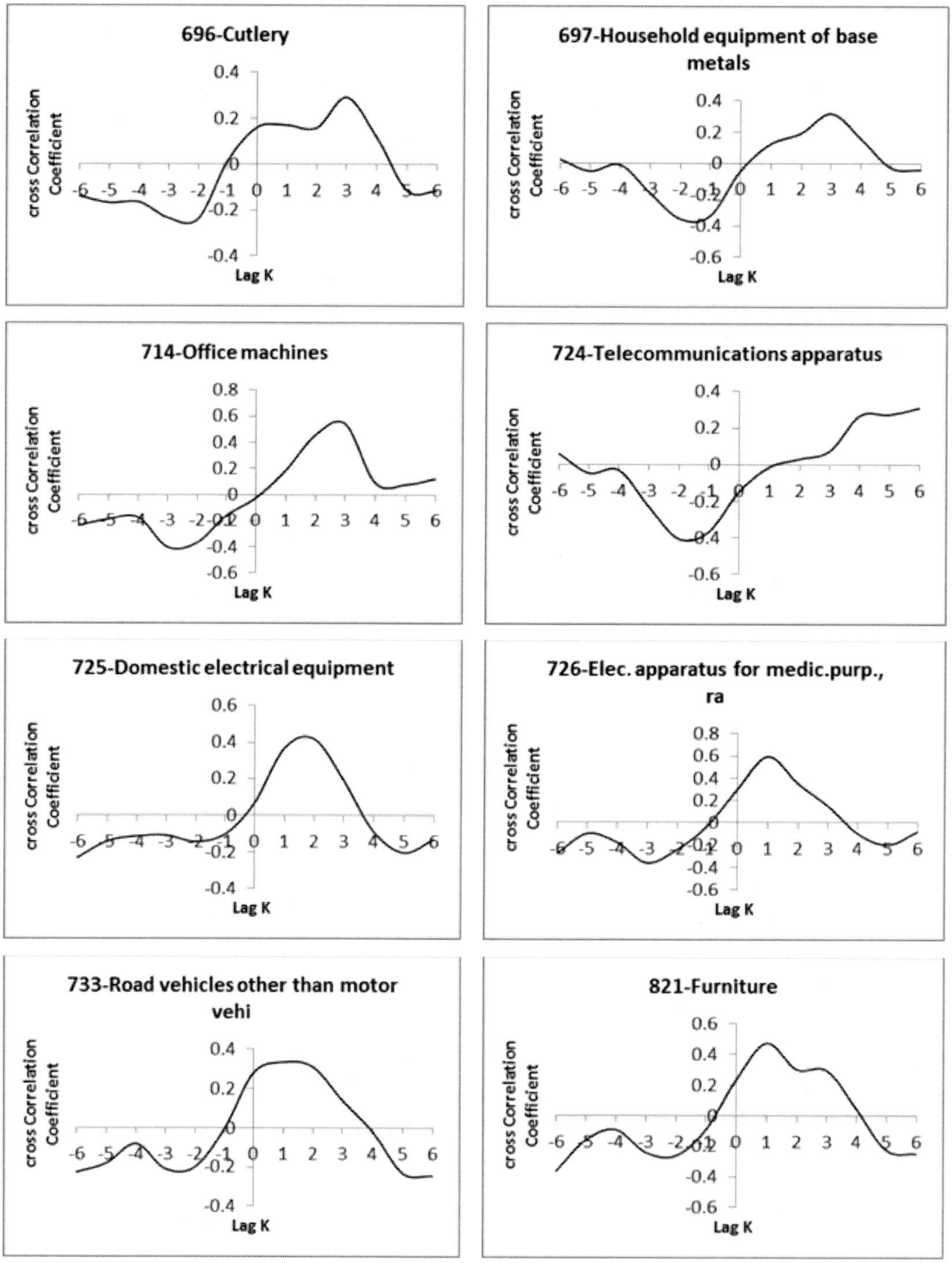

Figure 3. S-Curves in Industries that Support the Pattern (Continued).

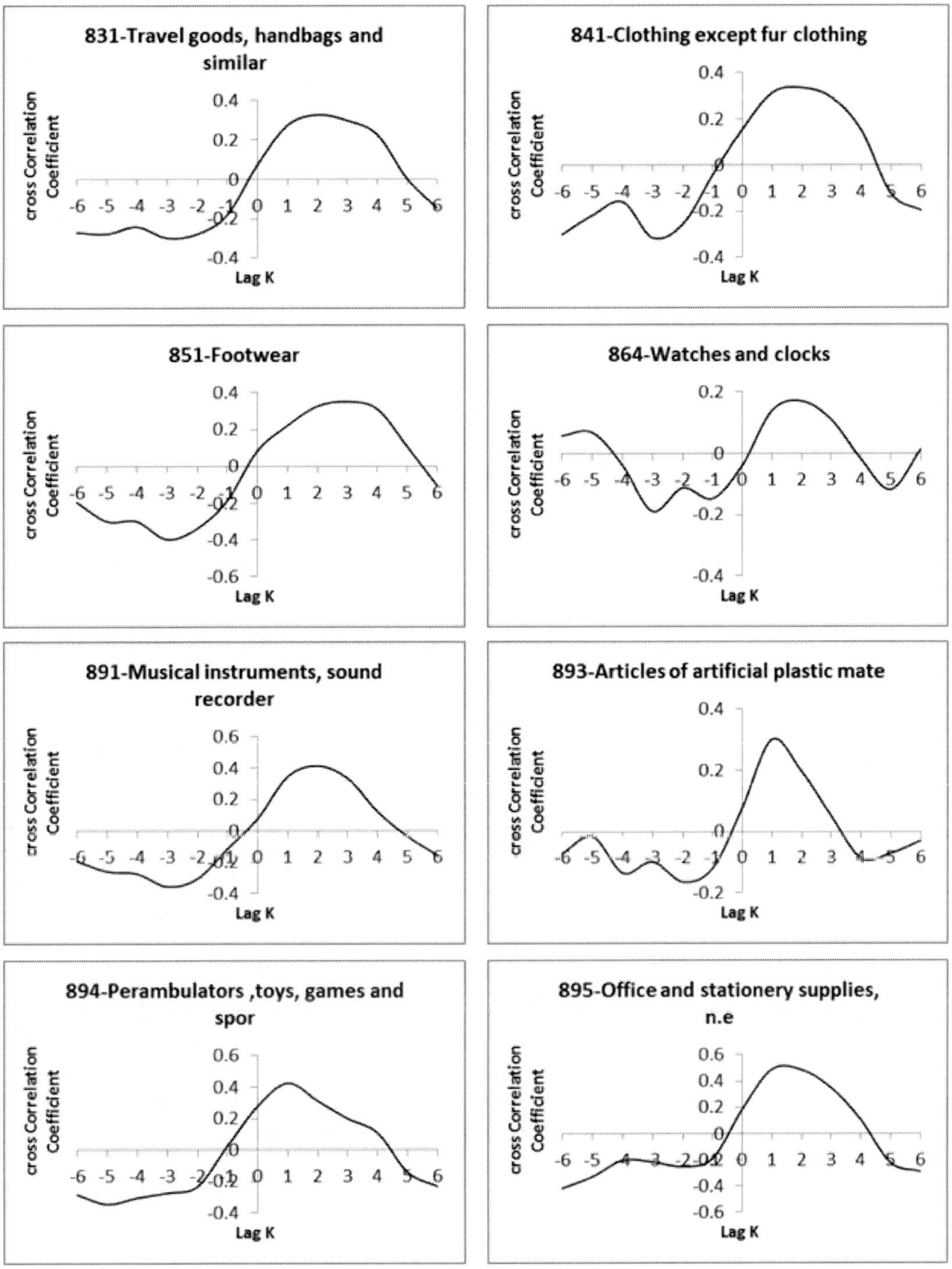

Figure 3. S-Curves in Industries that Support the Pattern (Continued).

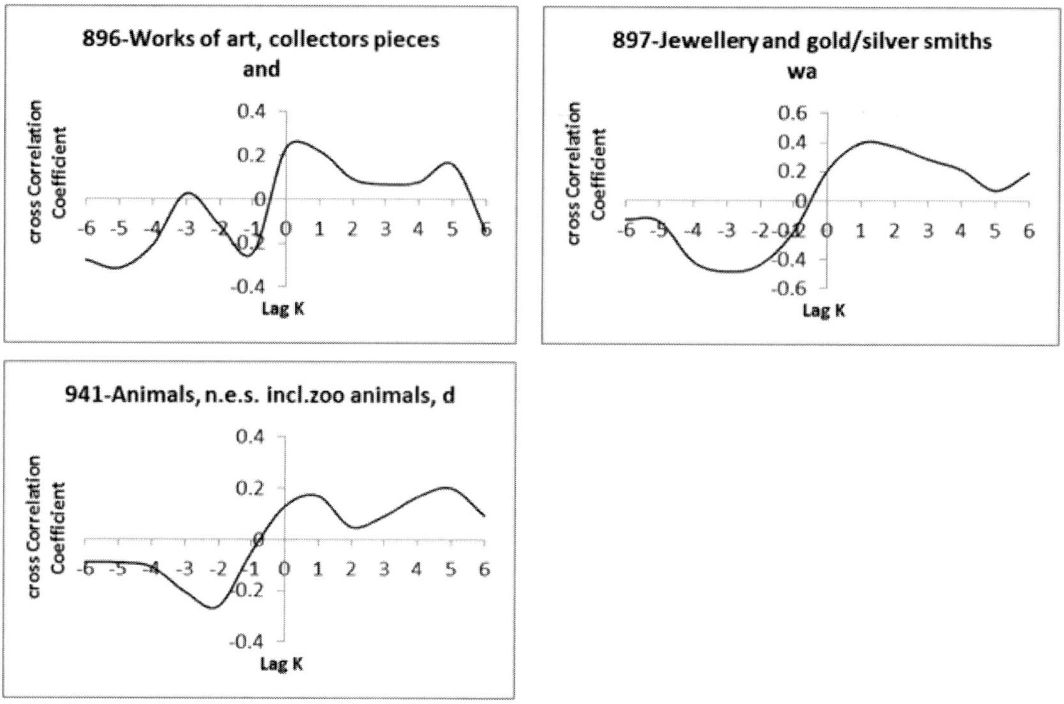

Figure 3. S-Curves in Industries that Support the Pattern (Continued).

Summary and Conclusion

The S-Curve hypothesis basically postulates that while cross-correlation coefficients between current exchange rate and future trade balance should be positive, the same correlation between past values of the trade balance and the current exchange rate is negative. When the concept was originally introduced by Backus *et al.* (1994) it was tested for 11 industrial countries using aggregate trade data between each country and rest of the world. Couple other studies tested the hypothesis by using data from developing world.

In this chapter we investigated the experience of Korea with the S-Curve. When we used aggregate trade flows of Korea with the rest of the world, we were able to support the S-Curve, implying that real depreciation of the won will improve Korean aggregate trade balance. However, in order to identify industries that contribute strongly to the S-pattern, we disaggregated Korean aggregate trade flows by industry and examined the experiences of 150 industries that trade between Korea and rest of the world. The S-Curve was confirmed in almost 1/3rd of the industries majority of which were small.

References

Backus, D.K., Kehoe, P.J., and Kydland, F.E. 1994, "Dynamics of the Trade Balance and the Terms of Trade: The J-Curve?" *The American Economic Review,* Vol. 84, pp. 84-103.

Bahmani-Oskooee, M. 1985, “Devaluation and the J-Curve: Some Evidence from LDCs”, *The Review of Economics and Statistics,* Vol. 67, pp. 500-504.

Bahmani-Oskooee, M. 1989, “Devaluation and the J-Curve: Some Evidence from LDCs: Errata”, *The Review of Economics and Statistics,* Vol. 69, pp. 553-554.

Bahmani-Oskooee, M. and M. Malixi, 1992. "More Evidence on the J-Curve from LDCs," *Journal of Policy Modeling*, Vol. 14, pp. 641-653.

Bahmani-Oskooee, M. and Ratha, A. 2004, “Dynamics of the U.S. Trade with Developing Countries”, *Journal of Developing Areas*, Vol. 37, pp. 1-11.

Bahmani-Oskooee, Mohsen., and Ratha, A. 2007a, “The S-Curve Dynamics of US Bilateral Trade”, *Review of International Economics.* Vol. 15, pp. 430-439.

Bahmani-Oskooee, Mohsen., and Ratha, A. 2007b, “Bilateral S-Curve between Japan and her Trading Partners”, *Japan and the World Economy*, Vol. 19, pp. 483-489.

Bahmani-Oskooee, M. and S. Hegerty (2010), “The J- and S-Curves: A Survey of the Recent Literature”, *Journal of Economic Studies*, Vol. 37, pp. 580-596

Hsing, Han-Min, 2005. “Re-Examination of J-Curve Effect for Japan, Korea and Taiwan”, *Japan and the World Economy*, Vol. 17, pp. 43-58.

Hsing, H-M., and Andreas Savvides, 1996. “Does a J-Curve Exist for Korea and Taiwan?”, *Open Economies Review*, Vol. 7, pp. 127-145.

Lal, A. K. and Lowinger, T.C. (2002), “The J-Curve: Evidence from East Asia”, *Journal of Economic Integration*, Vol. 17, pp. 397-415.

Parikh, Ashok and Shibata, Miyuki (2004), “Dynamics of the Relationship between the Terms of Trade and the Trade Balance in developing Countries of Asia, Africa, and Latin America,” Journal of Quantitative Economics, vol. 2, 104-21.

Senhadji, Abdelhak S. (1998), “Dynamics of the Trade Balance and the Terms of Trade In LDCs: the S-Curve” *Journal of International Economics,* Vol. 46, pp. 105-131.

Wilson, Peter. (2001), “Exchange Rates and the Trade Balance for Dynamic Asian Economies-Does the J-Curve Exist for Singapore, Malaysia and Korea?”, *Open Economies Review*, Vol. 12, pp. 389-413.

In: Exchange Rates in Developed and Emerging Markets
Editor: Mohsen Bahmani-Oskooee
ISBN: 978-1-62808-164-0

Chapter 4

A MICROSTRUCTURAL EFFECT OF JAPANESE OFFICIAL INTERVENTION IN THE YEN/DOLLAR FOREIGN EXCHANGE MARKET

Hiroya Akiba[1,*], Yoshihiro Kitamura[1], Shinichi Matsuda[2], and Ayano Sato[3]

[1]Waseda University, Tokyo, Japan
[2]Niijima Gakuen Junior College, Gunma, Japan
[3]Takasaki City University of Economics, Gunma, Japan

ABSTRACT

This study adopts a microstructural approach to examine the effect of Japanese official intervention in the yen/dollar foreign exchange market. Our empirical results show that the number of informed traders after the series of interventions is significantly larger and the degree of the market maker's reaction to the order flow and the cost of informed trading in the post-intervention period are significantly smaller than those in the pre-intervention one. This finding implies that frequent and intense intervention promotes competition among the informed traders. We interpret these data to conclude that this competition lowers the degree of information asymmetry in the market.

JEL Classification: D82; E58; F31

Keywords: intervention in the foreign exchange market; microstructure in the foreign exchange market

---

* Corresponding author. 1-6-1 Nishi-Waseda, Shinjuku-ward, Tokyo 169-8050, JAPAN *E-mail address*: hiroya@waseda.jp

INTRODUCTION

This paper adopts a microstructural model and examines the effect of Japanese official intervention in the yen/dollar markets. The main contribution of this study is that we estimate the structural model directly, not with a reduced-form equation, and we show how the intervention affects the microstructures in the markets. Our empirical approach adopts a sophisticated theoretical model and provides an empirical explanation of the microstructural effects of the intervention.

The Japanese monetary authority frequently intervened in the yen/dollar markets from January 2003 to March 2004. As shown in Ito (2005a), the interventions in this period were unannounced, but the total amount of intervention was unprecedentedly large, exceeding 35 trillion yen. However, since that period, the Japanese authority did not intervene until September 15, 2010, although many economists and market participants have often called for intervention against the over-appreciation of the yen/dollar exchange rate. The likely reason that the authority chose not to intervene is their skepticism about the effects of foreign exchange (FX hereafter) interventions in the long-term or even short-run horizon, except in the case of coordinated interventions among central banks, such as the Plaza Accord. Indeed, there has been a prolonged argument among researchers over the effectiveness of official intervention because of the inconsistency between theoretical analyses and empirical evidence (Jurgensen, 1983; Edison, 1993; Sarno and Taylor, 2001).

At the theoretical level, most studies consider whether sterilized FX intervention has an impact on the exchange rate through the portfolio balance (Dominguez and Frankel, 1993) and/or signaling channels (Mussa, 1981; Stein, 1989). Sarno and Taylor (2001) provide a brief summary of theoretical and empirical studies on this topic and conclude that the effect of sterilized FX intervention remains an ongoing controversy in economics. Although sterilized intervention does not affect the fundamentals (e.g., the interest rate), it may have a portfolio balance effect when the intervention assets are imperfect substitutes. The second (signaling) channel considers sterilized intervention as a signal regarding a future change in monetary policy. However, this view has not been supported by historical events (see Lyons, 2001, p.226). Traditionally, these two effects have mainly been analyzed within a macroeconomic framework. Although these models depict the essential features of the FX market and FX rate determination, it is a commonly held view that their empirical explanatory powers are quite marginal. This indicates that these traditional approaches miss certain key features of FX rate determination.

Recently, unlike the previous studies based on these macroeconomic approaches, a new approach, the so-called microstructure approach, is developing, with an emphasis being directed to the examination of official intervention in an FX market. This new approach has been facilitated by high-frequency data from FX markets, which has only recently been made available. The microstructure approach, the definition of which appears in Lyons (2001, pp. 5-9), allows us to assume a heterogeneity with regard to FX participants and asymmetric information among them. In contrast with the microstructure approach, the macroeconomics approach in FX markets generally assumes homogeneity and a lack of private information among market participants. Rime (2003) points out that it is reasonable to assume that FX participants have different views and information related to the future exchange rate at least over the short time horizons.

Recent empirical works examine how intervention affects FX market microstructure using high frequency data (Evans and Lyons, 2005; Dominguez, 2003; Payne and Vitale, 2003; Chari, 2007; Kim, 2007; Pasquariello, 2007). Dominguez (2003) uses the Deutsche mark/U.S. dollar and the Japanese yen/U.S. dollar data in an event-study approach and finds that certain traders know that the U.S. Federal Reserve is intervening in those markets at least one hour prior to the public release of the information regarding the intervention. Chari (2007) shows that official intervention leads to increased volatility, and the bid-ask spread is wider after interventions using the Japanese yen/U.S. dollar high frequency data in conjunction with Reuters news reports. This increased volatility after an intervention indicates that the intervention gives rise to different interpretations among market participants about the effect of the intervention (heterogeneity). Payne and Vitale (2003) adopt a vector auto regressive (VAR) approach using 15-minute interval data for the Swiss franc/U.S dollar. Their empirical results imply that market participants are able to anticipate central bank interventions and that an intervention has a significant impact on the exchange rate if it is concerted. These studies suggest that private information may exist in FX markets or that market participants might have different expectations about the effects of an intervention. We interpret these studies as evidence supporting the microstructure approach in studying FX interventions.[12] Moreover, unlike the extant literature, most of which estimates reduced-form equations (e.g., Dominguez, 2003; Payne and Vitale, 2003), we directly estimate the structural model depicting the microstructure in the yen/dollar markets. We believe that this approach allows us to provide more strict interpretations of our empirical results.

Additionally, one of the seminal studies of order flow analysis, Evans and Lyons (2005), argues that order flow data conveys information in FX markets and affect price-setting behavior. They also suggest that an intervention, which gives rise to order flows, would change the market equilibrium, although they do not use intervention data directly. Scalia (2008) tests the effectiveness of intervention using the Czech koruna/euro exchange rate on the basis of Evans and Lyons (2002), and finds that news of the intervention increases the price impact of order flows. Following these order flow approaches, our analysis emphasizes the role of order flow in affecting the exchange rate.

Taking advantage of the recent developments in the microstructure approach to FX intervention, this paper attempts to investigate the effects of Japanese intervention policy from January 2003 to March 2004. During this period, the Japanese monetary authority always implemented interventions unannounced, so-called secret interventions, although market participants may have been aware of it. Frenkel, Pierdzioch and Stadtmann (2005) compare the effects of announced and unannounced interventions by the Japanese monetary authority and conclude that only the latter have significant effects on the yen/dollar exchange rate. Consequently, the purpose of our study is especially to examine whether these secret interventions make the FX market more transparent, taking into account heterogeneous behavior and information asymmetry among market participants using a microstructure model, while most of the preceding studies focus on whether official intervention affects the exchange rate level or volatility. Given FX intervention in the studied period, we examine whether and how the microstructure in the FX market changes by comparing several

[12] As *private information*, we mainly consider information about macroeconomic fundamentals, including official intervention. We discuss inside information in an FX market in subsection 3.2.

underlying variables of market microstructure before and after the frequent intervention during that period.

When we estimate our model, we only use information concerning the fact that the Japanese monetary authority implemented frequent interventions and not information regarding the amounts of intervention during the period. In other words, we consider the frequent interventions to be the structural break point of the market microstructure of the yen/dollar FX market and split our sample. This enables us to compare the market microstructure before and after the frequent intervention. Our ultimate interest lies in whether an intervention changes the market microstructure and if an intervention affects exchange rates via this microstructural change. To answer the former question, we suggest our approach to estimating the effects of an intervention on the market microstructure. We hope that our work will give novel measures to evaluate the latter question in future research although we restrict ourselves to answering the former question here.

We use the procedure developed by Foster and Viswanathan (1995), which applies the simulated method of moments (SMM) to estimate the system of equations describing the equilibrium of Kyle (1985) or Admati and Pfleiderer (1988). Kyle (1985) and Admati and Pfleiderer (1988) analyze how information is incorporated into prices in the stock market when market participants have different information. In these models, order flows play a crucial role in price discovery.[13] To our knowledge, we are the first to apply these ideas (models) to an FX market to analyze the microstructure effects of interventions. That is, we examine how intervention in FX market eliminates asymmetric information between market makers and traders during our sample period, and we investigate whether intervention makes the market more efficient.[14]

Our main results are succinctly summarized as follows: we suggest that the number of informed traders increases after an intervention, and this increase lowers the extent of asymmetric information between market makers and informed traders. To demonstrate this result, we examine the sign of the derivative of the market maker's sensitivity to order flow with respect to the number of informed traders. The sign condition depends on the following two effects: an adverse selection effect faced by market makers, and a competition effect among informed traders. We find that the latter effect is relatively significant in the yen/U.S. dollar FX market. This finding suggests that the competition among informed traders reveals private information rapidly and makes market efficient. Therefore, an increase in the number of informed traders makes the impact of current order flow smaller because the reaction of uninformed market makers who observe market order flows and set bid and ask rates becomes smaller. This result is consistent with the empirical finding by Reitz, Stadtmann and Taylor (2010).

The remainder of this paper is organized as follows. The microstructure models developed by Kyle (1985) and Admati and Pfleiderer (1988) and the estimation method applied by Foster and Viswanathan (1995) are described briefly in Section 2. Section 3 is devoted to explanations of our sample data and the presentation of our empirical results. Our main concern, i.e., how the behavior of FX market participants is influenced by intervention, is discussed. Section 4 concludes the paper.

---

[13] Price discovery refers to a process in which a price reflects private information.

[14] Efficiency is defined as a situation in which FX rates reflect all available information instantaneously. In other words, there is no private information to exploit in FX markets.

1. The Microstructure Model and Estimation Method

Following Kyle (1985) and Foster and Viswanathan (1995), we assume there are three types of participants in the FX market: a risk neutral informed trader, an uninformed (noise or liquidity) trader and a risk-neutral competitive market maker.[15] Only an informed trader can observe a signal about private information, but an uninformed trader and a market maker are unable to observe the private information at time t. Private information is information that is relevant to FX rates and costly to acquire, which becomes public information in the next period t +1. Therefore, informed traders who pay the cost can exploit their informational advantage for only one period. In this study, traders are categorized as informed traders if they pay the cost to acquire private information, which is unknown to all traders at period t. Therefore, the number of informed traders is endogenous in this model.[16] Following Admati and Pfleiderer (1988) and Foster and Viswanathan (1995), we consider $\tilde{F}_t$, which can be understood as the fundamental value or efficient price for the exchange rate level. However, this value is not always the traded price $\tilde{p}_t$. $\tilde{p}_t$ is set by a market maker to clear the market based on the total current order flow $\tilde{\omega}_t$ and the past trading history, including all past public information until t, $\tilde{\Delta}_t$. The informed trader observes a signal of private information $\tilde{\delta}_t$ at period t. $\tilde{\delta}$ is private information which becomes useless one period after it is observed. Therefore, past private information set $\tilde{\Delta}_{t-1} = (\tilde{\delta}_1, \cdots, \tilde{\delta}_{t-1})$ are public information at period t. $\tilde{\omega}_t$ is composed of the uninformed traders' order flow l_t and the informed traders' orders $n_t I_t$. n_t is the number of informed traders and I_t is an order flow of a representative informed trader in time t. Also, $\tilde{\omega}_t$ is only observed by a market maker at period t, but a market maker cannot identify the two components of which $\tilde{\omega}_t$ is composed separately. This means that the market maker is unable to discern each component of the order flow. In equilibrium, a risk neutral, competitive market maker whose expected profit is zero $\{[E(\tilde{p}_t - \tilde{F} \mid \tilde{\Delta}_{t-1}, \tilde{\omega}_t] = 0\}$ is assumed to follow a linear pricing rule as below:

$$\begin{aligned} \tilde{p}_t &= E(\tilde{F} \mid \tilde{\Delta}_{t-1}) + \lambda_t \tilde{\omega}_t \\ &= \sum_{k=1}^{t-1} \tilde{\delta}_k + \lambda_t \tilde{\omega}_t \end{aligned} \tag{1}$$

where λ_t represents the impact of the current order flow $\tilde{\omega}_t$ on the corresponding exchange rate level and the sensitivity of the exchange rate, as set by the market maker, with respect to the current order flow. In this sense, λ_t captures an adverse selection problem between informed traders and market makers or the degree of market transparency. Intuitively, when the signal which informed traders observe is relatively less noisy, an increasing in informed

[15] We do not consider the endogenous behaviour of the monetary authority.

[16] An informed trader produces a better forecast than public information alone (Lyons 2001, p.26). In FX markets, leveraged investors are likely to generate such private information regarding macroeconomic fundamentals because they pursue profits by investing money into forecasting the fundamentals (e.g., Osler, 2009).

traders makes the market maker set λ_t to be larger in order to protect him or her against informed traders because that less noisy signal enlarges information asymmetry between informed and uninformed traders in order to protect themselves against informed traders. Thus, equation (1) means that the price set by a market maker is equal to the expectation of $\tilde{F}_t$, conditional on past public information observed by period t-1 plus an adjustment term $\lambda_t\tilde{\omega}_t$ that reflects the friction from asymmetric information.

A risk neutral, informed trader plays a strategic role in this model and determines her order flow I_t to maximize her expected profit $\{[E(\tilde{F}_t - p_t(\tilde{\Delta}_{t-1}, \tilde{\omega}_t)]I_t \mid \tilde{\Delta}_{t-1}, s_t\}$, subject to past public information and the private information signal (s_t), but uninformed traders place orders randomly because they have liquidity needs not directly related to gains from financial assets. Specifically, we assume the stochastic processes of the fundamental level of the exchange rate ($\tilde{F}_t$), the uninformed trader's order flow (l_t) and private information signal ($\tilde{\delta}_t$) as follows.

$$\tilde{F}_t - \tilde{F}_{t-1} = \tilde{\delta}_t = \Gamma_t \sigma_a \upsilon_t^a \tag{2}$$

$$l_t = \Gamma_t \sigma_b \upsilon_t^b \tag{3}$$

$$s_t = \tilde{\delta}_t + \varepsilon_t = \Gamma_t \sigma_a \upsilon_t^a + \Gamma_t \sigma_d \upsilon_t^d, \tag{4}$$

$$\ln(\Gamma_t) = A + \gamma \ln(\Gamma_{t-1}) + \sigma_\zeta \tag{5}$$

where $\upsilon_t^o \sim N(0,1)$, $o = a,b,d$. σ_q $(q = a,b,d,\zeta)$ A and γ are constant. ε_t is an informed trader's signal noise. These variables are independent of each other. Γ_t is a latent variable that governs the conditional heteroskedasticity in the volatility in the model, as assumed by Foster and Viswanathan (1995).

Using equations (1), (2), (3) and (4), we obtain the market maker's sensitivity as follows:

$$\lambda_t = \frac{\sigma_a^2}{\sigma_a^2(1+n_t)+2\sigma_d^2}\sqrt{\frac{n_t(\sigma_a^2+\sigma_d^2)}{\sigma_b^2}}. \tag{6}$$

Similarly, the reaction of an informed trader to the signal is given as:

$$\beta_t = \sqrt{\frac{\sigma_b^2}{n_t(\sigma_a^2+\sigma_d^2)}}. \tag{7}$$

By differentiating equation (1), we obtain the following equation:

$$\Delta p_t = \tilde{p}_t - \tilde{p}_{t-1} = \tilde{\delta}_t + \lambda_t\left[n_t\beta_t s_t + l_t\right] - \lambda_{t-1}\left[n_{t-1}\beta_{t-1}s_{t-1} + l_{t-1}\right]. \tag{8}$$

As shown by Foster and Viswanathan (1995) and Admati and Pfleiderer (1988), the expected profit of each informed trader in equilibrium, $\pi_t = \lambda_t \operatorname{var}(l_t \mid \Delta_{t-1}) / n_t$, equals the cost c that traders must pay to become an informed trader. With this condition, we obtain the following equation:

$$\begin{aligned} c &= \pi_t \\ &= \frac{\lambda_t E\left[\Gamma_t^2 \mid \Delta_{t-1}\right]\sigma_b^2}{n_t} \\ &= \frac{E\left[\Gamma_t^2 \mid \Delta_{t-1}\right]\sigma_a^2}{\sigma_a^2(1+n_t)+2\sigma_d^2}\sqrt{\frac{(\sigma_a^2+\sigma_d^2)\sigma_b^2}{n_t}}. \end{aligned} \tag{9}$$

Given numerical values for the conditional expectation of Γ_t^2 and other parameters, equation (9) implicitly defines the number of informed traders (n_t). With equation (5), the assumption of a log-normal distribution for Γ_t enables us to simulate the conditional expectation of Γ_t^2 (see equation (19) in Foster and Viswanathan, 1995).

We can discuss the relation between λ and the number of informed traders, which is calculated using equation (9). Admati and Pfleiderer (1988) indicate that the effect of informed trading on the impact of the order flow depends on the following condition:

$$\text{sign}\left(\frac{\partial \lambda_t}{\partial n_t}\right) = \text{sign}[\sigma_a^2(1-n_t)+2\sigma_d^2]. \tag{10}$$

Equation (10) implies that an increase in the number of informed traders has two effects. The first effect is explained by the adverse selection problem faced by market makers. Because the probability that the market makers may face disadvantageous deals increases with the number of informed traders, the sensitivity of market makers to order flow increases with the number of informed traders; therefore, the market makers need to hedge against their expected losses caused by deals with the informed traders.

For large value of σ_d^2 and small value of n_t, the effect of adverse selection dominates that of intensive competition among informed traders: when the signal noise gets much larger from the entry of informed traders, the market maker sets a larger λ_t. Meanwhile, the second effect is due to intensive competition among informed traders. The competition among them intensifies if the number of informed traders increases. Consequently, this competition decreases the market asymmetry and lowers the cost of trading because the central limit theorem tells that an increasing in informed traders contributes to the convergence of the mean of signal to true fundamental value. This indicates that competition possibly lowers the signal noise. This property enables the market maker to observe order flows that contain more precise information about the fundamentals and therefore lower λ.

Following Foster and Viswanathan (1995), the trading volume in each period V_t is computed as half of the orders from the informed traders, plus half of the orders from liquidity traders, plus half of the orders traded with the market maker:

$$V_t = \frac{1}{2}|n_t\beta_t s_t| + \frac{1}{2}|l_t| + \frac{1}{2}|n_t\beta_t s_t + l_t| \tag{11}$$
$$= \frac{\Gamma_t}{2}\left[|n_t\beta_t(\sigma_a\upsilon_t^a + \sigma_d\upsilon_t^d)| + |\sigma_b\upsilon_t^b| + |n_t\beta_t(\sigma_a\upsilon_t^a + \sigma_d\upsilon_t^d) + \sigma_b\upsilon_t^b|\right].$$

By substituting both equations (6) and (7) into equations (8) and (11), the price change and volume equations are expressed with the seven parameters ($\sigma_a, \sigma_b, \sigma_d, \sigma_\zeta, A, \gamma$ and c) and random variables. Next, given arbitrary parameters for equations (8) and (11), generated random variables give the simulated price change and trading volume. With these values, we calculate simulated moments for the SMM procedure, which are useful when it is difficult to estimate parameters by direct inference.[17] Following Table 1 in Foster and Viswanathan (1995), we use the same 52 moments to estimate the parameters. In our simulation, we draw 100,000 simulated values (or equivalently, we generate 10^5 random variables (υ^a, υ^b and υ^c). Let Θ be the vector of parameters that we estimate. Let Θ^* be the true parameters that are consistent with the observed data. When we define $f_i^{\Theta^*}$ and f_j^{Θ} to be the ith and j^{th} observed and simulated moments respectively, we define the mean difference between these as follows:

$$g_T(\Theta) = \frac{1}{T}\sum_{i=1}^{T} f_i^{\Theta^*} - \frac{1}{10^5}\sum_{j=1}^{10^5} f_j^{\Theta}, \tag{12}$$

where T is sample size. The SMM procedure finds a $\hat{\Theta}$ that minimizes the following quadratic function:

$$g_T(\Theta)' W g_T(\Theta), \tag{13}$$

where W is the inverse of the Newey-West estimator, the lag truncation parameter of which is $T^{1/3}$ (see Davidson and MacKinnon, 2004, p.362). If the simulation size is large enough, it is well-known that the SMM estimator will have little efficiency loss compared to the GMM estimator (see Foster, Richardson and Smith, 1993; Carrasco and Florens, 2002). The following section explains the data set for the SMM estimation and also shows the estimation results.

2. Empirical Results

2.1 Data

For the empirical analysis, we obtain the trading data for the spot exchange rate from EBS (Electronic Broking Service).[18] In the EBS market, we never have an established market

---

[17] See, for example, Gourieroux, Monfort and Renault (1993) and Gallant and Tauchen (1996).

[18] We use the EBS Data Mine Level 2.0, which is a dataset including one second time-sliced best bid/offer with volume, lowest given and highest paid and actual volumes.

maker who sets a price to clear the market. In this study, we assume a dealer to be a market maker who observes current order flows on the EBS screen and posts the best bid and/or ask prices. To examine the effect of FX intervention by the Japanese monetary authority, we focus on the Japanese yen/U.S. dollar FX rate. Hereafter, the yen/dollar refers to the spot yen rate quoted against the United States dollar. The sample period runs from December 30, 2002 to April 2, 2004. Throughout this period, the Japanese monetary authority frequently intervened into the yen/dollar FX market (see Ito, 2005b).

We exclude from our sample all data collected after 20:00 GMT in each day, as trading activity during these hours is minimal. Data from weekends is also excluded. Following Foster and Viswanathan (1995), we convert the original dataset into 30-minute intervals. We employ the quote midpoint of the best bid and ask rates observed at the end of each interval as a price p. The unit of trading volume is one million U.S. dollars. We sum the reported trading volumes for both the bid and ask sides in each interval, and we obtain the variable for trading volume V.

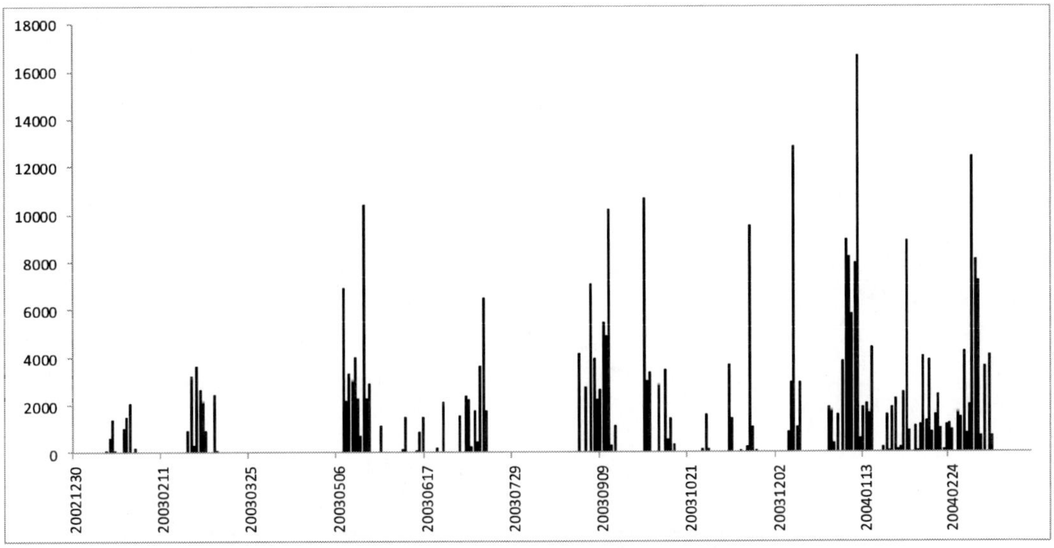

Source: Ministry of Finance, Japan.

Note: Figures on the vertical axis are the amount of daily intervention (in hundreds of million Japanese yen), December 30, 2002 to April 2, 2004.

Figure 1. Intervention.

Figure 1 shows the volume of intervention executed by the Japanese Ministry of Finance at a daily frequency. The days when interventions were undertaken follow the disclosures of the Japanese Ministry of Finance, which has disclosed its daily intervention record since April 1991. Figure 1 shows that the Japanese authority intervened heavily in the yen/dollar market throughout the sample period. We find the three periods during which the degree of the intensity of the Japanese intervention is high: (1) from January 15, 2003 to March 7, 2003, (2) from May 8, 2003 to July 16, 2003 and (3) from 29 August, 2003 to March 16, 2004. After the third period, the Japanese monetary authority did not intervene in the yen/dollar market until September 15, 2010. Ito (2005a) suggests that the Japanese monetary authority had different motivations for interventions during the third period and the two other periods; in the first and second period, the Japanese monetary authority intervened in the yen/dollar market to assist in the Japanese economic recovery, but in the third period, the Japanese monetary authority fought speculative pressures on the appreciation of the yen. In this study, we arrive at the following question: what is the result of intensive intervention conducted to alleviate long-term speculative pressure? Alternatively, how does intervention influence the FX market? To address this issue, we focus on the pre- and post-days of the third period. In other words, we examine whether the market microstructures are significantly different between the pre- and post-days of the third period. If the structure changed, we could possibly conclude that the Japanese interventions during the third period were effective to a certain extent. We hope that this attempt leads us to obtain a new evaluation method for the effect of FX intervention policy, which is still a controversy in the recent literature. Additionally, we examine whether intervention affects the number of speculators before and after the third period. If the number of speculators decreases, the intervention may be successful.

To examine the effects of FX intervention in the first and second periods, we have also performed additional estimations of our structural model for each of the 16 months in our full sample. However, these results do not enable us to make meaningful interpretations. Therefore, we only report the result for the third period. The result of the monthly estimation is available upon request.

2.2. Estimation Results

As mentioned above, we compare the market microstructure before and after the third period. We set the 13 days from August 12, 2003 to August 28 as the pre-day, and the other 13 days from March 17, 2004 to April 2, 2004 as the post-day (weekends excluded). The reason why we adopt 13 days for comparison is that the last day of our sample is April 2, 2004. The last day allows us to have 13 business days after the last intervention on March 16, 2004.

Table 1. Estimation Results

	Pre 13 days	Post 13 days
	Estimates	Estimates
σ_a	0.211	0.287
σ_b	392.556	678.884
σ_d	3.273	4.516
σ_ς	0.691	0.820
γ	0.047	0.056
A	-2.560	-3.258
c	5.844	3.780
χ^2	53.260 (.186)	51.822 (.225)
NOB	454	454

Note: χ^2 is a test statistic, the null of which is that all 52 moments [equation (13)] are equal to zero. The figures in parentheses are the p-values for the statistics. NOB is the number of observations. Pre (post) 13 days refers to the 13 days before (after) the series of interventions that were conducted from 29 August, 2003 to March 16, 2004.

Table 1 shows the estimated SMM parameters for the pre- and post-days. The χ^2 row presents the chi-square test statistics, the null hypothesis of which is that all 52 moment equations are equal to zero [$g_T = 0$ in equation (12)]. Under the null, it is known that $Tg_T^{'}Wg_T$ follows a χ^2 distribution with 45 degrees of freedom (52 moments minus the seven parameters). The figures in parenthesis show p-values for these statistics and mean that the null hypotheses for both the pre-days and post-days are not rejected. Therefore, this finding [$g_T = 0$ in equation (12)] may allow us to conclude that our models are well estimated in both periods. Alternatively, to evaluate our model specification, it is also possible to obtain the standard errors for the estimators with the asymptotic distribution of the SMM estimator. However, as mentioned in Foster and Viswanathan (1995), the small-sample properties of our approach are not known for models as complex as ours. Therefore, we omit reporting standard errors for the estimators and adopt a chi-square test to evaluate our model specification.

Table 2. Descriptive Statistics for Simulated Data

	Pre 13 days					Post 13 days					
	Mean	Median	S.D.	Min.	Max.	Mean	Median	S.D.	Min.	Max.	*t-stat.*
Δp	6.59E-05	-1.65E-04	0.092	-1.319	1.477	5.79E-05	-1.14E-04	0.081	-1.670	1.850	0.021
$\lambda(\times 1000)$	0.145	0.145	9.43E-07	0.145	0.145	0.120	0.120	6.18E-06	0.120	0.121	1.3E+06 ***
β	11.768	11.768	1.18E-04	11.750	11.768	13.538	13.538	0.001	13.206	13.538	4.8E+05 ***
n	103.430	103.430	0.002	103.430	103.746	122.798	122.798	0.022	122.798	129.061	2.8E+05 ***
l(absolute figure)	27.171	16.620	33.541	1.80E-04	721.801	24.060	13.102	34.460	1.39E-04	941.235	20.46 ***
$l(<0)$	-26.991	-16.608	33.311	-721.801	-0.001	-23.873	-13.098	34.254	-941.235	-0.001	14.57 ***
ε	-3.22E-04	4.32E-04	0.360	-6.154	8.768	-2.71E-04	2.52E-04	0.282	-6.183	9.635	0.04
V	289.209	180.606	349.993	0.023	10843.912	277.852	154.674	395.636	0.026	16345.600	6.80 ***
$\sigma_a^2(1-\bar{n})+2\sigma_d^2$	-6.366					-6.132					

Note: This table presents the descriptive statistics for the simulated data with the estimated parameters. The simulation is executed with 105 random variables. Δp and V are defined using equations (8) and (11), respectively. λ is the impact of the order flow [equation (6)]. n is the number of informed traders. l is the absolute value for the uninformed traders. l(<0) corresponds to the uninformed traders who buy the yen against the U.S. dollar. ε is a noise component in signal. The row $\sigma_a^2(1-\bar{n})+2\sigma_d^2$ shows the results of the condition from equation (10), where σ_a and σ_d are the estimated parameters reported in Table 1 and $\bar{n}$ is the mean of the proxies for informed trading that are generated by the simulation. t-stat is a test statistic, the null of which is that the mean of the simulated data for the pre 13days is equivalent to that of post 13 days. For example, t-stat for V is (277.85-289.20)/(395.632/105-349.992/105)=6.80.

*** Refers to statistical significance at the 1 percent level.

Table 2 shows the descriptive statistics for the simulated model parameters. The estimated parameters generated by the simulations enable us to calculate the impact of the order flows and the number of informed traders. For example, the rows *n* and λ in Table 2 present the descriptive statistics of the number of informed traders and the degree of the impact of the order flows. We draw 100,000 random variables in our simulation, and, therefore, the number of the simulated model parameters is basically 100,000.

First, the row $\sigma_a^2(1-\bar{n})+2\sigma_d^2$ of Table 2 shows the results of the condition in equation (10), where σ_a and σ_d are the estimated parameters reported in Table 1, and $\bar{n}$ is the mean of the proxies for the number of informed traders that are generated by the simulation. In both the pre-13 days and post-13 days in the third intervention period, these values are negative, indicating that the impact of order flows on a market maker's pricing is a *decreasing* function of informed trading because of the competition among traders, which is the second effect of two effects explained in the above section. As the negative sign in equation (10) does not change as a result of the intervention, it seems that this captures the fundamental nature of the exchange rate market structure. Namely, this finding implies that unlike an equity market, there is no analogue to inside information in FX markets (Ito, Lyons and Melvin, 1998). In FX markets, the market participants who accurately predict the variables regarding macroeconomic fundamentals, such as the unemployment rate, GDP and the interest rate, are informed traders (Osler, 2009).[19] Initially, there would be different expectations or views regarding macro information among the traders. However, if the competition among the informed traders who try to accurately predict the fundamental variables relevant to FX rates continues, they would eventually reach a consensus. This property implies that an increase in the number of informed traders enhances the revealing speed and accuracy of information regarding the fundamentals of FX rates. Therefore, an increase in the number of informed traders sweeps away asymmetric information regarding the fundamentals of the FX rate and lowers the degree of the adverse selection of the market makers. This competition among informed traders may reduce market dispersion (different opinions among market participants). To put it differently, the finding makes a market maker quote aggressively and leads to a smaller λ in the FX market.

Table 2 also indicates that the number of informed traders (n) increases after the third period and the number of uninformed traders ($|l|$) decreases after that point. This finding could be interpreted as follows. In Table 1, the cost to become an informed trader c becomes much lower after an intervention than it was before. This leads us to suggest that intervention lowers the cost of informed trading and encourages market participants to become informed traders. Conversely, why does intervention lower the cost of informed trading? Before an intervention, the prospects related to the future movements of the FX rate are relatively uncertain in the yen/dollar FX market. This property is supported by the evidence that the standard deviation of signal noise (ε) of the pre-13 days is greater than that of the post-13 days in Table 2. This result is consistent with the one in Reitz, Stadtmann and Taylor (2010), who find that foreign exchange intervention by the Japanese Ministry of Finance dampens expectation heterogeneity. Under the market conditions during the pre-13 days, market participants may consider informed trading to be so costly because noise factors continue to be dominant over the fundamentals in determining current FX rates. However, once intervention gives the market participants a strong message that the authority regards the current movement of FX rate as undesirable, and this message reduces the uncertainty about the future FX market, thereby lowering the cost of gathering information. To state the matter differently, intervention helps informed traders to observe signals about the fundamentals accurately. As a result, most uninformed traders before the third period become informed

[19] Of course, it is a common view that the variables regarding economic fundamentals are useless to predict intraday FX rate movements. However, in turn, it is also a common view that those variables are *useful* to predict FX rate movements in the medium and long run (Cheung and Chinn, 2001). Moreover, the market survey of Cheung and Chinn (2001) reveals that interest rates and surprise macroeconomic announcements always appear to be important for FX rates. Bearing these notions in mind, we consider that it is always profitable to predict the variables regarding economic fundamentals.

traders after that period because any market participant can easily become an informed trader. Table 2 shows that the mean of the number of informed traders, n_t, significantly increases (by 17 percent) after the third frequent intervention period, and the mean of the absolute number of uninformed traders, $|l_t|$, decreases by 13 percent.

It is also clear from observing the figures for the impact of order flows that intervention makes the FX market more transparent. If intervention makes the market transparent, we expect that the degree of adverse selection, λ, becomes smaller after an intervention. The mean of λ (the market maker's sensitivity to an order flow of one billion U.S. dollars, buying against the yen) in the post-intervention days, 12 pips, is lower than that of the pre-days, 14.5 pips in Table 2, and the difference between the two values is statistically significant at the one percent level. The estimated λ is so small that the FX market is transparent throughout the sample period, and the estimated λ is 2.5 pips lower (0.025 yen) in March, 2004 compared to that in August, 2003. Meanwhile, reaction of informed traders to the signal, β, in post-13days is 177 pips larger (1.77 yen) than that in pre-13days. This finding indicates that informed traders feel confident of their own signals and become aggressive. This evidence means that frequent intervention makes the FX market more transparent and efficient without adverse selection. To test the robustness of our result, we change the initial values for the SMM, and we confirm that the main results remain unchanged; the cost of informed trading and λ decrease and the number of informed traders increases after an intervention. Therefore, we conclude that the third period intervention promotes transparency in the yen/U.S. dollar FX market.

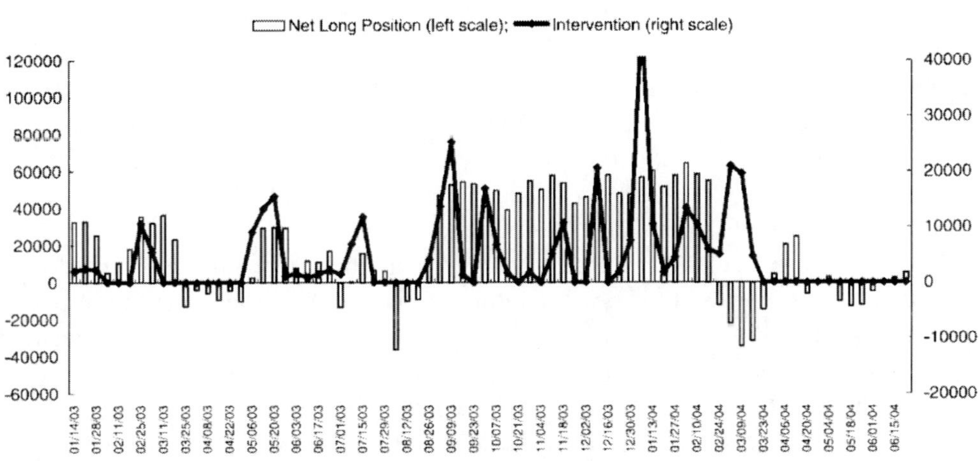

Source: Ito (2005a) Chicago Mercantile Exchange International Monetary Market.
Note: Futures position and intervention, January 14, 2003 to June 15, 2004.

Figure 2. Future Position and Intervention.

Additionally, Ito (2005a) suggests that the intervention during our sample period was practiced in part to fight the speculative pressures on the appreciation of the yen. Figure 2 is replicated from Ito (2005a). The bars in Figure 2 show the net long positions of yen currency futures (against the U.S. dollar) at the Chicago Mercantile Exchange (weekly frequency). The beginning of the intervention during the third period corresponds to the increasing net long position, and the long positions are offset at the end of the intervention. Ito (2005a) suggests that if the Japanese monetary authority intended to reduce the speculative pressure on the appreciation of the yen during the third period, the movements on the line charts, which are the amounts of intervention, may tend to coincide with those of the bars in Figure 2.

In our study, the total number of traders is defined as the sum of the informed and uninformed traders, and some of these traders may be motivated by speculation.[20] This assumption may allow us to consider that number as proxy for speculation. As shown in Table 2, the sum of $|l|$(absolute figure) and n is 130.6 in the pre-13day period and 146.86 in post-13 day period. Namely, the number of traders increases from before to after the third period. This finding indicates that intervention may induce the speculative buying of the Japanese yen if we consider the number of traders as proxy for speculation. In fact, it is reasonable to think that intervention induces speculation if we take a view that the effect of intervention is transitory; although intervention does depreciate the yen, and this effect is only transitory, market participants buy the yen following the intervention causing a short-lived depreciation in the yen, and the traders will sell it after the reverse appreciation of the yen. When only uninformed traders are inefficient not to hedge their position, their transactions may be due to noisy speculation but not hedge demand. This case enables us to consider the number of uninformed traders as proxy for speculation and to reach the opposite conclusion: intervention in the third period succeeded in dampening speculation.

CONCLUSION

In this paper, we have examined how heavy intervention by the Japanese monetary authorities affected the behavior of FX market participants from 2003 to 2004 and whether intervention changes the FX market microstructure. For this purpose, using the quoted yen/dollar high frequency data extracted from EBS Data Mine Level 2.0, we estimate the degree of the market maker's reaction to the order flow and the number of both informed and uninformed traders by the procedure of Foster and Viswanathan (1995).

Our empirical results show that the number of informed traders after the intensive intervention period becomes significantly larger, and the degree of the market maker's reaction to the order flow and the cost of informed trading after the intervention period are significantly smaller than those before the intervention. This finding implies that frequent and intense intervention increases the number of informed traders, and this increase promotes competition among the informed traders. The competition enhances market transparency; therefore, the market maker would not expect to suffer large losses from trade with informed investors. As a result, the degree of the market maker's reaction to an order flow becomes relatively low. That is, frequent and heavy intervention might serve to help promote market transparency. This result is consistent with the findings of Reitz, Stadtmann and Taylor (2010).

In addition, we find that the number of traders (or speculators) after the intervention period is significantly larger than that observed before the intervention. This finding leads us to interpret that the intervention helped to induce speculation rather than suppress it in the

[20] In this study, speculation is defined as a risky action seeking arbitrage profits. This includes the case where a market participant takes a long (short) position on currency futures, expecting appreciation (depreciation) of the spot rate (i.e., an arbitrage profits trader).

sample period. However, if we consider the number of uninformed traders as proxy for speculation, the result is reversed.

This paper focuses on the microstructural effect and not the macroeconomic effect of intervention. Therefore, the future research should include both microstructure and macroeconomic views to evaluate the effects of intervention policy in FX markets.

ACKNOWLEDGMENTS

We appreciate the helpful comments of Shiro Yabushita, Hideki Konishi, Koji Shirai and the seminar participants at the 2010 workshop at Waseda University. We would also like to express our gratitude to Junko Shimizu, Toshiaki Watanabe and other participants in the 2011 Japanese Economic Association Spring Meeting. All errors, however, are entirely ours. This research is supported by a GLOPE II from Waseda University and Jyoseikin of Takasaki City University of Economics.

REFERENCES

Admati, A. R., and Pfleiderer, P., 1988. A Theory of Intra-Day Patterns: Volume and Price Variability. *Review of Financial Studies* 1(1), 3-40.

Carrasco, M., and Florens, J.P., 2002. Simulation Based Method of Moments and Efficiency. *Journal of Business and Economic Statistics* 20(4), 482-492.

Chari, A., 2007. Heterogeneous Market-Making in Foreign Exchange Markets: Evidence from Individual Bank Responses to Central Bank Intervention. *Journal of Money, Credit and Banking* 39(5), 1134–1161.

Cheung, Y.W., and Chinn, M. D., 2001. Currency Traders and Exchange Rate Dynamics: A Survey of the US Market. *Journal of International Money and Finance* 20(4), 439-471.

Davidson, R., and MacKinnon, J.G., 2004. *Econometric theory and methods*. New York: Oxford University press.

Dominguez, K. M., and Frankel, J.A., 1993. Does Foreign Exchange Intervention Matter? The Portfolio Effect. *American Economic Review* 83(5), 1356-1369.

Dominguez, K. M., 2003. The Market Microstructure of Central Bank Intervention. *Journal of International Economics* 59 (1), 25-45.

Edison, H., 1993. The Effectiveness of Central Bank Intervention: A Survey of the Literature after 1982. *Princeton University Special Papers in International Economics No. 18.*

Evans, M. D.D., and Lyons, R. K., 2002. Order Flow and Exchange Rate Dynamics. *Journal of Political Economy* 110(1), 170–180.

Evans, M.D. D., and Lyons, R. K., 2005. Are Different-Currency Assets Imperfect Substitutes? In *Exchange Rate Economics: Where Do We Stand*? P. De Grauwe ed., Cambridge, MA: MIT Press, 1-38.

Foster, F. D., and Viswanathan, S., 1995. Can Speculative Trading Explain the Volume-Volatility Relation? *Journal of Business and Economic Statistics* 13 (4), 379-396.

Foster, F. D., Richardson, M., and Smith, T., 1993. Small Sample Properties of Simulated Method of Moments Estimators. *Working paper, Duke University, Fuqua School of Business.*

Frenkel, M., Pierdzioch, C., Stadtmann, G., 2005. The effects of Japanese foreign exchange market interventions on the yen/U.S. dollar exchange rate volatility. *International Review of Economics & Finance* 14(1), 27-39.

Gallant, A. R., and Tauchen, G., 1996. Which Moments to Match?, *Econometric Theory* 12(4), 657-681.

Gourieroux, C., Monfort, A., and Renault, E., 1993. Indirect Inference. *Journal of Applied Econometrics* 8, S85-S118.

Jurgensen, P., 1983. *Report of the Working Group on Exchange Market Intervention.*Washington D.C.: U.S. Department of the Treasury.

Kim, S.J., 2007. Intraday Evidence of Efficacy of 1991–2004 yen Interventions by the Bank of Japan. *Journal of International Financial Markets, Institutions and Money* 17(4), 341-360.

Kyle, A. S., 1985. Continuous Auctions and Insider Trading. *Econometrica* 53(6), 1315-1335.

Ito, T., 2005a. Interventions and Japanese Economic Recovery. *International Economics and Economic Policy* 2(2), 219-239.

Ito, T., 2005b. The Exchange Rate in the Japanese Economy: The Past, Puzzles, andProspects. *Japanese Economic Review* 56(1), 1-38.

Ito, T., Lyons, R. K., and Melvin, M. T., 1998. Is There Private Information in the FX Market? the Tokyo Experiment. *Journal of Finance* 53(3), 1111-1130.Lyons, R. K., 2001. *The Microstructure Approach to Exchange Rates*. Cambridge, MA: The MIT Press.

Mussa, M., 1981. The Role of Official Intervention. *Group of Thirty Occasional Papers No. 6.* New York: Group of Thirty.

Osler, C. L., 2009. Foreign Exchange Microstructure: A Survey of the Empirical Literature. *Forthcoming Encyclopedia of Complexity and System Science*: Springer.

Pasquariello, P., 2007. Informative Trading or Just Costly Noise? An Analysis of Central Bank Interventions. *Journal of Financial Markets* 10(2), 107-143.

Payne, R., and Vitale, P., 2003. A Transaction Level Study of the Effects of Central Bank Intervention on Exchange Rates. *Journal of International Economics* 61(2), 331-352.

Reitz S., Stadtmann G., and Taylor M. P., 2010. The Effects of Japanese Interventions on FX-forecast Heterogeneity. *Economics Letters* 108(1), 62-64.

Rime D., 2003. New Electronic Trading Systems in Foreign Exchange Markets. In *New Economy Handbook.* Derek C. Jones, ed.: Academic Press.

Sarno, L., and Taylor, M. P., 2001. Official Intervention in the Foreign Exchange Market: Is It Effective and, If so, How Does It Work? *Journal of Economic Literature* 39(3), 839-868.

Stein, J. C., 1989. Cheap Talk and the Fed: A theory of Imprecise Policy Announcements. *American Economic Review* 79(1), 32-42.

Scalia, A., 2008. Is Foreign Exchange Intervention Effective? Some Micro analytical Evidence from the Czech Republic. *Journal of International Money and Finance*27(4), 529-546.

In: Exchange Rates in Developed and Emerging Markets
Editor: Mohsen Bahmani-Oskooee
ISBN: 978-1-62808-164-0

Chapter 5

DUAL-CURRENCY SYSTEM AS A WAY TO RELIEVE THE CRISIS OF SOME EURO ZONE COUNTRIES

Adam Koronowski*
Institute Corona Mariae, Poland

ABSTRACT

Some euro zone member countries are severely hit by a crisis which combines recession, deep fiscal imbalances, fragility of the financial sector and balance of payments deficits. Although the origins and manifestations of the crisis are intricate and not identical amongst the countries, the present problems importantly stem from loss of competitiveness due to economic dynamics triggered by the introduction of the common currency. Since eliminating this problem within the monetary union is impossible through currency devaluation and it is improbable and at least very costly in the case of "internal devaluation" there are reasonable opinions that leaving the euro zone must be an unavoidable solution for countries like Greece. However an exit would be also very costly in economic and political terms. This chapter presents an alternative solution which is a dual currency system; reintroducing a national currency while remaining a member of the euro zone.

INTRODUCTION

The chapter is aimed at presenting a concept of relieving the problems envisaged by some member counties of the euro zone, Greece in particular. The concept is far from past and present efforts to soothe the situation, which may possibly turn out to be insufficient. The central idea of the solution suggested in this paper is an introduction of a dual-currency system which would consist of both the euro and a reintroduced national currency, a new "drachma".

* Email: A.R.Koronowski@gmail.com

The concept originates from an analysis of the roots of the present crisis, which include a severe loss of international competitiveness of the countries most hit by the crisis, and of its character which has a strong balance-of-payments aspect. This analysis leads to a conclusion that devaluation (as opposed to “internal devaluation”) may be crucial to solving the problems.

Since devaluation is impossible without a national currency its reintroduction is an option considered in some scenarios of future developments in the monetary union. These scenarios include, for example, the projects short-listed for the Wolfson economics prize in 2012 and the one eventually rewarded. However, reintroduction of a national currency in place of the euro brings about many problems of legal and economic nature related to the necessary redenomination of assets and liabilities. This usually finds a reflection in a proposal to make the change in conspiracy. Although being an act of legal abuse, deeply unfair and demolishing any remaining credibility, this would not invalidate many of the legal and economic problems of redenomination and could thus be far from an “orderly” exit. It could possibly only help avoid panic and related capital outflows before the change if it were successfully kept in secret (what would be problematic).

Reintroduction of a national currency while a country remains in the monetary union allows not to open the Pandora box of redenomination, to preserve the basic institutional and legal structure of the euro zone and at the same time to grasp the advantages of devaluation. A dual-currency system might be a long-lasting facility but it could also be a temporary step both towards a complete and orderly exit from the monetary union or a return to the single, common currency.

WHY REINTRODUCTION OF A NATIONAL CURRENCY MAY BE NECESSARY

To justify an opinion that a reintroduction of a national currency in some countries of the euro zone may turn unavoidable, it is worth paying some attention to the roots and character of the present crisis in the European Monetary Union.

Before the present crisis erupted and before public finances of some member countries of the European Union get beyond control there had been some tensions within the euro area. In 2008 new problems emerged and captured public interest but these old tensions did not necessarily disappeared; conversely, they seem to be closely interlinked with the present fiscal and banking crisis of some EU member countries.

The mechanism of these tensions started in some countries of the monetary union when economic agents, particularly consumers, reacted to a decline in interest rates due to entering the euro area. As a result the economy became overheated and inflation was slightly but persistently higher in these countries than the average for the euro area (early analysis: European Commission, 2001). Eventually, it brought about considerable “real exchange rate” appreciation or loss of international competitiveness (European Commission, 2005, Wyplosz, 2006, 2006(b)). Current account deficits emerged/increased. As foreign liabilities grew, possibilities to further accumulate the debt and run current account deficits came closer to a limit. In the absence of foreign exchange rate it eventually called for a decline in private and/or public spending. As a consequence the economy stagnated and excessive public deficits emerged (Koronowski, 2009) .

The most problematic PIIGS countries (Portugal, Italy, Ireland, Greece, Spain) match the above scenario. In 1999 – 2006 the competitiveness of the economy (versus other countries of the euro area) declined by 27% for Italy, by 12% for Spain and by 10% for Greece. (Wyplosz, 2006b) Portugal and Ireland also suit the general pattern although some additional factors played a role there. In particular, Portugal for a period of time experienced fall in profits in export sectors and as a consequence weakening exports, rather than rising export prices and deteriorating competitiveness (IMF, 2006, Basto, 2007).

Such cyclical developments had been observed and described in the literature on fixed exchange rate nominal anchors in stabilization programs; in that case boom and bust cycles used to end with a currency crisis.[21]

The role of balance-of payments imbalances in the euro zone crisis has been recognized, although in a rather weak form, by the European Commission (2009, p. 193): "The loss of the exchange rate as an adjustment instrument may imply protracted periods of self-reinforcing destabilising dynamics due to price and wage rigidities. Current account imbalances and net foreign asset positions can in turn play an important role in a context of exacerbated tensions in financial markets."

Visser (1995, p. 136) discussed the same problem much earlier in the context of the theory of optimum currency areas. In his critique of Ingram's opinion that a high degree of financial integration should be an argument in favor of a currency area (a criterion of the optimum currency area) Visser wrote: "If, for instance, diverging cost developments cause chronic sizeable current-account imbalances, wealth holders may at some point refuse to accumulate the debt of the deficit country. Capital inflows dry up and speculative attacks against the currency of the deficit country are to be expected, forcing a devaluation." Visser formulates his reservations in the traditional optimum currency area terms of fixed exchange rates and possible devaluations. In a monetary union there couldn't be a speculative attack against a currency or devaluation but wealth holders may still refuse to further accumulate the debt of the deficit country, in particular its government or financial institutions. In this juncture, there is no exchange rate risk which could spur investors to sell the currency of the deficit country but credit risk matters and it is even exacerbated by the absence of the exchange rate adjustment mechanism; it would be very difficult to service (foreign) debt as long as there is no improvement in the current account, no reasonable economic growth and no sufficient domestic savings. The problem of excessive debt may pertain to both public and private agents. However, government bond markets would be usually most liquid and would react most abruptly. Moreover, current account deficits and stagnating economy has a strong negative impact on public finances and crucially diminishes any room for fiscal maneuver. Imposing higher taxes on private agents who barely service their own debts and who still borrow even more in spite of tough market conditions would be rather difficult and dangerous. Any attempt to cut public spending would badly influence incomes and worsen the situation of private borrowers and financial institutions, too.

Although fiscal disequilibria and weak banking systems draw most attention during the crisis in the euro zone, balance of payments imbalances may be a crucial factor. Closer

[21] For more about the cycles see Kiguel, Liviatan (1992), Calvo, Vegh (1992), Santaella, Vela (1996), Khamis (1996).

analysis shows that countries which experienced most market pressure and which in particular were subject to major rating downgrades had not only poor fiscal situation but also – and probably first of all – high or extreme and persistent current account deficits and very big negative net international investment positions (Koronowski, 2011). This is the case of Greece, Spain and Portugal for example. Among PIIGS countries an exception is Ireland which had its government bonds spreads roaring in spite of a fairly good external position. In this case other factors, particularly exorbitant exposure to financial system losses and related fiscal expenditures, seem to have played a major role.

A different example of the role of balance of payments versus fiscal stance is United Kingdom where fiscal deficits recorded double-digit levels but the country did not experience a major fiscal tensions; it also preserved strong external position accommodated with deep depreciation of the British pound. The fiscal situation of the United Kingdom (comprising both deficits and debts) was worse than that of Spain. Also Belgium did not experience much market pressure in spite of its public debt comparable with that of Greece or Italy and rather high public deficits; again the country had no balance-of-payments deficits or high negative international investment position. Conversely, Spain had even lower public debt than "benchmark" Germany or an average for the European Union and the euro zone – it did not help the country to avoid a strong crisis as the country faces considerable balance of payments imbalances (also other factors matter there, in particular a real estate bubble). Italy has been "saved" although it reached a very high public debt level; however, it had still moderate current account deficits, quite good net international investment position and not particularly high public deficits.

These examples are far from a broad and deep presentation of the meaning of payments versus fiscal imbalances. They anyway show, firstly, that current accounts matter a lot for the severity of the crisis and market sentiments. Secondly, there is no direct link between fiscal situation and external position. Although "twin deficits" mechanism may have played sometimes an important role, the developments in the private sector seem to be meaningful. Current account deficits and foreign debt may result from high spending and borrowing of households during the boom phase (indeed, they do - compare: Koronowski, 2011). Fiscal deterioration may be an effect of a contraction during the bust phase and the crisis.

It is important to notice that, firstly, public deficits and debts do not provide a sufficient explanation of the credibility crisis and the balance of payments must be taken into account and – secondly – public spending is not the only one and sometimes not even the most important reason for payments imbalances. The causality between public deficits and payments deficits is more complicated in the above examples then the concept of "twin deficits" would suggest. Although high public expenditures and resulting public deficits may have caused rising foreign trade deficits in some PIIGS countries (in Greece, in particular) it seems also true that loss of international competitiveness and economic slowdown resulted in difficulties to keep public finances under control. Moreover, markets seem to be much more indulgent with respect to fiscal imbalances if only countries preserve a fair external position.

In these days it eventually seems fairly uncontroversial that the euro zone experiences major problems due to loss of competitiveness by some member countries. This can be reversed by "internal devaluation" or by devaluation; however, the latter is impossible unless there is a national currency.

What concerns "internal devaluation" it is not – in theory – impossible. In social and political practice it is rather difficult, very costly and improbable. An example where it worked or at least where huge payments imbalances were erased is Estonia. The country managed to turn its current account deficit of above 17% of GDP in 2007 into a surplus of 4.5% of GDP two years later. However, GDP contracted by 5.1% in 2008 and again by 16.1% in 2009. Unemployment rate reached almost 17% in 2010. It is also important that labor productivity decreased in 2008 and 2009; it may sound nice that productivity should grow fast where competition has been lost and current account deficit is excessive but it does not happen even in countries undertaking major balance of payments alignments. Neither acceptance of such a cost of economic contraction, nor fast rise in productivity seems to be a viable option for countries like Greece.

In effect, reintroduction of a national currency at a devalued exchange rate may turn out to be the only solution in the present conundrum. Contingency plans for euro zone exit occur. In particular, several scenarios of a break-up of the European Monetary Union have been presented for Wolfson Economics Prize in 2012. In the next part of the paper I will refer, among others, to these scenarios to discuss why it would be so difficult to exit from the euro zone.

Is an Orderly, Low-Cost Exit from the European Monetary Union Possible?

In this chapter only a situation when a single country exits the euro zone and the monetary union and the euro continue to exist is considered. This attitude could be applied to more than one country as long as it does not mean a complete break-up process which would make the euro cease to exist or split into "southern" and "northern" euro. Even so leaving the euro zone would be a very complicated process of legal, political, economic and technical dimensions.

An important legal aspect is a lack of any provisions which would regulate or explicitly allow for an exit from the monetary union. Leaving the euro zone would violate the Treaties and would demand leaving the European Union. However, a mild interpretation of the European law suggests that "the view that there are no circumstances under which a government can exit the euro-zone without also leaving the EU is probably not as robust as widely assumed". (Bootle, 2012) There is no formal mechanism for expelling a country from the EU (unlike the procedure for voluntary withdrawal under Article 50). Nevertheless, other EU members could simply refuse to cooperate with a country which leaves the euro zone, impose fines and suspend its membership rights. A unilateral decision to leave the monetary union would make little sense and would create political tensions.

Vast legal problems could result from denomination of assets and liabilities. There is a reasonable position that obligations governed by the law of the exiting country could be denominated according to the well established rule of Lex Monetae and any financial instruments governed by foreign law could not be legally denominated; such an attempt would only lead to court disputes and add uncertainty to the process. (Nordvig and Firoozye, 2012)

Denomination, even if planned in secrecy and introduced unexpectedly, which seems rather difficult, might necessitate introducing capital controls to avoid disruptive flows. For example, expectations of considerable depreciation of the new national currency and boosted uncertainty and risk should lead to massive sales of domestic (denominated) assets and capital outflow. However, "one immediate stumbling block is that any country that seeks to impose capital controls would be in clear breach of its existing treaty obligations. After all, the free flow of people, goods and capital is fundamental to the EU. These capital controls could therefore be overturned in the European courts and even in the national courts of the exiting country". "There is a provision (Article 59) which might allow the temporary imposition of capital controls for a period not exceeding six months, if approved by the Commission and the ECB and agreed by a qualified majority of states. (…) However, it may be impossible to build the required amount of support in advance without forewarning everyone that capital controls are coming". (Bootle, 2012)

All the above legal problems cause major political challenges, both domestic and international. Denomination would bring about huge redistribution of wealth and one should not expect that losers would not protest fiercely. Also keeping inflationary pressures under control and at the same time stabilizing the banking sector could be politically tricky. With respect to foreign affairs, to leave the euro zone and stay in the EU would necessitate full cooperation of other EU member states and a commonly shared "innovative" interpretation of the Treaties. Support from European institutions, including ECB, might be crucial for minimizing unnecessary disruption. Capital controls, as noticed above, might be introduced only with general consent of the EU member states – or at least should be instantaneously approved after having been imposed. It is difficult to imagine how all these arrangements could be made in secrecy.

Secrecy is a political problem itself. It has an ominous meaning for democratic process and control, credibility of country authorities and public support for undertaken measures. It is impossible to imagine that a wide political inter-party consultations or parliamentary debate on whether and how to leave the euro could be kept secret. The decision would bring about an immense effect in terms of wealth redistribution. The secret and authoritarian way in which the authorities would impose huge losses on big groups of citizens would demolish any public credibility of the authorities; credibility which would be crucial for next steps in the process of balancing and stabilizing the economy. Political destabilization would almost inevitably follow. It is very bitter that the European integration led to conundrums which provoke solutions of the martial law type or evoke the communist regimes. Such actions must not be acceptable.

In spite of that the secrecy of leaving the euro is a crucial feature of the process as envisaged in all papers short-listed for the Wolfson Economics Prize. It is even more embarrassing when one takes into consideration that all these papers admit that secrecy would be impossible to sustain.

Redenomination of financial instruments would have immense economic effects for the government, financial institutions, enterprises and households in the exiting country and abroad.

In the case of the government the most important effect would be a decline in the value of the public debt expressed in euros. The most of it is governed by the domestic law (for Greece compare: Nordvig and Firoozye, 2012) and it could be redenominated and subsequently depreciated, possibly also due to inflation. How the public debt would change in terms of GDP, except for inflationary depreciation of its real value, is a more complicated issue; much of GDP elements would change with denomination. Also budgetary incomes would be in drachmas. Interest rates would probably go much higher and refinancing terms would worsen.

A positive effect for the fiscal position should rather come from medium- and long-term economic growth and equilibrium regained due to reintroduction of the national currency.

Redenomination of public debt would have, however, a strong impact on financial institutions in the exiting country and abroad. This would bring about huge losses and currency mismatch in the balances of financial institutions. (However, denomination of deposits would alleviate the pressures.) The very existence of many banks and avoiding a systemic collapse would probably necessitate immense capital injections from the government and enormous liquidity support from the central bank. Of course the room for maneuver by the government would be very limited at best. No doubt, foreign support for an action which would severely hit financial institutions abroad in an ultimately uncontrolled manner should not be expected.

In the case of industrial enterprises the impact of denomination of financial instruments would be certainly differentiated. It would depend on the level of debt incurred and its legal governance. Of course the share of domestic and foreign proceeds would matter for the current financial situation of individual enterprises; generally speaking exporters should find their situation improved.

When it comes to households they would rather loose in effect of denomination; they are net wealth holders of assets governed by domestic law (Bootle, 2012). This could not only spur political discontent but also depress spending and hinder economic recovery.

The scale of denomination and revaluation of financial instruments, its impact on particular types of agents and their mutual influence (for example impact of households failure to service its credits on banks and on government support for banks) is difficult to assess precisely. Some general remarks are presented in the literature (for example Bootle, 2012, Nordvig and Firoozye, 2012) but much is left vague. This adds to the uncertainties and risks associated with leaving the euro. Probably there are some secret contingency projections prepared in central banks or governments and also with respect to their own position in major financial institutions.

The last dimension of reintroducing a national currency is technical. Its nexus is printing and minting new banknotes and coins. Of course the problem with it is secrecy. It would be quite a simple task if it could be done openly and orderly. Another difficult aspect related to cash is euro in circulation. It could not be simply denominated (it is physical euro anyway), it can't be stamped (no one would stamp euro banknotes as they preserve their value as the euro). Actually, it is impossible to introduce new coins and banknotes or maintain old ones representing the new currency (stamped euros) unexpectedly, orderly and quickly enough. This gives rise to some proposals of specific solutions, for example a period of non-cash payments in the new currency and cash payments in euros (Bootle, 2012). It would be rather difficult to conduct, having in mind the exchange rate changing freely and possibly fast. It is difficult to imagine people having their wages paid in drachmas but withdrawing the receipts from their accounts as euro cash. Most probably an immediate result would be a bank run. Also non-cash transactions nominated in the new currency could be quite problematic. No doubt they would need a period of intensive preparations, including changes in software systems.

According to Dobbs (2012) "a bigger challenge would be that multinational corporations and financial institutions would need time to adjust their systems and accounts for the new currency. As a reference, two years were allowed between the euro exchange rates being locked and the launch of the euro as legal tender, including the use of physical notes and coins. (…) (A)n overnight redenomination is therefore not possible and there would need to be some hiatus period of a minimum of three months up to the formal launch of the new currencies. During that period, consumers, corporations and speculators are likely to try to move their cash and savings that will be redenominated in the new (…) currency to financial institutions where they will remain in euros. They would have an incentive to withdraw and hoard old euro notes in cash. And if capital controls were imposed, as would seem necessary, euro notes could still be smuggled over the border, though the governments could try to force the notes to be redenominated (stamped – A.K.). These capital controls are illegal under EU law, resulting in potentially years of litigation".

The remarks in this part of the chapter are not intended to extensively present all problems and risks and assess the full costs of leaving the monetary union. My aim here is only to notice that legal, political, economic and technical problems related to exiting from the euro zone are enormous and interconnected. The solution I present in the next part allows to avoid them; it makes little sense to devote to much attention and effort to discuss these problems and costs in this chapter. Naturally, the solution proposed is not completely risk and cost free, either.

A Solution: To Reintroduce a National Currency and Stay in EMU

In the first part of the chapter I argued that a reintroduction of a national currency at a devalued exchange rate is a necessary step to regain the balance and growth in the economies of the euro zone most hit by the present crisis. In the second part I shortly presented the severe problems and immense costs which would accompany leaving the monetary union. In this juncture neither to stay in nor to leave seems a good option. However, in this part I am going to suggest a solution which breaks through from this dilemma; a country can reintroduce a national currency and stay in EMU.

The understanding of the dilemma is leading to efforts to find a third way – the idea presented in this paper is one of them. Another proposal has been made by Le Grand (2012). In his opinion "One way of overcoming at least some of these problems would be the following. At a given moment in time, a deficit country withdraws from the euro and denominates all its financial transactions in a temporary currency at a given exchange rate. It then immediately rejoins the euro but at a weaker exchange rate. Denote this QIR, for quit and instantly rejoin". "This form of QIR would be a devaluation with the same beneficial consequences for improving a country's competitiveness, but without all the practical problems associated with introducing a new currency". In the assessment of this proposal I fully agree with Bootle (2012) who argues that "an additional question regarding the form of a break-up is whether it is possible for a country to leave the euro-zone on a temporary basis, in order to improve its competiveness, before then returning to the currency union. (…) Suffice it to say here that we do not view that as a realistic option nor is the idea of an overnight technical deflation which did not need painful adjustment over a long period. The notion of some clever, technical trick that offers an escape from the nasty choice of external devaluation or internal deflation is a chimera".

In fact it is difficult to imagine an effective and sustainable denomination/deflation declared overnight without firmly introducing a new currency. With respect to financial instruments, including deposits and all forms of debt governed by domestic law, it would be identical with a generally declared default on all obligations on the one hand, and a form of a partial expropriation with regard to financial assets on the other hand. It would create economic costs and risks and political tensions which would otherwise associate denomination into a new currency and it would be very doubtful in legal terms and certainly lead to lots of litigation and legal chaos. It is highly improbable that this kind of denomination could bring about a sustainable decrease in the level of wages and prices set on a free market without any actual change of currency. In this sense QIR would be eventually completely ineffective as an instrument to improve competitiveness. As QIR assumes leaving the euro zone (although only temporary, for a very short period of time) it does not resolve the problems of breach of Treaty obligations and resulting political disputes. QIR would merely allow to avoid the costs of printing new cash but this is certainly too little to justify this unfortunate proposal.

I argue here for not leaving the euro zone but at the same time reintroducing a national currency. Such a change would not be associated with any denomination of existing euro nominated financial instruments, liabilities or assets. Conversely, it should be clearly and credibly declared in advance that the new currency would be used only for new transactions after it has been introduced. Since the reintroduction of a national currency would not alter any earlier contracts there would be no reason for bank run, capital outflow or secrecy to avoid associated problems. There would be no political tension resulting from financial losses due to denomination on the one hand and secrecy on the other hand. Cash could be openly prepared in advance what should help to orderly manage the process. Prices should be obligatory quoted in the new drachma which would be declared a legal tender. The drachma would be freely convertible into the euro (and officially and directly rather only to the euro) but the new currency would be in practice used only domestically.[22]

The exchange rate would be flexible, set on the market; preparations to establish necessary infrastructure could be made in advance of the D-day, the day when the new currency would be introduced. There would be no one step devaluation but a process of market depreciation. The starting rate would be 1:1 for simplicity, transparency and avoiding any sense of administratively forced change of economic conditions.

The introduction of the new currency would not compromise any existing domestic or international legal and financial obligations, in particular the country would in full respect all its obligations (and rights) as a member of the European Monetary Union (including Target2 balances). The new money would supplement the common currency and replace it only where it should become a legal tender domestically. This might be considered as a legal trick not being in compliance with the spirit of the Treaties but it should fairly be not considered a breach of the European law, at least not to the same degree as an declared exit from the monetary union. It should help reach international political consensus and gain cooperation. Moreover, any capital controls would be unnecessary and not introduced and the country could respect all its obligations as a member of the European Union and its single market.

[22] The new drachma would operate in a way similar to currencies convertible internally, although in a formal sense it could be fully convertible. A good example of how internal convertibility can accommodate free international trade and capital movement is the currency regime of Polish złoty in early 90's of the last century.

The country would stay in the monetary union and it would use a domestic currency additionally; it would operate under a dual currency system.

However, a reintroduction of the national currency, even within the dual currency system, brings about some risks and costs, too.

The aim to reintroduce the national currency is to improve competitiveness. Hence the drachma must depreciate and thus make wage costs and prices of domestic products expressed in the euro fall. Some depreciation would be desirable but there could be too much of a good thing. A positive aspect of the problem is that there would be no existing drachmas or drachma nominated assets that could become subject to massive sales. Conversely, on the first day there would be no drachmas and all agents obliged to use them to pay wages or taxes or perform any transactions where the drachma would be the only legal tender would have to exchange euros being in their possession for the new currency. Of course the central bank could sell them without limits at the given rate 1:1. If the exchange rate at a moment depreciated on the free exchange market too much the bank could fairly easily intervene (buy) on the shallow drachma market; in principle it could easily buy back the entire emission, which should make the value of drachma soar. At an early stage of functioning of the dual currency system the central bank would have in fact a full control over the exchange rate. It could use it to dose the depreciation at an optimum rate.

An important aspect of this process is credibility. It should be clear that the new currency is not going to be junk money. The exchange rate should not fall quickly or even it should stay perfectly stable for a period of time. However, it should be also clear that the new currency is going to depreciate against the euro; the external devaluation is the mechanism to gain so much needed improvement in competitiveness.

Another aspect of credibility is inflation. Any increase in drachma prices and wages would dent the improvement in competitiveness due to depreciation. Moreover, in the situation when all obligations existing on the D-day would remain nominated in euros (or foreign currencies) inflation would not make their real value fall. There would be no "debt depreciation", in particular with regard to the public debt due. Hence it is clear that inflation has no positive effects, which is not so unambiguous in the case of a redenomination covering excessive public financial obligations. This unequivocal attitude towards inflation could support credibility both in terms of the exchange rate and price stability.

However, there remains a tricky issue of managing the process of an optimum external depreciation and keeping inflation possibly low at the same time. The emission of drachmas would consist in the sale of the new currency for the euro. As I have argued above the central bank would have much discretion with respect to the exchange rate. At the beginning the rate could be stable but soon it should start depreciating slowly. The drachma emission system would be similar to an "informal crawling currency board system" with the monetary policy still run within the Eurosystem.[23] There would be certainly no excessive capital inflow into drachma nominated assets which could make the new money supply get out of control and cause inflationary pressures as for example in the case of Estonia's currency board (Koronowski, 2012). Drachmas would be demanded only to the extent they should serve transactions as a legal tender.

---

[23] This dual currency system would only be similar to a currency board; in particular, the national central bank would exchange its liabilities to euro-area credit institutions denominated in euro for liabilities denominated in drachma and not buy or sell euro as a foreign reserves currency. Moreover, the national central bank would perform euro monetary policy as a part of the Eurosystem.

A relative role of the drachma versus the euro is very important. Leaving to much room for quoting prices and performing transactions in the euro would make the introduction of the new currency of little importance and economic agents would continue to use the euro as the main unit of account. The result would be general indexation of all prices quoted in the drachma by the rate of exchange rate depreciation; inflation of drachma prices would wipe off any positive impact depreciation could have on competitiveness. This is why the drachma should be declared the only legal tender in most transactions in retail, all transactions in wholesale trade, for public obligations (taxes), wages and remunerations. It should be also clear that all respective prices are denominated by law into the drachma at the official rate, 1:1 on the D-day. Information campaign should be an important part of reintroducing the national currency so that desirable expectations and attitudes emerge.

The fact that the denomination would not pertain to liabilities and assets existing on the D-day does not mean that the introduction of the new currency would not have an important impact on financial situation of many economic agents. In particular, many of them, including the government, would stay with euro nominated assets but would get most of its future incomes in drachmas. The drachma could be freely exchanged for the euro but at a depreciated rate. This might make servicing the debt difficult by many firms, households and – last but not least – the government. The result could be growing problems in the financial sector. However, there would be no losses and negative effects due to balance sheet currency mismatch triggered by a denomination of assets and liabilities and devaluation; this could be possibly more devastating, especially in the financial sector and in the case of many firms. Moreover, if the problems become too severe the central bank could use its power to control – slow down or reverse - the rate of depreciation.[24]

It should be underlined here that depreciation should improve competitiveness and thus make export incomes grow, boost the economy and eventually bring about higher tax incomes to the budget. Of course it is impossible to precisely assess the respective developments, particularly so in a draft sketch presented in this paper.

Any proposals of exit from the monetary union assume denomination of financial instruments governed by the domestic law. This is – together with devaluation of the new currency – a form of default. In comparison with this situation a lack of denomination of financial instruments in the proposition presented in this paper it is a major difference. It does not mean that I am convinced that a default on public debt would not be a necessary element of rebalancing the economy. However, it can always be arranged – and agreed – on a "regular basis" instead of being unilaterally declared with respect to all classes of financial instruments governed by domestic law. The latter solution imposes huge and uncontrollable losses on many agents, especially financial institutions abroad. This may be a source of major problems. The idea presented in this paper leaves instead room for a default as an orderly, negotiated debt restructuring, potentially selective, restricted to government debt. This should have much less adverse effects for creditors as well as the credibility of the defaulting country's authorities.

Summing up, the major risk associated with the dual currency system as suggested in this paper is that it possibly could fail in efficient providing real depreciation of the new currency and improvement in competitiveness. The design and performing of the policy of

[24] Let's notice that in the case of drachma inflation the problem would be generally negligible; the difficulties emerge only when depreciation is an effective instrument to improve competitiveness.

denomination should allow for desirable depreciation and at the same time low inflation and hence should minimize the risk. Since the drachma could be only bought in exchange for the euro (euro denominated assets) and abundant capital inflow would be highly improbable there would be no excessive emission of the new currency and prices (or their domestic components which matter) should be fairly stable. This does not have to be much affected by the fact that the drachma would be sold at a devalued price for the euro.

However, the national central bank, being able to supply its own money, could use these powers to meet other targets. In particular, it could decide to inject liquidity in drachmas into the financial institutions through refinancing operations where acceptable collateral could include underperforming assets, also denominated in the drachma.[25] Such expansive policy could be aimed at strengthening the financial institutions or it could also have some aspect of quantitative easing. Moreover, the central bank in the dual-currency system could go even further and recapitalize commercial banks providing newly created drachmas in exchange for property rights. This of course would be very far from conservative attitudes towards the role of the central bank and much beyond the role of lender of last resort. However, when the task of recapitalization in face of possible systemic collapse could not be undertaken by the indebted government these attitudes might bleak.

Whatever is a possible scope for traditional and non-conservative expansionary monetary policy with respect to providing the drachma, I am convinced that these possibilities should be resigned. The basic aim of the dual currency system should be to bring about real depreciation so any additional targets and related monetary expansion which could boost inflation should be given up. Monetary policy should be performed within the structure of the Eurosystem and the drachmas should be provided only in exchange for the euro or euro denominated assets (in this respect the system would resemble a currency board).

The dual-currency system, as described above, could in principle be preserved permanently. However, it also gives opportunities, firstly, to eventually exit from the euro zone in an orderly manner or, secondly, to give up and withdraw the emission of the national currency, denominate all prices back to the euro and remain a member of the monetary union with a single and common currency system. In the first situation, the change could be very swift. The central bank should simply start performing monetary policy in drachmas instead of its actions as a member of the Eurosystem. Any denomination would not be needed, no secrecy necessary, the national currency, including cash, would have been already introduced. In the second case the country could also fairly easily become a "normal" member of the euro zone. The central bank would only have to declare that the drachma is converted into the euro at a given exchange rate, equal to the market rate on the day of conversion. This way all prices denominated in the drachma would be redenominated into the euro. The central bank would continue to perform all its actions as a member of the Eurosystem and it would stop providing the national currency via purchases of the euro and euro denominated assets. It should absorb existing drachma cash; this should be easy as its emission was a result of earlier purchases of the euro (assets). The ECB could help go through the process smoothly. Drachma banknotes and coins could for a period of time circulate representing the euro.

I must emphasize that the second scenario is very far from QIR mentioned earlier. Firstly, the country does not exit from the monetary union although, secondly, it reintroduces its

[25] Any active monetary policy performed in the national currency would enhance doubts concerning anyway ambiguous membership of the country in the euro zone.

national, parallel currency. Thirdly, the dual currency system may last quite long so that necessary adjustment can fully take place.

How long a country would preserve a dual-currency system and whether it eventually would exit the euro zone or conversely give up the national currency does not have to be determined in time when the dual-currency system is introduced. It could be subject to further analysis of the past developments and new perspectives, it means on the reassessment of the role of the single currency.

CONCLUSION

Improving external competitiveness and rebalancing current accounts is a major factor behind any successful solution of the present problems of euro zone countries most hit by the crisis. This target cannot be met in the monetary union through currency devaluation and "internal devaluation" does not seem a possible and reasonable option, either. This reasoning leads to a conclusion that an exit from the euro zone may turn out to be an unavoidable step to solve the problems. Contingency plans for leaving the euro zone emerge; in particular several papers have been presented as submissions for the Wolfson Economics Prize, which presented alternative scenarios of an orderly exit from or break-up of the monetary union. This kind of research proves that leaving the euro zone would be a complex process in political, economic and legal terms and it would cause high costs. These economic costs and political and legal clashes can be avoided if a country obeys its obligations as a member of the euro zone and does not leave the monetary union but at the same time reintroduces a national currency so that a dual currency system is established. In this system the national central bank performs monetary policy in the euro as a member of the Eurosystem and national currency is a domestic legal tender freely convertible to the euro at a floating but controlled exchange rate. A carefully managed process can lead to a gradual nominal and real depreciation of the currency and thus improved competitiveness. The dual currency system can be a long lasting solution, it also allows to resign the national currency and use again only the euro or – conversely – to resign the euro and exit the euro zone in an open, honest and orderly manner.

BIBLIOGRAPHY

Basto, R.B. , *The Portuguese Experience with the Euro – Relevance for New EU Member Countries*, Bank i Kredyt, No 11-12/2007

Bootle, R., *Leaving the euro: A practical guide*, a submission for the Wolfson Economics Prize MMXII by Capital Economics, 2012, (http://www.policyexchange.org.uk/images/WolfsonPrize/wep%20shortlist%20essay%20-%20roger%20bootle.pdf)

Calvo, G. A. and Vegh, C. A., *Inflation Stabilization and Nominal Anchors*, in Barth, R.C. and Wong, C.H. (ed.) *Approaches to Exchange Rate Policy*, IMF, 1992

Dobbs, C., *The NEWNEY approach to unscrambling the Euro*, a submission for the Wolfson Economics Prize MMXII, 2012, (http://www.policyexchange.org.uk/images/WolfsonPrize/newney%205%20jun.pdf)

European Commission (2001), *Policy adjustment in the euro-area countries: the risk of overheating*, in *The EU Economy: 2001 Review*, Directorate General for Economic and Financial Affairs

European Commission (2005), *Growth differences in the euro area*, in *Quarterly Report on the Euro Area*, II 2005, Directorate General for Economic and Financial Affairs

European Commission (2009), *Public Finances in EMU*, 2009, European Economy 5/2009

IMF, *Portugal: Selected Issues*, IMF Country Report No. 06/386, October 2006

Khamis, M., *Credit and Exchange Based Stabilization*, IMF Working Paper WP/96/51, 1996

Kiguel, M. and Liviatan, N., *The Business Cycle Associated with Exchange Rate Based Stabilizations*, The World Bank Economic Review, vol. 6, no 2, 1992

Koronowski, A., *Divergent business cycles as an effect of a monetary union*, International Economics and Economic Policy, vol. 6 no 2, 2009.

Koronowski, A. *On a Hidden Aspect of the Credibility Crisis in the European Union*, Research in World Economy, Vol. 2, No. 1, April 2011.

Koronowski, A, 2012, *Estonian and Hungarian economic policies before and during the crisis; virtue unrewarded and profligacy unpunished*, Research in World Economy, Vol. 3, No. 1, March 2012.

Le Grand, J., *QIR and EMU, A Proposal for Managing a Member State's Departure from the European Monetary Union*, Submission for the Wolfson Economics Prize, 2012, (http://www.policyexchange.org.uk/images/WolfsonPrize/wep%20special%20mention%20-%20julian%20le%20grand.pdf)

Nordvig, J., Firoozye, N., *Rethinking the European monetary union*, Wolfson Economics Prize 2012 – Final Submission, (http://www.policyexchange.org.uk/images/WolfsonPrize/nordvig%20-%20rethinking%20european%20monetary%20union.pdf)

Santaella, J. A.and Vela, A. E., *The 1987 Mexican Disinflation Program: An Exchange Rate Based Stabilization?,* IMF Working Paper WP/96/24, 1996

Wyplosz, Ch.(2006), *European monetary union, the dark side of a major success*, Economic Policy, April 2006 pp. 207-261, 2006.

Wyplosz, Ch. (2006b), *Diverging tendencies of competitiveness. Briefing notes to the Committee for Economic and Monetary Affairs of the European Parliament,* 2006.

Visser, Hans, *A guide to international monetary economics*, Edward Elgar, Cambridge, 1995.

In: Exchange Rates in Developed and Emerging Markets ISBN: 978-1-62808-164-0
Editor: Mohsen Bahmani-Oskooee

Chapter 6

Do Nominal Devaluations Lead to Real Devaluations? Evidence from Emerging Economies

Mohsen Bahmani-Oskooee[1,*] and Sahar Bahmani[2]
[1]Center for Research on International Economics And the Department of Economics, University of Wisconsin-Milwaukee, Milwaukee, WI, US
[2]Department of Economics, University of Wisconsin-Parkside, Kenosha, WI, US

Abstract

A country devalues its currency with an expectation that it will gain international competitiveness and increase its net exports. However, the inflationary effects of devaluation could curtail its favorable effects unless nominal devaluation leads to real devaluation. In this chapter we use nominal and real effective exchange rates data from China, Croatia, Bulgaria, Czeck Republic, Estonia, Hungary, Latvia, Lithuania, Poland, Romania, Russia, Slovakia, and Slovenia to determine whether nominal devaluations have led to real devaluations. We find the answer to be in the affirmative in the short run. The short-run effects last into the long run only in five countries including China.

I. Introduction

In his presidential bet to the White House, republican candidate Mitt Romney often said if he is elected as the President of the U.S., he will label China as "currency manipulator". What Romney meant was that in order to gain international competitiveness, China intervenes in its foreign exchange market in order to keep value of the yuan low against the dollar. When yuan is cheap, all Chinese exports to the U.S. become cheap and China exports more and runs trade surplus against the U.S. On the other hand, cheap yuan means an expensive dollar which

* Corresponding author: bahmani@uwm.edu.

makes U.S. exports or Chinese imports expensive in terms of yuan; hence it contributes to domestic inflation in China. It is possible that over time part or all of the gain in competitiveness is siphoned off by domestic inflation. Thus, if we are to measure the international competitiveness, we must incorporate changes in prices to changes in the nominal exchange rate. The resulting measure is consistent with the concept of the real exchange rate. Therefore, if devaluation or depreciation of the nominal exchange rate is to stimulate exports or improve the trade balance, it must lead to depreciation in the real exchange rate.

Several studies in the literature have investigated the link between the nominal and the real exchange rate. Examples are: Vaubel (1976), Connoly and Taylor (1976, 1979), Bruno (1978), and Edwards (1988, 1994) who concluded that nominal devaluations lead to real devaluations only in the short run. Other studies used cointegration analysis and showed that in some countries the nominal and the real exchange rate have a long-run relation, hence nominal devaluations leads to real devaluations. Examples in this later group are: Bahmani-Oskooee and Miteza (2002), Joyce and Kamas (2003), Holmes (2004), Bahmani-Oskooee and Gelan (2006), and Bahmani-Oskooee et al. (2008) who have considered the experiences of many developing countries including those in Africa and Latin America and have provided some support for the link between the nominal and the real exchange rate in the long run.

In this chapter we investigate whether the nominal and real effective exchange rates of China do have a long-run relationship and whether nominal devaluation in China leads to real devaluation so that China can enjoy gain in international competitiveness. We also extend our analysis to 12 other emerging economies. The list includes Bulgaria, Croatia, Czeck Republic, Estonia, Hungary, Latvia, Lithuania, Poland, Romania, Russia, Slovakia, and Slovenia. For this purpose, in Section II we outline the methodology. In Section III we report our findings and in Section IV we conclude.

II. The Model and Method

In analyzing the link between the nominal and real exchange rate, one question is should we concentrate on the bilateral rate or effective exchange rate. Since the effective exchange rate measures performance of one country's currency against the currencies of its trading partners, it is highly desirable to concentrate on effective rates. The effective exchange rates these days are constructed by different organizations such as the International Monetary Fund (IMF) or Bank for International Settlement (BIS) for almost all countries. The difference between the two sources is that while the former organization uses fixed trade weights to construct indexes of effective exchange rates, the later organization allows the weight to change over time so that the dynamic changes in the size of trade is accounted for. While all previous research has used IMF data to address the link between the nominal and the real exchange rate, we use data from BIS.

Let N*EX* denote the nominal effective exchange rate and R*EX* denote the real effective rate. Since the main purpose is to determine whether nominal devaluation leads to real devaluation, we follow previous research and concentrate on a log-linear model as in equation (1):

$$LnREX_t = \alpha + \beta LnNEX_t + \varepsilon_t \tag{1}$$

where ε is an error term. If a decline in *NEX*, i.e., a nominal depreciation, is to lead to a decline in *REX,* or a real depreciation, we expect the estimate of β to be positive. However, estimate of β yields the long-run effects of nominal exchange rate on the real rate. In order to judge the short-run effects also, we need incorporate short-run dynamics by expressing (1) in an error-correction modeling format. To this end we follow the bounds testing approach of Pesaran *et al.* (2001) an error-correction model outlined by equation (2):

$$\Delta LnREX_t = a + \sum_{K=1}^{n1} b_K \Delta LnREX_{t-K} + \sum_{K=1}^{n2} c_K \Delta LnNEX_{t-k} + \delta_1 LnREX_{t-1} + \delta_2 LnNEX_{t-1} + \mu_t \tag{2}$$

The difference between this model and Engle-Granger specification is that the lagged error term from (1) is replaced by the linear combination of lagged level variables in (2). Furthermore, this approach offers a one-step estimation of equation (2) to infer the short-run as well as the long-run effects of changes in the nominal exchange rate on the real exchange rate whereas, Engle-Granger approach involves two steps. Once (2) is estimated, the short-run effects are reflected in the estimates of c_k's and the long-run effects in the estimate of δ_2 that is normalized on δ_1. However, for the long-run effects not to be spurious, Pesaran *et al.* (2001) propose establishing joint significance of lagged level variables as a sign of cointegration. To do so, they recommend applying the standard F test with new critical values that they tabulate. Since the critical values account for degree of integration of all variables, there is no need for pre-unit-root testing as long as variables are either integrated of order zero, I(0) or I(1). Indeed, they prove that variables could be combination of I(0) and I(1) which is the case in most macro variables. Finally, to make sure that adjustment between the two exchange rates is toward long run equilibrium, long-run estimates are used to form an error-correction term using (1). The linear combination of lagged level variables in (2) is then replaced by the constructed lallged error-correction term, say, ECM_{t-1} and the resulting specification is estimated one more time using the lag structure as before. If adjustment is to be toward long-run equilibrium values, a significantly negative coefficient for ECM_{t-1} is expected (Bahmani-Oskooee and Ardalani, 2006).

III. The Empirical Results

In this section we estimate equation (2) for China, Croatia, Bulgaria, Czeck Republic, Estonia, Hungary, Latvia, Lithuania, Poland, Romania, Russia, Slovakia, and Slovenia using monthly data over the period January 1994-November 2012.[26] In order to get an idea about the relation between the nominal and real effective exchange rate, we plot them in Figure 1.

It is clear from Figure 1 that the two exchange rates move in harmony only in the cases of China, Czeck Republic, Estonia, Lithuania, Latvia, and Slovk Republic. However, we should

[26] As mentioned before the data comes from the Bank for International Settlements (BIS) web site: http://www.bis.org/statistics/eer/index.htm.

estimate equation (2) and show that these relationships are not spurious to which we turn next.

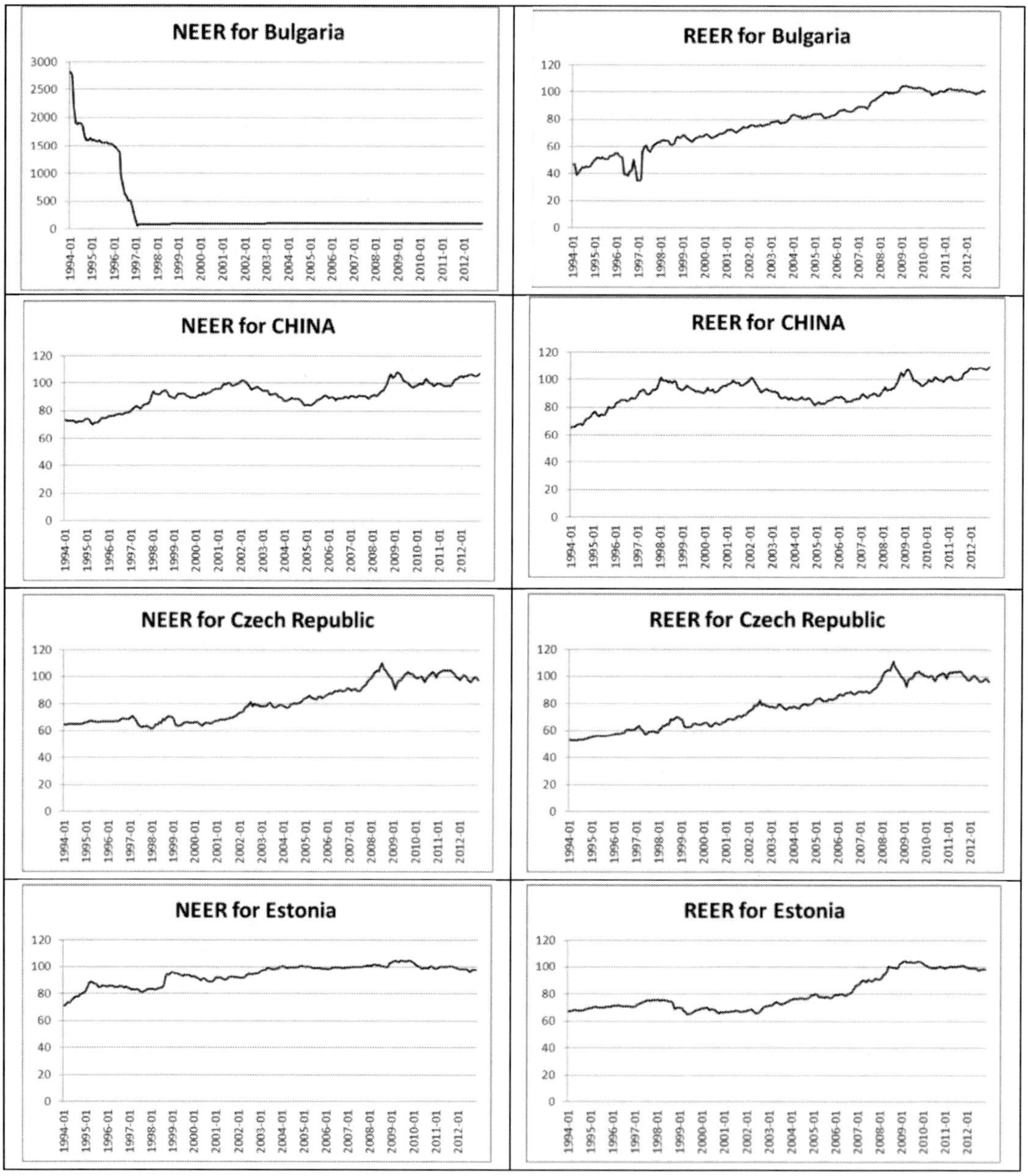

Figure 1. (Continued).

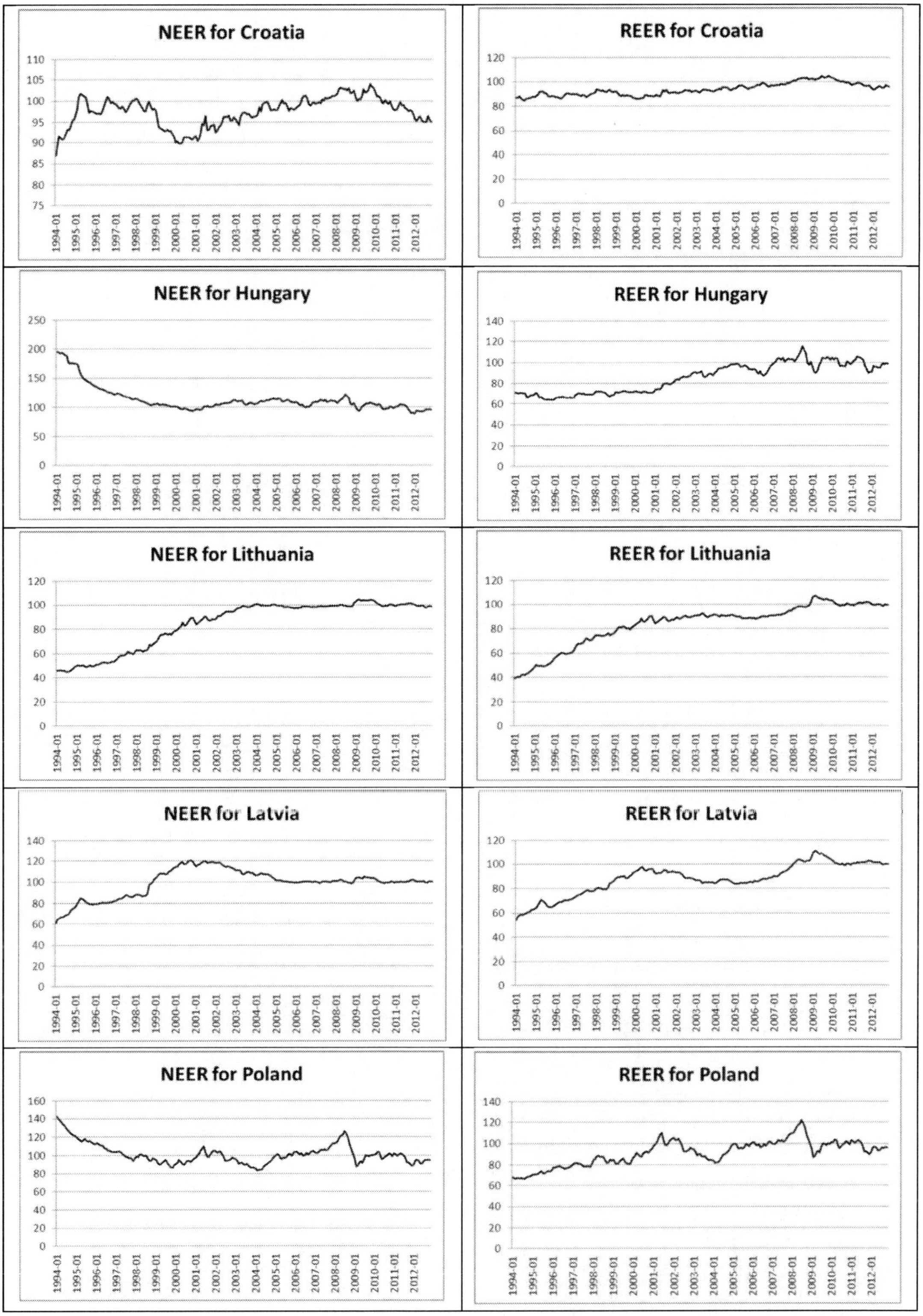

Figure 1. (Continued).

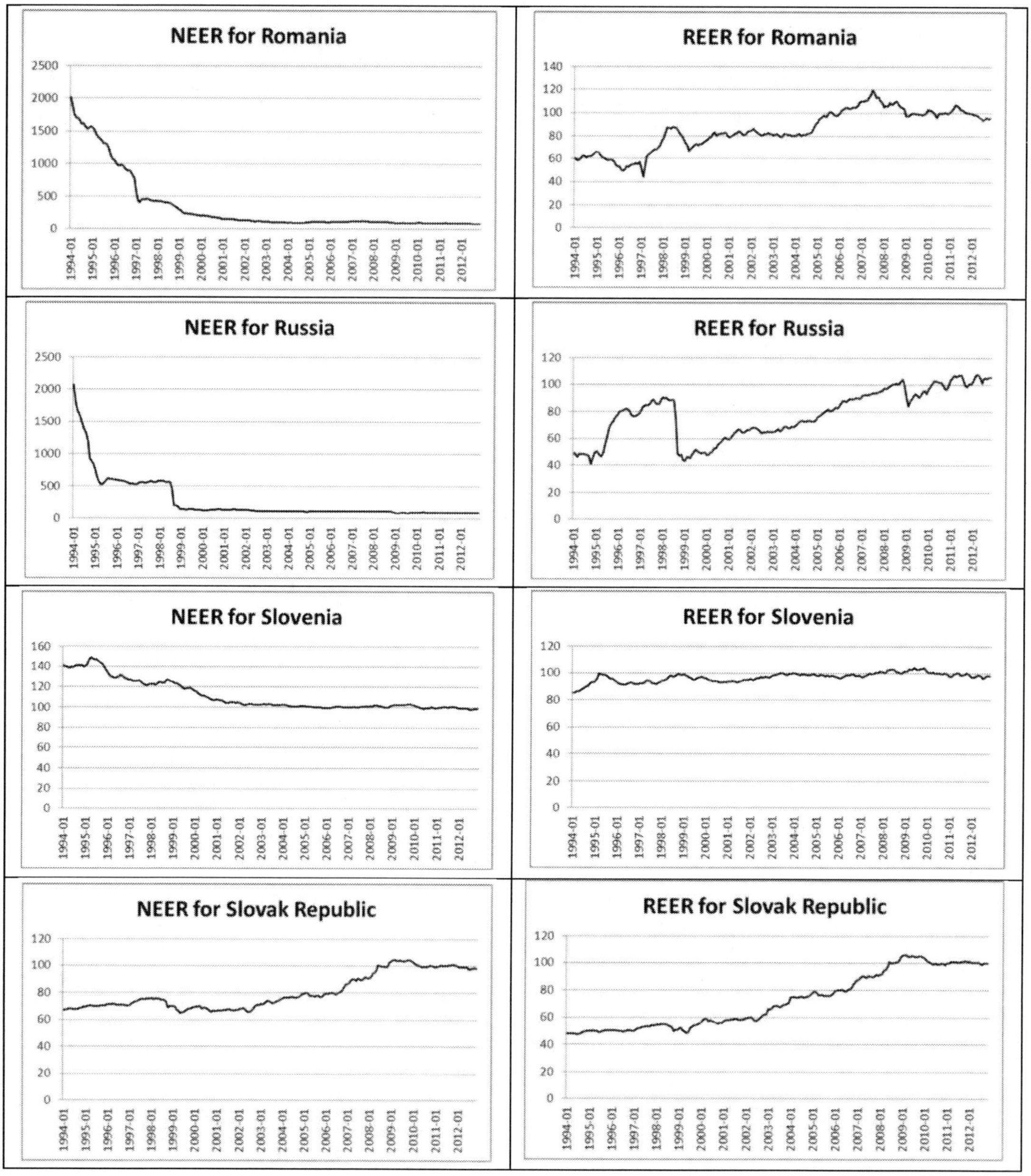

Figure 1. The Nominal (NEER) and Real (REER) Effective Exchange Rates.

Since data is monthly, a maximum of 12 lags are imposed on each first-differenced variable in equation (2) and Akaike's Information Criterion (AIC) is used to select the optimum number of lags in each case. The results for each optimum model of each country are reported in Table 1.

Table 1. Coefficient Estimates of Error-Correction Model (2) and Diagnostics

Panel A: Short-Run Coefficient Estimates

	Bulgaria	China	Croatia	Czeck Republic	Estonia	Hungary	Latvia	Lithuania	Poland	Romania	Russia	Slovak Republic	Slovenia
$\Delta LnREX_{t-1}$	0.31 (4.02)	0.37 (5.52)	0.01 (0.29)	-0.06 (0.92)	0.18 (2.62)	0.07 (1.03)	0.18 (2.73)	0.21 (3.07)	0.15 (2.31)	0.24 (3.52)	0.46 (6.39)		0.13 (1.96)
$\Delta LnREX_{t-2}$	-0.36 (4.02)	-0.12 (1.62)	-0.05 (1.35)	0.02 (0.25)	0.05 (0.79)	-0.05 (0.78)	0.13 (1.83)	0.10 (1.39)	-0.01 (0.20)	0.32 (4.33)	0.08 (1.03)		-0.08 (1.28)
$\Delta LnREX_{t-3}$	-0.27 (3.11)	-0.02 (0.25)	-0.09 (2.36)	-0.02 (0.36)	0.14 (2.04)	0.05 (0.82)	0.14 (2.05)		0.06 (0.98)	0.10 (1.33)	-0.17 (-2.35)		-0.13 (2.80)
$\Delta LnREX_{t-4}$	0.29 (3.31)	-0.13 (1.83)	0.04 (1.12)	-0.14 (2.35)		0.07 (1.16)	0.02 (0.51)		0.20 (3.10)	-0.16 (2.13)	0.14 (1.98)		
$\Delta LnREX_{t-5}$	-0.35 (3.99)	0.30 (4.46)	-0.07 (1.82)	0.02 (0.38)		-0.27 (4.45)	-0.10 (2.35)		-0.13 (2.07)	0.10 (1.73)	0.11 (1.74)		
$\Delta LnREX_{t-6}$	0.35 (3.78)	-0.45 (7.10)		0.54 (9.14)		-0.11 (1.77)			-0.21 (3.35)	0.04 (0.90)	0.04 (2.11)		
$\Delta LnREX_{t-7}$	-0.1 (0.91)	0.27 (4.06)		0.09 (1.30)		-0.31 (4.90)			-0.03 (2.17)	0.03 (0.77)			
$\Delta LnREX_{t-8}$	-0.46 (4.46)	-0.13 (1.92)		-0.18 (2.47)		0.12 (1.86)				0.03 (0.83)			
$\Delta LnREX_{t-9}$	-0.19 (1.62)	-0.02 (0.28)								-0.01 (0.17)			
$\Delta LnREX_{t-10}$	0.14 (1.76)	-0.12 (1.68)								0.09 (2.67)			
$\Delta LnREX_{t-11}$		0.34 (5.24)											
$\Delta LnNEX_{t}$	0.31 (10.38)	1.06 (27.24)	0.93 (24.23)	0.97 (39.13)	0.91 (22.20)	0.97 (45.29)	0.80 (18.18)	0.85 (21.43)	1.01 (60.89)	0.81 (24.01)	0.61 (43.12)	0.10 (20.99)	0.98 (17.17)
$\Delta LnNEX_{t-1}$	-0.26 (7.38)	-0.46 (5.34)		0.01 (0.18)	-0.22 (2.98)	-0.06 (0.93)	-0.12 (1.70)	-0.21 (3.06)	-0.18 (2.51)	-0.48 (7.15)	-0.29 (6.53)	0.04 (0.93)	-0.28 (3.00)
$\Delta LnNEX_{t-2}$	0.10 (2.64)	0.20 (2.22)		-0.02 (0.22)	-0.11 (1.48)	0.04 (0.67)	-0.05 (0.76)	-0.09 (1.34)	-0.004 (0.05)	-0.30 (3.95)	-0.07 (1.46)	0.03 (0.56)	0.19 (2.15)
$\Delta LnNEX_{t-3}$	-0.05 (1.12)	-0.08 (0.84)		-0.003 (0.05)	-0.15 (2.05)	-0.07 (1.11)	-0.22 (3.39)	-0.06 (1.52)	-0.05 (0.78)	0.04 (0.50)	0.08 (1.78)	-0.03 (0.67)	

Table 1. (Continued)

	Bulgaria	China	Croatia	Czeck Republic	Estonia	Hungary	Latvia	Lithuania	Poland	Romania	Russia	Slovak Republic	Slovenia
$\Delta LnNEX_{t-4}$	-0.18 (4.44)	-0.20 (2.23)		0.09 (1.34)		-0.07 (1.12)		-0.04 (1.52)	-0.20 (2.91)	0.19 (2.53)	-0.10 (2.30)	-0.07 (1.41)	
$\Delta LnNEX_{t-5}$	0.04 (0.87)	-0.37 (4.20)		-0.044 (0.70)		0.24 (3.84)		-0.07 (1.13)	0.12 (1.77)	-0.09 (1.36)	-0.1 (2.39)	0.02 (0.38)	
$\Delta LnNEX_{t-6}$	-0.04 (1.00)	0.49 (5.91)		-0.51 (8.05)		0.09 (1.33)		0.02 (1.75)	0.24 (3.53)			0.004 (0.08)	
$\Delta LnNEX_{t-7}$	0.16 (4.42)	-0.31 (3.58)		-0.09 (1.24)		0.25 (3.87)		-0.12 (0.50)				-0.02 (0.45)	
$\Delta LnNEX_{t-8}$	0.06 (1.60)	0.19 (2.20)		0.14 (1.90)		-0.12 (1.88)						0.0002 (0.01)	
$\Delta LnNEX_{t-9}$	-0.11 (3.01)	-0.01 (0.16)				-0.02 (0.70)						-0.19 (3.98)	
$\Delta LnNEX_{t-10}$	-0.12 (2.73)	0.091 (1.06)				0.0009 (0.04)							
$\Delta LnNEX_{t-11}$	-0.04 (1.62)	-0.33 (4.28)				-0.05 (2.48)							
Panel B: Long-Run Coefficient Estimates													
LnNEX	-0.40 (1.25)	0.64 (2.58)	0.88 (0.84)	0.89 (5.02)	1.02 (3.19)	1.21 (3.97)	-1.13 (0.58)	0.28 (1.18)	0.70 (4.72)	-0.16 (4.74)	-0.01 (0.06)	3.14 (1.57)	0.05 (0.64)
Constant	6.69 (3.67)	1.63 (1.44)	0.58 (0.12)	0.52 (0.66)	-0.13 (0.09)	-0.92 (0.66)	9.90 (1.07)	3.30 (3.03)	1.40 (2.07)	5.34 (32.02)	4.70 (4.99)	-10.01 (1.07)	4.39 (13.20)
Panel C: Diagnostics													
F	1.39	1.72	0.36	2.73	12.47	20.56	1.90	10.20	25.77	8.45	2.91	2.13	18.71
ECM_{t-1}	-0.01 (1.05)	-0.02 (1.73)	-0.01 (1.06)	-0.02 (2.07)	-0.02 (3.97)	-0.02 (4.96)	-0.005 (1.08)	-0.02 (2.48)	-0.03 (6.12)	-0.04 (4.09)	-0.01 (1.83)	0.004 (0.83)	-0.05 (3.96)
$Adj.\ R^2$	0.77	0.82	0.74	0.91	0.76	0.92	0.71	0.76	0.96	0.80	0.94	0.72	0.64

Notes: Numbers inside parentheses are the absolute value of t-ratios.

The F statistic is for testing the joint significance of lagged level variables (or cointegration) in each model. At the 10% level of significance, the upper bound critical value is 4.78. This comes from Pesaran *et al.* (2001, Table C1, Case III, p.300).

As can be seen from Table 1, for each country the results are reported in three panels. While Panel A reports the short-run coefficient estimates, Panel B reports the long-run estimates. Finally, diagnostic statistics are reported in Panel C. From Panel A we gather that in each case there is at least one significant coefficient obtained for the nominal effective exchange rate, implying that indeed nominal devaluation leads to real devaluation in the short-run. Interestingly, most of the impact takes place sooner since the current values of the change in the nominal effective exchange rate carries the largest short-run coefficient. In order to determine in how many countries the short-run effects last into the long run, we shift to Panel B. It appears that the nominal effective exchange rate carries a positive and highly significant coefficient only in the results for China, Czeck Republic, Estonia, Hungary, and Poland. Therefore, in the long run only these five countries will gain competitiveness. However, for our long-run results to be valid, we should establish cointegration to which we turn next.

From Panel C the results of the F test for joint significance of lagged level variables in (2) or cointegration reveals that our calculated F statistic is greater than its critical value of 4.78 in the cases of Estonia, Hungary, and Poland. In other cases we can rely upon the negative and significant coefficient obtained for ECM_{t-1}. Finally, estimated models seem to enjoy a good fit since size of the adjusted R^2 is high.

SUMMARY AND CONCLUSION

Intervention in the foreign exchange market by many countries to drive down the value of their currencies is said to be one way to gain international competitiveness in order to stimulate next exports and enjoy economic growth. However, inflationary effects of devaluation or depreciation may hurt the competitiveness gains in the long run unless we establish that any nominal depreciation leads to real depreciation.

A country that is often accused of engaging in currency manipulation is China. In this chapter we wonder whether nominal devaluation or depreciation of yuan leads to its real depreciation, hence international competitiveness gain. In addition to China, we also consider experiences of 12 other emerging economies. The list, therefore, includes China, Croatia, Bulgaria, Czeck Republic, Estonia, Hungary, Latvia, Lithuania, Poland, Romania, Russia, Slovakia, and Slovenia. Monthly nominal and real effective exchange rates over the period January 1994-November 2012, as well as the bounds testing approach, is used to investigate the short-run as well as the long-run effects of changes in the nominal effective exchange rate on the real rate.

We find that nominal devaluation leads to real devaluation in all 13 countries in the short run. However, the short-run effects last into the long run only in five countries including China. These findings suggest that not every country can benefit from currency devaluation in the long run. Therefore, it is necessary to use other policies to address a country's trade position in the long run such as product differentiation, improved quality, export diversification, import tariff, export subsidy, etc.

REFERENCES

Bahmani-Oskooee, M. & Miteza, I. (2002). "Do Nominal Devaluations Lead to Real Devaluations in LDCs?", *Economics Letters*, Vol. *74*, 385-391.

Bahmani-Oskooee, M. & Miteza, I. (2003). "Are Devaluations Expansionary or Contractionary: A Survey Article," *Economic Issues*, Vol. *8*, Part 2, 1-28.

Bahmani-Oskooee, M. & Ratha, A. (2004). "The J-Curve: A Literature Review", *Applied Economics*, Vol. *36*, 1377-1398.

Bahmani-Oskooee, M. & Ardalani, Z. (2006). "Exchange Rate Sensitivity of U.S. Trade Flows: Evidence from Industry Data", *Southern Economic Journal*, Vol. *72*, 542-559.

Bahmani-Oskooee, M. & Gelan, A. (2006). "On the Relation Between Nominal Devaluation and Real Devaluation: Evidence from African Countries," *Journal of African Economies*, forthcoming.

Bahmani-Oskooee, M., Hegerty, S. & Kutan, A. (2008). "Do Nominal Devaluations Lead to Real Devaluations? Evidence from 89 Countries", *International Review of Economics and Finance*, Vol. *17*, 644-670.

Brada, J. C., Kutan, A. M. & Zhou, S. (1997). "The Exchange Rate and the Balance of Trade: The Turkish Experience", *Journal of Development Studies*, Vol. *33*, 675-692.

Bruno, Michael. (1978). "Exchange Rates, Import Costs, and Wage-Price Dynamics." *Journal of Political Economy*, Vol. *86*, 379-403.

Connolly, Michael & Dean Taylor, (August 1976). "Adjustment to Devaluation with Money and Non-Traded Goods," *Journal of International Economics*, Vol. *6*, 289-298.

Edwards, Sebastian (1988). "Exchange Rate Misalignment in Developing Countries." World Bank Occasional Papers, No. 2, New Series, The Johns Hopkins University Press.

Edwards, Sebastian (1994). "Exchange Rate Misalignment in Developing Countries." in R. Barth and C. Wong (eds.), Approaches to Exchange Rate Policy: Choices for Developing and Transition Economies: International Monetary Fund, Washington, DC.

Engle, R. F. & Granger, C. W. J. (1987). "Cointegration and Error Correction: Representation, Estimation, and Testing," *Econometrica*, Vol. *55*, 251-76.

Holmes, Mark J. (2004). "Can African Countries Achieve Long-Run Real Exchange Rate Depreciation Through Nominal Exchange Rate Depreciation?" *The South African Journal of Economics*, Vol. *72*, 305-323.

Joyce, J. P. & Kamas, L. (2003). "Real and Nominal Determinants of Real Exchange Rates in Latin America: Short-Run Dynamics and Long-Run Equilibrium", *Journal of Development Studies*, Vol. *39*, 155-182.

Kamas, L. (2001). "Monetary and Exchange Rate Policy in Colombia: Effects on the Real Exchange Rate in the 1990s", *Journal of Development Studies*, Vol. *38* (2001), 131-166.

Pesaran, M. H., Shin, Y. & Smith, R. J. (2001). "Bounds Testing Approaches to the Analysis of Level Relationships," *Journal of Applied Econometrics*, Vol. *16*, 289-326.

Santos-Paulino, A. U. (2002). "Trade Liberalization and Export Performance in Selected Developing Countries", *Journal of Development Studies*, Vol. *39*, 140-164.

Vaubel, Roland (1976). "Real Exchange Rate Changes in the European Community: The Empirical Evidence and its Implications for European Currency Unification." *Weltwirtschaftliches Archiv*, Vol. *112*, 429-470.

In: Exchange Rates in Developed and Emerging Markets
Editor: Mohsen Bahmani-Oskooee
ISBN: 978-1-62808-164-0

Chapter 7

FOREIGN EXCHANGE RATES AND STOCK PRICES: EVIDENCE FROM MAJOR AFRICAN MARKETS

Odongo Kodongo[1,*] and Kalu Ojah[2]

[1]Department of Business Studies, Jomo Kenyatta University of Agriculture and Technology, Nairobi, Kenya

[2]Graduate School of Business Administration, University of the Witwatersrand, Johannesburg, South Africa

ABSTRACT

We study the short- and long-run dynamic relationships between currency markets and stock markets in five major African countries, for the period between January 1997 and May 2011. Our bivariate cointegration tests indicate no long-run relationship between the two markets in all the countries. However, in multivariate cointegration tests, we find that the world equity market (represented by the US stock market), provides information that drives both foreign exchange and stock markets of African countries; thus, causing a strong long-run relationship between these two markets. Stability tests show that parameter estimates are unstable particularly during the 2001/3 world recession and the 2007/9 global financial crisis periods, suggesting that African markets are exposed to external shocks. Furthermore, multivariate Granger-causality tests show that causality between the two markets is country-dependent. Interestingly, neither the "flow" channel nor the "stock" channel relationship between exchange rates and stock prices is supported by our results.

JEL Classification: F21; F31; F36

Keywords: Africa, stock markets, foreign exchange markets, cointegration

* Corresponding author: Tel.: +254 73 418 2471; E-mail: kodongo03@gmail.com.

1. INTRODUCTION

Africa's financial markets have witnessed many policy reforms in recent years. In particular, there has been a visible attempt to develop new stock markets in the continent and to modernize and grow existing ones with a view to enhancing their operating capacity (e.g., see Bekaert, Harvey and Lundblad, 2003). From international investors' perspective, these developments have expanded the frontiers for portfolio diversification. Similarly, there have been many changes in Africa's foreign exchange markets geared largely towards making them more market-driven. Market-driven exchange rates are more volatile and have the potential to increase the risk of international investments (Murinde and Poshakwale, 2004; Pan, Fok and Liu, 2007; Ooi, Wafa, Lajuni, and Ghazali, 2009).[27] Coupled with these reform measures has been the internationalization of capital markets, whose direct implications have been the gradual opening up of capital markets of many countries to foreign investments and the cross-listing of equities.

These reform measures have been implemented concurrently and have bred varied outcomes and consequences for macroeconomic stability. For instance, in many countries where the reform measures have been implemented, an increment in the flow of cross-border investment funds, increased volatility in stock market performance indicators and instability in the foreign exchange rates have been observed (Granger, Huangb and Yang, 2000; Bekaert, Harvey and Lundblad, 2003; Pan, Fok and Liu, 2007; Ooi, Wafa, Lajuni, and Ghazali, 2009; Muller-Platenberg, 2010 and Kodongo & Ojah, 2012). These observations raise some fundamental questions: Is there a linkage between stock market volatility and foreign exchange rate fluctuations? Is it rational to undertake policy reforms touching on stock markets and currency markets concurrently? We address these issues in some of Africa's major capital markets by investigating the causal interactions between stock market prices and foreign exchange rates. Ajayi, Friedman and Mehdian (1998) argue that movements in the equity and currency markets may be related because of some underlying economic variables that systematically affect both markets, leading to convergence of some expectations among market participants. We investigate whether developments in the world stock markets (proxied by the US) represent such underlying variables for Africa's equity and foreign exchange markets.

Intuitively, the volatility of exchange rates has implications for stock market prices. Appreciations in the exchange rate of a country's currency make the country's assets more expensive from foreigners' perspective and therefore adversely affect the competitiveness of its exporting firms; this in turn may cause the country's stock prices to fluctuate downwards. These effects are reversed for importing firms (and country's stock prices). This intuition is premised on the assumption that foreign exchange rate risk is unconditionally priced in the stock markets. However, the empirical evidence on this conjecture remains inconclusive (Carrieri and Majerbi, 2006; Kodongo and Ojah, 2011). The intuition has been shown to hold in some empirical studies. Using monthly stock indexes and exchange rates of six industrial economies, Ma and Kao (1990) find results suggesting that currency appreciation depresses

[27] In related studies, Apergis, Zestos and Shaltayev (2012) have shown that market fundamentals have long-run and short-run relationships with the exchange rate; Ioannidis and Kontonikas ((2008) have shown that monetary policy shifts significantly affect stock returns.

the stock market of an export-dominant economy, while it boosts the stock market for an import-dominant economy.

Being the least explored by both foreign investors and researchers, Africa's capital markets present an interesting platform for studying the nature of the linkages between foreign exchange rates and stock prices. We examine these linkages using monthly foreign exchange rate and stock price data of five major African financial markets: Egypt, Kenya, Mauritius, Morocco, and South Africa, for the period 1997:01 through 2011:05. The countries are all open, in varying degrees, to international trade and investments, and have some of the most viable capital markets in the African continent.[28] These countries share many common features although they also have substantial differences in terms of size of the economy, degree of development, rate of growth and maturity of financial markets.

Like many economies in the world, they all have economic and financial linkages with the US (a conventional proxy for world's capital market)[29] and are therefore affected by developments in the US economy. Indeed, Kodongo and Ojah (2012) have shown that the global financial crisis of 2007/2009, precipitated by the US financial crunch, affected trade and investment flows of these African countries significantly. Further, IMF (2009: pp. 3 - 6) shows that the global financial crisis caused a sharp drop in the stock markets and a drastic depreciation of currencies of many African countries. It attributes these effects to two main channels of transmission, namely: reduced inflows from abroad; and spillovers into the real economy, which translated into tighter credit conditions impacting trade finance adversely. It is therefore useful to understand the exact nature of the linkages between and among exchange rates, equity prices and the world capital market. The existence of these linkages will be of interest to stock market investors as well as policy mandarins. For instance, knowledge of these linkages could inform the formulation of policies to guard against contagion from world capital markets to Africa's foreign exchange and stock markets as well as strengthen the tools used in the fight against financial crises that may result from such contagion.

The rest of this paper is organized as follows. Section 2 reviews selected extant literature on the relationship between the two asset prices. Section 3 develops the methodology and presents the empirical strategy. Section 4 discusses the empirical findings. Section 5 concludes.

2. Related Literature

Theoretical foundations for the relationship between foreign exchange rate fluctuations and stock market price volatility can be traced to classical economics. Models of exchange rate determination based on the "flow-concept" (such as Dornbusch and Fischer, 1980) posit that foreign exchange rate changes affect international competitiveness and trade balance position. These effects are manifested in the country's real output and, by extension, firms' stock prices, through the influence of present and future cash flows. From a microeconomic viewpoint, exchange rate movements affect firms' values directly, if they are involved in

[28] Country choice is also guided by data availability. Consistent monthly data are available only after January 1997.

[29] Examples of studies which have used the US stock market as a proxy for world's capital market include Hatemi-J and Irandoust (2002), Yua and Nieh (2009), Phylaktis and Ravazzolo (2005) and Diamandis and Drakos (2011).

cross-border trade activities, and indirectly, for some firms not involved in external trade but whose competitiveness may be hinged on foreign exchange rate changes. Scholars such as Aggarwal (1981) espouse the view that such effects manifest themselves in the firms' stock and bond prices through their impact on future cash flows. Anticipated changes in asset values influence their risk profiles which, in turn, affect investors' portfolio allocation decisions. From this traditional viewpoint, currency changes are expected to drive stock market prices. The traditional flow model has been criticized on the grounds that it lacks a dynamic perspective and fails to recognize the interrelatedness of the current account, the financial account and international payments (Müller-Plantenberg, 2010).

On the other hand, monetary economists also present arguments that imply that stock price changes affect the behavior of foreign exchange rates movements. Using a model in which the price of stocks substitutes for the real interest rate in the determination of aggregate demand, Gavin (1989) paints a picture in which innovations in stock prices influence the behavior of foreign exchange rates and money demand through its impact on liquidity and wealth. Similarly, "stock-concept" or portfolio balance models of asset equilibrium argue that current account imbalances can affect exchange rates by shifting the residence of wealth between regions with different portfolio preferences. Specifically, portfolio balance models relate excess demand for stocks of external assets to expected yields of those assets and determine current and expected future exchange rates as elements of expected asset yields (Dooley and Isard, 1979). At the micro-level, Granger, Huangb and Yang (2000) describe the working of the portfolio balance model thus: a decrease in stock prices causes a reduction in the wealth of domestic investors, in turn leading to a lower demand for money with ensuing lower interest rates. The lower interest rates encourage capital outflows ceteris paribus, in turn causing currency depreciation. Thus, the portfolio balance approach views foreign exchange rates like the price of any traded commodity determined by the market mechanism: lower asset yields or worsening of a country's investment climate causes capital flight and lead to a decline in the demand for the country's currency.

In addition to these theoretical postulates, several studies have documented the existence of correlation between foreign exchange rate changes and stock price returns both at the macro level (Ajayi and Mougoue, 1996; Hatemi-J and Irandoust, 2002) and at the micro level (Khoo, 1994; Donnelly and Sheehy, 1996). The interaction between innovations in foreign exchange markets and stock market price changes has also attracted many studies. A sample of studies in developed equity markets show mixed findings on the issue. Upon examining data for six major industrialized countries, Ma and Kao (1990) find that a high currency value generates a favorable transaction exposure that creates excess demands for domestic stocks. Bahmani-Oskooee and Sohrabian (1992) find bidirectional causality between stock prices and foreign exchange rates for the US market whereas Ratner (1993) finds no relationship between the underlying long-term stochastic properties of the US stock market prices and foreign exchange rates. Similarly, Nieh and Lee (2001) find no evidence of long-run relationship between stock prices and exchange rates in the G-7 countries. In contrast, Hatemi-J and Irandoust (2002) and Stavárek (2005) find predominantly unidirectional causalities, with the direction running from stock prices to exchange rates, respectively for the Swedish and EU and US markets. However, Morley (2002) finds that the relationship reflects differences in financial system across countries. More recently, Yau and Nieh (2009) use threshold-ECM Granger-causality tests to show that no short-run causal relationship exists between stock prices and exchange rates for Japan and Taiwan. However, they find that in the long run a positive causal relationship exists that runs from either the Japanese or US exchange rate to the stock prices of Taiwan. Using dynamic conditional correlation coefficient analysis, Horng et al. (2010) find results indicating that exchange rate volatility positively affects the Japanese stock market.

Studies that have appeared in the literature from across emerging markets also present inconclusive findings. The early study of Abdalla and Murinde (1997) reports unidirectional causality from exchange rates to stock prices in Korea, Pakistan and India but supports the portfolio balance theory for the Philippines. Murinde and Poshakwale (2004) report conflicting results for the pre-euro and post-euro periods for European emerging financial markets of Hungary, Czech Republic and Poland. Phylaktis and Ravazzolo (2005) find that stock and foreign exchange markets are positively related in the Pacific Basin, and that the US stock market acts as a conduit for these linkages. For the period after the devaluation of the Brazilian currency, Tabak (2006) finds evidence supporting the portfolio balance viewpoint upon using linear Granger causality tests and impulse response functions; however, his nonlinear causality tests yield results supportive of the traditional flow viewpoint. Pan, Fok and Liu (2007) find mixed causality results for different East Asian markets in different periods and conclude that the linkages between the foreign exchange and stock markets vary across economies, depending on exchange rate regimes, the trade size, the degree of capital control, and the size of equity market.

Recent studies in the emerging markets continue to present varied findings. Aydemir and Demirhan (2009) find evidence of bidirectional causal relationship between exchange rate and all stock market indexes of Turkey. Ooi, Wafa, Lajuni, and Ghazali (2009) document results supportive of the portfolio balance viewpoint in both pre- and post-Asian currency crisis periods of 1997 for Thailand, but only in the post-crisis period for Malaysia. For China, Zhao (2010) finds neither stable long-term equilibrium relationship nor mean spillovers between the real effective exchange rate and stock price; however, there is bidirectional cross-volatility spillover effects between the two markets, indicating that past innovations in the stock market have effect on future volatility in the foreign exchange market, and vice versa. Tian and Ma (2010) report evidence of cointegration between the foreign exchange and stock markets in China. Diamandis and Drakos (2011) document findings suggesting that stock and foreign exchange markets in Argentina, Brazil, Chile and Mexico are positively related and that the U.S. stock market acts as a channel for these links.

In Africa's markets, two studies stand out. Using the exponential-GARCH model with Ghanaian data for the period 1995:1 through 2005:6, Adjasi, Harvey and Agyapong (2008) find a negative relationship between foreign exchange rate volatility and stock market returns in the long run and a positive relationship in the short run.

Their study defines exchange rates as the British pound (foreign currency) price of the Ghanaian cedi (domestic currency) so that depreciations in the local currency cause by a downward sloping exchange rate curve. Dube (2008) investigates the empirical validity of the monetary model of the South African rand-US dollar exchange rate using the ARDL Bounds test. In the model, tested with data for the period 1995:1 through 2006:12, money supply, income and interest rate are augmented by stock market prices. Among other findings, their results support the existence of a long-run relationship between exchange rates and stock prices, suggesting that models of exchange rate determination should be expanded to include stock market prices in addition to the usual bond prices.

An important observation about the two investigations in Africa is that they both cover one country's financial markets. To this extent, they are narrow in scope and might fail the external validity test. Our study attempts to achieve generalization by covering five of the major financial markets cutting across Africa's sub-Saharan and Northern regions. We use the cointegration analysis and multivariate VEC-Granger causality tests to examine these relationships. Parameter constancy is examined using the Hansen and Johansen (1999) recursive estimation method.

3. EMPIRICAL PROCEDURES

3.1. The Basic Model

Assuming a world of two countries, we model the relationship between domestic (African country) and foreign (world) stock prices and the exchange rate thus:

$$I_t^{AC} = \beta_0 + \beta_1 S_t^{AC} + \beta_2 I_t^{US} + \varepsilon_t \quad (1)$$

where I_t^{AC} and I_t^{US} are, respectively, the natural logarithms of the African country and USA (world representative) stock market indexes at time *t*, both expressed in real terms; S_t^{AC} is the natural logarithm of the dollar real exchange rate of the African country's currency at time *t*; and ε_t is the disturbance term. The real exchange rate is defined as the nominal exchange rate adjusted by the CPI of the USA relative to the CPI of the African country. The real exchange rate is suitable for our analysis because it is a better measure of a country's competitive position than the nominal exchange rate (Chow, Lee and Solt, 1997), especially in the context of African countries where purchasing power changes can be high and volatile.

The sensitivity term (β_1) measures the linkage between real exchange rates and domestic stock prices taking into consideration the influence of foreign stock price changes. Consider the portfolio balance approach where stock prices are expected to lead exchange rates: an increment in US stock prices may cause the expected yields on US stocks to decline relative to those in an African country. All else constant, this causes an increment in the demand for the stocks of the African country and portfolio capital flows from the US into the African country; this results in increased demand for the African country's currency causing its value to appreciate relative to the US dollar ($\beta_1 > 0$).

3.2. Cointegration Test

We test for cointegration using the maximum likelihood procedure of Johansen (1995). The approach is based on estimating the pth order Vector Autoregressive (VAR) model in *n* variables:

$$Y_t = \mu + \sum_{i=1}^{p} \pi_i Y_{t-i} + \varepsilon_t \tag{2}$$

where Y_t is the *n*-vector of variables; μ is the *n*-vector of drift terms; π_i is an $n \times n$ matrix of parameters to be estimated; $t = 1, 2, \dots, T$. Since levels of time series Y_t might be non-stationary, equation (2) is usually transformed into a dynamic vector error correction model (VECM) of the form:

$$\Delta Y_t = \mu + \pi Y_{t-1} + \sum_{i=1}^{p-1} \Gamma_i \Delta Y_{t-i} + \varepsilon_t \tag{3}$$

where $\pi = -\left(I - \sum_{i=1}^{p} \pi_i\right)$ and $\Gamma_i = -\sum_{i=1}^{p-1} \pi_i$. Now suppose that Y_t contains some non-stationary *I*(1) time series components; in order to get the stationary error term ε_t, the term πY_{t-1} must be stationary. This requires that πY_{t-1} must contain $r < n$ cointegrating relationships. Now, if the VAR(*p*) process in equation (3) has unit roots, then the matrix π has reduced rank given by $\text{rank}(\pi) = r < k$. Thus, there exists $(n \times r)$ matrices α and β each with rank *r*, such that $\pi = \alpha\beta'$. Johansen (1995) argues that testing for cointegration of system (3) is equivalent to checking out the rank of the matrix π. In practice, one estimates π and its eigenvalues and then determines the number of distinct cointegrating vectors by checking the significance of the resulting eigenvalues. We perform the significance test using Johansen's *trace* statistic:

$$\lambda_{trace}(r_0) = -T \sum_{i=r+1}^{n} \ln\left(1 - \hat{\lambda}_i\right) \tag{4}$$

where T is number of observations; r_0 is the anticipated number of cointegrating vectors and $\hat{\lambda}_i$ are the estimated eigenvalues. This statistic tests the null hypothesis, $H_0: r \le r_0$ against the alternative, $H_1: r > r_0$, such that *r* is the number of distinct cointegrating vectors.

3.3. Causality Test

We use the multivariate Granger causality tests to understand the nature of the relationships between the exchange rate and stock market prices. A simple multivariate Granger causality methodology for exploring the dynamics of cointegrating systems has been proposed in the literature (Toda and Yamamoto, 1995; Dolado and Lütkepohl, 1996). The methodology, designed to avoid biases occasioned by preliminary tests for unit roots and cointegration, allows one to test linear or nonlinear restrictions on the coefficients by estimating a vector autoregression in levels (LVAR) and applying the Wald criterion, paying little attention to the integration and cointegration properties of the time series data (Toda and Yamamoto, 1995). The Wald test has standard asymptotic χ^2 distribution under general conditions.

Suppose the true (or some information criterion estimated) lag order is known to be $p\ (\geq 1)$. This procedure involves fitting an LVAR of the order $(p+1)$, then performing the test for causality using a standard Wald test on the least squares estimators of the first *p* VAR coefficient matrix: the $(p+1)$th coefficients are redundant and are not expected to be statistically different from zero.[30] Including redundant information in the system may cause inefficiency and power loss in the tests. However, evidence from Monte Carlo tests shows that power losses for the Wald causality test are relatively minor in trivariate or higher-order systems, for moderate to large sample sizes, and for systems with large true lag orders (Giles and Williams, 1999).

Following Phylaktis and Ravazzolo (2005), we implement this method by fitting a trivariate LVAR system. We begin by re-writing the VECM in equation (3) as an LVAR:

$$Y_{it} = \Phi_{i0} + \Phi_{i1} Y_{i,t-1} + \dots + \Phi_{ip} Y_{i,t-p} + \varepsilon_{it} \tag{5}$$

where, for each country k $(k = 1, \dots, n)$, Φ_{ij} $[j = 1, \dots, (p-1)]$ are $(m \times m)$ matrices of coefficients; Φ_{i0} is an m-vector of constants; m is the number of variables in the system (three in our case). Thus, for each of the African countries under investigation in this study, the VAR takes the following form:

$$\begin{bmatrix} I_{AC,t} \\ S_{AC,t} \\ I_{US,t} \end{bmatrix} = \begin{bmatrix} \Phi_{10} \\ \Phi_{20} \\ \Phi_{30} \end{bmatrix} + \begin{bmatrix} \Phi_{11}(L) & \Phi_{12}(L) & \Phi_{13}(L) \\ \Phi_{21}(L) & \Phi_{22}(L) & \Phi_{23}(L) \\ \Phi_{31}(L) & \Phi_{32}(L) & \Phi_{33}(L) \end{bmatrix} \cdot \begin{bmatrix} I_{AC,t-1} \\ S_{AC,t-1} \\ I_{US,t-1} \end{bmatrix} + \begin{bmatrix} \varepsilon_{AC,t} \\ \varepsilon_{S,t} \\ \varepsilon_{US,t} \end{bmatrix} \tag{6}$$

where Φ_{i0} are intercept terms for each equation *i*; and Φ_{ij} are coefficient parameters to be estimated; *L* is the lag operator; and ε_{it} are the normally distributed disturbance terms.

Consistent with the proposal of Dolado and Lütkepohl (1996), we choose the lag structure (p) through the Wald test and fit the model with one extra lag, $p+1$. Coefficient estimates are obtained using the ordinary least squares estimation. Enders (1995) explains that such estimators are consistent, and asymptotically efficient. To formally test our causality hypotheses, we use the Wald test on the first p VAR coefficients. Thus, to check whether the "stock" channel holds for a particular country, we test the restrictions: $\Phi_{13}(L) = 0$, $\Phi_{21}(L) = 0$ and $\Phi_{23}(L) = 0$. The "flow" channel is tested through the restrictions:

[30] Dolado and Lütkepohl (1996) argue that the non-standard asymptotic properties of the Wald test on the coefficients of cointegrated VAR systems are due to singularity of the asymptotic distribution of the least squares estimators. They explain that their methodology gets rid of the singularity by fitting a VAR whose order exceeds the true order and proceed to show that the procedure leads to a nonsingular asymptotic distribution of the relevant coefficients, overcoming problems associated with standard tests and their complicated non-standard limiting properties.

$\Phi_{12}(L) = 0$, $\Phi_{13}(L) = 0$ and $\Phi_{23}(L) = 0$. The restrictions $\Phi_{12}(L) = 0$, $\Phi_{13}(L) = 0$ and $\Phi_{21}(L) = 0$, $\Phi_{23}(L) = 0$ are used to test for the combined transmission mechanism of "flow" and "stock" channels (see also, Phylaktis and Ravazzolo, 1995; and Diamandis and Drakos, 2011).

3.4. The Data

In this paper, we investigate the relationship between real exchange rates and stock market prices for the African region, represented by Egypt and Morocco (North Africa) and Kenya, Mauritius and South Africa (sub-Saharan Africa). Observations are sampled at monthly intervals and cover the period 1997:01 through 2011:05. National stock market indexes for Kenya and Mauritius are obtained from the International Financial Statistics database (IFS) of the International Monetary Fund; they are denominated in local currency. Market indexes for Egypt, Morocco, South Africa and the USA are obtained from *MSCI Barra*, in local currency units. Both *MSCI Barra* and IFS indexes are value-weighted and are calculated with dividends reinvested; they are largely consistent with each other.[31]

The end-of-month nominal rates of exchange between the US dollar and the selected African currencies are obtained from the IFS. The nominal exchange rate is defined as the domestic (African country) currency price of the US dollar. We convert nominal exchange rates into real exchange rates using consumer price indices (CPI) obtained from IFS. In our analysis, we use the logarithms of the real exchange rate, defined as $ln\left(RER_{\frac{AC}{\$}}\right) = ln(CPI_{AC}) - ln\left(NER_{\frac{AC}{\$}}\right) - ln(CPI_{USA})$, where *NER* is the nominal exchange rate. This transformation takes us away from the definition used earlier for the nominal exchange rate. In the relationship that results here, appreciations in the real value of the local currency are represented by an upward sloping real exchange rate curve.

We begin the analysis by highlighting the key characteristics, including the official liberalization dates of the various stock markets investigated. Similarly, we highlight the exchange rate systems in place in the foreign exchange markets of the sampled countries. Table 1 reports these facts. It is clear from the table that all the markets are considered liberalized during the period of investigation. Although it would be interesting to compare pre- and post-liberalization periods, data paucity would not permit this endeavor. The exchange rate systems for the majority of the countries are flexible enough to allow us to explore the nexus between changes in exchange rates and stock price movements. However, for countries operating non-floating foreign exchange regimes, our tests examine the effects of foreign exchange restrictions on the links between foreign exchange and stock markets.

Trend analysis of the data shows a general positive relationship between stock market prices and real exchange rates in all the countries, suggesting that real exchange rate appreciations are associated with stock price increments in these markets. For South Africa, it is important to point out the existence of a marked negative relationship between the two prices between 1997 and mid-2002. Appreciations in the domestic currency also tend to be associated with stock price declines in Kenya during the period between 2005 and 2011. We

[31] Our correlation analysis yields a coefficient of 98.7% between *MSCI Barra* Mauritius indices and the *IFS* indices for 2002:5-2011:05. For Kenya, the correlation coefficient is 95.7% over the same period.

also observe that a positive relationship generally exists between domestic stock market prices and stock prices of the US. This is particularly clear for Kenya, Morocco and South Africa for the entire study period and for all the countries around 2002/3 and 2008/9 periods, when the stock market declines in the US coincide with bear markets in the five African countries.

Table 1. Key information on Africa's stock and foreign exchange markets

	Market liberalization year‡	Foreign ownership limit	Dividend and capital repatriation	Equity market capitalization§ (billions of US $)	Country competitiveness†		Exchange rate system#
					Index	Rank	
Egypt	1992	100%	free	84.27	4.0	81	Managed float since Jan 1993
Kenya	1995	75%	free	13.37	3.6	106	Managed float since Oct 1993
Mauritius	1994	100%*	free	5.68	4.3	55	Managed float since July 1994
Morocco	1988	100%	free	69.29	4.1	75	Crawling peg since Jan 1991ǂ
South Africa	1996	100%	free	1,010.06	4.3	54	Managed float since Jan 1995

‡ Dates are those reported in Bekaert, Harvey and Lumsdaine (2002) except for Mauritius whose liberalization date is obtained from the African Development Bank website: http://www.afdb.org/fileadmin/uploads/afdb/Documents/Publications/24108404-EN-MAURITIUS.PDF

§ Market capitalization, as of end of 2010, is obtained from the websites of the respective stock exchanges.

† World Economic Forum (2011). Country competitiveness is measured through a combination of performance on a variety of pillars, including financial markets development, market size, innovation, infrastructural development, goods and labor markets efficiency, among others. Countries are rated on an index ranging from 1 (lowest) to 7 (highest). Country competitiveness may play a role in attracting foreign capital.

The information on exchange rate systems is sourced from Kamar and Bakardzhieva (2005) for Egypt; Ndung'u (1999) for Kenya; Commission of the European Communities (2004) for Morocco; www.emerging-markets-online.com for Mauritius; Dube (2009) for South Africa.

* No one foreign investor may hold a controlling stake in any Mauritius firm or more than 15% of the total ownership interest of a Mauritius sugar firm.

ǂ The basket of currencies was undisclosed until April 2001, when it was formally announced that the basket would henceforth be composed of the euro (80%) and the US dollar (20%).

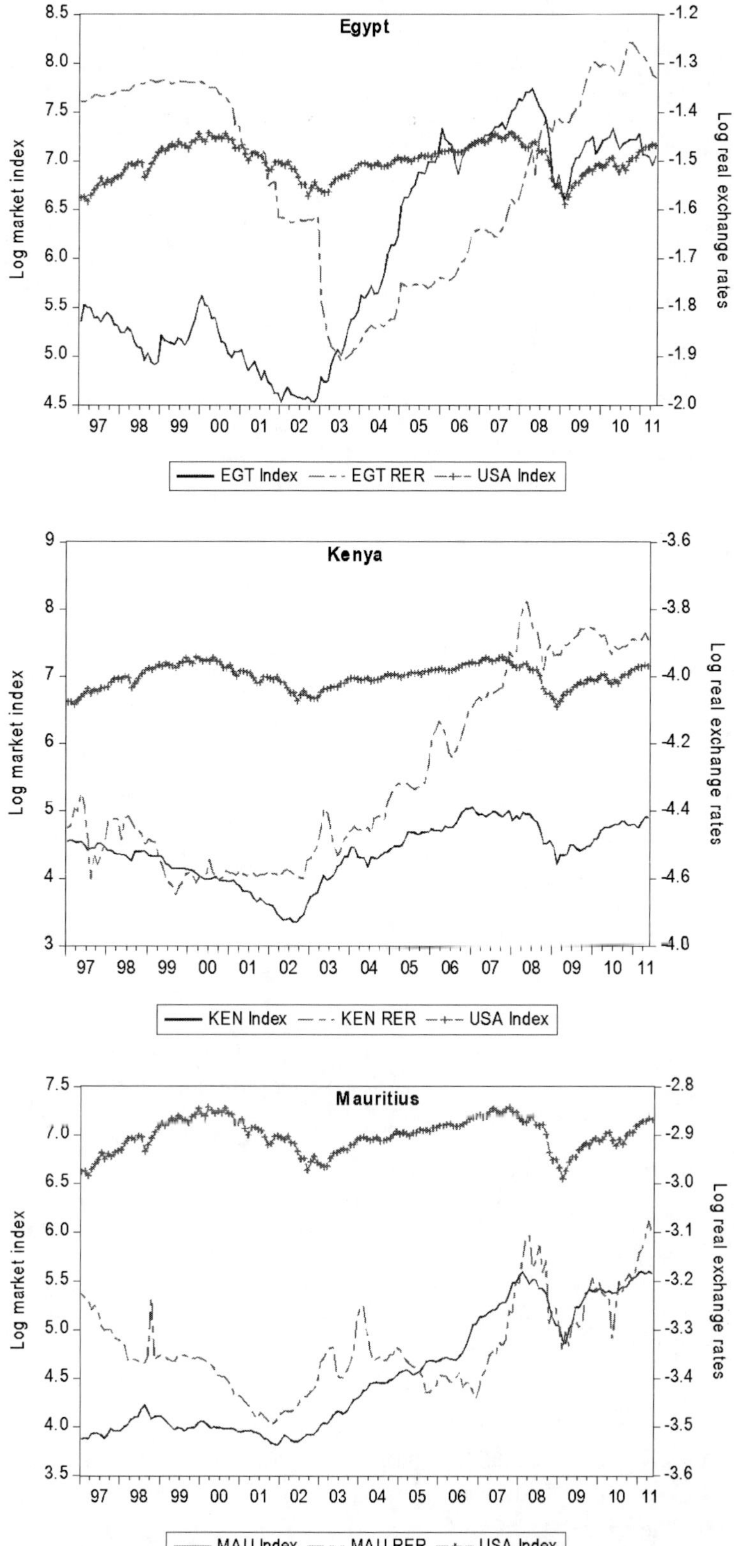

Figure 1. (Continued).

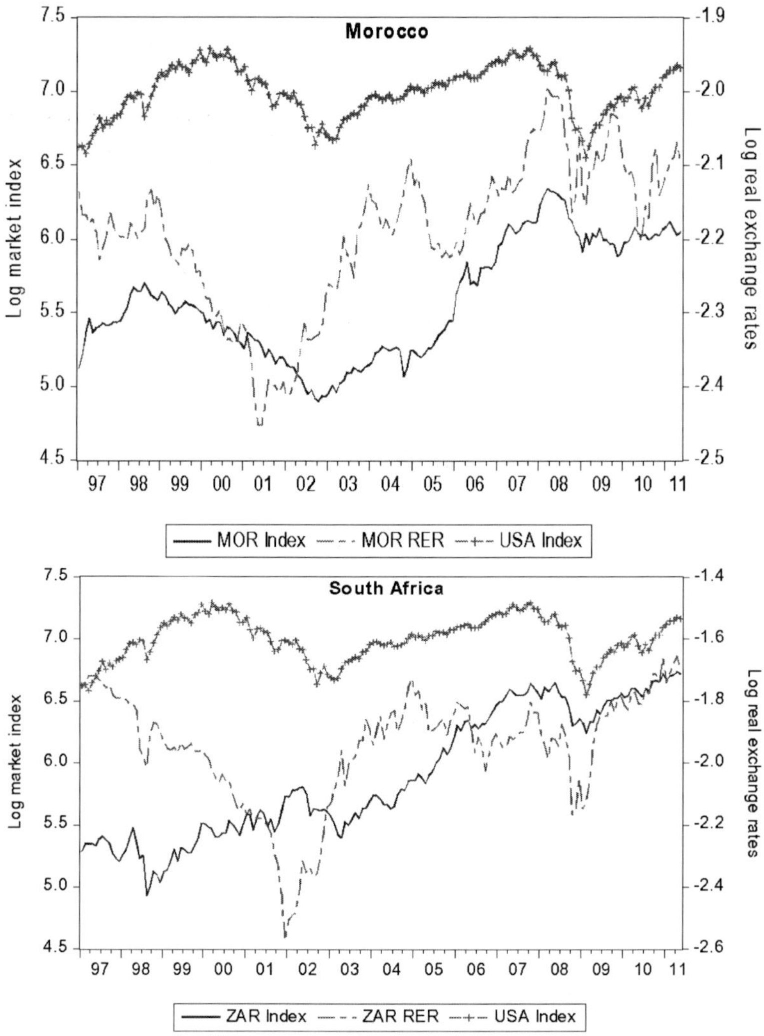

Prefixes EGT, KEN, MAU, MOR and ZAR represent Egypt, Kenya, Mauritius, Morocco and South Africa, in that order. RER is real exchange rate. Thus, EGT RER, for instance means the real exchange rate of Egypt.

Figure 1. Trends in stock market indexes and real exchange rates.

4. EMPIRICAL RESULTS

4.1. Results of Cointegration Tests

Before performing tests of cointegration, we investigate the time series properties of the data by conducting unit root tests. Table 2 contains results of these tests. Both Phillips-Perron and augmented Dickey-Fuller tests show that all the variables are stationary only after being differenced once. Therefore, to avoid spurious cointegration outcomes, we conduct our cointegration tests in first differences.

Table 2. Unit root tests results

	Variable	Augmented Dickey-Fuller		Phillips-Perron	
		Level	1st difference	Level	1st difference
Country					
Egypt	Market index	-1.97	-5.66***	-1.67	-10.90***
	Real exchange rate	-0.88	-5.63***	-0.66	-11.53***
Kenya	Market index	-1.98	-5.69***	-1.86	-11.65***
	Real exchange rate	-2.36	-4.77***	-2.20	-10.34***
Mauritius	Market index	-2.39	-5.13***	-1.91	-8.92***
	Real exchange rate	-2.15	-15.07***	-2.40	-15.01***
Morocco	Market index	-1.14	-8.60***	-1.29	-12.72***
	Real exchange rate	-2.17	-7.31***	-2.46	-12.00***
South Africa	Market index	-2.72	-13.44***	-2.72	-13.45***
	Real exchange rate	-1.92	-12.41***	-2.00	-12.41***
USA	Market index	-2.72	-6.43***	-2.56	-11.59***

All variables are in logs. Stationarity tests are conducted with a deterministic trend. Critical values (based on MacKinnon, 1996) are: 1%, -4.01; 5%, -3.44; and 10%, -3.14.

The cointegration tests use Johansen's *trace* statistic with the number of observations, T, adjusted as in Reimers (1992), to correct for small sample bias. We conduct the tests separately for each of the five African countries using a system of the three variables: the domestic stock market index, the real exchange rate, and the USA stock market index (the proxy for the rest of the world). Results, presented in Table 3, show that the null hypothesis of no cointegration among the three variables is rejected, at the 5% significance level, for Egypt, Mauritius and South Africa. Further, there are three cointegrating relationships for Egypt and one cointegrating relationship for Mauritius and South Africa. However, at the 1% level, the three variables also have one cointegrating vector for Egypt. We fail to reject the hypothesis of no cointegration among the three variables for Kenya and Morocco.

Next, we estimate the long-run cointegrating vectors for the system of three variables. Results are reported in Table 4. In all the cases, the results show a positive relationship between the stock markets and the real exchange rate. The long-run relationship between African stock markets and the USA stock market are positive for Kenya, Mauritius and Morocco but negative for Egypt and South Africa. Negative coefficients may be interpreted to mean the absence of integration between two markets.

Further, we conduct a test for the exclusion of each of the variables from the cointegrating vector. Results are reported in Table 5. The table shows that for all countries but Kenya, we fail to reject the hypothesis that the USA stock market can be excluded from the cointegrating vector. Thus, it is apparent that the USA stock market is not participating in the cointegrating relationship for most of the countries. Conversely, the restriction that the real exchange rate has a coefficient of zero in the cointegrating vector is rejected for all the countries.[32] Thus, for the three countries (Egypt, Mauritius and South Africa) that exhibit a cointegrating relationship among the three variables, it is apparent that the observed relationship exists largely between real exchange rates and domestic stock prices.

[32] As a further robustness check, we run cointegration tests with the Euro area stock market as the world proxy, for the period January 1999 to May 2011. For all countries, our tests fail to reject the hypothesis of no cointegration. Results of these tests are presented in Table 8.

Table 3. Trace statistics for Johansen's cointegration tests

	H_0: r = 0	H_0: r ≤ 1	H_0: r ≤ 2
Country			
Egypt	37.14**	18.65**	6.56**
Kenya	24.26	6.23	0.01
Mauritius	30.36**	11.34	0.53
Morocco	20.92	8.87	0.26
South Africa	47.00**	14.10	0.02
Critical values (5%)	29.68	15.41	3.76
(1%)	35.65	20.04	6.65

The table reports Johansen's likelihood ratio (trace) statistics for the number of cointegrating vectors, *r*, shown. For each country, the statistic tests the null hypothesis that there are at most zero, one and two cointegrating vectors, respectively. ** denotes the rejection of the null at the 1% significance level. Critical values generated by Osterwald-Lenum (1992) have been used. A two-lag structure, chosen through Wald tests, has been employed for all countries but Mauritius, which has three lags.

Table 4. Long-run cointegrating vector for: $I_t^{AC} = \beta_0 + \beta_1 S_t^{AC} + \beta_2 I_t^{US} + \varepsilon_t$

	β_0	β_1	β_2
Country			
Egypt	92.77	27.00	-6.49
		(4.13)	(-0.93)
Kenya	-2.71	1.18	1.74
		(4.21)	(4.21)
Mauritius	20.81	7.89	1.44
		(6.45)	(2.26)
Morocco	13.06	4.55	0.36
		(5.28)	(0.72)
South Africa	28.96	4.86	-1.94
		(5.54)	(-2.15)

The table presents coefficients of the error correction term with *t*-statistics in parentheses. Johansen's normalization is done with respect to the domestic stock price index. The constant term in the cointegrating equation is not directly estimated in the trend specification but is rather extracted from other estimates; thus, the *t*-statistic for the parameter is not calculated.

Table 5. Exclusion tests for I_{AC}, S_{AC} and I_{US}

	I_{AC}	S_{AC}	I_{US}
Country			
Egypt	0.26	5.88**	0.47
Kenya	8.44***	6.49**	9.04***
Mauritius	7.35**	8.06***	2.11
Morocco	3.26*	3.40*	0.13
South Africa	8.38***	16.52***	2.52

The table reports chi-square values (one degree of freedom) of Likelihood Ratio tests for the restriction that the variable specified has a coefficient of zero in the cointegrating vector. *, ** and ***, respectively, denote rejection of the null at the 10%, 5% and 1% significance levels.

The veracity of this inference, is assessed by examining the cointegration between the domestic stock prices and the real exchange rate in a bivariate VAR setup. Results, reported in Table 7, show the absence of cointegration between the two variables for all countries but Egypt. Thus, it appears that the existence of cointegration between stock market prices and the foreign exchange rates of these countries is driven by information from the US stock market. This lends credence to the inference that the five African equity markets studied here are, at least, partially integrated with the US stock markets. The conjecture of partial integration may be justified by information flow. All the five markets are tracked by the International Finance Corporation, MSCI Barra as well as other major international stock markets analysts. Similarly, the stock markets of these countries also have websites where trading information, such as changes in market capitalization, yields and prices are regularly updated. Thus, foreign portfolio managers with an interest in these markets can easily obtain the desired information from any of these sources. Further, due to its relatively higher information efficiency and dominance, US stock market developments spread quickly and inform trading, around the world, both of stocks and other assets such as foreign currency. For instance, declines in US stock prices may reduce Diaspora remittances to Africa, eliciting depreciations of African currencies and reduced foreign investment flows into Africa's bourses. These patterns may recur over time, causing a long-run positive relationship between the two domestic markets driven by US market developments.

Last, we examine the stability, over time, of parameters obtained in the trivariate cointegration tests. That is, we check whether temporal developments in the financial markets may have had a significant influence on the behavior of estimated parameters over the study period. In this regard, we use tests proposed by Hansen and Johansen (1999). We concentrate the short-run parameters out of the analysis (i.e., eliminate them by setting them equal to their full sample values) and focus only on the recursive estimates of the long-run parameters.[33] Standard errors (at the 95% confidence level) of the recursive estimates are obtained on the basis of the full sample. We run the tests using the eigenvalues obtained from the Johansen's (1995) Fixed Information Maximum Likelihood (FIML) cointegration.[34] We run the tests in two levels. First, we evaluate the time path of λ_1, the largest positive eigenvalue in the FIML cointegration. An evaluation of the time path of the eigenvalue λ_i can be seen as an evaluation of the *i*th column of the estimated adjustment coefficients and the *i*th column of the estimated cointegrating vectors (Hansen and Johansen, 1999); therefore, changes in the estimated adjustment coefficients and cointegrating vectors will be reflected in changes in the estimated eigenvalues. Second, a formal test of the constancy of both the estimated adjustment coefficients and the estimated cointegrating vectors over time is performed as a test of constancy of λ_1 using the statistic:

$$\mathcal{T}(\xi_1^{(\tau)}) = \frac{\tau}{T}\left|\frac{\xi_1^{(\tau)} - \xi_1^{(T)}}{\hat{\sigma}_{11}}\right| \qquad (7)$$

[33] Another way of performing these tests is to re-estimate both the long-run and the short-run parameters recursively. Because the two tests give us results that are qualitatively similar, we present only results for tests with short-run parameters concentrated out.

[34] Hansen and Johansen (1999) explain that a unique relationship exists between the eigenvectors, the adjustment coefficients (α) and the cointegrating vectors (β) that can be exploited to allow the use of eigenvectors to test the stability of estimated parameters.

where $\xi_1^{(\tau)} = \ln\left(\frac{\lambda_1^{(\tau)}}{1-\lambda_1^{(\tau)}}\right)$, τ is the size of the sample used in the recursive estimation, T is the full sample size and $\hat{\sigma}$ represents the standard error of estimate. The null hypothesis of stability is rejected if $\mathcal{T}(\xi_1^{(\tau)})$ exceeds the 5% critical value. The statistic has a standard asymptotic chi-square distribution. We use the critical values in Ploberger et al. (1989).

Time paths of the eigenvalues with the 95% bands are displayed in Figure 2. The figure shows that in all the five cases, bigger point estimates are obtained in the early parts of the sample period compared with the rest of the period. Further, the period around 2001-2003 had a bigger impact on parameter estimates for Egypt, Kenya and South Africa. This coincides with the period of world recession (see for example United Nations, 2002) and, for Kenya, it also coincides with the economic turbulence caused by political uncertainty arising from the first multi-party elections of 2002. We also observe, in the case of Egypt, that the period around 2006/2008 had a substantial impact on the parameter estimates. This period roughly corresponds with the boom in the country's stock markets and currency appreciation, ascribed to huge inflows of foreign direct investments and the resulting large foreign currency reserves.[35]

Figure 3 shows the time paths of the test statistics in equation (7). We observe that the hypothesis of parameter constancy is rejected for Morocco, but not rejected for all the other countries. The time paths of the test statistics for Mauritius and Morocco show substantial instability throughout the study period. Further, parameters for Egypt, Kenya and Morocco show remarkable instability during 2008/10 period, an observation that may be explained by the global financial crunch. From these stability tests results, Kenya, with its estimated parameters showing volatility around two major periods of turbulence in the world markets, appear to exhibit higher sensitivity to developments in the world financial markets than the other countries. This inference seems consistent with results for the parameter exclusion tests (Table 5), which show that Kenya is the only country whose data rejects the hypothesis that the US stock market can be excluded from the cointegration relationship. Overall, however, our results show that the model captures very well major economic events in, and effects of changes in the world markets in the economies of, these countries during the study period.

4.3. Results of Multivariate Granger Causality Tests

We now provide results of the multivariate Granger causality tests. First, we provide evidence of bivariate causality from the US stock markets to stock markets of African countries (test of the restriction $\Phi_{13}(L) = 0$); from real exchange rates to the domestic stock markets (test of the restriction $\Phi_{12}(L) = 0$); from domestic stock markets to real exchange rates (test of the restriction $\Phi_{21}(L) = 0$) and from Africa's stock markets to US stock markets

[35] According to AfDB/OECD (2008), Egypt's foreign direct investment (FDI) rose to unprecedented levels in 2006/07, making it the top FDI recipient in Africa. FDI inflows reachedUSD11 billion, contributing to a 63 per cent improvement in the overall balance of payments in 2006/07.This resulted in international reserves exceeding USD 30 billion, which represented more than ten months of import cover. The share prices of major Egyptian firms recorded unprecedented increases during 2007, and the Cairo and Alexandria Stock Exchange index of 30 leading shares (CASE 30) stood at 8 688, up 30 per cent from its level at end-of-2006.

(test of the restriction $\Phi_{31}(L) = 0$). These relationships are examined using the methodology proposed by Dolado and Lütkepohl (1996). Results are provided in Table 6.

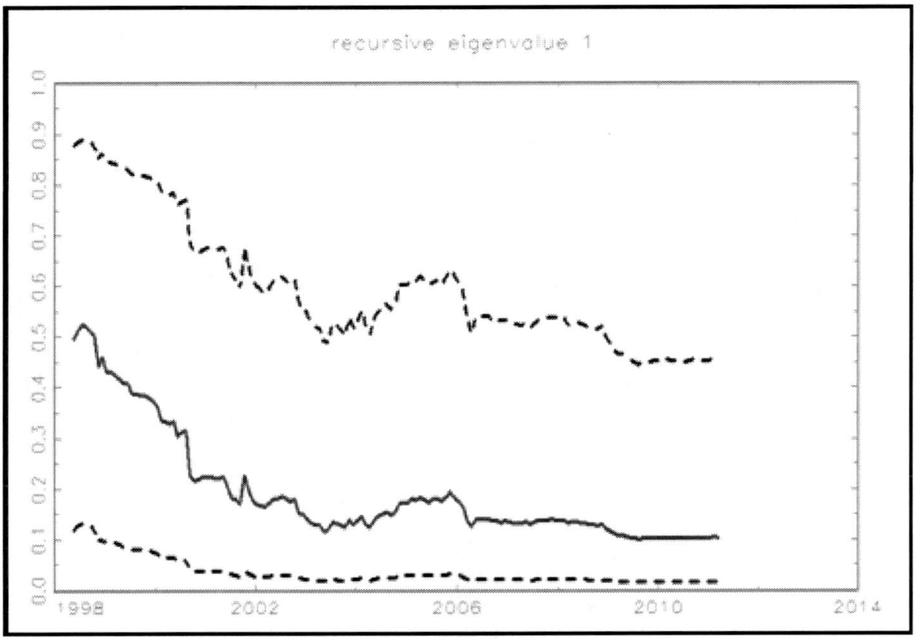

(a) Egypt

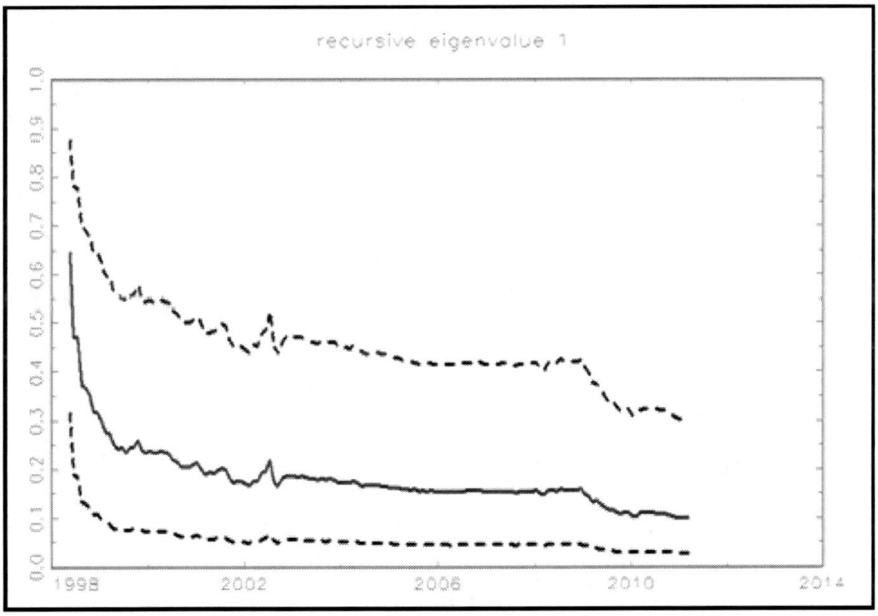

(b) Kenya

Figure 2. (Continued).

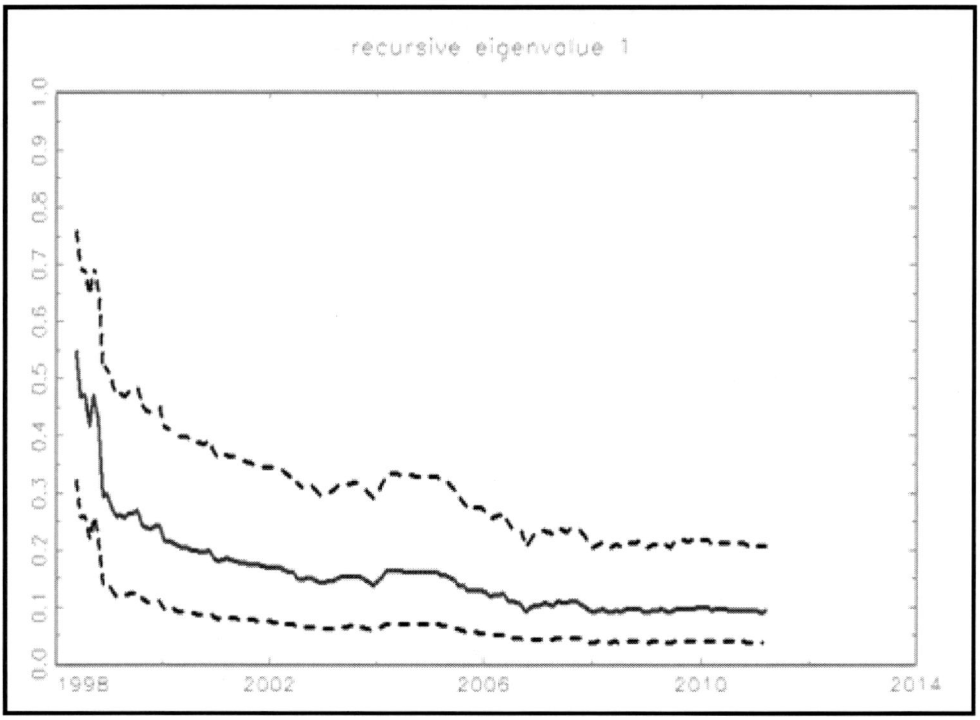

(c) Mauritius

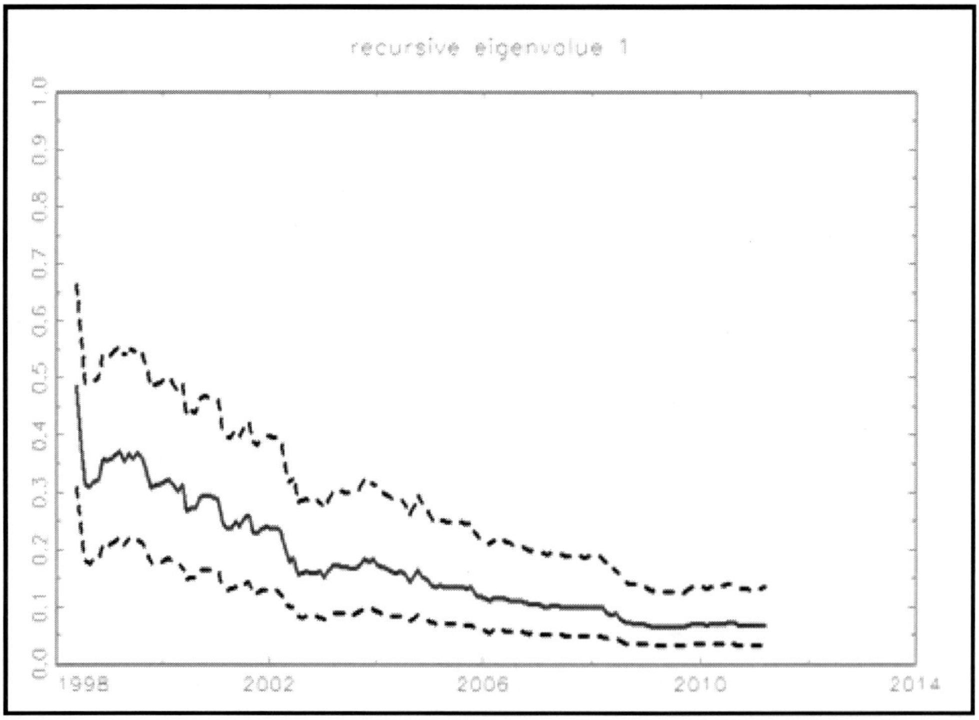

(d) Morocco

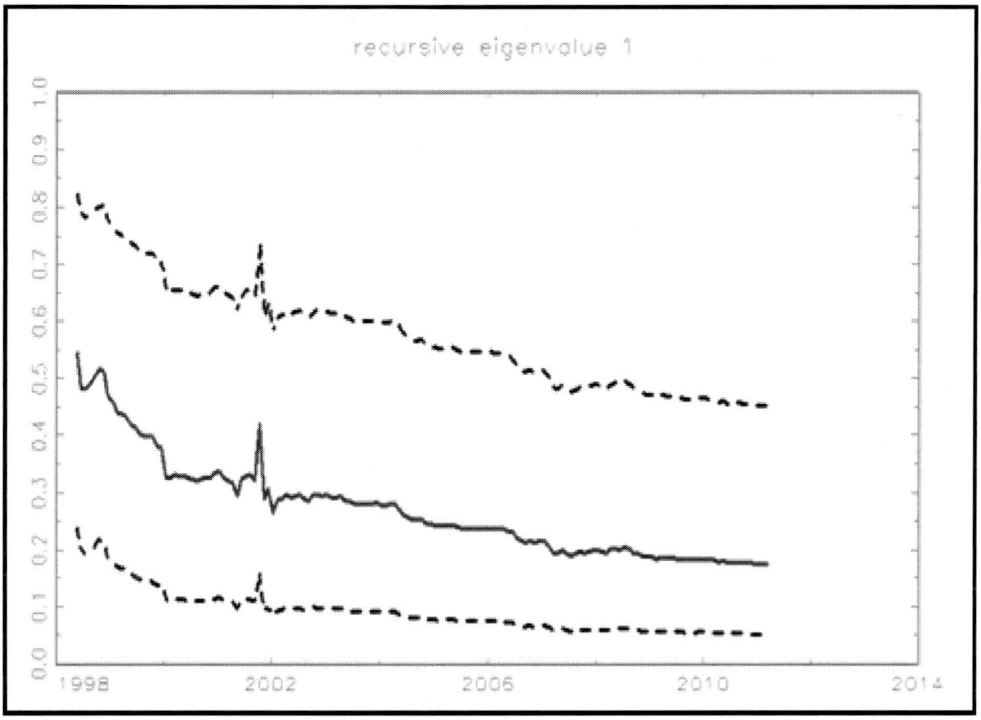

(e) South Africa

The solid line is the time path for the eigenvalue. The dashed lines are the 95% confidence bands.

Figure 2. Time path for eigenvalues.

Table 6. Results of multivariate Granger causality tests

		$\Phi_{12}(L) = 0$	$\Phi_{13}(L) = 0$	$\Phi_{21}(L) = 0$	$\Phi_{23}(L) = 0$	$\Phi_{31}(L) = 0$
Country						
Egypt	$\chi^2(2)$ p-value	5.834* (0.05)	1.768 (0.41)	0.906 (0.64)	0.858 (0.65)	3.078 (0.21)
Kenya	$\chi^2(2)$ p-value	3.065 (0.22)	0.024 (0.99)	6.160* (0.05)	2.535 (0.28)	12.691*** (0.00)
Mauritius	$\chi^2(3)$ p-value	5.877 (0.12)	22.33*** (0.00)	10.651** (0.01)	5.238 (0.11)	5.673 (0.13)
Morocco	$\chi^2(2)$ p-value	0.230 (0.89)	3.207 (0.20)	2.278 (0.32)	2.488 (0.29)	4.872* (0.09)
South Africa	$\chi^2(2)$ p-value	0.961 (0.62)	4.862* (0.09)	0.365 (0.83)	0.395 (0.82)	5.762* (0.06)

Explanation of the restrictions is provided in equation 6. The number of degrees of freedom for the chi-square distribution is the number of lags used in the VAR. ***, ** and *, respectively, denote rejection of the null hypothesis at 1%, 5% and 10% significance levels.

Table 6 shows that the restriction $\Phi_{13}(L) = 0$ is rejected only for Mauritius and South Africa, two of the countries for which cointegration among the three variables was found. Therefore, changes in equity prices in the US stock market seem to have a direct significant influence on the prices of stocks traded in the stock markets of these two countries. It is also evident that real exchange rates drive stock price movements (the restriction $\Phi_{12}(L) = 0$ is rejected) only in Egypt while domestic stock prices drive real exchange rates (the restriction $\Phi_{21}(L) = 0$ is rejected) only in Kenya and Mauritius. Surprisingly, tests results show that in three of the five countries, we reject the hypothesis that causality does not move from African stock markets to US stock markets (i.e., we reject the restriction $\Phi_{31}(L) = 0$). We believe that this surprise finding may be explained by expectations. Financial markets developments in the US typically lead to or coincide with financial markets developments in other regions. Therefore, an anticipated decline in the US stock markets may cause investors to believe that stock markets in Africa will decline following the US decline. Because of the perception of relatively higher liquidity and country risks in Africa, international investors are likely to liquidate their long positions in Africa's stocks ahead of similar action in respect of their long positions in US stocks. The expectations-stimulated closing off of long positions will pile a downward pressure on Africa's stock markets before they cause US stock markets to decline. Similarly, because relatively high risk investment destinations such as African countries yield better equity returns, anticipated growth in the US stock market may trigger a rush to buy into such markets well ahead of the boom that would sure follow the US stock market upturn.

Table 7. Bivariate cointegration between real exchange markets and stock markets in Africa

Panel A: Long-run cointegrating vector for: $I_t^{AC} = \beta_0 + \beta_1 S_t^{AC} + \varepsilon_t$		
	β_0	β_1
Country		
Egypt	23.30	11.28 (3.10)
Kenya	10.17	1.35 (2.46)
Mauritius	30.56	7.73 (4.27)
Morocco	16.38	4.93 (4.61)
South Africa	15.19	4.75 (2.26)
Panel B: Trace statistics for Johansen's cointegration tests		
	H_0: r = 0	H_0: r ≤ 1
Country		
Egypt	23.00**	11.29**
Kenya	3.82	0.01
Mauritius	11.36	1.40
Morocco	10.49	0.49
South Africa	5.42	0.03
Critical values (1%)	20.04	6.65

t-values in parentheses. ** denotes rejection of the null at 1%.

(a) Egypt

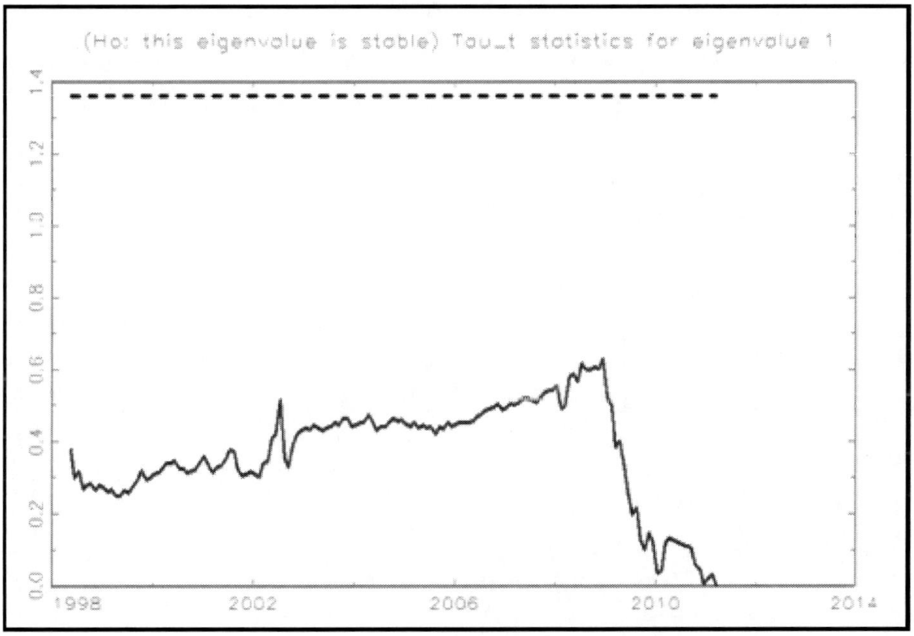

(b) Kenya

Figure 3. (Continued).

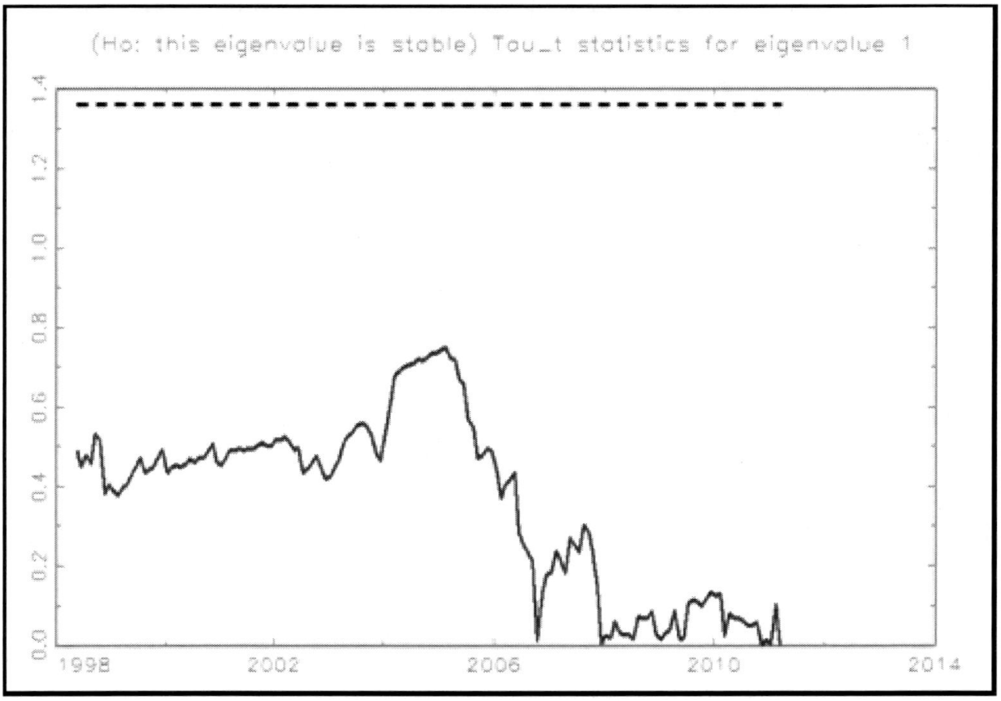

(c) Mauritius

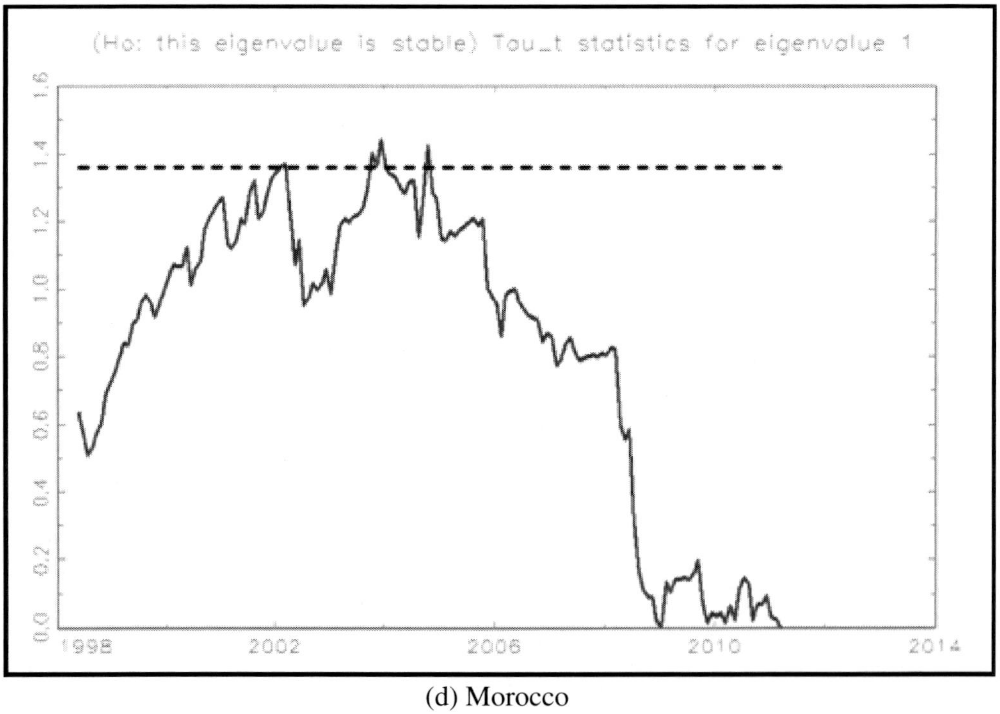

(d) Morocco

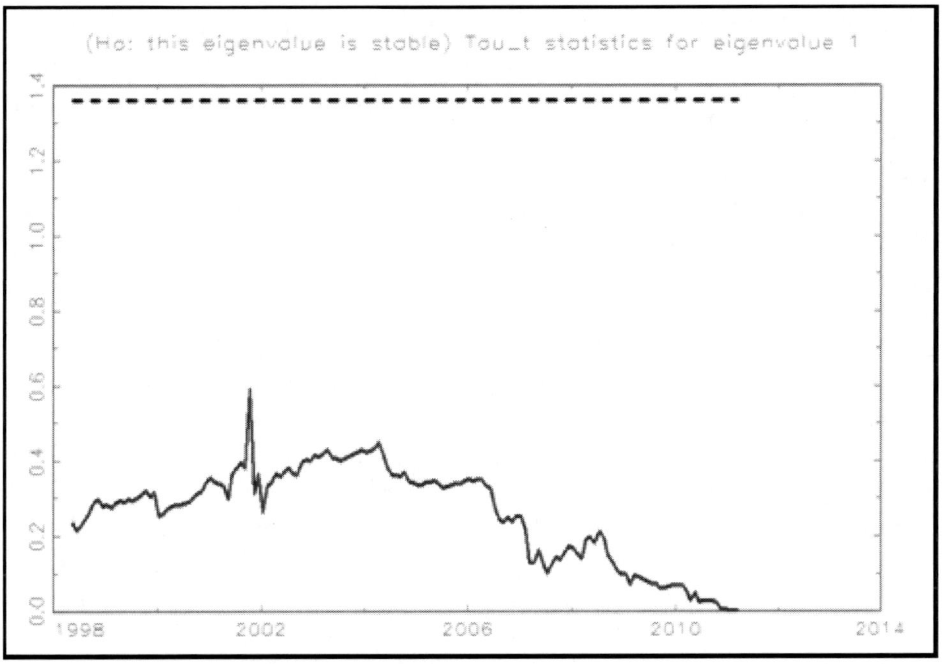

(e) South Africa

The dashed line is the 5% critical value. Critical values developed by Ploberger et al. (1989) are used.

Figure 3. Time path for test statistics for eigenvalues.

Table 8. Cointegration tests with the Euro area stock market as the world market proxy

Trace statistics for Johansen's cointegration tests (Euro area stock market as the world proxy)			
	H_0: r = 0	H_0: r ≤ 1	H_0: r ≤ 2
Country			
Egypt	28.90	10.24	1.16
Kenya	28.95	11.02	0.61
Mauritius	13.70	3.33	0.00
Morocco	22.89	7.43	0.01
South Africa	28.59	13.58	0.04
Critical values (1%)	35.65	20.04	6.65

Secondly, we provide evidence on the "flow" and "stock" channels. Neither the restrictions $\Phi_{12}(L) = 0$, $\Phi_{13}(L) = 0$ and $\Phi_{23}(L) = 0$ (the flow channel), nor the restrictions $\Phi_{13}(L) = 0$, $\Phi_{21}(L) = 0$ and $\Phi_{23}(L) = 0$ (the stock channel) are rejected for any of the five countries. Thus, none of the hypothesized channels can explain the nexus between stock markets and real exchange rates in any of the five African countries. These results are inconsistent with those of Phylaktis and Ravozzolo (2005) for Asian countries and Diamandis and Drakos (2011) for Latin American countries.

CONCLUSION AND POLICY IMPLICATIONS

Is there a linkage between stock market volatility and foreign exchange rate fluctuations in some of Africa's major markets? Is it rational to undertake policy reforms touching on the stock markets and currency markets concurrently in these major markets? Our analyses do not provide definite answers to these questions. First, in bivariate cointegration tests, we do not find sufficient evidence to conclude that the two variables have a long-run relationship in the countries investigated. Further, the hypothesis that the two variables do not Granger-cause each other (in bivariate tests) is not rejected for most of the countries. The absence of cointegration and causality in bivariate studies is indicative of the suggestion that policy reforms can be undertaken concurrently in the two markets without fear of non-optimal outcomes in the economies of these countries.

Second, when movements in the world markets (as proxied by the US equity market) are incorporated in the analysis, there is strong evidence that the real exchange rate plays an important role in influencing long-run changes in the equity prices of all the five countries. Thus, there is a dynamic relationship between the two key financial markets variables that is contingent upon developments in the world financial markets. This finding reasonably justifies the conclusion that Africa's equity markets are partially integrated with the world markets (in agreement with Kodongo and Ojah, 2012). The policy consequence of this finding is that developments in Africa's stock and currency markets ought not to be analyzed in isolation but as joint participants in developments in the world financial markets. We infer from this finding that stock and foreign exchange markets in Africa appear to be vulnerable to external shocks and contagion. Thus, policy makers and market regulators are called upon to ensure proper surveillance to detect sources and timing of shocks from external financial markets and to put in place structures that would ensure timely interventions to counter the effects of such shocks on domestic markets. Further, market regulators must ensure that domestic stock and foreign exchange markets participants have full confidence in these markets so as to discourage them reacting to developments in external markets in a manner that may present harmful consequences to these markets.

Our finding that the US (proxy for the world) stock markets do not play a significant role in the cointegrating vector may be ascribed to several factors, including perceived country risk, size of capital markets (market capitalization), as well as deepness of the financial markets. As the market capitalization statistics show, many of the capital markets we have investigated here are quite small by world standards (see also Allen, Otchere and Senbet, 2011). Small size capital markets are associated with perceived risk of illiquidity, which, combined with home bias, may discourage international investors from taking advantage of available portfolio investment opportunities in such markets. Similarly, if political risk of these countries is perceived to be high, it may be a disincentive to international investors. To this extent, therefore, these countries' financial markets may not be attracting foreign investor participation proportionate with their capacity to absorb international capital.

Thus, it would appear that measures that have been put in place by various governments and private financial markets players in Africa to improve on information availability, further liberalize financial markets and adopt more flexible foreign exchange regimes have not been effective in achieving full integration of Africa's financial markets with financial markets elsewhere in the world. A policy implication of this is that there is need to do more in terms of technology consumption, and innovation to make Africa's financial markets deeper and broader and more attractive to international investors. To this end, the introduction of American Depository Receipts (ADRs), country funds and risk management products such as financial derivatives is advised. Studies by Phylaktis and Ravazzolo (1995) and Diamandis and Drakos (2011) have shown that the existence of such instruments has helped to increase integration between Southeast Asian and Latin American financial markets, respectively, with financial markets elsewhere in the world.

ACKNOWLEDGMENT

The authors thank Søren Johansen for advice on parameter stability tests.

REFERENCES

Abdalla, I. & Murinde, V. (1997). Exchange Rate and Stock Price Interaction in Emerging Financial Markets: Evidence on India, Korea, Pakistan and the Philippines. *Applied Financial Economics*, *7*, 25-35.

Adjasi, C., Harvey, S. K. & Agyapong, D. (2008) Effect of Exchange Rate Volatility on the Ghana Stock Exchange. *African Journal of Accounting, Economics, Finance and Banking Research*, *3*, 28–47.

AfDB/OECD. (2008). *The African Economic Outlook 2008*. Paris: OECD Development Centre.

Aggarwal, R. (1981). Exchange Rates and Stock Prices: A Study of the US Capital Markets under Floating Exchange Rates. *Akron Business and Economic Review*, *12*, 7–12.

Ajayi, R. A., Friedman, F. & Mehdian, S. M. (1998). On the Relationship between Stock Returns and Exchange Rates: Tests of Granger causality. *Global Finance Journal*, *9*, 241–251.

Ajayi, R. A. & Mougoué, M. (1996). On the Dynamic Relation between Stock Prices and Exchange Rates. *Journal of Financial Research*, *2*, 196–207.

Allen, F., Otchere, I. & Senbet, L. W. (2011) African Financial Systems: A Review. *Review of Development Finance*, *1*, 79–113.

Apergis, N., Zestos, G. K. & Shaltayev, D. S. (2012) Do market fundamentals determine the Dollar–Euro exchange rate? *Journal of Policy Modeling*, *34*, 1-15.

Aydemir, O. & Demirhan, E. (2009) The Relationship between Stock Prices and Exchange Rates: Evidence from Turkey. *International Research Journal of Finance and Economics* (Issue 23), 207–215.

Bahmani-Oskooee, M. & Sohrabian, A. (1992). Stock Prices and the Effective Exchange Rate of the Dollar. *Applied Economics*, *24*, 459–464.

Bekaert, G., Harvey, C. R. & Lumsdaine, R. L. (2002) Dating the integration of world equity markets. *Journal of Financial Economics*, *65*, 203-247.

Bekaert, G., Harvey, C. R. & Lundblad, C. (2003). Equity Market Liberalization in Emerging Markets. *Journal of Financial Research*, *26*, 275–299.

Carrieri, F. & Majerbi, B. (2006) The Pricing of Exchange Risk in Emerging Stock Markets. *Journal of International Business Studies*, *37*, 372–391.

Chow, E. H., Lee, W. Y. & Solt, M. S. (1997) The Exchange Rate Risk Exposure of Asset Returns. *Journal of Business*, *70*, 105–123.

Commission of the European Communities. (2004). Country Report: Morocco. Commission Staff Working Paper No. SEC(2004).

Diamandis, P. F. & Drakos, A. D. (2011) Financial Liberalization, Exchange Rates and stock Prices: Exogenous Shocks in four Latin American Countries. *Journal of Policy Modeling*, *33*, 381–394.

Dolado, J. J. & Lütkepohl, H. (1996) Making Wald Tests for Cointegrated VAR Systems. *Econometric Reviews*, *15*, 369–386.

Donnelly, R. & Sheehy, E. (1996) The Share Price Reaction of UK Exporters to Exchange Rate Movements: an Empirical Study. *Journal of International Business Studies*, *27*, 157–65.

Dooley, M. P. & Isard, P. (1979). The Portfolio Balance Model of Exchange Rates. International Finance Discussion Paper No. 141, Federal Reserve Board, Washington DC.

Dornbusch, R. & Fisher, S. (1980) Exchange Rates and The Current Account. *American Economic Review*, *70*, 960–971.

Dube, S. (2008). Stock Prices and the Exchange Rate in a Monetary Model: A ARDL Bounds Testing Approach using South African Data. *African Finance Journal*, *10*, 1–26.

Dube, S. (2009). Capital Inflows and Profit Remittances: A Causality Analysis for the South African Economy. *African Finance Journal*, *11*, 1–24.

Enders, W. (1995). *Applied Econometric Time Series*, 2nd edition. New York: Wiley.

Gavin, M. (1989). The Stock Market and Exchange Rate Dynamics. *Journal of International Money and Finance*, *8*, 181–200.

Giles, J. A. & Williams, C. L. (1999). Export-led Growth: A Survey of the Empirical Literature and Some Non-Causality Results. Working Paper EWP9901, University of Victoria.

Granger, C. W. J., Huangb, B.-N. & Yang, C-W. (2000). A Bivariate Causality Between Stock Prices and Exchange Rates: Evidence from Recent Asian Flu. *Quarterly Review of Economics and Finance*, *40*, 337–354.

Hansen, H. & Johansen, S. (1999) Some Tests for Parameter Constancy in Cointegrated VAR-Models. *Econometrics Journal*, *2*, 306-333.

Hatemi-J, A. & Irandoust, M. (2002). On the Causality between Exchange Rates and Stock Prices: A Note. *Bulletin of Economic Research*, *54*, 197–203.

Horng, W.-J., Hsu, L.-H. & Hsu, H.-H. (2010). Dynamic Associated Analysis of Japan's Stock Market and Exchange Rates: DCC and EGARCH model. International Conference on Management and Service Science (MASS), 24-26 August 2010.

IMF (2009). Regional Economic Outlook: Sub-Saharan African Financial Systems and the Global Financial Crisis: Impact, Risks, and Policy Priorities. May 2009. http://www.imf.org/external/country/nga/rr/2009/051809E.pdf.

Ioannidis, C. & Kontonikas, A. (2008). The impact of monetary policy on stock prices. *Journal of Policy Modeling*, *30*, 33–53.

Johansen, S. (1995). *Likelihood-based Inference in Cointegrated Vector Autoregressive Models*. Oxford: Oxford University Press.

Kamar, B. & Bakardzhieva, D. (2005). Economic Trilemma and Exchange Rate Management in Egypt. *Review of Middle East Economics and Finance*, *3*, 91–114.

Khoo, A. (1994). Estimation of Foreign Exchange Exposure: An Application to Mining Companies in Australia. *Journal of International Money and Finance*, *13*, 342–363.

Kodongo, O. & Ojah, K. (2011). Foreign Exchange Risk Pricing and Equity Market Segmentation in Africa. *Journal of Banking and Finance*, *35*, 2295–2310.

Kodongo, O. & Ojah, K. (2012). Real Exchange Rates, Trade Balance and Capital Flows in Africa. *Journal of Economics and Business*, *66*, 22–46.

Ma, C. K. & Kao, G. W. (1990). On Exchange Rate Changes and Stock Price Reactions. *Journal of Business Finance and Accounting*, *27*, 441–449.

MacKinnon, J. G. (1996). Numerical Distribution Functions for Unit Root and Cointegration Tests. *Journal of Applied Econometrics*, *11*, 601–618.

Morley, B. (2002). Exchange rates and stock prices: implications for European convergence. *Journal of Policy Modeling*, *24*, 523–526.

Müller-Plantenberg, N. (2010). Balance of Payments Accounting and Exchange Rate Dynamics. *International Review of Economics and Finance*, *19*, 46–63.

Murinde, V. & Poshakwale, S. (2004). Exchange Rate and Stock Price Interactions in European Emerging Financial Markets before and after the Euro. www.ssrn.com/abstract=493543

Ndung'u, N. S. (1999). *Monetary and Exchange Rate Policy in Kenya*. Research Paper 94, African Economic Research Consortium, Nairobi.

Nieh, C.-C. & Lee, C.-F. (2001). Dynamic Relationship Between Stock Prices and Exchange Rates for G-7 Countries. *Quarterly Review of Economics and Finance*, *41*, 477–490.

Ooi, A.-Y., Wafa, S. K., Lajuni, N. & Ghazali, M.F. (2009). Causality between Exchange Rates and Stock Prices: Evidence from Malaysia and Thailand. *International Journal of Business and Management*, *4*, 86–98.

Osterwald-Lenum, M. (1992). A Note with Quantiles of the Asymptotic Distribution of the Maximum Likelihood Cointegration Test Statistics. *Oxford Bulletin of Economic and Statistics*, *54*, 461–471.

Pan, M.-S., Fok, R. C.-W. & Liu, Y. A. (2007). Dynamic Linkages between Exchange Rates and Stock Prices: Evidence from East Asian Markets. *International Review of Economics and Finance*, *16*, 503–520.

Phylaktis, K. & Ravazzolo, F. (2005). Stock Prices and Exchange Rate Dynamics. *Journal of International Money and Finance*, *24*, 1031–1053.

Ploberger, W., Krämer, W. & Kontrus, K. (1989). A New Test for Structural Stability in the Linear Regression Model. *Journal of Econometrics*, *40*, 307–318.

Ratner, M. (1993). A Cointegration Test of the Impact of Foreign Exchange Rates on US Stock Market Prices. *Global Finance Journal*, *4*, 93–101.

Reimers, H. E. (1992). Comparisons of Tests for Multivariate Cointegration. *Statistical Papers*, *33*, 335–346.

Stavárek, D. (2005). Stock Prices and Exchange Rates in the EU and the USA: Evidence of their Mutual Interactions. *Czech Journal of Economics and Finance*, *55*, 141–161.

Tabak, B. M. (2006). The Dynamic Relationship between Stock Prices and Exchange Rates: Evidence for Brazil. *International Journal of Theoretical and Applied Finance*, *9*, 1377–1396.

Tian, G. G. & Ma, S. (2010). The Relationship between Stock Returns and the Foreign Exchange Rate: The ARDL Approach. *Journal of the Asia Pacific Economy*, *15*, 490–508.

Toda, H. Y. & Yamamoto, T. (1995). Statistical Inference in Vector Autoregressions with Possibly Integrated Processes. *Journal of Econometrics*, *66*, 225–250.

Ugbebor, O. O. & Olubusoye, O. E. (2004). Testing the Purchasing Power Parity Hypothesis for the Nigerian Foreign Exchange Markets. http://www.commerce.uct.ac.za/economics/Conferences/2004/AES2004Conference/Papers/Ugbebor.pdf

United Nations (2002). World Economic Situation and Prospects 2002. Department of Economic and Social Affairs and United Nations Conference on Trade and Development, United Nations, New York.

Yau, H.-Y. & Nieh, C.-C. (2009). Testing for Cointegration with Threshold Effect between Stock Prices and Exchange Rates in Japan and Taiwan. *Japan and the World Economy*, *21*, 292–300.

Zhao, H. (2010). Dynamic Relationship between Exchange Rate and Stock Price: Evidence from China. *Research in International Business and Finance*, *24*, 103–112.

In: Exchange Rates in Developed and Emerging Markets
Editor: Mohsen Bahmani-Oskooee
ISBN: 978-1-62808-164-0

Chapter 8

ON THE OPTIMAL EXCHANGE RATE POLICY FOR THE GCC COUNTRIES

Almukhtar Al-Abri*
Department of Economics and Finance, Sultan Qaboos University,
Alkodh, Oman

ABSTRACT

This chapter extends the new Keynesian small open economy model to evaluate alternative exchange rate arrangements for a small oil-exporting economy. A number of recent stylized facts are incorporated, such as, the increasing counter-cyclicality of oil-exporters with the US economy, the increasing volatility of the US dollar vis-à-vis other major currencies, and the increasing trade of oil-exporters with the Euro area, East Asia, and Japan. In addition, by employing a three-country general equilibrium model, we analyze movements of the anchor currency against other major currencies and the consequences for the pegging country. In this respect, the model suggests that a basket peg is more welfare-improving compared to a unilateral peg. Further, the variance of the currency in which oil-price is denominated came as an important determinant in welfare analyses. These conclusions have important policy implication, particularly for the Gulf Cooperation Council (GCC) countries as they consider alternative monetary arrangements.

Keywords: GCC countries, exchange rate regimes, monetary policy, New Keynesian small open economy model

1. INTRODUCTION

The Gulf Cooperation Council (GCC) countries, comprised of Bahrain, Kuwait, Oman, Qatar, Saudi Arabia, and the United Arab Emirates (UAE), share a common economic structure with hydro-carbon sector representing an annual average of 45% of national output

* Corresponding author: Tel: (968) 92833012, Fax: (968) 24414043, Email: asalabri@squ.edu.om.

and an annual average of 90% of governmental revenues in the period 2000–2010, IMF (2011).[36] For the last four decades, the GCC countries have had no independent monetary policy due to the unilateral pegs of their national currencies to the US dollar. Nonetheless, these pegs have supported GCC countries' record of strong economic performance over those four decades. However, given the progress, albeit slow, of these countries in diversifying their economies, promoting non-oil exports, and developing their financial sectors, the need for monetary policy autonomy might arise in the future. The choice of the exchange rate regime came to the forefront during the period 2003-2008 when inflation accelerated among the GCC countries, which coincided with a period of prolonged US dollar depreciation against major currencies. This is to say that the long standing period of stable domestic prices in GCC countries, attributed largely to the GCC's pegging their currencies to the US dollar, no longer stood ground as a result of the depreciating US dollar which has received much of the blame for the accelerating inflation among the GCC.

Previous studies analyzed the optimality of pegging the GCC national currencies to the US dollar. For example, Squalli (2011) extends the central bank loss function employed by Berger et al. (2001) and find a weak support for continuing with the US dollar peg for the largest economies of the GCC region (Saudi Arabia, Qatar, and UAE) in terms of stabilizing inflation and output. Coudert et al. (2011) highlight the rising concern that fluctuations in crude oil-prices often result in large misalignments of pegged currencies in oil-exporting countries due to burgeoning oil wealth and massive capital inflows. For example, the surge in crude oil-prices during 2000 – 2007 caused substantial real appreciations of oil-exporters' currencies. Since the exchange rate is fixed, the adjustment came through inflationary pressures. To avoid such undesirable adjustment, Frankel (2005) suggests pegging the national currencies of oil exporters to the international crude oil-price. Alternatively, Engel (2009) suggests including currency misalignment as a target for monetary policy beside inflation and output gap.

This chapter offers a holistic approach of investigating the choice of optimal exchange rate regime for the member countries of the GCC. The new Keynesian small open economy model is extended to include three countries, a small commodity-exporting country (Home) and two large foreign countries. The second foreign country is needed to incorporate the decline in the US share in global economy. In addition, a second foreign country is added to model the impact on the home country's welfare of possible long-run misalignment of the US dollar (hence, currencies pegged to the US dollar) vis-à-vis major world currencies. A number of recent stylized facts are also incorporated in our model, such as, the increasing counter-cyclicality of oil-exporters with the US economy, the increasing volatility of the US dollar vis-à-vis other major currencies, and the increasing trade of oil-exporters with the Euro area, East Asia, and Japan.

The rest of the chapter is organized as follows: Section 2 lays out the model and its assumptions. Section 3 presents the solution of the model under different pricing schemes. Section 4 compares the welfare results under fixed and flexible exchange rate regimes and the factors that affect the level of welfare. Some conclusions follow.

[36] The exception was the United Arab Emirates and Bahrain where hydrocarbons constitute relatively smaller share of output and governmental revenues, IMF (2011).

2. THE MODEL

The model follows the base models developed by Obstfeld and Rogoff (1995, 1996, 2000) and the later extensions by others (e.g. Devereux and Engel (1998, 2003); Corsetti and Pesenti (2005); Galí and Monacelli (2005); and Adolfson et al. (2007)). The model considers three countries: one home country and two foreign countries, where the home country is assumed to be small and the two foreign countries are assumed to be large. The home country produces one local non-traded composite good and exports one primary commodity, oil, and imports and consumes a traded composite good, which is produced in the two foreign countries, and its local composite nontraded good. The home country is small so that it is a price taker in both the primary commodity market and the traded composite consumption good market. Each of the two foreign countries produces two goods, a composite consumption good, which is consumed by the three countries, and a local nontraded consumption good. The two foreign countries import part of their oil consumption from the home country. The need to add a third country to the standard two-county new open economy model is motivated as follows. If we think of the first foreign country as the United States, then the second foreign country (say rest of the world, rest of the OECD countries, or the Euro Area for approximation) is needed to incorporate the decline in the US share in global economy. In addition, a second foreign country is added to model the impact of possible long-run misalignment of the US dollar vis-à-vis major world currencies. Table 1. shows the decline in trade shares of Gulf Cooperation Council (GCC) Countries with the United States to other countries, such as Europe, China, and Japan.

Consumers

Households in the three countries get utility by consuming the composite traded and non-traded consumption goods and holding real money balances, which provide them with liquidity services. The utility function exhibits also the disutility of efforts or labor. We assume that the home country's money is held only by the home agents and the foreign countries' monies only by the foreign agents. Each country has an infinitely lived representative household with identical preferences over a composite consumption good that is produced in the two foreign countries only and a composite local-nontraded consumption good that is produced in each country for local consumption. At any particular time t the home and the foreign households maximize the sum of their discounted expected one period utilities. The present discounted value of lifetime utility of a domestic resident is

$$U_t = E_t \sum_t^{\infty} \beta^t \left[u(C_t) + \chi v(\frac{M_t}{P_t}) - \varsigma(L_t) \right] \tag{1}$$

where E_t is the expectation operator given the information available at the beginning of period t. β is the intertemporal discount factor. χ is the weight of real balances in the agent's utility. M_t denotes the nominal money stock that the individual acquires at the beginning of period t and then holds through the end of the period. P_t is the consumption price index which is defined below. The same preferences are valid for the two foreign countries' representative agent. In the following, we will use the superscripts F1 and F2 to differentiate the two foreign countries variables from their home country counterparts.

Table 1. Import partners of GCC countries in 2000 and 2009 (% of total imports)

Country\Import Partner Countries	United States		United Kingdom		Japan		China		European Union	
	2000	2009	2000	2009	2000	2009	2000	2009	2000	2009
Bahrain	12.6	8.0	5.8	4.4	3.9	5.2	1.5	5.7	25.5	28.4
Kuwait	12.1	11.2	7.8	4.0	8.7	7.2	4.7	9.0	32.9	29.9
Oman	5.4	6.5	5.8	2.3	18.1	15.0	1.9	4.8	19.3	17.1
Qatar	10.3	13.1	7.8	5.5	11.0	7.9	3.0	4.2	35.5	35.6
Saudi Arabia	19.0	12.8	6.4	4.9	10.3	6.4	3.9	10.7	32.8	32.4
United Arab Emirates	7.9	8.8	8.1	4.0	9.6	4.7	8.1	13.5	37.4	25.3

Source: Direction of Trade Statistics (DOT) and IMF.

We assume that all individuals in the model are indexed by $j \in [0,1]$. The interval $j \in [0, n_1]$ consists of agents in the home country; each receives oil revenue from her government and produces a non-traded consumption good $z' \in [0, n_1]$. The intervals $j \in (n_1, n_2)$ and $j \in (n_2, 1]$ consist of foreign agents in foreign country one and foreign country two respectively; each of whom produces two goods, a traded consumption good $z \in (n_1, n_2)$ and $z \in (n_2, 1]$, and a non-traded consumption good $z' \in (n_1, n_2)$ and $z' \in (n_2, 1]$ respectively. The real consumption index for the home agent is

$$C_t(j) = \frac{C_{T,t}(j)^{\gamma} C_{N,t}(j)^{1-\gamma}}{\gamma^{\gamma}(1-\gamma)^{1-\gamma}} \tag{2}$$

where $C_{T,t}(j)$ denotes the home agent's consumption index of traded goods and $C_{N,t}(j)$ denotes the home agent's consumption index of nontraded goods. The same thing is valid for the foreign gent's consumption indexes in the two foreign countries. We assume here that agents in the three countries consume the same basket of traded and nontraded goods. We also assume that the elasticity of substitution between the composite goods of traded and nontraded goods and the elasticity of substitution between the traded goods of foreign country one and foreign country two are both unity. The consumption indexes of traded goods and local nontraded goods are each defined as follows

$$C_{T,t}(j)=\frac{\left(C_{T,t}(F1,j)\right)^{\eta}\left(C_{T,t}(F2,j)\right)^{1-\eta}}{\eta^{\eta}\left(1-\eta\right)^{\eta}} \tag{3}$$

$$C_{T,t}(F1,j)=\left[\left(\frac{1}{n_{F1}}\right)^{\frac{1}{\phi}}\int_{n1}^{n2}c_{T,F1}^{F1}(z)^{\frac{\phi-1}{\phi}}dz\right]^{\frac{\phi}{\phi-1}},\quad C_{T,t}(F2,j)=\left[\left(\frac{1}{n_{F2}}\right)^{\frac{1}{\phi}}\int_{n2}^{1}c_{T,F2}^{F1}(z)^{\frac{\phi-1}{\phi}}dz\right]^{\frac{\phi}{\phi-1}} \tag{4}$$

$$C_{N,t}(j)=\left[\left(\frac{1}{n_{H}}\right)^{\frac{1}{\phi}}\int_{0}^{n1}c_{N,t}(z')^{\frac{\phi-1}{\phi}}dz'\right]^{\frac{\phi}{\phi-1}} \tag{5}$$

$$C_{N,t}^{F1}(j)=\left[\left(\frac{1}{n_{F1}}\right)^{\frac{1}{\phi}}\int_{n1}^{n2}c_{N,t}^{F1}(z')^{\frac{\phi-1}{\phi}}dz'\right]^{\frac{\phi}{\phi-1}} \tag{6}$$

where $c_{T,F1}(z), c_{T,F2}(z),$ and $c_{N,t}(z')$ are the home consumption of traded good z produced at foreign country one and foreign country two and nontraded good z' respectively. Foreign country one counterparts are defined analogously. $C_{T,t}(F1,j)$ and $C_{T,t}(F2,j)$ are the consumption of the home agent of the composite traded consumption goods produced in foreign country one and two respectively. $\eta=\frac{n_{F1}}{n_{F1}+n_{F2}}$ is the proportion of trade consumption goods imported from foreign country one. The above consumption functions exhibit the constant-elasticity-of-substitution (CES), where ϕ is the price elasticity of demand faced by each monopolist and equal to the elasticity of substitution between distinct goods of a given composite good. We assume that $\phi>1$ to ensure interior equilibrium with a positive output level. We henceforth omit the use of the index j for simplicity.

Let $P_{T,t}(z)$, $P_{T,t}^{F1}(z)$, and $P_{T,t}^{F2}(z)$ denote the home-currency and the two foreign-currencies price of the traded good z produced by the two foreign countries. And let $P_{N,t}(z')$ denote the home-currency price of the local-nontraded good z' produced by the home agent. Similarly, $P_{N,t}^{F1}(z')$ and $P_{N,t}^{F2}(z')$ denotes the foreign-currencies price of the local-nontraded good z' produced by each of the two foreign countries. The consumption-based home and foreign price indexes are then given by

$$P_t = (P_{T,t})^{\gamma}(P_{N,t})^{1-\gamma} \quad \text{and} \quad P_t^{F1} = (P_{T,t}^{F1})^{\gamma}(P_{N,t}^{F1})^{1-\gamma} \qquad (7)^{37}$$

where $P_{T,t}$ is the home-currency price of one unit of the composite consumption good and $P_{N,t}$ is the home-currency price of one unit of the local-nontraded good produced by the home country. The price indexes for the home country are given by (the indexes for foreign country 1 and foreign country 2 follow analogously)

$$P_{T,t}(F1) = \left[\left(\frac{1}{n_{F1}}\right)\int_{n1}^{n2}\left[S^{F1}P_{T,t}^{F1}(z)\right]^{1-\phi}dz\right]^{\frac{1}{1-\phi}}, \quad P_{T,t}(F2) = \left[\left(\frac{1}{n_{F2}}\right)\int_{n2}^{1}\left[S^{F2}P_{T,t}^{F2}(z)\right]^{1-\phi}dz\right]^{\frac{1}{1-\phi}} \qquad (8)$$

$$P_{N,t} = \left[\left(\frac{1}{n_H}\right)\int_0^{n1}P_{N,t}(z')^{1-\phi}dz'\right]^{\frac{1}{1-\phi}}; \qquad (9)$$

Since we assume identical individuals who solve the same allocation problem, we can aggregate prices as $P_{T,t}^{F1} = P_{T,t}^{F1}(z)$ and $P_{T,t}^{F2} = P_{T,t}^{F2}(z)$, which allows us to define

$$P_{T,t} = \left(\left(S_t^{F1}P_{T,t}^{F1}\right)^{\eta}\left(S_t^{F2}P_{T,t}^{F2}\right)^{1-\eta}\right) \qquad (10)$$

where: $\eta = \frac{n_{F1}}{n_{F1}+n_{F2}}$ as previously defined.

The home agents' demand for the traded consumption good z is given by

$$c_{T,t}(z) = \gamma\left[\frac{P_{T,t}(z)}{P_{T,t}}\right]^{-\phi}\left(\frac{P_t}{P_{T,t}}\right)C_t \qquad (11)$$

Using the law-of-one-price condition and taking a population-weighted average of the home country's and the two foreign countries' demands, we find the total demand for traded good z is

$$y_{T,t}^d(z) = \left[\frac{P_{T,t}(z)}{P_t}\right]^{-\phi}C_{T,t}^W \qquad (12)$$

where $C_{T,t}^W$ is the total consumption of the traded goods in the three countries. The home agents' demand for local nontraded good z' is given by,

[37] The derivations of these price indexes are provided in Obstfeld and Rogoff (1996, Ch. 10).

$$c_{N,t}(z') = \left(\frac{P_{N,t}(z')}{P_{N,t}} \right)^{-\phi} \frac{P_t}{P_{N,t}} C_t \quad (13)$$

To obtain closed-form solutions, a functional form for the utility function is needed. we assume that $u(C_t)$ exhibits a constant relative risk aversion (CRRA) with degree of risk aversion ρ, that is $u(C_t) = \frac{C_t^{1-\rho}}{1-\rho}$. Also, the utility of the real money balances takes the logarithmic form $v(\frac{M_t}{P_t}) = \log(\frac{M_t}{P_t})$. Efforts enters the utility function in a linear form $\varsigma(l_t) = L_t$

Production Technologies

The home agent j produces only one good, the local nontraded good $z' \in [0, n_1)$, where the only input is labor. That is,

$$Y_{N,t}(z') = \theta_t L_{N,t}(z') \quad (14)$$

where θ_t denotes the home country-specific productivity shock to non-traded technology. $L_{N,t}$ is the employment of labor in nontraded good production. In addition, the home agent receives her share from oil revenue, where oil is uniquely endowed in the home country. we assume first that the market for oil is perfectly competitive. In this case, the price of oil, denoted by $P_{O,t}^{F1}$, is exogenously determined outside the home country and, we further assume that it is denominated in the currency of foreign country one. In terms of home currency, the nominal revenue of a home agent from production (oil and finished non-traded goods) is

$$R_t = S_t^{F1} P_O^{F1} O_t^H(z) + P_{N,t}(z') Y_{N,t}(z') \quad (15)$$

we assume that the home country redistributes its oil revenue among its people in lump-sum payments. In the real world, the supply of any internationally traded commodity is influenced by many factors. To keep the model as simple as possible, we assume that the home country takes the price of oil as given and exports the quantity of oil that meets the foreign country's demand for oil. For simplicity, we assume the cost of extracting oil is zero. More realistic modeling of oil supply should take into consideration the oligopolic structure of the oil market. That is, oil supply shocks can be decomposed into price and quantity shocks. The quantity of oil supplied has two separate components: a deterministic component that relates to OPEC announced production and a stochastic component that refers to non-OPEC members; we focus on price shocks and assume that quantity shocks are minimal.

The foreign agent j (in each of the two foreign countries) produces two goods, a traded consumption good z and a local nontraded good z'. For the production of the traded consumption good, we assume that the only inputs are oil and labor and that the foreign agent has monopoly power in producing this good. To introduce price rigidity into the model, we assume that prices are set one period in advance and before information about the foreign and home countries money supplies is known. We further assume that capital stock is constant. Thus, the analyses of this study best characterize the short to medium term. The production function of traded good z produced by a foreign agent takes the form

$$Y_{T,t}^{F1}(z) = \theta_t^{F1} O_t^{F1}(z)^{\alpha} L_{T,t}^{F1}(z)^{1-\alpha} \quad 0 < \alpha < 1 \tag{16}$$

where $O_t^{F1}(z)$ is the quantity of oil imported from home country and used for the production of good z. $L_{T,t}^{F1}(z)$ is labor employment in the production of traded good z. The demand for oil can be solved from the foreign agent's problem, which is:

$$O_t^{F1}(z) = \left(\frac{\alpha}{1-\alpha}\right)^{1-\alpha} \left(\frac{P_t^{F1}}{P_O^{F1}} \left(C_t^{F1}\right)^{\rho}\right)^{1-\alpha} \left(\frac{Y_{T,t}^{F1}(z)}{\theta_t^{F1}}\right) \tag{17}$$

The production of local nontraded good z' is identical to that of the home agent, which takes the form

$$Y_{N,t}^{F1}(z') = \theta_t^{F1} L_{N,t}^{F1}(z') \tag{18}$$

Thus, in terms of foreign currency, the revenue of an agent in foreign country one is

$$R_t^{F1} = P_{T,t}^{F1}(z) Y_{T,t}^{F1}(z) + P_{N,t}^{F1}(z') Y_{N,t}^{F1}(z') \tag{19}$$

It can be seen that the home country and each of the two foreign countries are asymmetric in terms of their revenue from production activities. The resource constraints that equate the quantities demanded and supplied of each good are:

$$Y_{N,t}(z') = \int_0^{n1} c_{N,t}^j(z')dj \tag{20}$$

$$Y_{T,t}^{F1}(z) + Y_{T,t}^{F2}(z) = \int_0^{n1} c_{T,t}^j(z)dj + \int_{n1}^{n2} c_{T,t}^j(z)dj + \int_{n2}^{1} c_{T,t}^j(z)dj \tag{21}$$

$$Y_{N,t}^{F1}(z') = \int_{n1}^{n2} c_{N,t}^{j}(z')dj \qquad (22)$$

Introducing Price Rigidity

To introduce the simplest form of price rigidity into the model, we assume that agents choose the nominal price of their goods, traded and nontraded, one period in advance and before information about monetary, productivity, and oil-price shocks are realized. Prices fully adjust to all shocks after one period. One could justify this rigidity of prices as an institutional constraint such as menu costs. We should distinguish here between two schemes of export invoicing or price settings, producer currency pricing and local currency pricing.

Producer currency pricing

Under producer currency pricing, each producer sets the price of the traded good z in her own currency. In this case, the optimal price setting is:

$$P_{T,t}^{F1}(z)_{PCP} = \left(\frac{\phi}{\phi-1}\right)\frac{E_{t-1}\left[\left(\frac{\left(P_t^{F1}\right)^{1-\alpha}\left(C_t^{F1}\right)^{1-\alpha\rho}}{\theta_t^{F1}\alpha^{\alpha}(1-\alpha)^{1-\alpha}}\right)\left(P_{O,t}^{F1}\right)^{\alpha}\right]}{E_{t-1}\left(C_t^{F1}\right)^{1-\rho}} \qquad (23)$$

$$P_{T,t}^{F2}(z)_{PCP} = \left(\frac{\phi}{\phi-1}\right)\frac{E_{t-1}\left[\left(\frac{\left(P_t^{F2}\right)^{1-\alpha}\left(C_t^{F2}\right)^{1-\alpha\rho}}{\theta_t^{F2}\alpha^{\alpha}(1-\alpha)^{1-\alpha}}\right)\left(S_t^{F2F1}P_{O,t}^{F1}\right)^{\alpha}\right]}{E_{t-1}\left(C_t^{F2}\right)^{1-\rho}} \qquad (24)$$

This means that foreign country one does not face any exchange rate risk in pricing its traded goods since it imports oil in its own currency and exports its finished goods in its own currency too. The same thing is not true for foreign country two. It is exposed to exchange rate risk because it imports oil denominated in foreign country one's currency.

Local currency pricing

However, under local currency pricing, each producer of traded good z sets the price of her good in the currency of the buyer. In this case, the optimal price setting is:

$$P_{T,t}(z)_{LCP,Fj} = \left(\frac{\phi}{\phi-1}\right)\frac{E_{t-1}\left[\left(\frac{\left(P_t\right)^{1-\alpha}\left(C_t\right)^{1-\alpha\rho}}{\theta_t^{Fj}\alpha^{\alpha}(1-\alpha)^{1-\alpha}}\right)\left(P_{O,t}\right)^{\alpha}\right]}{E_{t-1}\left(C_t\right)^{1-\rho}} \qquad (25)$$

Producers in the two foreign countries will choose the same price to charge agents in the home country. Equation (25) shows that the foreign exchange risk is not included in the firms' pricing decisions. The home country's agent is immune to nominal exchange rate fluctuations since she buys imported goods in her own currency. Although the nominal exchange rate between the two foreign countries seems to be relevant given the fact that oil is denominated in foreign country one's currency, it turns out that all nominal exchange rates cancel-out when prices are expressed in the home country's currency.[38] Finally, the choice of currency pricing is irrelevant for the price of the local nontraded good, which is optimally set by the home agent's as (those of foreign country one and foreign country two follow analogously)

$$P_{N,t} = P_{N,t}(z) = \left(\frac{\phi}{\phi - 1}\right)\frac{E_{t-1}\left(\frac{P_t C_t}{\theta}\right)}{E_{t-1}\left(C_t^{1-\rho}\right)} \tag{26}$$

The Budget Constraints

To simplify, the model contains six financial assets. Money, denominated in each currency of the three countries, and interest-bearing riskless private bonds denominated in the home country's currency and the two foreign countries' currencies. We assume that there are complete asset markets- agents of each country can purchase state-contingent nominal bonds for each state of the world.[39] In the literature, free capital mobility is approximated by the complete asset markets assumption. We further assume that there are restrictions set forth by each country allowing residents to hold only home money. Thus, the representative individual is confined to holding her own country's money and interest-bearing claims on home agents and foreigners denominated in the bond issuer's currency.[40] The representative consumer in the home country receives income from oil revenue distributed in lump-sum fashion by the government and from return on foreign bond holdings. She picks consumption, money holdings, non-traded-good-production labor inputs, and holdings of a foreign bond to maximize utility. The individual's financing constraint for any date t in real terms is given by

$$\frac{B_{H,t+1}}{P_t} + \frac{S_t^{F1}B_{F1,t+1}}{P_t} + \frac{S_t^{F2}B_{F2,t+1}}{P_t} + \frac{M_t}{P_t} = (1+r_t)\frac{B_{H,t}}{P_{t-1}} + (1+r_t^{F1})\frac{S_t^{F1}B_{F1,t}}{P_{t-1}}$$
$$+ (1+r_t^{F2})\frac{S_t^{F2}B_{F2,t}}{P_{t-1}} + \frac{M_{t-1}}{P_t} + \frac{R_t}{P_t} - C_t - T_t \tag{27}$$

where B_H, B_{F1} and B_{F2} denote the net private holdings of bonds issued by home agents and foreign agents, respectively, and denominated in the bond issuer's currency. S_t^j is the

[38] Although we assume LCP for the consumption good, the low of one price still hold for the oil price across countries since oil is denominated in foreign country one's currency.

[39] We omit state-contingent notations for ease of exposition.

[40] Relaxing this assumption does not change the qualitative results of this paper.

nominal exchange rate between the home country and foreign country j (expressed as units of the home country's currency per units of foreign country j's currency). R_t is given in Equation (15). T_t denotes the lump-sum taxes paid to the government, r_t^{F1} and r_t^{F2} are the foreign real interest rates, and M_{t-1} is home nominal money holdings at the beginning of period t. In nominal terms, the budget constraint for the home individual can be written, in terms of home currency, as[41]

$$B_{H,t+1} + S_t^{F1} B_{F1,t+1} + S_t^{F2} B_{F2,t+1} + M_t = (1+i_t) B_{H,t} + (1+i_t^{F1}) S_t^{F1} B_{F1,t} + (1+i_t^{F2}) S_t^{F2} B_{F2,t} + M_{t-1} + R_t - P_t C_t - P_t T_t \tag{28}$$

In the nominal budget constraint above, the nominal yield i_t^j is paid at the beginning of period t and is known at period $t-1$. The representative agent in each of the two foreign countries will pick consumption, money holdings, bond holdings, and labor and oil inputs to maximize utility. The real budget constraint for the foreign individual can be written as

$$\frac{B_{F1,t+1}^{F1}}{P_t^{F1}} + \frac{B_{H,t+1}^{F1}}{S_t^{F1} P_t^{F1}} + \frac{B_{F2,t+1}^{F1}}{S_t^{F2F1} P_t^{F1}} + \frac{M_t^{F1}}{P_t^{F1}} = (1+r_t^{F1}) \frac{B_{F1,t}^{F1}}{P_{t-1}^{F1}} + (1+r_t) \frac{B_{H,t}^{F1}}{S_t^{F1} P_{t-1}^{F1}} + (1+r_t^{F2}) \frac{B_{F2,t}^{F1}}{S_t^{F2F1} P_{t-1}^{F1}} + \frac{M_{t-1}^{F1}}{P_t^{F1}} + \frac{R_t^{F1}}{P_t^{F1}} - C_t^{F1} - T_t^{F1} \tag{29}$$

In nominal terms, the budget constraint for the foreign representative agent in foreign country one can similarly be written as

$$B_{F1,t+1}^{F1} + \frac{B_{H,t+1}^{F1}}{S_t^{F1}} + \frac{B_{F2,t+1}^{F1}}{S_t^{F2F1}} + M_t^{F1} = (1+i_t^{F1}) B_{F1,t} + (1+i_t) \frac{B_{H,t}}{S_t^{F1}} + (1+i_t^{F2}) \frac{B_{F2,t}}{S_t^{F2F1}} + M_{t-1}^{F1} + R_t^{F1} - P_O^{F1} O_t^{H} - P_t^{F1} C_t^{F1} - P_t^{F1} T_t^{F1} \tag{30}$$

The nominal interest rate for the home-currency denominated bonds on date t is defined as

$$(1+i_t) = E_t \left[\frac{P_t}{P_{t-1}} (1+r_t) \right] \tag{31}$$

[41] We use the notation of Obstfeld and Rogoff (1996, Ch.10). In this case, M_t is nominal balances accumulated during period t and carried over into period $t+1$, while $B_{F1,t}$, for example, denotes bonds accumulated during period $t-1$ and carried over into period t.

with an analogous definition for each of the two foreign-currencies nominal interest rates. Also, because we assume complete asset markets, real interest rates are equal, or $r_t = r_t^{F1} = r_t^{F2}$. The nominal interest rate and the exchange rate are tied together by the uncovered interest rate parity condition,

$$(1+i_t) = E_t\left[\frac{S_{t+1}^{F1}}{S_t^{F1}}(1+i_t^{F1})\right] = E_t\left[\frac{S_{t+1}^{F2}}{S_t^{F2}}(1+i_t^{F2})\right] \tag{32}$$

Government Budget Constraint

We assume that the revenue of the home government comes from taxes, seignorage, and oil revenue. However, it remits all revenue (including oil) to its people in lump-sum fashion. Thus, its budget constraint in per capita terms is (assuming zero government purchases)

$$0 = T_t + \frac{M_t - M_{t-1}}{P_t} \tag{33}$$

The foreign government budget constraint is

$$0 = T_t^{F1} + \frac{M_t^{F1} - M_{t-1}^{F1}}{P_t^{F1}} \tag{34}$$

We assume that the three governments do not issue bonds. Since our main focus is on monetary policy, We assume no government expenditures to avoid any stabilization role that might be played by fiscal policy, particularly for the home country where oil revenues are collected by the government.

Effects of Exchange Rates on Prices

The issue of export invoicing is at the center of the debate in the new open economy literature. Three price-setting mechanisms are considered in the literature, Producer-Currency Pricing (PCP), Local-Currency Pricing (LCP), and Pricing-To-Market (PTM). In PCP, producers set prices in their own currency. In this case, the price that foreigners pay for domestic goods, and the price that home residents pay for foreign goods fluctuate when the exchange rate changes. Under PCP, purchasing power parity holds at all times (for the traded goods sector), since there is only one price set in producer's currency for each good. In LCP, producers set the price in the consumers' currency. That is, producers charge two prices-one to residents of their own country, and another to residents of the other country. In this case, prices consumers face do not respond at all to exchange rate changes. Finally, in PTM, producers segment international markets for their goods, such that they can, at least over some time horizon, charge different prices to different national markets according to these markets' demand conditions. Under both the LCP and the PTM, purchasing power parity does not hold. This is because under this form of price stickiness, exchange rate changes do not lead to proportional changes in import prices, leaving short-run deviations from the law of one price. Since the import prices are pre-set in the importer's rather than the exporter's currency, the exchange rate pass-through to import prices is zero. As we discussed in section 1 of this chapter, the issue of the effects of price setting on the choice of the exchange rate regime was formally analyzed by Devereux and Engel (1998, 2003).

Thus, for the composite consumption good, we compare the welfare measure of alternative exchange rate regime using the two assumptions of price-setting, PCP and LCP. However, for the price of oil, to make the model tractable and to be consistent with the empirical evidence we discussed earlier, we assume that it is denominated in the currency of foreign country 1.

Monetary Policies/Exchange Rate Regimes and Shocks

We assume that the three economies are subject to three kinds of exogenous shocks; real oil price shocks, money supply shocks (nominal shocks), and productivity shocks (real shocks). We assume that all three shocks follow log-normal distributions. For oil price shocks, and to account for persistence, we assume that the log of real oil price follows an AR(1) process of the form:

$$p^{r}_{O,t} = \varphi p^{r}_{O,t-1} + \varepsilon_t \tag{35}$$

where $0 \leq \varphi \leq 1$, and ε_t is mean zero i.i.d. normally distributed random variable with variance σ^2_ε. The real price of oil is defined as the international price of oil denominated in foreign country one converted to local currency by the nominal exchange rate and divided by the country's respective consumer price index. Similarly, the productivity shocks can be represented by the following form:

$$\log\theta_t = \delta\log\theta_{t-1} + u_t \tag{36}$$

$$\log\theta_t^{F1} = \delta\log\theta_{t-1}^{F1} + u_t^{F1} \tag{37}$$

$$\log\theta_t^{F2} = \delta\log\theta_{t-1}^{F2} + u_t^{F2} \tag{38}$$

where $0 \le \delta \le 1$, and u_t, u_t^{F1}, and u_t^{F2} are mean zero i.i.d. normally distributed random variables with variances σ_u^2, $\sigma_{u^{F1}}^2$, and $\sigma_{u^{F2}}^2$ respectively. We also follow Devereux and Engel (2003) in distinguishing between two alternative monetary/exchange rate arrangements, fixed exchange regime and flexible exchange regime. The log money supply for the three countries is given by:

$$m_t = m_{t-1} + \omega(s_t^* - E_{t-1}s_t^*) + a_1 u_t + a_2 u_t^{F1} + a_3 u_t^{F2} + a_4 \varepsilon_t + v_t \tag{39}$$

$$m_t^{F1} = m_{t-1}^{F1} + b_2 u_t^{F1} + b_3 u_t^{F2} + b_4 \varepsilon_t + v_t^{F1} \tag{40}$$

$$m_t^{F2} = m_{t-1}^{F2} + \omega^f (s_t^{F2F1} - E_{t-1}s_t^{F2F1}) + c_2 u_t^{F1} + c_3 u_t^{F2} + c_4 \varepsilon_t + v_t^{F2} \tag{41}$$

where: $s_t^* = ks_t^{F1} + (1-k)s_t^{F2}$, $0 < k < 1$. The values $k = 1$ and $k = 0$ correspond to the special cases when the home country respectively fixes its nominal exchange rate with foreign country one only or foreign country two only. v_t, v_t^{F1}, and v_t^{F2} are mean-zero i.i.d. normally distributed random disturbances to money supply with variances σ_v^2, $\sigma_{v^{F1}}^2$, and $\sigma_{v^{F2}}^2$ respectively. Each money supply equation is a reaction function for the four shocks, except for the home country, which has to react to its own productivity shocks. For simplicity, we assume that the parameters of the reaction function are exogenous in this model. Quantitative estimation of these parameters should consider determining them optimally from the model (i.e., as a function of the other parameters and shocks), a step beyond the scope of this chapter.

The reaction parameters in the money supply rule are assumed to be exogenous (e.g. determined from historical records). The money supply equation for the home country and foreign country two allows the distinction between two exchange rate regimes depending on the value of ω and ω^f respectively. When $\omega, \omega^f \to 0$, the monetary authority does not intervene in the exchange market, allowing the exchange rate to adjust freely, thus, we have a flexible exchange regime. The money supply in this case is exogenous. However, as $\omega, \omega^f \to -\infty$, there is full intervention in the exchange market by the monetary authority to maintain the exchange rate at its parity. In this case, the exchange rate is not allowed to adjust and we have a fixed exchange regime. The money supply in this case is endogenous. To simplify the search for model solutions, we assume that the shocks in this model are not correlated.

The relevance of the choice of the exchange rate regime between the two foreign countries can be motivated as follows. If we think of foreign country one as the United States, we could think of the third country as the rest of the OECD countries. Thus, s_t^{F2F1} is the exchange rate of a weighted average of the currencies of OECD countries against the US dollar. The argument for including the exchange rate policy in the money supply reaction function is that of Sevensson (1999). If the foreign countries adopt a flexible exchange rate regime and follows an inflation-targeting objective, then optimal monetary policy needs to respond to exchange rate movements because such movements carry information about future inflation. Also, since the home agent's share of revenue from oil exports are denominated in the currency of foreign country one, and since she consumes the traded good of the other two countries, her consumption will be affected by movements in the nominal exchange rate between the two foreign countries.

Using the three monetary policy rules above, we can obtain an explicit solution for the composite exchange rate (in logs) of the home country with the rest of the world,

$$\left(s_t^* - E_{t-1}s_t^*\right) = \left(\frac{a_1}{1-\omega}\right)u_t + \left(\frac{a_2 - \tilde{a}_2 - \omega^f (a_2 - b_2)}{(1-\omega)(1-\omega^f)}\right)u_t^{F1} + \left(\frac{a_3 - \tilde{a}_3 - \omega^f (a_3 - b_3)}{(1-\omega)(1-\omega^f)}\right)u_t^{F2}$$
$$+ \left(\frac{a_4 - \tilde{a}_4 - \omega^f (a_4 - b_4)}{(1-\omega)(1-\omega^f)}\right)\varepsilon_t + \left(\frac{1}{1-\omega}\right)v_t + \left(\frac{(\omega^f - k)v_t^{F1} - (1-k)v_t^{F2}}{(1-\omega)(1-\omega^f)}\right) \quad (42)$$

where $\tilde{a}_j = kb_j - (1-k)c_j$. The solution of the composite exchange rate reveals that the home country, by fixing its exchange rate (i.e. $\omega \to -\infty$), it can offset the local monetary and productivity shocks only. For the foreign monetary, productivity, and oil price shocks, the home composite exchange rate will be affected by its own choice of the exchange rate regime as well as that of foreign country two. Table 2. summarizes the effects of a one-unit shock in each of the seven shocks on the home country's composite exchange rate with the rest of the world, when other shocks are shut-off.

Table 2. The impact of shocks on the nominal exchange rate of the home country

Home Regime	**Foreign country two regime**	v_t	v_t^{F1}	v_t^{F2}	u_t	u_t^{F1}	ε_t
Flexible $\omega \to 0$	Flexible $\omega^f \to 0$	1	$-k$	$-(1-k)$	a_1	$(a_2 - \tilde{a}_2)$	$(a_4 - \tilde{a}_4)$
	Fixed $\omega^f \to -\infty$	1	-1	0	a_1	$(a_2 - b_2)$	$(a_4 - b_4)$
Fixed $\omega \to -\infty$	Flexible $\omega^f \to 0$	0	0	0	0	0	0
	Fixed $\omega^f \to -\infty$	0	0	0	0	0	0

where $\tilde{a}_j = kb_j + (1-k)c_j$. The home country can insulate its exchange rate from all shocks by fixing it against either one of the two foreign countries or a basket of both. In other cases, the choice of the nominal exchange rate between the two foreign countries matters for the effects of shocks on the nominal exchange rate of the home country. When foreign country two adopts a fixed exchange regime against foreign country one, then the former country's monetary policy will have no impact on the home country nominal exchange rate.

3. Model Solution

Following the literature, the endogenous variables of the model are obtained in closed-forms as a result of imposing a log-normality assumption for the distribution of the shocks hitting each economy. The equilibrium of the model for any monetary policy rule must satisfy: (a) the first order conditions for the utility maximization by home and foreign agents, (b) the risk sharing condition, (c) market clearing in inputs (labor and oil), composite consumption goods (traded and non-traded), bonds, and money, and (d) consolidated public sectors budget constraints.

The home country agent's optimal consumption and money holdings may be described by the following familiar conditions:

$$(1+i_{t+1}) = \frac{1}{\beta} E_t\left(\frac{P_{t+1}C_{t+1}^{\rho}}{P_t\, C_t^{\rho}}\right) \tag{43}$$

$$\frac{M_t}{P_t} = \chi\left(\frac{1+i_{t+1}}{i_{t+1}}\right)C_t^{\rho} \tag{44}$$

Foreign country one agent's optimal consumption, money holdings, and oil demand may similarly be described by the following conditions (those of foreign country two agent's are similar).

$$(1+i_{t+1}^{F1}) = \frac{1}{\beta} E_t\left(\frac{P_{t+1}^{F1}\left(C_{t+1}^{F1}\right)^{\rho}}{P_t^{F1}\left(C_t^{F1}\right)^{\rho}}\right) \tag{45}$$

$$\frac{M_t^{F1}}{P_t^{F1}} = \chi\left(\frac{1+i_{t+1}^{F1}}{i_{t+1}^{F1}}\right)\left(C_t^{F1}\right)^{\rho} \tag{46}$$

$$O_t^{F1}(z) = \left(\frac{\alpha}{1-\alpha}\right)^{1-\alpha}\left(\frac{P_t^{F1}}{P_{O,t}^{F1}}\left(C_t^{F1}\right)^{\rho}\right)^{1-\alpha}\left(\frac{Y_{T,t}^{F1}(z)}{\theta_t^{F1}}\right) \tag{47}$$

Equations (43) and (45) are the familiar stochastic Euler equations, while (44) and (46) are the money market clearing conditions. Equation (47) is the optimal demand for oil by the foreign country's agent. Also, from the bond holdings first order conditions, and due to the assumption of complete asset markets, we obtain the following risk-sharing condition

$$P_t\, C_t^{\rho} = S_t^{F1}P_t^{F1}\left(C_t^{F1}\right)^{\rho} = S_t^{F2}P_t^{F2}\left(C_t^{F2}\right)^{\rho} \tag{48}$$

Consumption is not equalized across countries since purchasing power parity (PPP) does not hold in this case due to the presence of nontraded goods. This property is discussed in detail by Corsetti and Pesenti (2005) and Devereux and Engel (2003).

Market Clearing Conditions

Both the consumption goods and the oil market clearing conditions are ensured in the derivation of the optimality conditions. The money market clearing condition is ensured by assuming that each country supplies the quantity of money demanded by its agents. The bond market clearing condition results from the zero net-foreign assets assumption, or

$$
\begin{aligned}
&n_{F1}B_{H,t}^{F1} + n_{F2}B_{H,t}^{F2} + n_H B_{H,t} = 0 \\
&n_{F1}B_{F1,t}^{F1} + n_{F2}B_{F1,t}^{F2} + n_H B_{F1,t} = 0 \\
&n_{F1}B_{F2,t}^{F1} + n_{F2}B_{F2,t}^{F2} + n_H B_{F2,t} = 0
\end{aligned}
\tag{49}
$$

Flexible Price Solution

The flexible price solution will serve as a benchmark for welfare evaluations. The flexible price solution is obtained by realizing that the pricing rules are valid in every state of the world and not just in expectations. We thus have

$$
C_t = \left(\frac{(\phi-1)\left(\alpha^{\alpha}(1-\alpha)^{1-\alpha}\right)^{\gamma}}{\phi} \right)^{\frac{1}{\rho(\alpha\gamma-1)}} \left(\frac{\left(\theta_t^{F1}\right)^{\gamma\eta}\left(\theta_t^{F2}\right)^{\gamma(1-\eta)}\left(\theta_t\right)^{1-\gamma}}{\left(p_{O,t}^{r}\right)^{\alpha\gamma}} \right)^{\frac{1}{\rho(\alpha\gamma-1)}}
\tag{50}
$$

Monetary neutrality is obtained in this case. As one expects, home consumption is higher with higher real oil price. Productivity shocks are positively related to consumption. The inter-country transmission of the productivity shocks is proportional to the trade proportions.

The expected value and the variance of log consumption for the home country under flexible prices are (assuming shocks follow log-normal process)

$$
E_{t-1}(c_t) = \frac{1}{\rho(1-\alpha\gamma)} \left\{ \Phi(t-1) - \frac{(1-\gamma)\sigma_U^2}{2} - \frac{\gamma\eta\sigma_{U_{F1}}^2}{2} - \frac{\gamma\eta\sigma_{U_{F2}}^2}{2} - \frac{\alpha^2\gamma\sigma_{\varepsilon}^2}{2} \right\} - \frac{1}{2}\sigma_c^2 + \Gamma_c
\tag{51}
$$

where: $\Phi(t-1) = -\alpha\gamma p_{o,t-1}^{r} + \gamma\eta\delta\log\theta_{t-1}^{F1} + \gamma(1-\eta)\delta\log\theta_{t-1}^{F2} + (1-\gamma)\delta\log\theta_{t-1}$

$$\sigma_c^2 = \frac{1}{(\rho(\alpha\gamma - 1))^2}\left\{\alpha^2\gamma^2\sigma_\varepsilon^2 + \gamma^2\eta^2\sigma_{U_{F1}}^2 + \gamma^2(1-\eta)^2\sigma_{U_{F2}}^2 + (1-\gamma)^2\sigma_U^2\right\} \tag{52}$$

Expected log consumption is decreasing in the volatility of consumption and in the volatility of productivity and real oil price shocks. The variance of log consumption is increasing in the volatility of real oil price and productivity shocks.

Producer Currency Pricing

Following the literature, when goods are invoiced in the producers' currency, the degree of pass-through from nominal exchange rates to import prices is one. In this case, shocks are transmitted through the nominal exchange rate. The explicit solution for the home agent's log consumption can be written in terms of the stochastic shocks and their variances as:

$$c_t = E_{t-1}(c_t) + \frac{1}{\rho}\left\{\Psi_1 v_t + \Psi_2 v_t^{F1} + \Psi_3 v_t^{F2} + \Psi_4 u_t + \Psi_5 u_t^{F1} + \Psi_6 u_t^{F2} + \Psi_7 \varepsilon_t\right\} \tag{53}$$

where: $\Psi_1 = \left(\frac{(1-\gamma)}{1-\omega}\right)$, $\Psi_2 = \left(\frac{\omega\omega^f - \gamma\omega^f - \omega((1-\gamma)k + \gamma\eta) + \gamma\eta}{(1-\omega)(1-\omega^f)}\right)$,

$$\Psi_3 = \left(\frac{\omega(1-(1-\gamma)k - \gamma\eta) - \gamma(1-\eta)}{(1-\omega)(1-\omega^f)}\right), \quad \Psi_4 = \left(\frac{(1-\gamma)a_1}{1-\omega}\right)$$

$$\Psi_j = \begin{pmatrix} \left(\frac{1-\gamma}{1-\omega}\right)a_j + \left(\frac{\omega\omega^f - \gamma\omega^f - \omega((1-\gamma)k + \gamma\eta) + \gamma\eta}{(1-\omega)(1-\omega^f)}\right)b_j \\ -\left(\frac{\omega(1-(1-\gamma)k - \gamma\eta) - \gamma(1-\eta)}{(1-\omega)(1-\omega^f)}\right)c_j \end{pmatrix}$$

$$j = 5,\ 6,\ and\ 7$$

where the expected value of the home country's log consumption is

$$E_{t-1}(c_t) = \frac{1}{\rho(1-\alpha\gamma)}\left\{\begin{array}{l} \Phi(t-1) - \frac{\gamma\eta\sigma_{S_{F1}}^2}{2} - \frac{\gamma(1-\eta)\sigma_{S_{F2}}^2}{2} - \frac{(1-\gamma)\sigma_U^2}{2} - \frac{\gamma\eta\sigma_{U_{F1}}^2}{2} \\ -\frac{\gamma\eta\sigma_{U_{F2}}^2}{2} - \frac{\alpha^2\gamma\sigma_\varepsilon^2}{2} - \frac{\sigma_V^2}{2} - \gamma(\rho^2\alpha^2 + \alpha\rho^2 - \alpha\rho)\sigma_c^2 \\ -(1-\rho-\gamma(1-\rho(\alpha+1)))\sigma_{mc} - \gamma(1-\rho(\alpha+1))(\sigma_{S_{F1}C} + \sigma_{S_{F2}C}) \\ +\Gamma_c \end{array}\right\} \tag{54}$$

where: $\Phi(t-1) = -\alpha\gamma p'^{r}_{o,t-1} + \gamma\eta\delta\log\theta^{F1}_{t-1} + \gamma(1-\eta)\delta\log\theta^{F2}_{t-1} + (1-\gamma)\delta\log\theta_{t-1}$

We can see that the expected value of log consumption for the home agent under producer currency pricing is negatively influenced by the volatility of the bilateral nominal exchange rate with each of the foreign countries weighted by the proportion of trade in traded goods. It is also negatively influenced by the variance of home and foreign productivity shocks and oil price shocks. It is also decreasing in the variance of log consumption. For $\rho(\gamma+1)<1$, the expected value of log consumption is decreasing with the covariance between home consumption and the bilateral nominal exchange rate with each of the two foreign countries. These covariances will probably be negative since a depreciation of the home currency against each of the two foreign currencies makes foreign imported goods more expensive, hence, lowers home consumption. Thus, they may offset the negative effect of the volatilities of the bilateral nominal exchange rates on log consumption. The home country's and foreign countries' monetary shocks affect the expected value of consumption through their effects on the variance of log consumption, as shown below. The variance of the home country's log consumption is:

$$\sigma_c^2 = \Psi_1^2\sigma_V^2 + \Psi_2^2\sigma_{V_{F1}}^2 + \Psi_3^2\sigma_{V_{F2}}^2 + \Psi_4^2\sigma_U^2 + \Psi_5^2\sigma_{U_{F1}}^2 + \Psi_6^2\sigma_{U_{F2}}^2 + \Psi_7^2\sigma_\varepsilon^2 \quad (55)$$

Higher volatility of each of the seven shocks, leads to higher consumption variance and lower expected log consumption. Thus, the influence of both the shocks and their variances on log consumption depends largely on the choice of the exchange rate regime and the reaction of the central banks in the three countries to the shocks. Table 3 summarizes the influence of each shock on log consumption, assuming other shocks are absent. Productivity shocks of foreign country two and oil price shocks have analogous impact on log consumption as that of foreign country one's productivity shocks, thus, we omit them for ease of exposition.

For a positive domestic monetary shock, log consumption will increase under a flexible exchange regime, and will have no effect under a fixed exchange rate regime. As we expect, under the flexible rate regime, the degree by which a domestic monetary shock affects log consumption is the proportion of nontraded goods in total consumption. This is no surprise, since domestic monetary policy can work through the local nontraded sector, the only production sector with labor/leisure choice in the home country. The impact of a positive foreign monetary shock on log consumption depends on the choice of the exchange rate regime between the two foreign countries. Foreign monetary shocks will affect the home country's consumption through its effect on the nominal exchange rate between home and each of the two foreign countries, which will be passed on to home's local prices. These results seem to be consistent with the literature. A positive foreign monetary shock that leads to a depreciation in the foreign currency and a higher foreign price level hurts home consumers in two ways: by decreasing their oil revenue purchasing-power and by increasing the price of imported goods when expressed in home currency. In summary, a fixed exchange rate regime can better stabilize log consumption against monetary shocks.

A positive domestic productivity shock in the nontraded sector increases log consumption only under a flexible exchange regime by the proportion of the nontraded sector in total consumption and has no impact under a fixed exchange regime. On the other hand, a positive foreign productivity shock increases log consumption under both regimes, flexible and fixed, with varying impacts depending on the response of the central banks in the two countries, assuming central banks accommodate productivity shocks by increasing the money supply. When the home country fixes its exchange rate, the influence of foreign productivity shocks on log consumption is determined only by the response of the foreign central bank to this shock. It can influence the impact of these shocks on its log consumption by choosing the appropriate weight k in the basket peg only when foreign country two adopts a flexible exchange rate regime against foreign country one. However, under a flexible exchange regime, home can influence the impact of productivity shocks by choosing optimal policy reaction coefficients $a_2, a_3,$ and a_4. Thus, the flexible exchange regime can better insulate log consumption from productivity shocks if the central bank of the home country is able to predict the response of the central bank in the foreign countries and act accordingly.

What has been said about foreign productivity shocks carries on to the real oil price shocks. The influence of a positive oil-price shock on log consumption will also depend on the response of the monetary authorities in the two countries to this shock and the choice of the exchange rate regime of both, the home country and foreign country two. The flexible exchange regime will better insulate log consumption against real oil-price shocks provided that the home central bank can zero the response of the foreign central banks. If the central bank of the foreign country does not respond to oil price shocks, then the impact of oil price shocks on home log consumption vanishes.

Table 3. The impact of shocks on log consumption of the home country under PCP

Home regime	Foreign country two regime	v_t	v_t^{F1}	v_t^{F2}	u_t	u_t^{F1}
Flexible $\omega \to 0$	Flexible $\omega^f \to 0$	$1-\gamma$	$\gamma\eta$	$\gamma(1-\eta)$	$(1-\gamma)a_1$	$(1-\gamma)a_2 + \gamma(\eta b_2 + (1-\eta)c_2)$
	Fixed $\omega^f \to -\infty$	$1-\gamma$	γ	0	$(1-\gamma)a_1$	$(1-\gamma)a_2 + \gamma b_2$
Fixed $\omega \to -\infty$	Flexible $\omega^f \to 0$	0	$((1-\gamma)k + \gamma\eta)$	$(1-\gamma)k + (1-\gamma\eta)$	0	$((1-\gamma)k + \gamma\eta)b_2 + (1-(1-\gamma)k - \gamma\eta)c_2$
	Fixed $\omega^f \to -\infty$	0	1	0	0	b_2

Table 3 also show that when the three countries are under a fixed exchange rate regime (when the home country and foreign country two chooses to fix their nominal exchange rate) then the impact of the shocks on home's log consumption is solely determined by the response of the independent-currency country, foreign country one.

Local Currency Pricing

With local currency pricing, we still have total expenditures on consumption equalized across countries due to the complete asset markets assumption. The degree of pass-through from nominal exchange rates to import prices is zero under LCP. Thus, the nominal exchange rate does not transmit shocks across countries. The log consumption of the home agent's is

$$c_t = E_{t-1}(c_t) + \frac{1}{\rho}\left\{\Gamma_1 v_t + \Gamma_2 v_t^{F1} + \Gamma_3 v_t^{F2} + \Gamma_4 u_t + \Gamma_5 u_t^{F1} + \Gamma_6 u_t^{F2} + \Gamma_7 \varepsilon_t\right\} \tag{56}$$

where: $\Gamma_1 = \left(\frac{1}{1-\omega}\right)$, $\Gamma_2 = \left(\frac{\omega(\omega^f - k)}{(1-\omega)(1-\omega^f)}\right)$, $\Gamma_3 = \left(\frac{-\omega(1-k)}{(1-\omega)(1-\omega^f)}\right)$, $\Gamma_4 = \left(\frac{a_1}{1-\omega}\right)$

$$\Gamma_j = \left(\left(\frac{1}{1-\omega}\right)a_j + \left(\frac{\omega(\omega^f - k)}{(1-\omega)(1-\omega^f)}\right)b_j - \left(\frac{\omega(1-k)}{(1-\omega)(1-\omega^f)}\right)c_j\right) \qquad j = 5,\ 6,\ and\ 7$$

The expected value of the home country's log consumption is

$$E_{t-1}(c_t) = \frac{1}{\rho(1-\alpha\gamma)}\left\{\begin{array}{l}\Phi(t-1) - \frac{(1-\gamma)\sigma_U^2}{2} - \frac{\gamma\eta\sigma_{U_{F1}}^2}{2} - \frac{\gamma\eta\sigma_{U_{F2}}^2}{2} - \frac{\alpha^2\gamma\sigma_{\varepsilon}^2}{2} - \frac{\gamma\sigma_V^2}{2} \\ -(1-\rho-\gamma(1-\rho(\alpha+1)))\sigma_{mc} - \gamma(\rho^2\alpha^2 + \alpha\rho^2 - \alpha\rho)\sigma_c^2 + \Gamma_c\end{array}\right\} \tag{57}$$

where: $\Phi(t-1) = -\alpha\gamma p_{o,t-1}^r + \gamma\eta\delta \log\theta_{t-1}^{F1} + \gamma(1-\eta)\delta\log\theta_{t-1}^{F2} + (1-\gamma)\delta\log\theta_{t-1}$

Differently from the case of producer currency pricing, the expected value of log consumption is not affected by the variance of the bilateral nominal exchange rate with each of the two foreign countries. The variance of the home country's log consumption is then:

$$\sigma_c^2 = \Gamma_1^2\sigma_V^2 + \Gamma_2^2\sigma_{V_{F1}}^2 + \Gamma_3^2\sigma_{V_{F2}}^2 + \Gamma_4^2\sigma_U^2 + \Gamma_5^2\sigma_{U_{F1}}^2 + \Gamma_6^2\sigma_{U_{F2}}^2 + \Gamma_7^2\sigma_{\varepsilon}^2 \tag{58}$$

To compare the two pricing schemes, the impact of a one unit shock in each of the shocks, shutting-off other shocks, on log consumption can similarly be summarized in Table 4.

As noted above, with local currency pricing, the degree of pass-through from nominal exchange rate to local prices is zero, since prices are already set in local currency. We can see that the impact of local monetary shock is higher under local currency pricing when the home country adopts a flexible exchange rate regime. Foreign monetary shocks have no impact on log consumption when the home country allows its nominal exchange rate to be fully flexible. For the foreign productivity shocks and real oil price shocks, the impact is solely determined by the response of the home central bank to these shocks if the latter allows the nominal exchange rate to be fully flexible. Given a freely flexible exchange rate between the two foreign countries, if the home country fixes its nominal exchange rate then the effect of foreign monetary shocks is determined by the weights of the composite nominal exchange rate against the two foreign countries. Similar analyses are valid for the foreign productivity and oil shocks. In summary, when consumption goods are priced in the home country's currency, the effects of monetary, productivity, and oil shocks on log consumption are generally lower and more controllable than when they are priced in the currency of the producers.

Under flexible exchange rate regime, the implications of local currency pricing on monetary policy are substantial. This is because changes in nominal exchange rates will not affect relative prices between domestic and imported goods. As noted by Devereux and Engel (2003), LCP is consistent with fixed exchange rate regimes when only traded goods are considered. However, recently Duarte (2004) show that a flexible exchange rate regime might still be advantageous in case of distinctive nontraded productivity shocks (specific country shocks). As shown in Table 4., the impact of foreign real shocks (productivity and oil price shocks) depends solely on the reaction of the home country's central bank when the latter adopts a flexible a flexible exchange rate regime. However, when it chooses a fixed exchange rate regime, the reactions of the foreign central banks will affect the log consumption of the home country. The home country's central bank cannot offset these reactions since money supply is endogenous under a fixed exchange rate regime.

4. Welfare Evaluations

The welfare criterion for choosing the optimal exchange rate regime under different assumptions about shocks is the conditional expected utility level, which depends on expected level of consumption, variance of consumption, and expected disutility of efforts. Following the literature, we ignore the utility from holdings of real money balances (assume $\chi \to 0$). This is because real money balances enter the utility function as a means to generate a demand for money. Since there are other ways to derive a demand for real balances (e.g. Cash-In-Advance method) it is safe to ignore utility from real balances in comparing welfare. Our welfare criterion is then:

$$EU_t = E\left(\frac{C_t^{1-\rho}}{1-\rho}\right) - E(L_t) \tag{59}$$

We assume that utility is the same each period (stationary). This is due to the complete markets assumption (free capital mobility) and the one period ahead pricing policies by agents (see Obstfeld and Rogoff (1998)).

Since we assume that the shocks follow log-normal distributions, the solution of the endogenous variables should follow log-normal distributions as well. Thus, we can express expected utility of consumption in terms of the mean of log consumption and the variance of log consumption ($E(C^{1-\rho}) = \exp(1-\rho)\left[E(c) + ((1-\rho)/2)\sigma_c^2\right]$).

Table 4. The impact of shocks on log consumption of the home country under LCP

Home Regime	Foreign country two regime	v_t	v_t^{F1}	v_t^{F2}	u_t	u_t^{F1}
Flexible $\omega \to 0$	Flexible $\omega^f \to 0$	1	0	0	a_1	a_2
	Fixed $\omega^f \to -\infty$	1	0	0	a_1	a_2
Fixed $\omega \to -\infty$	Flexible $\omega^f \to 0$	0	k	$1-k$	0	$kb_2+(1-k)c_2$
	Fixed $\omega^f \to -\infty$	0	1	0	0	b_2

To complete the welfare evaluation, we need to find the expected level of employment. For the home agent,

$$E(L_{N,t}) = \frac{(1-\gamma)(\phi-1)}{\phi} E(C_t^{1-\rho}) \tag{60}$$

Equation (60) shows that the expected level of efforts is a linear function of $E(C_t^{1-\rho})$. Thus, we can base our welfare analysis on utility from consumption. The welfare measure can then be reduced to

$$EU_t = \left(\frac{\phi-(1-\rho)(1-\gamma)(\phi-1)}{\phi(1-\rho)} \right) \exp(1-\rho)\left(Ec_t + \frac{(1-\rho)}{2}\sigma_c^2 \right) \tag{61}$$

Using (61), we can compare alternative monetary policy/exchange rate regime choice for the two pricing schemes (PCP and LCP). Equation (61) can be written in terms of the variances of the shocks and the covariances once we substitute for the expected value and the variance of log consumption. The expected utility is increasing in the variance of log consumption for any values of the risk aversion coefficient, ρ. The variance of log consumption is generally lower under LCP since the volatility of the nominal exchange rate is absent. In terms of expected log consumption, it is not clear which pricing-scheme dominates. This is because for producer currency pricing, the positive impact on expected consumption of the covariances between consumption and nominal exchange rates might offset the negative effects of nominal exchange rate volatility. Thus, it is unclear whether expected utility is higher under producer currency pricing. The question that needs to be addressed then is given the export-pricing scheme, what is the optimal exchange rate regime that maximizes the home agent's utility. We can observe that the home agents are better off under producer currency pricing adopting a flexible exchange rate regime. This is due to the standard argument in favor of a flexible exchange rate regime of active monetary policy. The central bank in the home country will have a free-hand to respond to the shocks. This is also true under local currency pricing, practically if the real foreign shocks are dominant.

However, given the information requirement to conduct optimal monetary policy, one should consider the choice of a fixed exchange rate regime for the home country as a second-best alternative. In this case, the home country is faced with the choice between fixing its exchange rate to one of the foreign countries or a basket of both. The relevant case to consider is when the two foreign countries are in a flexible exchange rate regime against each other.

Under producer currency pricing, the optimal weight (k) to fix the exchange rate against foreign country one is

$$k^{PCP} = \frac{\left(\frac{\gamma^2\eta}{1-\gamma}\right)\sigma^2_{V_{F1}} + \left(\frac{\gamma(1-\gamma\eta)}{1-\gamma}\right)\sigma^2_{V_{F2}} - \sum_{j=2}^{4}(b_j - c_j)(\gamma\eta b_j + (1-\gamma\eta)c_j)}{\gamma\left(\sigma^2_{V_{F1}} + \sigma^2_{V_{F2}}\right) + \sum_{j=2}^{4}(b_j - c_j)^2\sigma^2_j} \tag{62}$$

where $j = 2,3, and\ 4$, $\sigma^2_2 = \sigma^2_{U_{F1}}, \sigma^2_3 = \sigma^2_{U_{F2}}, and\ \sigma^2_4 = \sigma^2_{\varepsilon}$. The optimal weight is a complicated function of foreign monetary, productivity, and real oil price shock variances as well as the response functions of the foreign central banks to theses shocks. If the two foreign countries follow a random walk money supply rule (i.e. when the monetary rule does not respond to productivity or real oil price shocks) or if they respond equally to these shocks, then the optimal weight for the basket peg will merely reflect the relative variance of uncontrollable money supply shocks.

On the other hand, when we assume local currency pricing, the optimal weight to fix the exchange rate against foreign country one is

$$k^{LCP} = \frac{\sigma^2_{V_{F2}} - \sum_{j=2}^{4} c_j(b_j - c_j)}{\sigma^2_{V_{F1}} + \sigma^2_{V_{F2}} + \sum_{j=2}^{4}(b_j - c_j)^2\sigma^2_j} \tag{63}$$

Again, if we assume that the two foreign central banks will respond to own and foreign productivity shocks and oil shocks equally, or if they allow their money supply to follow a random walk process (i.e. they set their reaction parameters equal to zero), then the optimal weight to fix against foreign country one is the proportion of foreign country two's monetary shocks in the two foreign countries' monetary shocks. That is, the home country should put more weight to the country with less monetary disturbances. The determination of the optimal currency basket weight demands overwhelming information about the variance of the shocks and the expected response of foreign central banks. Thus, from (62) and (63), we conclude that in the case of a fixed exchange rate regime, a basket peg is better than a unilateral peg to the currency of one of the two foreign countries.

The choice of the monetary rule reaction coefficients depends on the exchange rate regime being adopted by the home country, on price-setting of imports (PCP vs. LCP), and on the reaction coefficients of the two foreign countries. In the case of a fixed exchange rate regime, the monetary policy will be directed toward maintaining the exchange rate at its parity. However, only under a flexible exchange rate regime will the home country have the freedom to respond to productivity and oil price shocks. Here, we solve for the optimal reaction coefficients for the home country's monetary rule. We assume that the three countries will be under a flexible exchange rate regime. The home country chooses its optimal reaction coefficients given the reaction coefficients of the other two countries.

$$a_1^{PCP} = 0,\ a_1^{LCP} = 0 \tag{64}$$

$$a_j^{PCP} = \frac{-\gamma(\eta b_2 + (1-\eta)c_2)}{1-\gamma},\ a_j^{LCP} = 0, \qquad j = 2, 3, \textit{and } 4 \tag{65}$$

For a positive home productivity shock that affects the nontraded sector, expected nontraded consumption will increase and expected prices will decrease, boosting the nominal interest rate. However, since the home country has no traded sector, the optimal response of the central bank is zero change in money supply. This is because an increase or a decrease in money supply will affect the nominal exchange rate with the two foreign countries. This in turn affects home country's consumption of traded goods. For a positive foreign productivity or oil price shock, the response of the home country's central bank will depend on the response of the two foreign countries to these shocks. For example, a higher oil price that is expected to be permanent will increase the home country's expected consumption due to higher revenue, but it will increase expected future prices due to the higher input costs in the foreign country. Since we assume prices are set one period in advance, consumption will increase this period leading to higher nominal interest rate. If we assume that the two foreign countries will respond positively to this shock, then the optimal response of the home country's central bank is to reduce the money supply.[42] We can see from (64) and (65) that a passive monetary policy (with respect to real shocks) is consistent with LCP. As noted above, allowing the nominal exchange rate to be flexible dominants a fixed exchange rate policy in terms of welfare. More specifically, a flexible exchange rate regime results in a lower variance of consumption under LCP, given the assumption of active monetary policies for the two foreign countries.

CONCLUSION

In this chapter, the optimal choice of exchange rate regime for the oil-exporting GCC countries is analyzed. The chapter extends the new Keynesian small open economy model to allow for a three-country, the home country and two foreign countries. The solution of the model shows that the optimal exchange rate regime for an oil-exporting country depends on pricing-schemes of its imports as well as the response of its trading-partners to their productivity shocks and to the oil-price shocks. Under both pricing-schemes, producer currency pricing and local currency pricing, a flexible exchange regime can improve the welfare of home agents provided that the central bank in the home country (the oil-exporting country) is able to predict both the shocks and the response of the foreign central banks to these shocks. This does not seem feasible given the current monetary and financial developments in the GCC countries. In other words, the impact of monetary, productivity,

[42] Devereux and Engel (2003) show that increasing the money supply is the optimal response of the central bank to a positive productivity shock (domestic or foreign) in a two-country model.

and oil price shocks on the utility of agents in an oil exporting county is lower when a fixed exchange rate regime is adopted and at the same time the response of the central bank in this country is passive to these shocks compared to the response of the central bank in the country with which it fixes its currency. Welfare analyses also show that, in the case of a fixed exchange rate regime, a basket peg is better than a unilateral peg to a single currency. Also, a fixed exchange rate regime is more welfare-improving the stable is the currency in which oil-price is denominated.

REFERENCES

Adolfson, M., Laseén, S., Lindé, J. & Villani, M. (2008). Evaluating an estimated new keynesian small open economy model. *Journal of Economic Dynamics and Control*, *32*(8), 2690-2721.

Berger, H., Jensen, H. & Schjelderup, G. (2001). To peg or not to peg? A simple model of exchange rate regime choice in small economies. *Economics Letters*, *73*, 161-167.

Corsetti, G. & Pesenti, P. (2005). International dimension of optimal monetary policy. *Journal of Monetary Economics*, *52*(2), 281-305.

Coudert, V., Couharde, C. & Mignon, V. (2011). Does euro or dollar pegging impact the real exchange rate? The case of oil and commodity currencies. *The World Economy*, *34*(9), 1557-1592.

Devereux, M. & Engel, C. (1998). Fixed versus floating exchange rates: how price setting affects the optimal choice of exchange rate regime. *National Bureau of Economics Research* Working Paper No. 6867 (Cambridge, MA:NBER).

Devereux, M. & Engel, C. (2003). Monetary policy in the open economy revisited: price setting and exchange rate flexibility. *Review of Economic Studies*, *70*, 765-783.

Dornbusch, R. (1973). Devaluation, money and non-traded goods. *American Economic Review*, *63*, 871-80.

Duarte, M. (2004). Monetary policy and the adjustment to country-specific shocks. *Federal Reserve Bank of Richmond*, Economic Quarterly, Volume *90*/2.

Engel, C. (2009). Currency misalignment and optimal monetary policy: A reexamination. *National Bureau of Economic Research* Working Paper No. 14829 (Cambridge, MA:NBER).

Frankel, J. (2005). Peg the export price index: a proposed monetary regime for small countries. *Journal of Policy Modeling*, *27*, 495-508.

Galí, J. & Monacelli, T. (2005). Monetary policy and exchange rate volatility in a small open economy. *Review of Economic Studies*, *72*(3), 707–34.

IMF. (2011). Gulf Cooperation Council Countries: Enhancing economic outcomes in an uncertain global economy. Middle East and Central Asia Department, International Monetary Fund, Washington, D.C.

Obstfeld, M. & Rogoff, K. (1995). Exchange rate dynamics redux. *Journal of Political Economy*, *103*(3), 624-660.

Obstfeld, M. & Rogoff, K. (1996). *Foundations of international macroeconomics*. Cambridge, MIT Press.

Obstfeld, M. & Rogoff, K. (1998). Risk and exchange rates. *National Bureau of Economic Research*, Working Paper No. 6694.

Obstfeld, M. & Rogoff, K. (2000). New directions for stochastic open economy models. *Journal of International Economics*, *50*(1), 117-153.

Sevensson, L. (1999). Inflation targeting as a monetary policy rule. *Journal of Monetary Economics*, *43* (3), 607-54.

Squalli, J. (2011). Is the dollar peg suitable for the largest economies of the Gulf Cooperation Council? *Journal of International Financial Markets, Institutions & Money*, *21*, 496-512.

In: Exchange Rates in Developed and Emerging Markets
Editor: Mohsen Bahmani-Oskooee
ISBN: 978-1-62808-164-0

Chapter 9

THE EFFECTS OF CENTRAL BANKS' INDEPENDENCE ON INFLATION OUTCOMES IN EMERGING COUNTRIES: DOES THE CHOICE OF EXCHANGE REGIME MATTER?

Jamal Bouoiyour[1,*] and Refk Selmi[2]
[1]CATT, Center of analysis and processing of data, University of Pau, France
[2]ESC, High School of Trade, University of Manouba, Tunisia

ABSTRACT

This chapter considers the benefits and the drawbacks of the choice of exchange regime on the central bank independence effects on inflation outcomes. The analysis of data of inflation, central bank independence, exchange regime either fixed or floating and other explanatory variables of twelve emerging countries from 1991 to 2009 provides strong support for the theoretical viewpoint, whereby regulatory separation exerts a substantial effect on inflation dynamic. More precisely, this study explores empirical evidence that low inflation outcomes may be achieved by setting up central bank independence which itself should be accompanied by pegged exchange regime. Furthermore, we note obviously that matter which classification is employed either de facto or de jure, the effect of regulatory separation on inflation outcomes is lower in countries operating under fixed exchange regime than those operating under floating peg. These results do not change substantively when changing the model (i.e. ordinary least squares with two-way fixed effects chosen by Hausman test and Arellano and Bond method or when including the multiplicative interaction terms) or when changing exchange classifications (i.e. de jure and de facto). This means that our results are robust.

JEL Classification: E31; E52; E58; F31

Keywords: Exchange regime, inflation, central bank independence

---

* Corresponding author: E-mail : jamal.bouoiyour@univ-pau.fr.

1. INTRODUCTION

The debates relative to the relationship between central banks' independence, exchange regime and inflation dynamic are not recent. The climate of high inflation has brought monetary authorities to worry about the possible effects of exchange rate movements on inflation. In particular, they worried about the possible formation of a vicious circle whereby high exchange rate fluctuations accentuate the expectations of higher inflation level in the future. Hence, the literature survey has developed a large consensus on the linkage between inflation outcomes, exchange regime, central bank's independence and other fundamentals[43] trying to identify the main concepts in inflation outcomes determinants framework.

Alogoskoufis and Smith (1991) found empirical evidence that exchange regimes matter for the persistence of inflation. They demonstrate that fixed exchange rate regime appears to be associated with negligible persistence of inflation volatility, while managed exchange regime is associated with very high inflation persistence. Among the same lines, Dani (2000) added that The institutional structure of the central bank hereafter may have an intense influence on dampening the inflation level when each country is operating under floating exchange system but with an important size portion of its banking sector (e.g. Dani, 2000). Perhaps more importantly, they show that independent central banks and fixed exchange regimes are institutional mechanisms that enable to keep a low level of inflation.

More recently, Colpelovitch and Singer (2007) confirm that the influence of separate agency to mitigate the inflationary pressures is conditional on the degree of flexibility of exchange rate and the size associated to banking sector. In almost the same vein, Guisinger and Singer (2010) argue that monetary authorities' attempt is to keep the stability of prices by adopting a fixed exchange rate system, i.e. this latter serve as a signal of government's lower inflation level.

Regardless of the approach taken, two issues have a great interest in international economics and a special attention from academics: Firstly, to determine the key determinants of inflation pressures, in particular, because in the short run, it is still difficult to identify the reasons behind an increase in inflation rate level and an excessive inflation volatility (e.g. Bleaney and Fielding (2002) and Alfaro (2005)). Secondly, to identify the impact of independent central banks on inflation rate and its evolution under different classifications of exchange regime (e.g. Guisinger and Singer, 2010), especially because central banks' independence in emerging countries is lower and reforms are infrequent (e.g. Cobham, 2012).

It is conceivable then that various theoretical and empirical studies demonstrate the capacity of central banks to choose the final goals of monetary policy to adjust its policy tools and to operate independent instruments freely in order to track its main objectives such as gradually reducing inflation (i.e. a high level of independence and especially more effective financial regulation of central banks are important to assure price stability). Various questions can be raised then: why do some emerging countries have separate agencies to supervise the central banks and others do not? What impact of supervision does it have on central banks' activities? Does independence of central banks matter in terms of linkage between exchange regime and inflation? Does regulatory separation make a different inflation behavior? What lessons can be drawn as regards the effect of financial regulation on the link between exchange regime and inflation outcomes?

---

[43] See Appendix A.

As stated above, several studies assess the question of the linkage between inflation, exchange regime and central bank independence in developed countries (e.g. Canavan and Tommasi (1997), Dani (2000), etc...) in comparison to the literature survey on the relationship between inflation pressures with the degree of democracy and banking sector size (e.g. Colpelovitch and Singer, 2007). Very few works have been advanced on central bank independence effects on inflation in emerging countries (e.g. Zare et al. (2012) and Cobham (2012)) and in our knowledge there are no studies on the relationship between inflation outcomes and regulatory separation by using a panel of emerging countries taking into account the effects of the effects of exchange regime, banking sector size and the level of democracy and then the multiplicative interaction terms between these variables.

To achieve this goal, we derive other testable questions which can bring additional explanations on the possible effects of regulatory separation on inflation dynamic as well as its interaction with the choice of exchange regime: What do central banks of emerging countries actually do? What role does pegged exchange regime play when it comes to the effect of central bank independence and inflation outcomes? What are the hallmarks of the choice of pegged exchange regime? Or what do peg exchange regime' gains in terms of the central bank independence's effect on inflation dynamic? More generally, do fixed or float exchange regime matter for inflation? Does an unfavorable choice of exchange regime can threaten central banks' independence effects on inflation outcomes? Can the inclusion of democracy and banking sector size make a difference?

Intuitively, this chapter will offer new perspectives on the determinants of inflation outcomes. More precisely, we want to know whether the link between inflation dynamic and financial regulation driver by the dependency or not of the central banks to separate agencies (e.g. Cukierman (1992), Maxfield (1997), Clark (2002), Bodea (2009), etc...) depends intensely on the choice of exchange regime. Hence, the main purpose here is to verify theoretically and empirically if inflation outcomes may be achieved by setting up independent central banks and if this is conditional on the choice of exchange regime as well as the degree of democracy and the banking sector size (e.g. Colpelovitch and Singer, 2007).

The remainder of this chapter proceeds as follows: Section 2 presents a brief overview of inflation trajectory and its interaction with central bank independence in 12 emerging countries [44](Algeria, Egypt, Jordan, Iran, Kuwait, Lebanon, Morocco, Oman, Qatar, Saudi Arabia, Sudan and Tunisia) depending on the choice of exchange regime either fixed or floating under two classifications (i.e. de jure versus de facto)[45]. Section 3 describes the data sets of selected emerging countries that we use to evaluate the relationship between inflation, exchange regime, central bank independence and other explanatory variables. This latter section presents our empirical results and robustness check by using ordinary least squares with two-way fixed effects chosen by Hausman test and Arellano and Bond method with and without multiplicative interaction terms. The last section concludes our paper.

---

[44] We choose here some emerging countries with different exchange regimes and central bank structures, but with almost the same inflation behavior.

[45] See Appendix B.

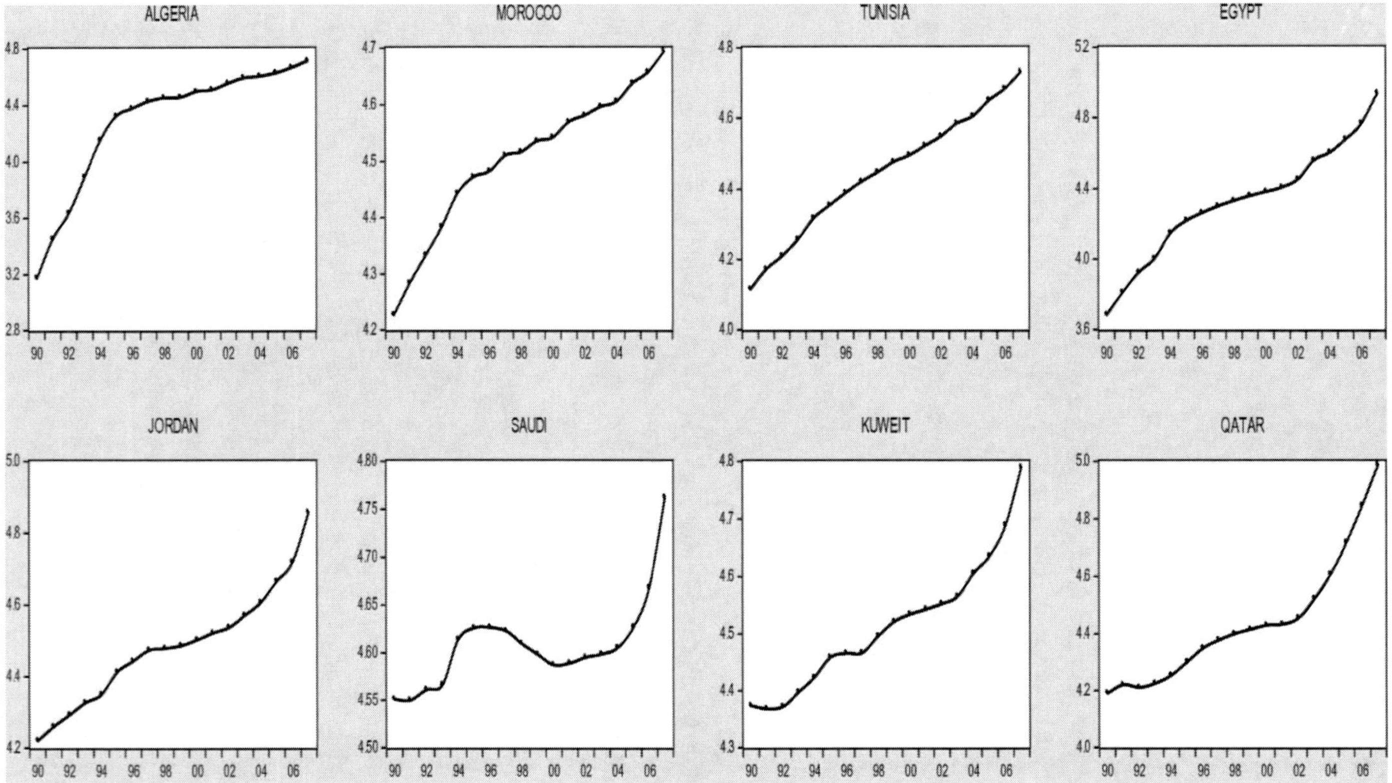

Figure 1. (Continued).

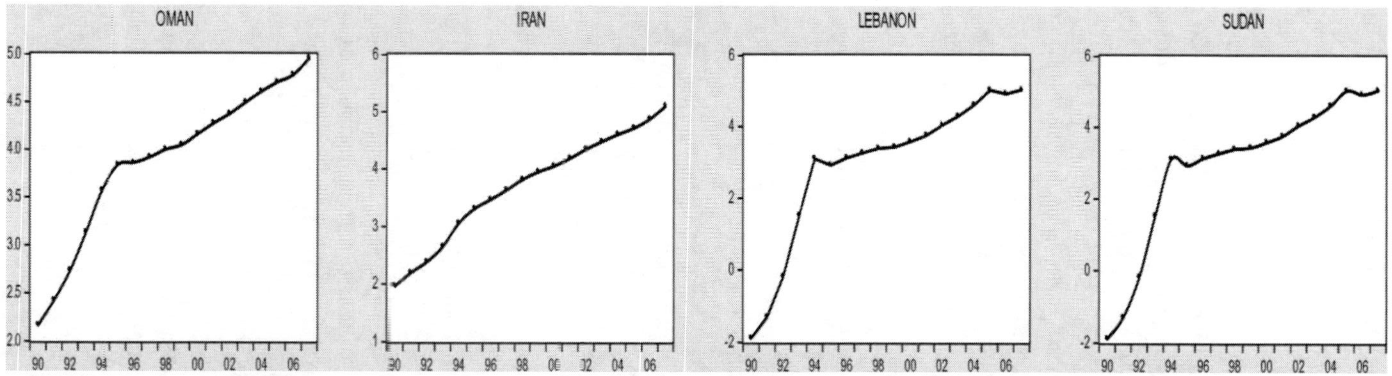

Source: Usherbrooke data (University of Canada): http://perspective.usherbrooke.ca/bilan/statistiques/2

Figure 1. Inflation evolution in selected emerging countries.

2. Central Bank Independence, Inflation Dynamic and Exchange Regime in Emerging Countries: An Update Overview

In emerging countries, the inflation surged quickly across the period from 1990 to 2009 (see Figure 1). This is mainly due to the geopolitical tension such as the Iranian-Iraqian wars in 1988 and Gulf war 1990-1991. In the early 2000s, we note that in the majority of considered countries, the inflation rate has declined. Hereafter, we note that inflation start to increase widely. This may be explained by exogenous shocks to the region, such as American-Iraqian tension in 2003, which led to higher price for oil, translating itself to other commodity prices on international market and then to exchange rates (see Bouoiyour and Selmi, 2012), reflecting stronger demand from emerging market countries.

Just as the main advantage of central bank independence may be that it allows monetary authorities to maintain stable prices closely associated as mentioned above to the choice of exchange regime, it will be crucial in the following to assess in detail this linkage.

2.1. Central Bank's Independence and Inflation Dynamic

In emerging countries, the central banks are the monetary authorities responsible for monetary and exchange policies which operate with various degrees of economic and political autonomy (see Figure 2). They dispose financial instruments that may be private or public to regulate the credit, exchange rate, interest rate and inflation level. They also implement restrictions on banking activities. However, central banks and regulatory agencies emerged as completely separate entities in very few emerging countries (e.g. Cobham, 2012).

Furthermore, it is not easy to determine the effect of regulatory separation on the evolution of inflation level. In this context and according to Copelovitch and Singer (2007) and Dumiter (2009), central bank independence is quite difficult to be assessed and quantified (i.e. there is no single definition or measure of this variable). Nonetheless, a large literature survey on this topic provides evidence that independent central banks foster less volatile inflation rates. Is this viewpoint absolutely true?

As our objective in this study is to clarify the importance of central banks' intervention either is dependent or independent as a key determinant of inflation outcomes, it is important first of all to describe the policies adopted by the central banks of the considered countries in our study period (i.e. from 1990 to 2009).

From 1990 to 1995, the Bank of Algeria is not independent. This is due to the fact that its economy was in bad shape. Many factors constrained the independence of Algerian Bank in that period, such as the high level of unemployment of 30%, a budget deficit of 8.7% and a deficit of balance of trade (e.g. Zaouache and Ilmane, 2008). However, these factors were relaxed in the year 2000; the dinar was more stable against the US dollar, the oil price increased leading to a favorable balance of trade.

In addition and in the considered period, the central banks of Egypt, Iran, Jordan and Lebanon are autonomous entities whose have as main functions to maintain economic stability and developing financial markets. Nevertheless, the central bank of Iran has given more independence in its bank supervisory in comparison to other countries in question (e.g. Cobham, 2012).

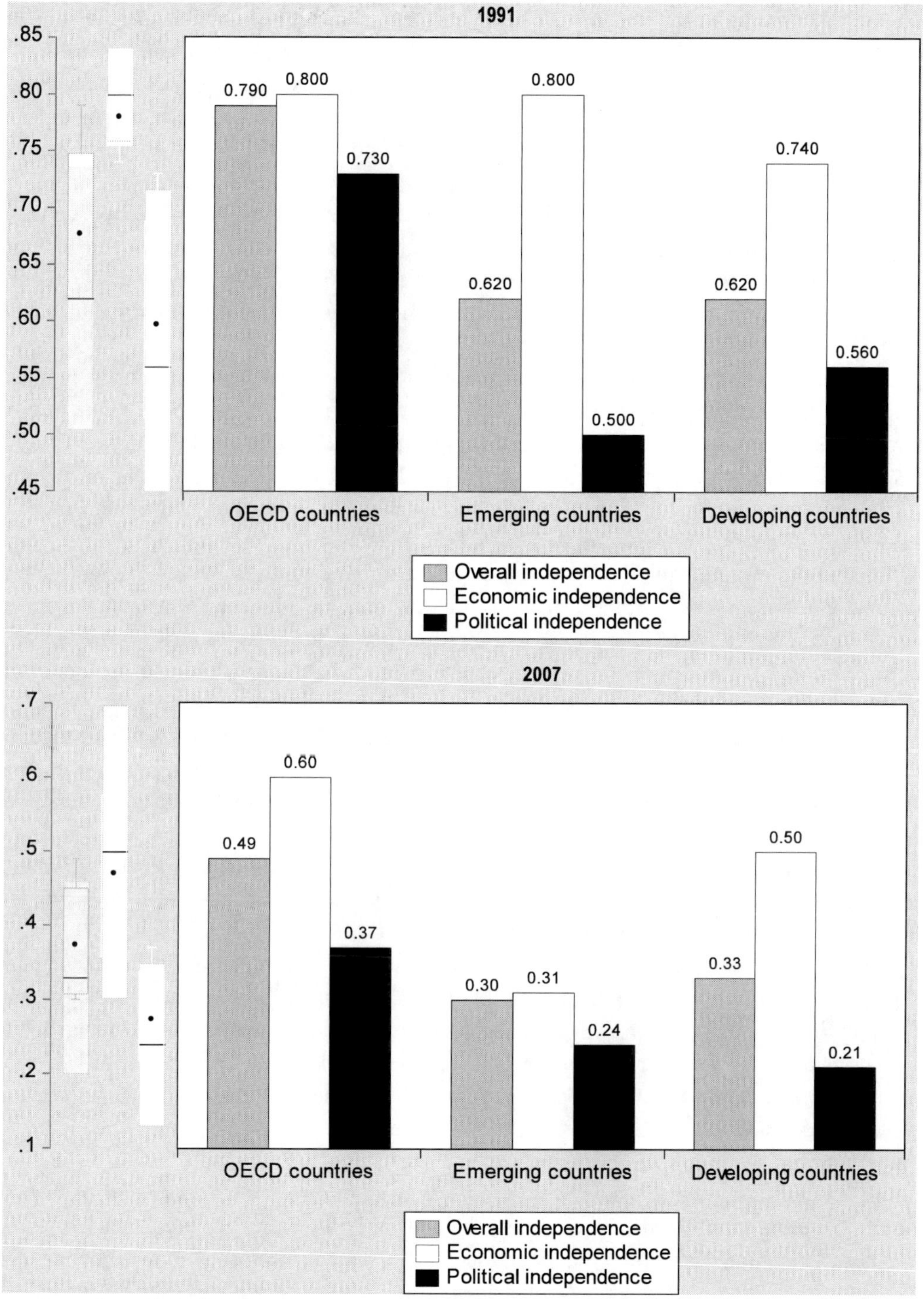

Source: Data from IMF (2006) and Arnone et al. (2008).

Figure 2. Central banks' independence by using GMT index.

Besides, in that period (i.e. from 1990 to 2009), the central banks of Morocco and Tunisia which have almost the same conduct in terms of exchange and monetary policies are autonomous like most of the emerging countries, trying to keep the inflation level in target to retain a competitive position in terms of trade performance (e.g. Bouoiyour and Selmi, 2012). Morocco tries to establish a new regulatory banking act for all credit institutions which succeed in reinforcing the power of the central bank in regulating and supervising the activities of credit institutions (e.g. Cobham, 2012). For Tunisian case, the banking legislation starts by modifying regulatory separation and supervision in 1994. Later on, an amendment which expands the central banks' activity takes place (e.g. Arnone et al. 2006).

Then, Kuwait, Oman, Qatar and Saudi Arabia implement a monetary policy capable of ensuring and achieving price stability and support their currencies either to facilitate a transition toward total convertibility into other currencies, especially the US dollar (cases of Kuwait, Qatar and Saudi Arabia) or to control the movements of nominal exchange rate into foreign exchange rates of its principal partners (case of Oman).

To some extent, the independence of central banks in emerging countries potentially depends on the organization of the banking system, the role of monetary policy, the degree of democracy and the management of the exchange rate. Indeed, the independence of central banks is difficult to be quantified.

To determine this degree, many indicators can be used, including Cukierman index and GMT index[46]. The first one is initiated by Cukierman (1991) presented in Figure 2 which confirms that the central banks' independence in emerging countries is very low with average around 6.28%. We also notice that the overall independence of the central banks of Egypt, Morocco and Tunisia were compared well with other emerging countries. The degree of independence in GCC countries (Kuweit, Qatar and Saudi Arabia) is the lowest in comparison to other emerging countries in question, except Algeria. The second one (e.g. Grilli et al. (1991) and Arnone et al. (2008) show that developed and OECD countries have progressed in terms of political autonomy than economic autonomy, contrary to emerging countries (see Figure 2). Concretely, this figure presents in detail the economic and political independence in the considered countries.

Hence by basing on this index, we show that Morocco and Tunisia which have a medium sized banking sector are characterized by an important level of economic independence. Algeria with its small banking sector considerably dominated by the public sector banks compared well to other countries in terms political independence. The Egypt's banking sector is large relative to the size of its economy distinguished during high economic independence and low political one. The same variable is scored for Iran characterized by a small banking sector considerably dominated by public sector element as having high economic independence and zero political independence, similar to Sudan's central bank independence. All considered GCC countries (i.e. Oman, Qatar, Saudi Arabia, and the UAE) are characterized by medium-sized banking sector (except Oman with small banking sector size) and high concentration, particularly the dominance of public sector (except Saudi Arabia with moderate concentration). In these countries, the central bank independence assessed by GMT index as having high economic independence and very low political independence. Saudi Arabia has an overall independence below the average of GCC countries (e.g. Cobham, 2012) but in terms of political independence, the UAE is well above that of Saudi Arabia.

[46] Various indicators of central bank independence are reported in Appendix C.

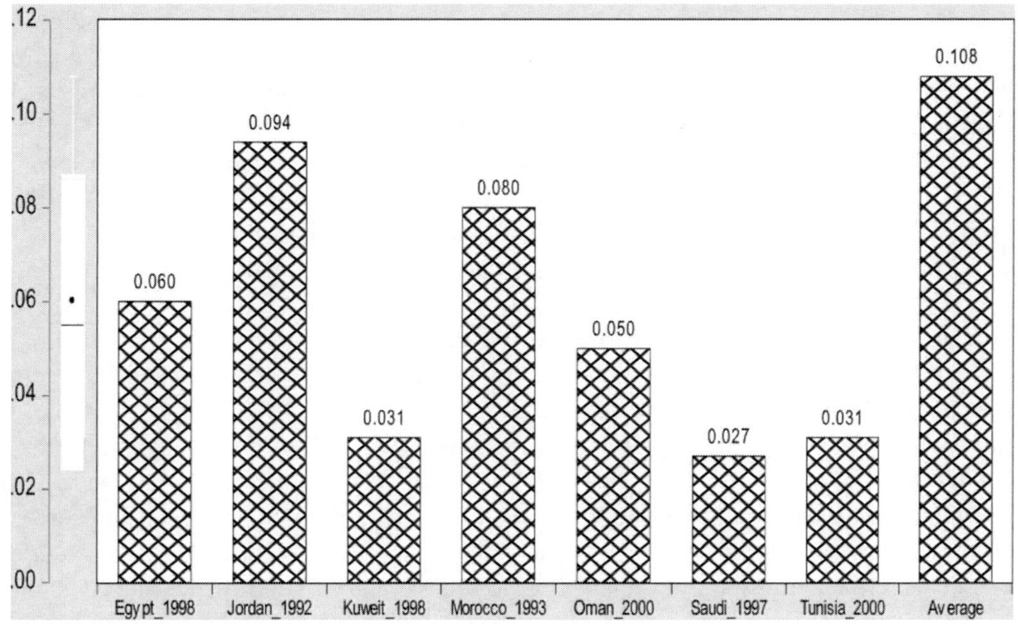

Source: Arnone et al. (2006).

Figure 3. Central Banks' independence in selected emerging countries.

2.2. Exchange Regime and Inflation Dynamic

The emerging countries have adopted various exchange regimes and have modified usually their choice. It is useful and valuable here to compare between de jure exchange rate regimes classified by the IMF and the de facto exchange rate regimes proposed by Reinhart and Rogoff (2004). This allows us to highlight the differences between the statements of the monetary authorities of emerging countries.

Let us start with Algeria. This small open economy adopts a managed float (pegged to euro) in terms of de jure classification, but in practice (i.e. de facto) the Algerian currency is more aligned with the US dollar. In Morocco and Tunisia, the exchange rates are pegged to the Euro, but not aligned to this latter. Nevertheless, the currencies of Jordan, Lebanon, Syria and Sudan are narrowly aligned in practice with the dollar. However, the Egyptian currency seems to be unaligned with the dollar as well as the euro (de facto). Similarly, Iran is distinguished by a managed float unaligned with the dollar (in practice). Still the GCC countries (mentioned above), in overall, these economies adopt hard pegged exchange rate system to the dollar except Kuwait which recently switch to a peg to a basket of currencies but "dollar still the largest component" (e.g. Cobham, 2012).

Furthermore and from Figure 3, we note that the percentage of emerging countries with de jure fixed exchange rates has been a steady decline since 1990, reflecting a level shift in favor of floating exchange regime from 1990 to 1995. Between 1999 and 2005, this percentage increase by a large gap from 30% to more than 50%. Since 2005, there is a decline from 52% to 47%. The increase in percentage observed between 1995 and 2005 reflects a shifting in favor of fixing exchange regime which may be mainly due to the fear of floating especially after the introduction of euro (the adoption of the euro by several emerging countries (e.g. Algeria, Morocco, Tunisia, etc…) can reverse according to Guisinger and Singer (2010) the overall trend. More interestingly, we note according to Figure 4, that over the last period from 1996 to 2007, the pegged exchange regime still the most adopted regime in emerging countries with 58.19% compared with 88.89% over the period 1977-1985. In contrast, we show an increase on the share of floating exchange regime from 8.15% percent over the period 1977-1985 to nearly 36% in the last sub-period. So, can governments in emerging countries obtain low inflation levels by limiting exchange movements?

To answer this question, it will be important to compare inflation performance under fixed, pegged and float exchange rate arrangements by using two exchange rate classifications (de jure and de facto). Hence, Figure 5 reveals obviously that the de jure and de facto classifications assign the lowest inflation outcomes to the fixed exchange rate and the highest ones associated to the floating exchange regime.

In contrast, Guisinger and Singer (2010) argue that de facto fixed exchange regime is not associated itself to lower inflation rate. More precisely, they advance that only the countries which linked their facto exchange regimes with de jure pronouncements can receive the benefits of inflation control. They explain this idea by the nonlinear nature which distinguishes the relationship between exchange regime and inflation which depends on the assumptions of other variables such as central banks' independence, democracy and banking sector size, etc… Therefore and because building credible monetary policy is a difficult task, especially in emerging countries (e.g. Arnone et al. 2006), it will be perhaps important to track the same line of Copelovitch and Singer (2007) and Guisinger and Singer (2010) by linking the interaction between central banks' independence, the choice of exchange regime and inflation outcomes with the degree of democracy and the size of banking sector.

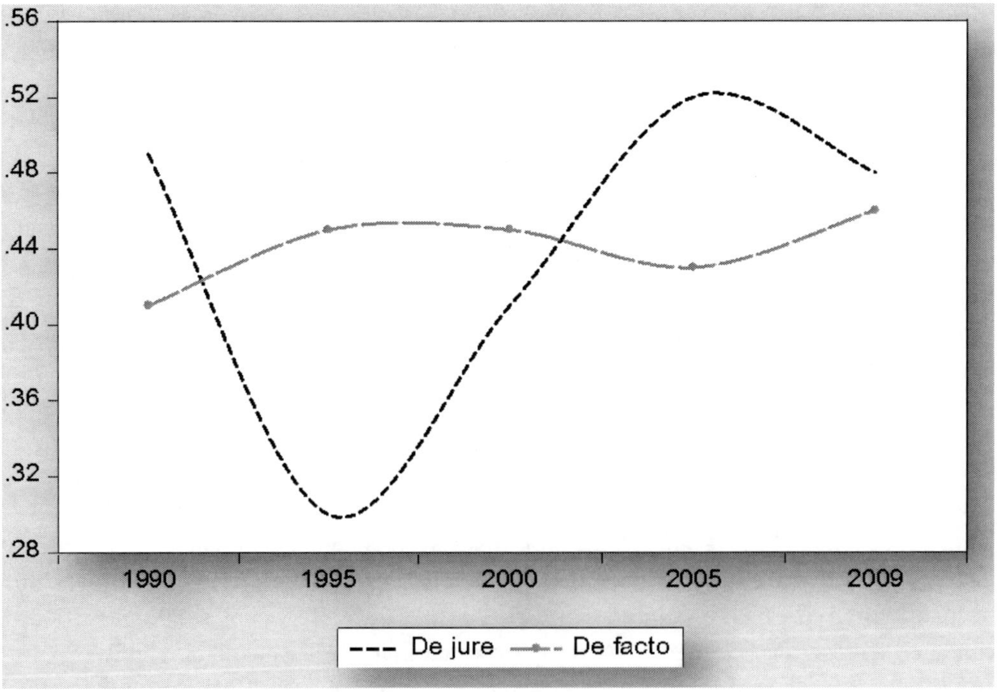

Source: IMF (multiple years) and Reinhart and Rogoff (2004).

Figure 4. The exchange regime's percentage adopted by emerging countries.

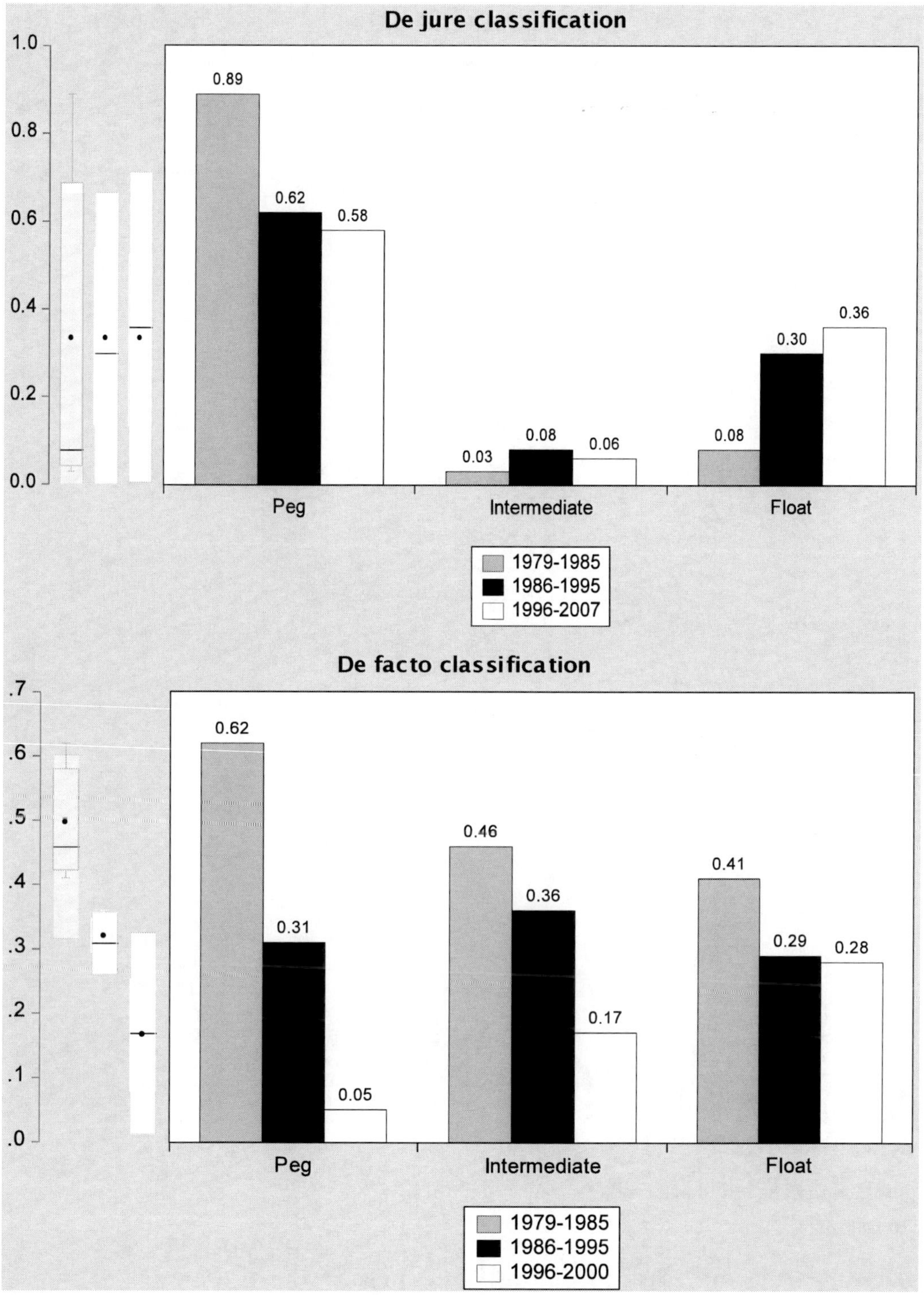

Source: For de facto classification, data are disponible in IMF (various issues). For de jure classification, we can see Sfia and Mouley (2009). We take into account here only to the emerging countries, especially the Middle East North African countries.

Figure 5. Exchange regimes in emerging countries.

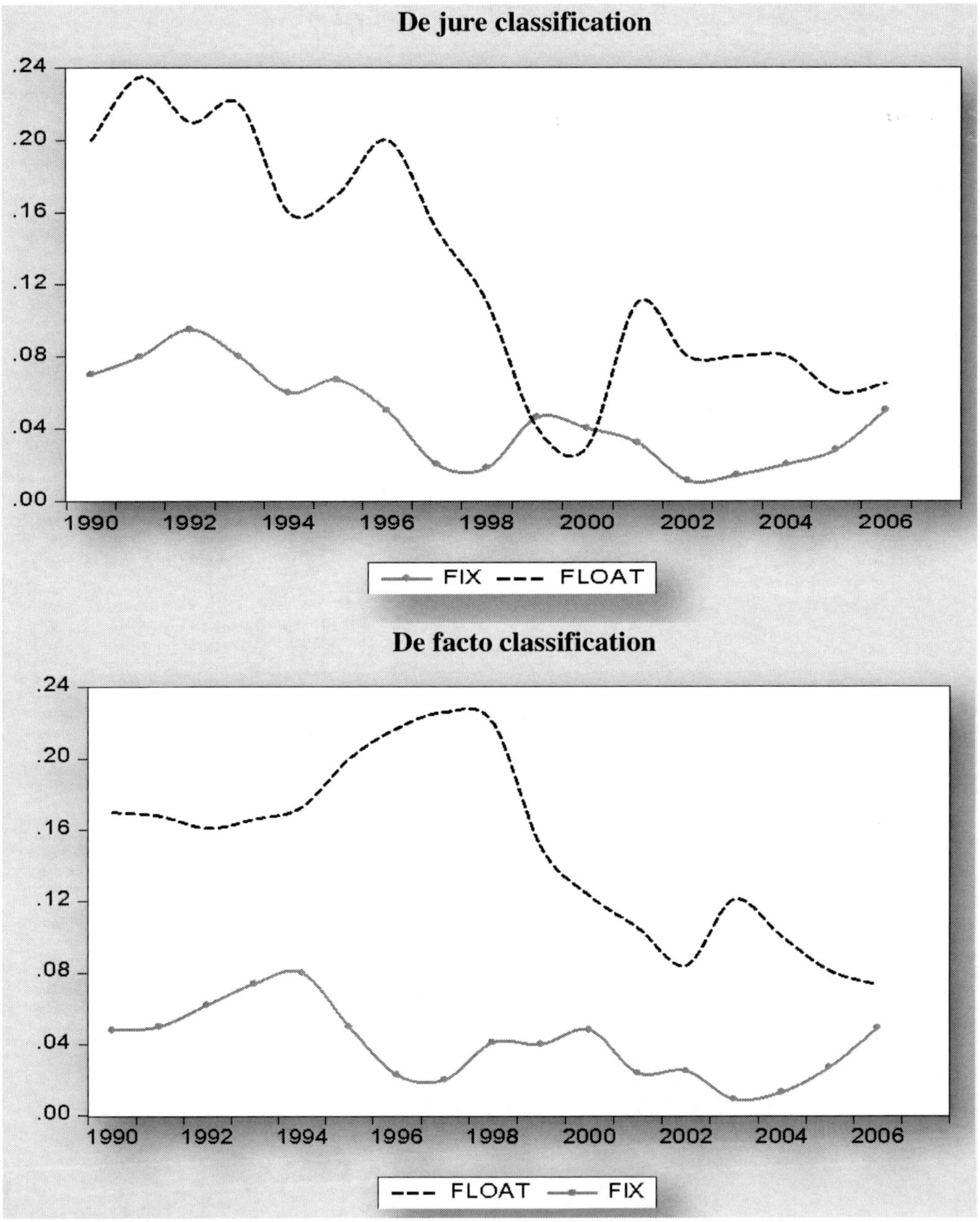

Source: IMF staff, various reports.

Figure 6. Inflation performance and exchange regime classifications.

2.3. Other Determinants of Inflation Outcomes

Rather than exchange regime and central bank independence which are explained at outset as potential fundamentals of inflation dynamic, there are other determinants which can affect it considerably. For example, it is assessed that under floating exchange regime, the monetary policy would be more vulnerable to the variability of international capital (e.g. Sfia and Mouley, 2009). Therefore, a high degree of capital openness (see Figure 7) would be likely associated with fixed exchange regime leading to low level of inflation outcomes. So, how do emerging countries with more open capital openness interact with inflation? Does capital account openness decrease inflation across emerging countries? And how has opening up the capital account affected inflation?

Furthermore, Copelovitch and Singer (2007) argue that democracy is better able than non-democracy to signal the intention of monetary authorities to keep the stability of prices. Figure 8 presents the level of democracy in the considered countries and indicates that they have not a good position compared to the world. Does this degree of democracy matter for inflation in emerging countries?

Guisinger and Singer (2010) hereafter confirmed that: "The logic is straightforward : the size of the banking sector is an excellent proxy for the potential magnitude of the career costs associated with bank instability", that is to say that the influence of the intervention of central banks on inflation may be less important when the banking sector size is relatively small. Copelovitch and Singer (2007) verified this argument for a panel of twenty three industrialized countries, remains hereafter to evaluate to what extent this viewpoint can be true in the case of emerging countries ?

Among the same context, Figure 9 illustrates the variation in the size of banking sector across the considered emerging countries. Theoretically and empirically (e.g. Copelovitch and Singer, 2007), the banking sector size can magnify the impact of central banks on inflation evolution which is conditional on the choice of exchange regime. Thus, a high level of banking sector size can mitigate the inflationary pressures. But, can the size of banking sector make a difference in terms of central banks and exchange regime effects on inflation outcomes in emerging countries?

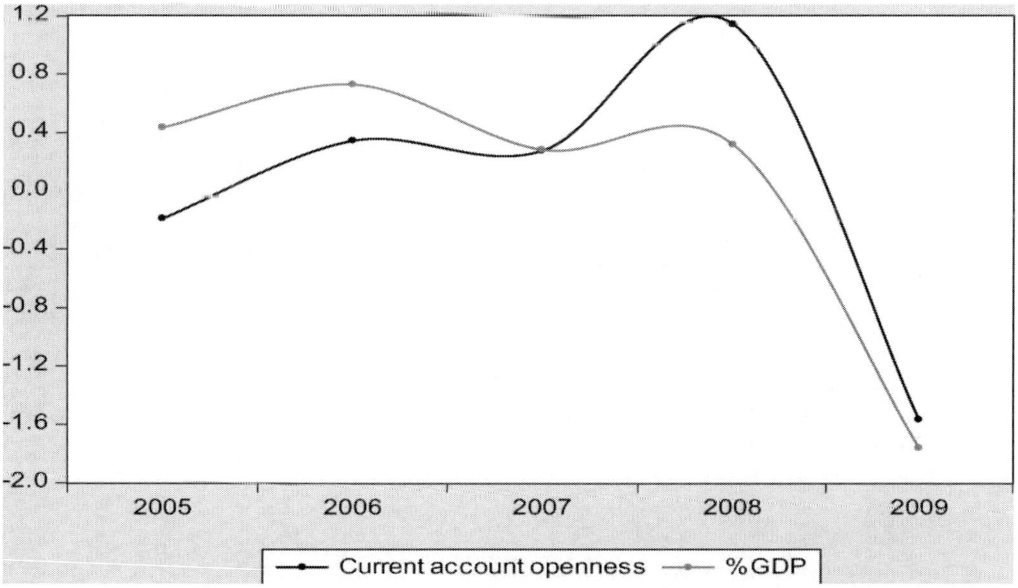

Source: International Monetary Fund.
Data disponible also at https://pwt.sas.upenn.edu/php_site/pwt61_form.php

Figure 7. Evolution of current account openness and GDP in emerging countries.

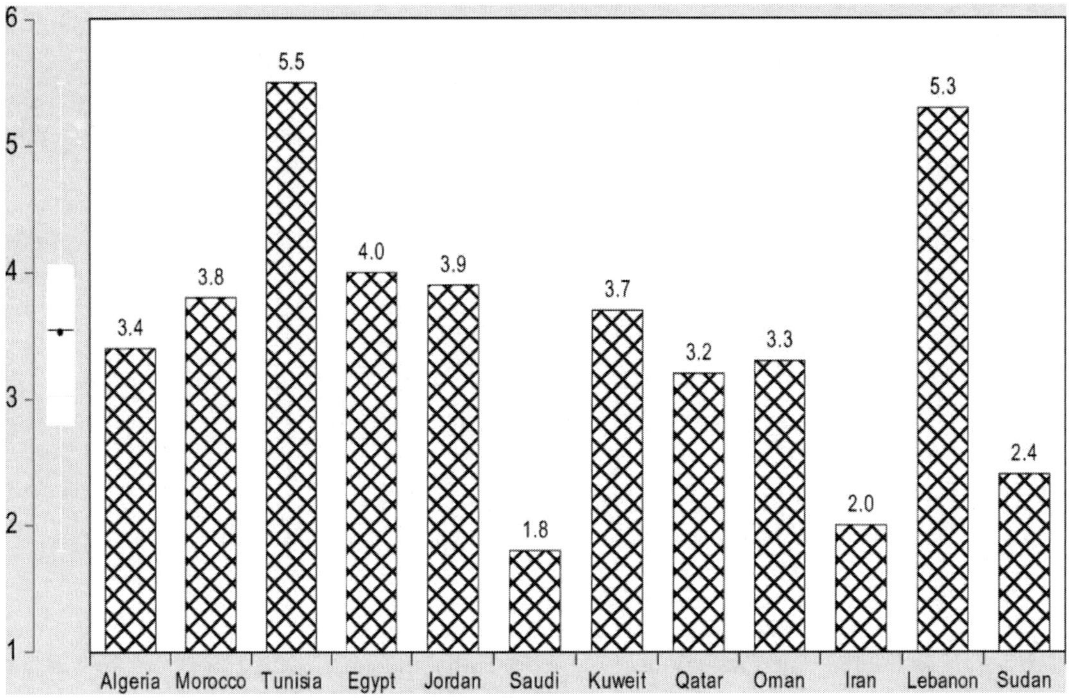

Source: Economist Intelligence Unit (EIU, 2011). http://www.sida.se/Global/About%20Sida/S%C3%A5%20arbetar%20vi/EIU_Democracy_Index_Dec2011.pdf

Figure 8. Democracy index in selected emerging countries.

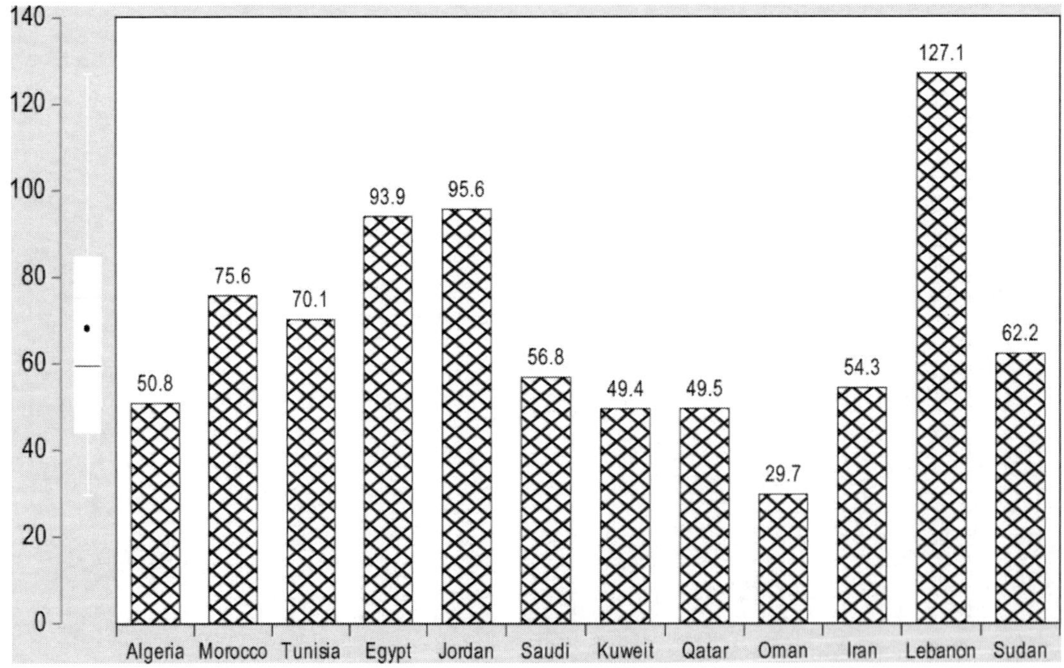

Note: Data from Econstats (http://www.econstats.com/ifs/NorGSc_Mor1_M.htm) and authors's calculations.

Figure 9. Banking sector size in selected emerging countries.

3. Empirical Analysis

3.1. Data and Methodology

To test if the financial regulation is an important factor influencing the monetary policy behavior (in particular, inflation dynamic) and its connection to exchange regime, we use a panel data of twelve emerging countries for the period from 1990 to 2009. Our methodology in this study follows an econometric model based on linear regression with panel corrected standard errors. The dependent variable is the logged five year average inflation rate. The Models 1 and 2 include as explanatory variables, exchange rate regime (i.e. the exchange regime variable takes the value 0 for floating exchange regime and managed float and 1 of fixed exchange regime[47]) by using two classifications strategies (de jure and de facto)[48], the log of GDP and that of GDP per capita, the capital account openness[49], the banking sector size (measured as a domestic private credits provided by the banking sector as a percentage of GDP) and regulatory separation[50] (i.e. a binary variable that takes the value 0 if the central bank is unified and a value 1 if there is a separate agency which supervises the central banks activity).

Thereafter and because we know that there are additional variables whose inclusion can outperform the model, we thought to add interactive term as the study of Copelovitch and Singer (2007). Hence to assess the fact that the effect of central bank independence on inflation outcomes is conditional on the exchange rate regime which itself depends intensely to the size of banking sector and democracy, we include in Models 3 and 4 relatively a two-way and three-way multiplicative interaction terms[51] which capture the effects associated to separate on inflation outcomes conditional upon the choice of exchange regime in the first time, and then to the combination between exchange regime, the banking sector size and the degree of democracy.

To regress inflation on exchange regime and regulatory separation taking into account other explanatory variables as like democracy and banking sector size, we thought to use the OLS method. Indeed, this latter is biased for panel, the OLS with fixed or variable effects can be more reasonable. Nevertheless, it is crucial here to address the possibility of endogeneity (i.e. to be clear, there are some reasons to expect that rather than fixed exchange regime can cause lower level of inflation, this latter can also cause exchange regime)[52].

In this context, Coudert and Doubert (2005) confirm that because of endogeneity of the exchange rate regime to inflation, a reverse causality in the inflation regression is more likely,

---

[47] The fixed exchange regime such as currency boards, hard pegs, etc….

[48] The data of exchange rate regimes' classifications are disponible in the IMF's annual report on exchange arrangements and exchange restrictions. See also Appendix B.

[49] This index is disponible in Usherbrooke data; higher values of this latter indicate greater degree of openness. http://perspective.usherbrooke.ca/bilan/statistiques/2

[50] Focusing on the perspective of central bank involvement in banking regulation (Cukierman (1992) and Copelovitch and Singer (2007)), we thought to use as indicator of central bank independence the Cukierman index based on annual observations of central bank involvement for each country, which presents a variable which takes into account the role of the central bank in banking regulation and supervision, noted (CBI). This latter is equal to: 0= if the central bank is not assigned the main responsibility for banking supervision and 1= if the central bank assigned the main responsibility for banking supervision. Data are disponible in IMF's report on regulatory banking sector.

[51] For details about multiplicative interction terms, we can see: http://homepages.nyu.edu/~mrg217/interaction.html.

[52] For more details about the problem of endogeneity, we can see Bouoiyour (2012).

as inflation may play a role in the choice of an exchange rate regime "a country could choose a fixed exchange rate because it already has a low inflation. The opposite mechanism could be true. A country could adopt a peg because of its high inflation, if it expects that the peg could bring more discipline and credibility to the government policy." In this case, the IV method can be more effective. This method consists in finding a variable that affects the exchange rate regime without impacting inflation, this is the instrumental variable. Since it is difficult and sometimes impossible to find this variable, we thought about using the Arellano and Bond method (GMM). In turn, this method assumes that lagged values of the dependent and independent variables also serve as valid instruments under certain restrictions.

3.2. Key Results

To evaluate the relationship between inflation, central bank independence, exchange regime and other determinants without and with interactive term, we use in the first step the Ordinary Least Squares method (OLS) with two-way fixed effects chosen by Hausman test without and with multiplicative interactive terms summarized in Tables 1 and 2, respectively. In the second step, we estimate the relationship in question using Arellano and Bond method (GMM) without and with interactive terms summarized relatively in Tables 4 and 5.

We should add here that we employ in these several models an alternative measure of exchange regime based on the IMF's de jure classification. Unlike this latter classification, we use another measure of exchange regime which is derived from a combination of foreign reserve activity and market exchange rates taking into account the chronologies associated to each countries (Reinhart and Rogoff, 2004). Intuitively, does exchange regime classification matter for the interaction between central bank independence and inflation dynamic?

3.2.1. OLS method

The results of OLS estimates without interactive terms are summarized in Table 1. We notice that the relationship between separate and inflation is statistically insignificant. This may be mainly due to the fact that the linkage between central banks' independence and inflation outcomes is considerably conditional on the choice of exchange regime either fixed or floating, the level of democracy and the size of banking sector as demonstrated by Copelovitch and Singer (2007). It remains then to verify if this viewpoint is true when we include interactive terms taking into account the latter variables.

Hereafter, we show a negative and significant effect of exchange regime (Fixed versus floating) under both classifications either de jure or de facto on inflation, i.e. the inflation levels are lower in countries which choose fixed exchange regimes than those which choose a more flexible exchange regime. In this context, Gupta (2007) argues that countries with severe inflationary pressures frequently choose to adopt a crawling peg regime or a managed float regime characterized by highly anchor in a stabilization objective. Our results are not necessarily built on this finding because the considered countries describe their exchange policies as flexible, which is associated to a high level of inflation while according to Sfia and Mouley (2009): "MENA countries describe themselves as floaters because that is what the International Monetary Fund (IMF) wants to hear, but in reality they intervene massively to adjust their exchange rates. Thus, we can define their attitude as fear of the IMF".

Table 1. OLS without Interactive Terms

Dependent variable: Log (Five year average inflation)		
	(1) ***De jure***	**(2)** ***De facto***
Constant	-4.014 (-1.180)	-6.215 (-1.027)
Separate	1.278 (1.074)	1.007 (1.051)
Exchange regime (Fixed=1 ; Floating=0)	-0.394* (-1.361)	-0.265 (-1.013)
GDP (log)	-0.251*** (-2.211)	-0.189** (-2.054)
GDP per capita (log)	-0.106 (-0.590)	-0.123 (-0.421)
Democracy	0.067 (0.420)	0.079 (0.631)
Current account openess	-0.017* (-1.467)	-0.024 (-1.103)
Banking sector size	0.004 (1.046)	0.001 (0.885)
R^2	0.41	0.33

Note: Panel corrected standard errors in parentheses; *p<=.10; **p<=.05; ***p<=.01.

Table 2. OLS with Interactive Terms

Dependent variable: Log (Five year average inflation)				
	(1) ***De jure***	**(2)** ***De jure***	**(3)** ***De facto***	**(4)** ***De facto***
Constant	-4.260 (-1.095)	-3.593** (-2.164)	-6.341*** (-3.240)	-6.593* (-1.712)
Separate	-1.109** (-2.642)	-0.408** (-2.309)	-1.122*** (-3.395)	-0.504* (-1.813)
Exchange regime (Fixed=1 ; Floating=0)	-0.482* (-1.642)	-0.384* (-1.550)	-0.313 (-1.122)	-0.384* (-1.550)
GDP (log)	-0.259** (-2.000)	-0.180*** (-3.241)	-0.192** (-2.392)	-0.153** (-2.623)
GDP per capita (log)	-0.106 (-0.582)	-0.067 (-0.853)	-0.101 (-0.673)	-0.092 (-0.589)
Democracy	0.061 (0.367)	-0.065* (-1.535)	0.083 (0.812)	-0.092* (-1.628)
Current account openess	-0.018* (-1.391)	-0.007* (-1.926)	-0.032 (-1.147)	-0.017** (-2.455)
Banking sector size	0.004 (1.038)	0.012 (0.589)	0.011 (1.206)	0.017 (0.522)
Exchange regime*Separate	-0.109 (-0.139)		-0.213** (-2.676)	
Exchange regime*Banking*Democracy*Separate		-0.004* (-1.414)		-0.005* (-1.525)
R^2	0.42	0.49	0.38	0.41

Note: Panel corrected standard errors in parentheses; *p<=.10; **p<=.05; ***p<=.01

Table 3. GMM without Interactive Terms

Dependent variable: Log (Five year average inflation)		
	(1) ***De jure***	**(2)** ***De facto***
Constant	-4.092** (-2.409)	-8.107 (-0.763)
Separate	-1.184*** (-7.241)	-0.622* (-1.724)
Exchange regime (Fixed=1 ; Floating=0)	-0.886* (-1.763)	-0.552 (-1.214)
GDP (log)	-0.258*** (-4.611)	-0.243** (-2.207)
GDP per capita (log)	0.054 (0.636)	0.060 (0.558)
Democracy	-0.048* (-1.647)	-0.035* (-1.481)
Current account openess	-0.009* (-1.513)	-0.012 (-0.788)
Banking sector size	0.002 (1.237)	0.005 (1.109)
J-Statistic	1.68 E-20	1.32 E-23

Note: Panel corrected standard errors in parentheses; *p<=.10; **p<=.05; ***p<=.01.

Table 4. GMM with Interactive Terms

Dependent variable: Log (Five year average inflation)				
	(1) ***De jure***	**(2)** ***De jure***	**(3)** ***De facto***	**(4)** ***De facto***
Constant	-3.634 (-1.945)	-1.902* (-1.055)	-8.015 (-0.945)	-8.103* (-1.621)
Separate	-1.124*** (-5.837)	-0.842*** (-3.415)	-0.634* (-1.806)	-0.626*** (-3.310)
Exchange regime (Fixed=1 ; Floating=0)	-0.889 (-0.701)	-0.461* (-1.485)	-0.577* (-1.586)	-0.560 (-0.533)
GDP (log)	-0.241*** (-3.820)	-0.178** (-2.927)	-0.250* (-1.718)	-0.247** (-2.122)
GDP per capita (log)	-0.053 (-0.630)	-0.063 (-0.784)	-0.069 (-0.555)	-0.066 (-1.027)
Democracy	-0.033* (-1.420)	-0.057* (-1.476)	-0.035** (-2.000)	-0.041* (-1.819)
Current account openess	-0.008* (-1.289)	-0.009* (-1.548)	-0.016* (-1.404)	-0.009* (-1.548)
Banking sector size	0.001 (1.200)	0.0053 (1.000)	0.007* (1.428)	0.009* (1.561)
Exchange regime*Separate	0.210 (0.592)		-0.099*** (-2.733)	
Exchange regime*Banking*Democracy*Separate		-0.031* (-1.466)		-0.052* (-1.404)
J-Statistic	4.90 E-19	9.88 E-17	1.37 E-23	1.86 E-23

Note: Panel corrected standard errors in parentheses; *p<=.10; **p<=.05; ***p<=.01.

Furthermore, it is remarkable that the coefficient associated to the economic growth is linked negatively and significantly to inflation level, i.e. an increase of GDP of emerging countries is accompanied by lower inflation. This confirms the idea whereby the countries characterized by a small size are more likely to be associated with fixed exchange regime and then would be accompanied with lower inflation outcomes (e.g. McKinnon, 1963). In the same vein, Sfia and Mouley (2009) advanced that the countries distinguished during a large size or more precisely high level of GDP are more associated to a floating exchange regime which is a key source of inflationary pressures.

Our results also reveal that democracy has a negative and significant effect on inflation dynamic; this can necessarily be due to the very bad position of the emerging countries in terms of the level of democracy (see Figure 8). Concretely, the lack of democracy can lead to political instability. Thus, the level of inflation will be necessarily affected by the extent of political instability, i.e. inflation will be higher in the countries with unstable policy. It is theoretically expected that high level of democracy is associated with lower inflation in lower inequality countries and with higher inflation in higher inequality countries (e.g. Cukierman et al. (1992) and Desai et al. (2003)).

Besides, our results also reveal that the expectation whereby a high degree of current account openness is necessarily linked to lower inflation outcomes is verified. This confirms the viewpoint of Gupta (2007) who shows that "By opening up the capital account, policymakers impart a signal to the private sector that it is willing to suffer the punishment of loose monetary policy in the form of capital outflow. Thus, it alters the private sector expectations about the future monetary policy, which is itself can be inflation reducing." However, we notice an unexpected relationship between banking sector size and logged inflation which is insignificant.

Let us now verify if the sign and significance of different coefficients associated to the various variables used still the same when we include interactive terms.

3.2.2. OLS with interactive terms

When we include the interactive term, we notice that the coefficient associated to central bank independence or separate is negative and highly significant in comparison to other explanatory variables used, but this is mainly conditional on the choice of exchange regime either fixed or floating (Models 1 and 3). This provides a strong support to the argument of Cukierman et al. (1992) who show that inflation outcomes are higher in countries with low central bank independence and that of Gupta (2007) who advance that "the freer is the central bank, the lower is inflation rate." Hence, we confirm empirically the result theoretically addressed whereby the regulatory separation can be a key fundamental of inflation dynamic in emerging countries.

Table 5. Predicted Inflation Values Conditional on the Choice of Exchange Regime

Exchange rate regime	Does central banks supervise banks?	Predicted average inflation	Confidence interval (95%)
Fixed	Yes (Separate=0)	6.38	4.67-7.12
Floating	Yes (Separate=0)	4.59	3.71-5.74

Although, when we combine the exchange regime, the democracy and the banking sector size variables as two-way or three way-interactive terms, we notice more intense relationship between central bank's independence and inflation. Hence, we show that the independence of central banks in emerging countries will be linked negatively and significantly to inflation level, but conditional to the choice of exchange regime, the degree of democracy and the size of banking sector.

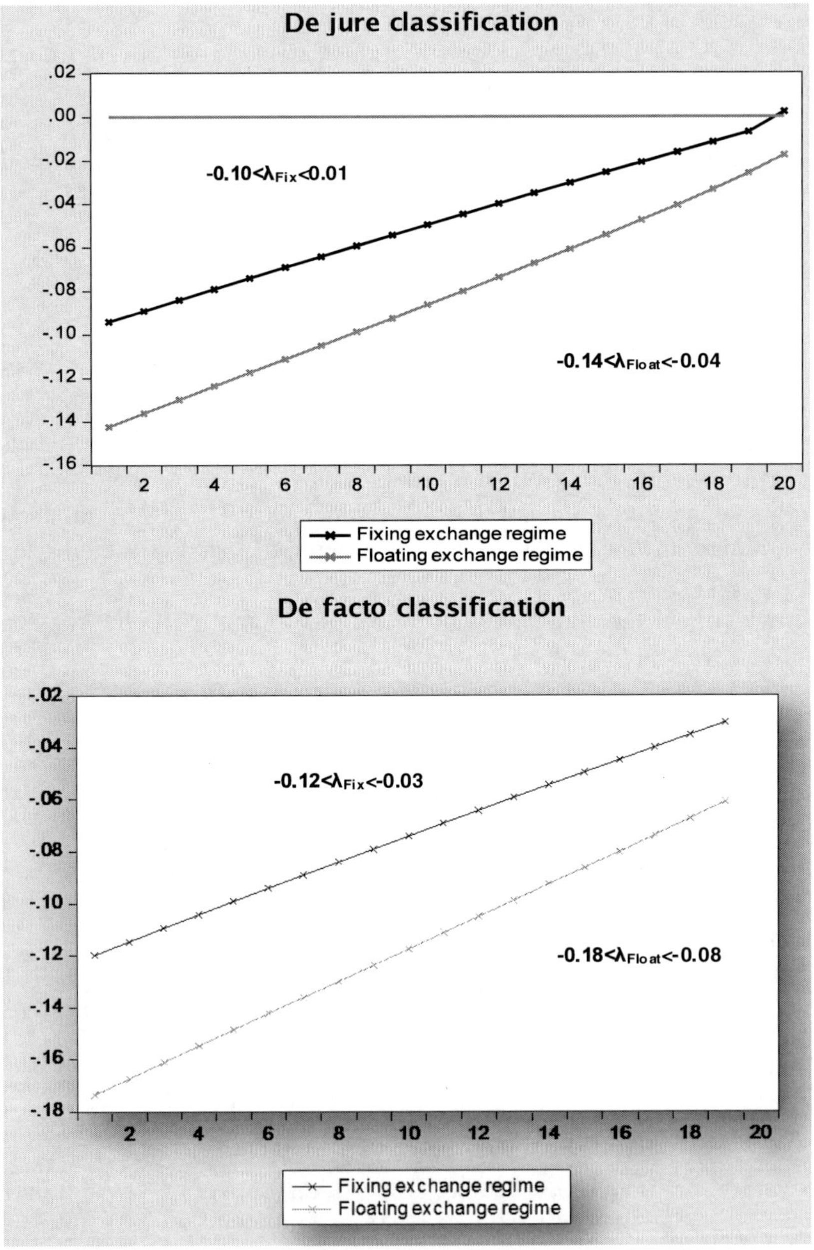

Note: For detailed analysis about the conditional marginal effects, we can see: http://homepages.nyu.edu/~mrg217/interaction.html.

Figure 10. Conditional marginal effects of central bank independence on inflation outcomes.

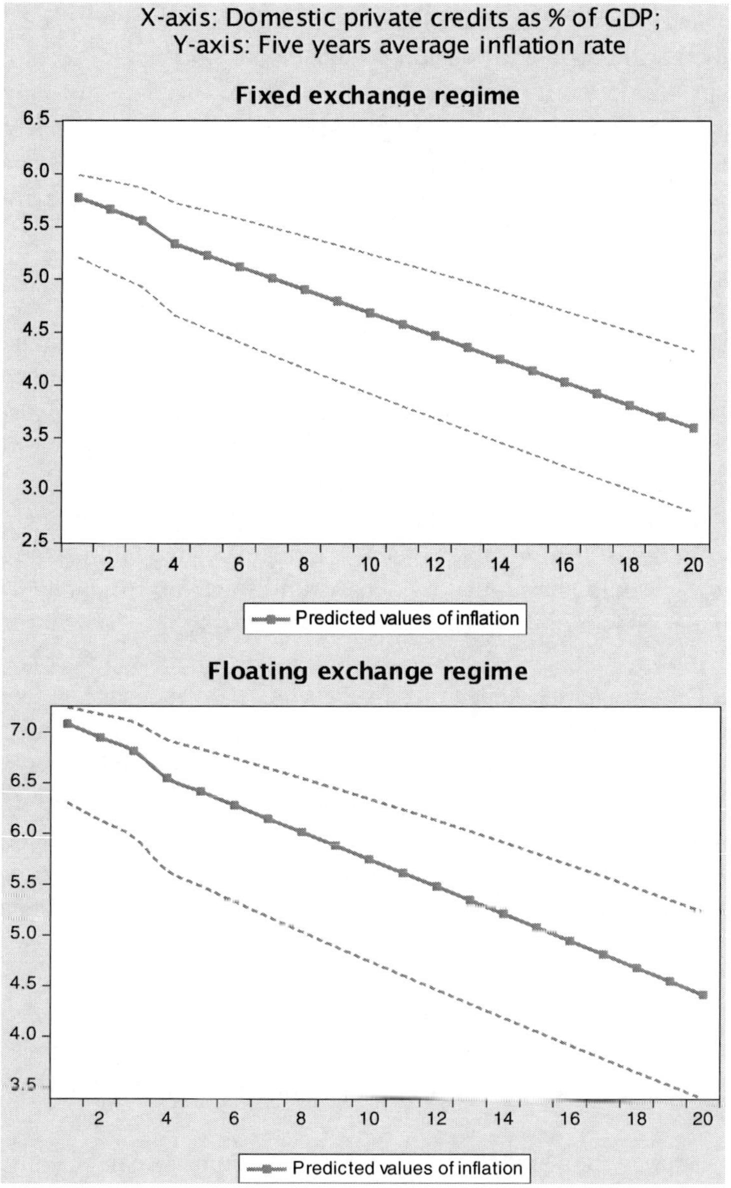

Note: Dashed lines indicate 95% confidence intervals. Calculations done by using Stata, Clarify software. For more details we can refer to: http://gking.harvard.edu/publications/clarify-software-interpreting-and-presenting-statistical-results.

Figure 11. Predicted values of inflation by banking sector size with central bank independence (de jure classification).

3.2.3. GMM method

Our previous results summarized in Table 1 (OLS without interactive term) show that there is not a significant linkage between regulatory separation and inflation either for fixed or floating exchange regimes. Table 2 (OLS with interactive terms) reveals that the effect of central bank independence on inflation outcomes of countries under fixed exchange regime are lower than those operating under flexible exchange regime (i.e. negative and significant coefficient associated to the variable exchange regime). These results appear robust when we use GMM method without interactive terms under both classifications in question, i.e. de facto and de jure (Table 3). It remains to verify if it is crucial to distinguish between the various classifications of exchange regime or only the choice of exchange regime (fixed or floating) matter when we analyze its relationship with inflation and central bank independence using GMM method with interactive terms to check the robustness of our results summarized in Table 1.

3.2.4. GMM method with interactive terms

By using GMM method with interactive terms, the results obtained support the hypothesis whereby the lower level of inflation is associated to greater central bank independence which is itself closely linked to fixed exchange regime. We also notice that the coefficient associated to exchange regime is negative and statistically significant (i.e. lower values imply that higher degree of exchange fixity decrease the inflation outcomes). We should add here that the results obtained above from OLS method with interactive term (two or three way) seem robust. From Tables 2 and 4, fixed exchange regime appears favorable in emerging countries to mitigate regulatory separation effects on inflation' levels under both classifications either de jure or de facto.

To confirm our results, we present in Figure 10 the marginal effects of regulatory separation on inflation average depending to the choice of exchange regime (Fixed versus managed or floating regime) under two classifications (i.e. de jure and de facto) trying to check the robustness of our results. We notice that the separation has a negative and significant effect on inflation dynamic under floating exchange rate regimes. Indeed, regulatory separation has a little influence on inflation outcomes under fixed exchange regimes in both de jure and de facto classification. Furthermore, the results reported in Table 5 strongly support this. We show that when the central banks supervise banks under floating exchange regime, the predicted average inflation is 6.38 at 95% confidence level. However, under fixed exchange regime, we notice that the predicted inflation average declines to 4.59.

CONCLUSION

A stable monetary policy aimed at low level of inflation rate can be considered as a main tool and an important condition for sustainable economic growth in emerging countries. The literature survey on this topic (e.g. Desai et al. (2003), Gupta (2007), etc…) considers that independent central banks have lower costs on inflation, but this dependency is conditional especially on the choice of exchange regime.

By analyzing a panel data from twelve selected emerging countries from 1990 to 2009, we show that the inflation outcomes of countries operating under fixed exchange regime are lower, but this should be accompanied by: (i) Independent central banks; (ii) more opening current account; (iii) high level of GDP; (iv) high level of democracy and (v) important size of banking sector.

More interestingly, our results reveal that regulatory separation has a little influence on inflation outcomes under fixed exchange regimes than under floating regimes for both considered arrangements, i.e. de facto and de jure classifications. Hence, lower inflation in emerging countries may be achieved by setting up independent central banks but depending to the choice of exchange regime either fixed or floating exchange regime. Our results appear robust using OLS and GMM methods without and with interactive terms and based on two classifications (i.e. de jure versus de facto).

Nonetheless and as we see contemporaneously, the procurement of a high level of democracy may be considered as a difficult task in the considered countries. Thereafter, the lack democracy which is between 1.77 and 5.33 in considered economies with ranks comparable to the rest of the world between 97 and 160[53] can threaten the central bank independence, inflation outcomes and exchange regime connection. Thus, to tend towards more autonomy of central banks with low degree of democracy and without potential preparation of the pass-through towards pure floating exchange regime will be insufficient to guarantee a continuously or a permanently lower inflation' levels.

Regardless of the results taken above, it seems also important in our own viewpoint to evaluate whether central bank independence is related to the linkage between exchange regime and inflation dynamic under financial crisis (i.e. currency, banking and debt crisis), that can spread to emerging countries affecting widely inflation outcomes. So, this chapter suggests additional questions for future research: Can a suitably independent central bank achieve stable or low levels of inflation under financial crisis? Does this depend on whether the countries in question chose fixed exchange regime or floating exchange regime? If it does, to what extent can emerging countries - that adopt pegged exchange regime[54] - achieve or establish reductions in inflation levels under financial crisis?

The answers to these several questions will automatically enhance our understanding on the interaction between inflation outcomes, the choice of exchange regime and central bank independence. By analyzing the impact of recent financial crisis on this last linkage, we can also detect an explicit nonlinear effect (i.e. structural breaks in the considered link). Whether or not this is the case, we cannot neglect the fact that the effect of regulatory separation on inflation is conditional on the choice of exchange regime either fixed or floating and critically depends on the banking sector size and the degree of democracy.

Appendix A. Predictions Concerning the Inflation Outcomes

Structural characteristics	Empirical predicted inflation
Fixed exchange rate regime	Low inflation average (Sfia and Mouley, 2009)
Floating exchange rate regime	High inflation average (Sfia and Mouley, 2009)
High GDP	Low inflation rate (McKinnon, 1963)
High democracy	Low inflation rate (Copelovitch and Singer, 2007)
High capital openess	Low inflation rate (Gupta, 2007)
Independence of central bank (Separate=1)	Low inflation rate (Copelovitch and Singer, 2007)
Dependence of central bank (Separate=0)	High inflation rate (Dumiter, 2009)
High banking sector size	Low inflation rate (Copelovitch and Singer, 2007)

[53] See Economist Intelligence Unit : http://www.sida.se/Global/About%20Sida/S%C3%A5%20arbetar%20vi/EIU_Democracy_Index_Dec2011.pdf

[54] The pegged exchange regime is the most adopted regime in the emerging countries in question.

APPENDIX B. CLASSIFICATIONS OF EXCHANGE REGIMES USED IN OUR STUDY

	Number assigned to category in fine grid	**Number assigned to category in coarse grid**
No separate legal tender	1	1
Pre announced peg or currency board arrangement	2	1
Pre announced horizontal band that is narrower than or equal to +/- 2%	3	1
De facto peg	4	1
Pre announced crawling peg	5	2
Pre announced crawling band that is narrower than or equal to +/- 2%	6	2
De facto crawling peg	7	2
De facto crawling band that is narrower than or equal to +/- 2%	8	2
Pre announced crawling band that is wide than or equal to +/- 2%	9	2
De facto crawling band that is narrower than or equal to +/- 5%	10	3
Moving band that is narrower than or equal to +/- 2%	11	3
Managed floating	12	3
Freely floating	13	4
Freely falling	14	5

Source : Reinhart and Rogoff (2004).

APPENDIX C. SOME INDEPENDENCE'S INDICATORS

Cukierman's index (CBI)
Focusing on the perspective of central bank involvement in banking regulation (Cukierman (1992) and Copelovitch and Singer (2007)), we can thought to another index, based on annual observations of central bank involvement for each country, which presents a variable which takes account into the role of the central bank in banking regulation and supervision, noted (CBI). This latter is equal to : 0= if the central bank is not assigned the main responsibility for banking supervision. 1= if the central bank assigned the main responsibility for banking supervision.
GMT index
This index is initiated by Grilli et al. (1991). It takes account on both political autonomy and economic autonomy of central banks (CB). **Political autonomy:** 1= Governor appointed without government involvement. 2= Governor appointed for more than 5 years. 3= Board appointed without government involvement. 4= Board appointed for more than 5 years. 5= No mandatory participation of government representatives in the board. 6= No governmental approval is required for formulating monetary policy.

GMT index
7= Requirements forcing CB to pursue monetary stability among its primary objectives.
Economic autonomy:
1= No automatic procedure for government to obtain direct credit facilities from CB.
2= Direct credit facilities extended at market rates.
3= Credit on a temporary basis.
4= Credit of limited amount.
5= CB does not participate in primary market for public debt.
6= CB is responsible for setting the Discount Rate.
7= CB has no responsibility for overseeing the banking sector and shares responsibility with other institutional entities.

REFERENCES

Arnone, M., Laurens, B. J. & Segalotto, J. -F. (2006). "*The Measurement of Central Bank Autonomy: Survey of Models, Indicators, and Empirical Evidence*," IMF Working Paper WP/06/227.

Alogoskoufis, G. & Smith, S. (1991). "The Phillips Curve, the Persistence of Inflation and the Lucas Critique: Evidence from Exchange Rate Regimes." *American Economic Review*, *81*, 1254-1271.

Alfaro, L. (2005). "Inflation, Openness, and Exchange Rate Regimes: The Quest for Short-term Commitment." *Journal of Development Economics*, 229-49.

Arnone, M., Laurens, B. J., Segalotto, J. -F. & Sommer, M. (2008). "*Central Bank Autonomy: Lessons from Global Trends*," IMF Staff Papers, *56*, 263-296.

Bleaney, M. & David Fielding, D. (2002). "Exchange Rate Regimes, Ináation and Output Volatility in Developing Countries." *Journal of Development Economics*, 233-45.

Bouoiyour, J. (2012). "Transferts de fonds, syndrome hollandaise et effets de seuil dans les pays MENA." *Annual conference of Femise*, Marrakech (November, 2012).

Bouoiyour, J. & Selmi, R. (2012). "Exchange volatility and trade performance in developing countries: What roles do differential commodity prices and crude energy uncertainties play?" Mimeo University of Pau.

Bodea, C. (2009). "Exchange Rate Regimes and Independent Central Banks: A Correlated Choice of Imperfectly Credible Institutions." Forthcoming. International Organization.

Canavan, C. & Tommasi, M. (1997). On the Credibility of Alternative Exchange Rate Regimes. *Journal of Development Economics*, *54* (1), 101-122.

Clark, W-R. (2002). "Partisan and Electoral Motivations and the Choice of Monetary Institutions Under Fully Mobile Capital." *International Organization*, *56* (4), 725-749.

Cobham, D. (2012). Monetary policy strategies, financial institutions and financial markets in the Middle East and North Africa: an overview. Working paper of Heriott-Watt University.

Copelovitch, P. & Singer, A. (2007). "Financial regulation, monetary policy and inflation in industrialized world." *Annual meeting of the Midwest political science association*.

Coudert, V. & Doubert, C. (2005). "Does exchange rate regime explain differences in economic results for Asian countries? *Journal of Asian economics*, vol *16*, n°5, October.

Cukierman, A. (1992). ''*Central Bank Strategy, Credibility, and Independence.* '' Cambridge Press.

Cukierman, A., Steven, W. & Bilin, N. (1992). ''Measuring the Independence of Central Banks and Its Effects on Policy Outcomes.'' *The World Bank Review*, *6* (3), 353–398.

Dani, R. (2000). *Exchange regimes and institutional arrangements in the Shadow of capital flows*. Harvard University.

Desai, R. M., Olofsgard, A. & Yousef, T. (2003). Democracy, inequality and inflation. *American political science review*, *97* (3).

Dumiter, F. C. (2009). "Central Bank independence and inflation targeting: The case of Romania." *The Romanian economic journal*.

Grilli, Vittorio, Donato Masciandaro & Guido Tabellini. (1991). "Political and Monetary Institutions and Public Financial Policies in the Industrial Countries." *Economic Policy*, *6* (2), 341-392.

Gupta, A. S. (2007). "*Does capital account openess lower inflation?*" Working paper n°191 of Indian council for research on international economic relations.

Guisinger, A. & Singer, D. A. (2010). Exchange Ratye Proclamation and Inflation Fighting Credibility, International Organization, Vol. *64*, n° 2, 313-337.

Maxfield, S. (1997). "*Gatekeepers of Growth: The International Political Economy of Central Banking in Developing Countries*." Princeton: Princeton University Press.

McKinnon, R. I. (1963). "Optimum currency areas," *American Economic Review*, *53*, 717-725.

Reinhart, C. M. & Rogoff, K. S. (2004). "The Modern History of Exchange Rate Arrangemnts: A Reinterpretation", *Quarterly Journal of Economics*, Vol. *119*, n°1, 1-48.

Sfia, D-M. & Mouley, S. (2009). "*Determinants of exchange practices in the MENA countries : Some further empirical results*." Working paper n°952 of the William Davidson Institute, University of Michigan.

Zare, E., Rahimi, M., Nademi, Y. & Heydarpour, E. (2012). " Central bank independence and inflation in Iran: New evidence with nonlinear approach." *Journal of Basic and Applied Scientific Research*, *2* (2), 1011-1014.

Zouache, A. & Ilmane, M-C. (2008). Central bank independence in a MENA transition economy: the experience of Algeria". Mimeo Birbeck, University of London.

In: Exchange Rates in Developed and Emerging Markets
Editor: Mohsen Bahmani-Oskooee
ISBN: 978-1-62808-164-0

Chapter 10

IS THERE A SCOPE TO CAPITALIZE ON EXCHANGE RATE FLUCTUATIONS? EVIDENCE FOR IRAN

Magda Kandil[1] and Ida A. Mirzaie[2]
[1]Western Hemisphere Department, International Monetary Fund, Washington, DC, US
[2]Department of Economics, Ohio State University, Columbus, OH, US

I. INTRODUCTION

There has been an ongoing debate on the appropriate exchange rate policy in developing countries. The debate focuses on the degree of fluctuations in the exchange rate in the face of internal and external shocks. Exchange rate fluctuations are likely, in turn, to determine economic performance. In judging the desirability of exchange rate fluctuations, it becomes, therefore, necessary to evaluate their effects on output growth and price inflation. Demand and supply channels determine these effects.

A depreciation (or devaluation) of the domestic currency may stimulate economic activity through the initial increase in the price of foreign goods relative to home goods. By increasing the international competitiveness of domestic industries, exchange rate depreciation diverts spending from foreign goods to domestic goods. As illustrated in Guittian (1976) and Dornbusch (1988), the success of currency depreciation in promoting trade balance largely depends on switching demand in proper direction and amount, as well as on the capacity of the home economy to meet the additional demand by supplying more good[55].

While the traditional view indicates that currency depreciation is expansionary, some theoretical views have suggested possible contractionary effects. Meade (1951) discusses this theoretical possibility. If the Marshall-Lerner condition is not satisfied, currency depreciation could produce contraction.[56] Hirschman (1949) points out that currency depreciation from an

[55] Empirical support of this proposition for Group 7 countries over the 1960-89 period is provided in Mendoza (1992).

[56] The Marshall-Lerner condition states that devaluation will improve the trade balance if the devaluing nation's demand elasticity for imports plus the foreign demand elasticity for the nation's exports exceed 1.

initial trade deficit reduces real national income and may lead to a fall in aggregate demand. Currency depreciation gives with one hand, by lowering export prices, while taking away with the other hand, by raising import prices. If trade is in balance and terms of trade are not changed these price changes offset each other. But if imports exceed exports, the net result is a reduction in real income within the country. Cooper (1971) confirms this point in a general equilibrium model.

Diaz-Alejandro (1963) introduced another argument for contraction following devaluation. Depreciation may raise the windfall profits in export and import-competing industries. If money wages lag the price increase and if the marginal propensity to save from profits is higher than from wages, national savings will go up and real output will decrease. Krugman and Taylor (1978) and Barbone and Rivera-Batiz (1987) have formalized the same views.

Supply-side channels further complicate the effects of currency depreciation on economic performance. Bruno (1979) and Wijnbergen (1989) postulate that in a typical semi-industrialized country where inputs for manufacturing are largely imported and cannot be easily produced domestically, firms' input cost will increase following a devaluation. As a result, the negative impact from the higher cost of imported inputs may dominate the production stimulus from lower relative prices for domestically traded goods. Gylfson and Schmid (1983) provide evidence that the final effect depends on the magnitude by which demand and supply curves shift because of devaluation.[57]

To summarize, currency depreciation increases net exports and increases the cost of production. Similarly, currency appreciation decreases net exports and the cost of production. The combined effects of demand and supply channels determine the net results of exchange rate fluctuations on real output and price.[58]

This paper revisits the relationship between exchange rate fluctuations and economic activity in Iran. The contribution of the theory is in treating the process of forming rational forecasts of the exchange rate. Recent experiences of currency crises have brought to the forefront the importance of anchoring agents' forecasts in the design of an appropriate exchange rate policy. Hence, the theory aims to separate the effects of anticipated shifts in the exchange rate from unanticipated deviations and agents' forecasts. The theoretical investigation introduces a model that decomposes movements in the exchange rate into anticipated and unanticipated components using rational expectations. Anticipated movement in the exchange rate is assumed to vary with agents' observations of macro-economic fundamentals, which determine changes in the exchange rate over time. Deviation in the realized exchange rate from its anticipated value captures the unanticipated component of the exchange rate.

In this context, the output supplied varies with unanticipated price movements and the cost of the output produced. Anticipated exchange rate movements determine the cost of the output produced. In contrast, unanticipated exchange rate movements determine economic conditions in three directions: net exports, money demand, and the output supplied.

[57] Hanson (1983) provides theoretical evidence that the effect of currency depreciation on output depends on the assumptions regarding the labor market. Solimano (1986) studies the effect of devaluation by focusing on the structure of the trade sector. Agenor (1991) introduces a theoretical model for a small open economy and distinguishes between anticipated and unanticipated movement in the exchange rate. Examples of empirical investigations include Edwards (1986), Gylfason and Radetzki (1991), Roger and Wang (1995), Hoffmaister and Vegh (1996), Bahmani (1998), Kamin and Rogers (2000), and Kandil and Mirzaie (2002, and 2003).

[58] For an analytical overview, see Lizondo and Montiel (1989).

The solution of the model demonstrates the effects of demand and supply channels on the output and price responses to unanticipated changes in the exchange rate. Based on theory's solutions, empirical models are formulated for output and price. The models incorporate demand and supply shifts as well as exchange rate shifts. Exchange rate fluctuations are assumed to be randomly distributed around a steady-state stochastic trend over time. This trend varies over time with agents' observations of macro-economic fundamentals. Positive shocks to the exchange rate indicate an unanticipated increase in the Foreign currency price of domestic currency, i.e., unanticipated currency appreciation. Similarly, negative shocks indicate unanticipated depreciation of the exchange rate.

The data under investigation are for Iran during 1971-2008. The real effective exchange rate for Iran is constructed as a weighted average of bilateral real exchange rates with major trading partners, with weights that represent the share of each trading partner in the total trade of Iran. The real bilateral exchange rate value is the value of the Iranian rial in terms of the trading partner currency, multiplied by the relative price between the two countries. Hence, the real effective exchange rate accounts for the relative prices in the domestic economy relative to foreign prices in the economies of major trading partners. The relative price channel is important to the analysis of exchange rate fluctuations given the high inflationary experience in developing countries, including Iran. Accordingly, the empirical investigation will combine the nominal exchange rate policy with movements in domestic price inflation relative to that of major international prices for trading partners to determine the implications of fluctuations in the real exchange rate on economic performance in Iran.

The results clearly illustrate the different effects of anticipated and unanticipated shifts of the exchange rate on the macroeconomy. Anticipated shifts have limited effects, which minimize the role of rational forecast in guiding production plans in many developing countries, including Iran. In contrast, unanticipated deviation of the realized exchange rate from agents' forecasts induce random fluctuations, with varying effects, positive or negative, on output growth and price inflation. Such fluctuations signal the importance of varying the exchange rate in line with agents' forecasts of fundamentals, striking an appropriate balance between necessary flexibility to ensure competitiveness while maintaining agents' confidence to hold domestic currency.

The remainder of the paper is organized as follows. Section II presents the theoretical model. Section III outlines the empirical models. Section IV presents empirical results. The summary and conclusion are presented in section V.

II. THEORETICAL BACKGROUND

In the real world, stochastic uncertainty may arise on the demand or supply sides of the economy. Economic agents are assumed to be rational. Accordingly, rational expectations of demand and supply shifts enter the theoretical model. Economic fluctuations are then determined by unexpected demand and supply shocks impinging on the economic system.

The paper introduces a macro-economic model that incorporates exchange rate fluctuations of the domestic currency. Fluctuations are assumed to be realized around a steady-state trend that is consistent with variation in macro-economic fundamentals over time. Uncertainty enters the model in the form of disturbances to both aggregate demand and aggregate supply. Within this framework, aggregate demand is affected by currency depreciation through exports, imports, and the demand for domestic currency, and aggregate supply is affected through the cost of imported intermediate goods. The model demonstrates theoretically that unanticipated currency depreciation decreases real output growth, via the effect on the supply side. However, the relationship between unanticipated currency depreciation and aggregate demand makes the final outcome inconclusive.

A. Aggregate Demand

The demand side of the economy is specified using standard IS-LM equations with a modification for an open economy. The specifications below describe equilibrium conditions in the Goods and Money markets. All coefficients are positive and throughout the paper, lower case denotes the logarithm of the corresponding level variable. The subscript *t* denotes the current value of the variable.

$$c_t = c_o + c_1 y_{dt},\ 0 < c_1 < 1 \tag{1}$$

$$y_{dt} = y_t - t_t \tag{2}$$

$$t_t = t_0 + t_1 y_t,\ t_1 > 0 \tag{3}$$

$$i_t = i_0 - i_1 r_t,\ i_1 > 0 \tag{4}$$

$$RE_t = \frac{S_t P_t}{P_t^*} \tag{5}$$

$$x_t = x_0 - x_1 \log\left(RE_t\right),\ x_1 > 0 \tag{6}$$

$$im_t = m_0 + m_1 y_t + m_2 \log\left(RE_t\right),\ m_1, m_2 > 0 \tag{7}$$

$$y_t = c_t + i_t + g_t + x_t - im_t \tag{8}$$

$$m_t - p_t = -\lambda\left[r_t + (E_t p_{t+1} - p_t)\right] + \phi y_t + \theta\left(E_t s_{t+1} - s_t\right),\ \lambda, \phi, \theta > 0 \tag{9}$$

Equations (1) through (8) describe equilibrium conditions in the Goods market. In equation (1), real consumption expenditure, *c*, varies positively with real disposable income, y_d. In equation (2), disposable income is defined to be the net of real income, *y*, minus taxes, *t*. In equation (3), real taxes are specified as a linear function of real income. In equation (4), real investment expenditure, i, varies negatively with the real interest rate, r. In equation (5), let the domestic price level be represented by P and the foreign price level in foreign currency by P^*. S denotes the spot price of domestic currency. It measures the number of foreign currency units per units of domestic currency. RE is the price of domestically produced goods and services relative to the prices of foreign produced goods and services, i.e., the real exchange rate of the domestic currency. When RE increases, the domestic currency appreciates in real terms. The value of RE measures the degree of competitiveness of foreign produced goods and services relative to those produced domestically.[59] In equation (6), real exports are related to an autonomous element, x_0, which rises when the income level abroad rises, and to relative prices. The inverse relationship between RE and x, in (6), refers to the fact that when the domestic price is higher relative to foreign goods, exports will decrease. In equation (7), real imports, im, are assumed to rise with the level of real income and the real exchange rate of the domestic currency. Equation (8) describes the equilibrium condition in the goods market. Real government spending, g, is assumed to be exogenous. The total expenditure by domestic residents in real terms (y) is the sum of real consumption expenditure (c), real investment (i), real government spending (g), and net exports (the real value of exports, x, minus the real value of imports, im).

Substituting all equations into the equilibrium condition for the goods market results in the expression for real income. It is a function of the exchange rate, the domestic price level, the foreign price level, and the domestic interest rate. This expression is the IS equation which describes the negative relationship between real income and the real interest rate.

In equation (9), equilibrium in the money market is obtained by equating the demand and supply of real money balances. The real money supply is determined by nominal balances, m, deflated by price, p. The demand for real money balances is positively related to real income and inversely related to the nominal interest rate. The nominal interest rate is defined as the sum of the real interest rate and inflation expectation at time t. $E_t s_{t+1}$ is the expected future value of the foreign currency at time t. It is assumed that citizens in each country must hold domestic money for transactions purposes but they may speculate by holding foreign money.[60] An unexpected temporary appreciation of the domestic currency in period t would lead to speculation of depreciation in period $t+1$ to restore the steady-state normal trend of the exchange rate, i.e., $(E_t s_{t+1} - s_t) < 0$.[61] Consequently, agents decrease the speculative demand for domestic currency, establishing a positive relationship between the demand for real money balances and agents' expectation of the exchange rate relative to the current value of the currency.

The LM equation is determined by the equilibrium condition in the money market. It establishes a positive relationship between real income and the real interest rate. Solving for the interest rate, r, from the LM equation and substituting the result into the IS equation results in the equation for aggregate demand.

---

[59] For a similar definition, see (Shone 1989).

[60] For a similar discussion, see (Buiter 1990).

[61] Agents are encouraged to dispose of domestic currency following unexpected appreciation.Alternatively, speculative attacks may start if agents perceive the exchange rate to be overvalued (e.g., in the event of a peg that cannot be sustained). Hence, the demand for domestic currency decreases.

B. Aggregate Supply

On the supply side, output is produced using a production function that combines labor, capital, energy and imported intermediate goods. When the currency depreciates (or is devalued), it is more expensive to buy intermediate goods from abroad. The price of energy is paid in dollars in order to isolate this variable from fluctuations in the exchange rate.

To illustrate, the level of gross domestic output, Q, is produced using a production function that combines imported intermediate goods, U, labor, L, and the capital stock, K. The production function is Cobb-Douglas in U and L, assuming fixed capital stock.[62] In addition, the production function is dependent on the energy price, Z. Accordingly, the supply-side of this economy can be summarized in equations (10) through (14) as follows:

$$Q_t = L_t^{\delta} U_t^{1-\delta} e^{-Z_t} \qquad (10)$$

$$Y_t = Q_t - RE_t U_t \qquad (11)$$

$$l_t^d = u_t - \eta\{w_t - p_t + z_t - \log\delta\}, \qquad \eta = \frac{1}{1-\delta} > 0 \qquad (12)$$

$$u_t = l_t + \frac{1}{\delta}\{\log(1-\delta) - z_t + \log(RE_t)\} \qquad (13)$$

$$l_t^s = \eta\log\delta + \omega\{w_t - E_{t-1}p_t\}, \qquad \omega > 0 \qquad (14)$$

Equation (10) specifies the level of gross domestic output produced, assuming complementary relation between the labor input and imported intermediate goods. Equation (11) defines domestic value added (output supplied) or the difference between gross domestic output and the amount of real intermediate imports.[63]

To derive the demand for inputs, the marginal product of L and U is calculated and the results are equated with the real cost of labor (the real wage) and the real price in domestic currency of imported intermediate goods (the real exchange rate). Taking log transformation of the first-order conditions and rearranging produces equations (12) and (13). The demand for labor varies negatively with the real wage and positively with imported intermediate goods. Similarly, the demand for imported intermediate goods increases with the labor input. The appreciation of currency decreases the real price of imported intermediate goods and, hence, increases the demand for these goods. Furthermore, a rise in the energy price decreases the demand for labor and imported intermediate goods.

---

[62] Fixing the capital stock excludes the possibility that depreciation may increase labor productivity by stimulating capital accumulation.

[63] This definition follows Agenor (1991) where he introduces a model and assumes intermediate goods are necessary for the production process and cannot be produced domestically.

Equation (14) hypothesizes a positive log-linear relationship between labor supply and expected real wage. The supply of labor increases with an increase in the nominal wage relative to workers' expected price at time *t-1*.

The nominal wage solution is obtained by equating labor demand and labor supply. Substituting the nominal wage into labor demand results in the solutions for employment and imported intermediate goods. Substituting for *l* and *u* into the log transformation of equation (10), results in an equation for gross domestic output supplied. Substituting the result into the log transformation of equation (11) results in an equation for the aggregate supply of domestic value added. For details of the model solution, see Kandil and Mirzaie (2003).

Aggregate supply has a direct positive relationship with output price surprises. Workers decide on labor supply based on their expectation of the aggregate price level. An increase in aggregate price relative to workers' expectations increases the demand for labor and, hence, the nominal wage. A rise in expected real wage increases employment and, hence, the output supplied. In addition, the aggregate supply moves positively with the foreign currency price of domestic currency. Currency appreciation decreases the cost of imported goods and increases the output supplied. Further, the output supplied varies negatively with changes in the energy price.[64]

C. Market Equilibrium

Internal balance requires that aggregate demand for domestic output be equal to aggregate supply of domestic output at full employment. It is assumed that demand and supply shifts in the model are constructed of two components: anticipated (steady-state) component and an unanticipated (random) component. The combination of demand and supply channels indicates that real output depends on unanticipated movements in the exchange rate, the money supply, government spending, and the energy price.[65] In addition, supply-side channels establish that output varies with anticipated changes in the exchange rate and the energy price.

Given demand-side channels, aggregate demand increases with an unexpected increase in government spending or the money supply, creating positive price surprises and, hence, increasing output and price in the short-run. The allocation of price surprises between output growth and price inflation is dependent on the slope of the short-run supply curve, as determined by elasticities underlying the supply side of the economy. Changes in the energy price, both anticipated and unanticipated, increase the cost of the output produced, decreasing output and raising prices.[66]

The complexity of demand and supply channels may determine the results of exchange rate fluctuations as follows:

---

[64] This assumption assumes the country is an energy importer. Of course, in oil producing country, like Iran, an increase in the energy price is likely to have a positive effect on the output supplied.

[65] With the exception of the energy price, shocks are assumed to fluctuate in response to domestic economic conditions or in response to external vulnerability, e.g., capital mobility or fluctuations in foreign reserves.

[66] The price level may rise unexpectedly in response to energy price shocks, creating incentives to increase the output produced. This channel moderates the reduction in output and the rise in price in response to energy price shocks. For a detailed theoretical illustration, see Kandil and Woods (1997). The moderating effect of the rise in price is further reinforced in the theoretical model through the increase in the real exchange rate, reducing the real cost of intermediate imported goods.

1. In the goods market, a positive shock to the exchange rate of the domestic currency (an unexpected appreciation) will make exports more expensive and imports less expensive. As a result, the competition from foreign markets will decrease the demand for domestic products, decreasing domestic output and price.
2. In the money market, a positive shock to the domestic currency (an unexpected temporary appreciation) relative to anticipated value, prompts agents to hold less domestic currency and decreases the interest rate. This channel moderates the contraction of aggregate demand and, therefore, the reduction in output and price in the face of a positive exchange rate shock.
3. On the supply side, a positive shock to the exchange rate (an unanticipated appreciation) decreases the cost of imported intermediate goods, increasing domestic output and decreasing the cost of production and, hence, the aggregate price level.[67]

III. Empirical Models

The empirical investigation analyzes annual time-series data of real output and price in Iran. The sample period for investigation is 1971-2008. Over time, it is assumed that real output growth and price inflation fluctuate in response to aggregate domestic demand shocks, energy price shocks and exchange rate shocks. Shocks are randomly distributed over the time span under investigation.

Exchange rate shocks are assumed to be distributed around an anticipated stochastic steady-state trend. This trend varies with agents' observations of macroeconomic fundamentals that are likely to determine the exchange rate.[68] Positive shocks to the price of domestic currency in foreign currency represent unanticipated appreciation around this trend. Negative shocks represent unanticipated currency depreciation. Over the time span under investigation, these shocks are assumed to occur with equal probability around the stochastic moving trend. Detailed econometric methodology is provided in Appendix A. Detailed description and sources of all data are described in Appendix B.

The model specification is based on the results of the test for non-stationarity of real output as follows:[69]

---

[67] Other supply-side channels may reinforce the negative effect of currency depreciation on the output supplied. Recent crises in developing countries have illustrated the mismatch effects of currency depreciation on balance sheets. Many developing countries rely on foreign sources of financing. Currency depreciation increases the cost of borrowing by raising the burden of foreign currency denominated liabilities. A higher cost of borrowing has an adverse effect on the supply-side of the economy, further reinforcing the negative effect on output growth and the positive effect on price inflation in the theoretical model.

[68] The theoretical model does not determine the exchange rate or other policy variables endogenously. Instead, the model is solved for the reduced forms that determine the responses to exogenous policy shocks. In theory, shocks approximate unanticipated components of policy shifts based on rational expectations. For example, an overvalued exchange rate represents an unanticipated currency appreciation around agents' expectation of what the exchange rate should be. Econometrically, the anticipated component varies with agents' observations of macro-economic fundamentals, as described in Appendix A.Random shocks capture exogenous fluctuations around the moving trend over time.

[69] For details, see Kwiatkowski et. al. (1992). Non-stationarity indicates that, real output follows a random-walk process. Upon first-differencing, the resulting series is stationary, which is the domain of demand and supply shifts, as specified in theory.

$$Dy_t = A_0 + A_1 E_{t-1}Dz_t + A_2 (Dz_t - E_{t-1}Dz_t) + A_3 E_{t-1} Dm_t + A_4 (Dm_t - E_{t-1}Dm_t) + A_5 E_{t-1} Dg_t + A_6 (Dg_t - E_{t-1}Dg_t) + A_7 E_{t-1} Drs_t + A_8 (Drs_t - E_{t-1}Drs_t) + A_9 EC_{t-1} + V^y_t \quad (15)$$

The test results are consistent with non-stationary real output. Given these results, the empirical model of real output is specified in first difference form where $D(.)$ is the first-difference operator.[70] Accordingly, all variables in the model enter in first-difference form. We also test for the non-stationarity of the energy price, the money supply, government spending and the exchange rate. Given evidence of non-stationarity, we test for co-integration between the non-stationary dependent variables and non-stationary independent variables. Given evidence of co-integration (see Table A2), we introduce an error correction term, EC_{t-1}, into the empirical model. The error correction term is the lagged value of the residual from regressing the non-stationary dependent variable on non-stationary, jointly co-integrated, right hand-side variables. The unexplained residual of the model is denoted by v^y_t. We test for the endogeneity of the exchange-rate and the measures of aggregate demand and supply (see Table A4). Given evidence of endogeneity, the forecast equations account for lagged values of variables proven to be statistically significant. Agents are expected to negotiate higher wages in anticipation of demand expansion. In turn, anticipated demand shifts are neutral.[71] Nonetheless, anticipated demand shifts may determine real output through their effects on anticipated real exchange rate.[72] Consequently, anticipated demand shifts may increase real output.

Let z_t be the log value of the energy price. Agents' expectation of a variable at time t based on information available at time $t-1$ is denoted by E_{t-1}. Based on theory's forecast, output growth is expected to vary negatively with changes in the energy price, both anticipated and unanticipated, at time $t-1$. Accordingly, $A_1, A_2<0$.[73] Two sources of domestic policies, government spending and the money supply, approximate demand shifts, where g_t and m_t denote the log values of government spending and the money supply. Unanticipated growth in government spending and the money supply increase aggregate demand, creating positive price surprises. Hence, $A_4, A_6>0$. Anticipated growth in government spending and the money supply may also increase real output growth. Accordingly, $A_3, A_5>0$.

---

[70] Given the non-stationarity of the estimated dependent variables (see Table A1), the empirical models are estimated in first-difference form. Hence, the anticipated component measures anticipated change in the policy variable. Shocks approximate unanticipated change (growth) in the policy variable.

[71] In the real world, institutional rigidity may interfere with agents' ability to adjust fully to anticipated demand shifts. In the labor market, contracts may be longer than one year, preventing wages at time t from adjusting fully to anticipated demand shifts at time $t-1$. Accordingly, anticipated demand shifts are not absorbed fully in price. Alternatively, institutional rigidity may be attributed to price rigidity in the product market. To reduce menu costs, producers may resort to adjusting prices at specific intervals over time. Given price rigidity, anticipated demand shifts at time $t-1$ may determine real output growth in the short-run. For a discussion of the implications of sticky-wage and sticky-price models, see Kandil (1996).

[72] Anticipated demand shifts increase price, increasing anticipated real exchange rate. This channel moderates anticipated increase in the real cost of imported intermediate goods, increasing the output supply.

[73] The energy price is measured by the international energy price. For oil exporting countries, like Iran, changes in oil price are likely to contribute positively to output growth. The increased capacity, following a rise in the energy price, is likely to moderate price inflation.

Finally, anticipated appreciation of the real exchange rate determines the cost of the output supplied. Let rs_t be the log value of the real exchange rate.[74] Based on Data availability, the exchange rate is measured by the real effective exchange rate, a weighted average of real exchange rates with respect to Iran's major trading partners.[75] Accordingly, a rise in the exchange rate indicates real appreciation of the domestic currency. As producers anticipate a lower cost of imported intermediate goods, in the face of currency appreciation, they increase the output supplied. Accordingly, $A_7>0$.

Unanticipated change in the exchange rate is likely, however, to determine both aggregate demand and supply[76]. Unanticipated currency appreciation, a positive shock to the exchange rate, decreases the cost of buying intermediate goods, increasing the output supplied. Concurrently, appreciation decreases net exports and the demand for domestic currency. The final effect remains indeterminate on aggregate demand, output, and price.

To establish robustness, the empirical model in (15) is reestimated, replacing specific demand shifts (government spending and the money supply) with a broad measure of aggregate demand (nominal GDP) as follows:[77]

$$\begin{aligned}Dy_t &= A_0 + A_1E_{t-1}Dz_t + A_2\left(Dz_t - E_{t-1}Dz_t\right) + A_3E_{t-1}Dn_t + A_4(Dn_t - E_{t-1}Dn_t)\\ &+A_5E_{t-1}Dg_t + A_6\left(Dg_t - E_{t-1}Dg_t\right) + A_7E_{t-1}Drs_t + A_8\left(Drs_t - E_{t-1}Drs_t\right) +\\ &A_9EC_{t-1} + v_t^y \end{aligned} \tag{16}$$

Here, n_t denotes the log of the nominal value of Gross Domestic Product. This broad measure combines a variety of demand shifts stemming from the goods or money markets. Accordingly, $A_3>0$, and $A_4>0$. Model estimation will then determine how important exchange rate fluctuations are, given all other shocks impinging on the aggregate economy.

To demonstrate fluctuations in the output price, an empirical model is specified as follows:

$$\begin{aligned}Dp_t &= B_0 + B_1E_{t-1}Dz_t + B_2\left(Dz_t - E_{t-1}Dz_t\right) + B_3E_{t-1}Dm_t + B_4(Dm_t - E_{t-1}Dm_t)\\ &+B_5E_{t-1}Dg_t + B_6\left(Dg_t - E_{t-1}Dg_t\right) + B_7E_{t-1}Drs_t + B_p\left(Drs_t - E_{t-1}Drs_t\right) + b_9EC_{t-1}\\ &+v_t^p \end{aligned} \tag{17}$$

Based on test results, output price is evident to be non-stationary for the various countries under investigation. Accordingly, the empirical model is specified in first-difference form.

---

[74] This measure captures shifts attributed to the nominal exchange rate, s, and the foreign price of imports, p*, in theory.

[75] The forecast equation of the exchange rate is explained in the econometric methodology appendix. The forecast equation is based on a formal causality test in which we test the significance of lags of variables that may be relevant to the exchange rte. Hence, we do take into account the endogeneity of the exchange rate with respect to growth and inflation. Having accounted for the lags of all variables that are relevant to agents' forecast, the shocks to the exchange rate are identified.

[76] Unanticipated currency appreciation may be the result of unanticipated shock that moves the exchange rate relative to its expected value. Alternatively, unanticipated appreciation may be consistent with an overvalued currency compared to agents' expectations that have adjusted downward in view of underlying macroeconomic fundamentals.

[77] This measure is likely to vary with a variety of shocks underlying aggregate demand: the money supply, government spending, velocity, consumption, investment, and external shocks attributed to fluctuations in the current and capital accounts.

Energy price shifts, both anticipated and unanticipated, increase the cost of the output produced and, hence, prices. Accordingly, B_1, $B_2>0$. Both anticipated and unanticipated demand shifts increase price inflation. Accordingly, B_3, B_4, B_5, $B_6>0$.

Given the effect of anticipated currency appreciation in increasing the output supplied, price inflation decreases and $B_7<0$.[78] An unanticipated appreciation of the domestic currency (a positive shock to the exchange rate) increases the output supplied and may decrease (net exports effect) or increase (money demand effect) aggregate demand. The former two channels are deflationary while the latter increases price inflation.

To establish robustness, the empirical model of price inflation is modified, replacing specific demand shifts with a broad measure of aggregate demand, nominal GDP shifts, as follows:

$$Dp_t = B_0 + B_1E_{t-1}Dz_t + B_2\left(Dz_t - E_{t-1}Dz_t\right) + B_3E_{t-1}Dn_t + B_4(Dn_t - E_{t-1}Dn_t)$$
$$+B_7E_{t-1}Drs_t + B_8\left(Drs_t - E_{t-1}Drs_t\right) + B_9EC_{t-1} + v_t^p \qquad (18)$$

Price inflation varies positively in the face of aggregate demand shifts, both anticipated and unanticipated. Accordingly, $B_3>0$ and $B_4>0$. Note that aggregate demand shifts are allocated between output growth in (16) and price inflation, in (18). Nonetheless, we estimate a separate equation for price to test the effects of exchange rate fluctuations while controlling for a broad measure of aggregate demand in the empirical model.

IV. Empirical Results

The results of estimating the empirical models of real output and price incorporating government spending and the money supply are presented in Table 1. These results indicate the effects of policy variables, as approximated by monetary, fiscal and exchange rate shifts, on output growth and price inflation. Table 2 contains the results of estimating the empirical models that incorporate nominal GDP as a proxy for aggregate demand. Table 3 contains summary statistics of the change in the real and nominal exchange rates, price inflation, and anticipated and unanticipated changes in the real exchange rate.

A. Fluctuations in the Face of Policy Shifts

Table 1 summarizes the evidence of estimating the empirical models in (15) and (17) for Iran.

Theory predicts that an increase in the energy price, both anticipated and unanticipated, increases the cost of the output produced. Hence, the output supplied decreases and price inflation increases. In oil-producing countries like Iran, however, an increase in the energy price is likely to cause an expansion in the output supplied and a reduction in price inflation.

[78] Anticipated shifts in the real exchange rate are function of lagged values of variables that enter the forecast equation, including its own lags. Hence, lagged values of domestic price are captured in anticipated currency shifts.

Anticipated and unanticipated changes in the energy price are generally insignificant on output and price in Iran.[79]

Theory predicts that agents adjust wages and prices in the face of anticipated monetary shifts, neutralizing their effects on output. Consistent with theory's predictions, anticipated monetary shifts are insignificant in determining real output growth in Iran. The inflationary effect of anticipated monetary shifts is also insignificant on price inflation in Iran.

Unanticipated monetary shifts are distributed between real output growth and price inflation with a coefficient that is dependent on the slope of the short-run supply curve. Output growth does not vary significantly in the face of unanticipated monetary shifts in Iran. Overall, the evidence indicates limited effects of monetary policy on real output growth and price inflation in Iran.

Consistent with neutrality, anticipated government spending appears also insignificant on output growth. Anticipated government spending does not accelerate price inflation significantly in Iran. Similarly, the real effect of unanticipated fiscal policy shocks are not significant in Iran. In contrast to theory's prediction, unanticipated shock to government spending has a negative significant effect on price inflation in Iran. The evidence attests that government spending has targeted capacity building over the years, easing binding constraints with a negative significant effect on price inflation.

Table 1. Nonlinear 3SLS Parameter Estimates, using money supply and Government spending

Output									
A0	**A1**	**A2**	**A3**	**A4**	**A5**	**A6**	**A7**	**A8**	**RH0**
-0.63	8.44	-0.08	0.15	-0.41	0.31	0.10	0.08	0.45	0.55*
(-0.08)	(0.07)	(-1.13)	(0.22)	(-1.26)	(0.66)	(0.72)	(0.44)	(0.67)	(2.75)
R-square: 0.50									
Price									
B0	**B1**	**B2**	**B3**	**B4**	**B5**	**B6**	**B7**	**B8**	**RH0**
0.06	0.04	-0.11	0.52	0.29	0.08	-0.37**	-0.48	0.06	0.52
(0.43)	(0.02)	(-0.86)	(0.30)	(0.63)	(0.16)	(-1.97)	(-0.75)	(0.43)	(1.28)
R-square: 0.35									

A0, B0 Intercept
A1, B1 Anticipated Energy Price
A2, B2 Unanticipated Energy Price
A3, B3 Anticipated Money Supply
A4, B4 Unanticipated Money Supply
A5, B5 Anticipated Gov. Spending
A6, B6 Unanticipated Gov. Spending
A7, B7 Anticipated REER
A8, B8 Unanticipated REER
A9 Error Correction
RH0 Serial correlation
* Significant at 5%.
** Significant at 10%.
t-ratios are in parenthesis

[79] It is worth noting that prices may be subject to controls that moderate or eliminate the effects of market shocks, as predicted by theory.

The exchange rate is measured by the real effective exchange rate. Accordingly, a rise in the exchange rate indicates real appreciation of the domestic currency.[80] Theory predicts that anticipated appreciation in the value of the domestic currency decreases the cost of imported goods and increases output growth. There is no evidence of significant output growth in Iran in the face of exchange rate shifts. Hence, the supply-side channel is not significant to transmit the effects of anticipated exchange rate shifts to the real economy.

Unanticipated fluctuations of the domestic currency affect the demand and supply sides of the economy. A positive shock to the exchange rate (an unanticipated appreciation) increases the output supplied and decreases money demand and net exports. The first two channels cause output expansion, while the latter causes output contraction. In contrast, price inflation is likely to decrease with the increase in the output supplied and the reduction in net exports. Consistently, the evidence for Iran is not significant regarding the output and price responses, implying inconclusive evidence on the direction of the effects of unanticipated currency appreciation.

B. Fluctuations in the Face of Aggregate Demand Shifts

Table 2 summarizes the evidence of estimating the empirical models in (16) and (18). The evidence remains robust concerning the insignificant effects of fluctuations in the energy price on economic performance in Iran.

Anticipated aggregate demand shifts are generally significant to stimulate output growth in Iran. In contrast, anticipated aggregate demand shifts are not significant on price inflation. Institutional rigidity prevents price adjustment in the face of unanticipated demand shifts, necessitating non-neutral effect on output growth. In contrast, unanticipated aggregate demand shocks increase price inflation significantly. Accordingly, price inflation accelerates in the face of aggregate demand shocks in Iran in the short-run. In contrast, price controls and capacity expansion mitigate the inflationary effect of aggregate demand on price inflation in the long-run..

Overall, the significant effects of aggregate demand shifts appear more pervasive compared to specific policy shifts. Hence, constraints on the demand side of the economy limit the transmission mechanism of specific policy shifts, namely fiscal and monetary, to the product market in Iran. Further, aggregate spending does not appear to be closely tied to monetary and/or fiscal policies.

The evidence remains robust concerning the limited effect of the supply-side channel in transmitting anticipated exchange rate shifts to the product market in Iran. Consistent with the effect of unanticipated currency appreciation in decreasing the cost of production, output expansion is significant in Iran.

The insignificant evidence provides further support for the complexity of demand and supply channels in determining the effects of exchange rate fluctuations, both anticipated and unanticipated, on price inflation in Iran.

---

[80] Throughout the paper, appreciation will describe increase in the foreign price of domestic currency attributed to either market forces or managed policy within a year.The estimation technique accounts for the endogeneity of the exchange rate with respect to domestic economic conditions. Exogenous shocks are attributed to domestic and/or external shocks.

Table 2. Nonlinear 3SLS Parameter Estimates, using nominal GDP.

Output								
A0	**A1**	**A2**	**A3**	**A4**	**A7**	**A8**	**A9**	**RH0**
-0.18	-0.62	0.02	1.29**	0.15	-0.17	0.13*	-0.37	0.67*
(-1.10)	(-0.54)	(0.37)	(2.09)	(0.91)	(-0.38)	(2.50)	(-1.38)	(2.24)
R-square: 0.79								
Price								
B0	**B1**	**B2**	**B3**	**B4**	**B7**	**B8**	**B9**	**RH0**
0.13	1.05	-0.07	0.02	0.87*	-0.66	-0.05	-0.56*	0.36
(0.96)	(0.84)	(-1.27)	(0.04)	(6.24)	(-1.07)	(-0.99)	(-2.61)	(-1.20)
R-square: 0.85								

A0, B0 Intercept
A1, B1 Anticipated Energy Price
A2, B2 Unanticipated Energy Price
A3, B3 Anticipated nominal GDP
A4, B4 Unanticipated Nominal GDP
A7, B7 Anticipated Real Effective Exchange Rate
A8, B8 Unanticipated Real Effective Exchange Rate
A9 Error Correction
RH0 Serial correlation
* Significant at 5%.
** Significant at 10%.
t-ratios are in parentheses

SUMMARY AND CONCLUSION

The analysis has focused on the effects of exchange rate fluctuations on Iran. To that end, the paper presents a theoretical rational expectation model that decomposes movements in the exchange rate into anticipated and unanticipated components. Anticipated changes in the exchange rate enter the production function through the cost of imported goods. Unanticipated currency fluctuations determine aggregate demand through exports, imports, and the demand for domestic currency, and determine aggregate supply through the cost of imported intermediate goods.

Let the exchange rate be the real price of the domestic currency in terms of a weighted average of currencies for major trading partners for Iran. Anticipated movements in the exchange rate are assumed to vary with agents' observations of macro-economic fundamentals determining changes in the exchange rate over time. A positive shock to the exchange rate, an unanticipated appreciation of the domestic currency, decreases net exports and money demand and increases the output supplied. Based on the strength of each channel, the combined effects of demand and supply channels may determine the direction of output and price adjustments in the face of currency fluctuations.

In general, Iran is characterized by a high degree of price flexibility in the face of unanticipated aggregate demand shifts. In contrast, capacity expansion has limited price adjustment to anticipated aggregate demand shifts in the long-run, producing non-neutral effects, i.e., significant real growth expansion. Nonetheless, the real and inflationary effects of specific policy shocks, fiscal and monetary, appear limited on output and price. Hence, demand-side constraints hinder the transmission mechanism of domestic policies to the product market. Further, aggregate spending does not appear to be closely tied to monetary and fiscal policies.

The limited effects of anticipated exchange rate appreciation on output growth and price inflation indicate that rational forecast of exchange rate movement is rather limited to gauge the strategy of agents in Iran. Hence, producers do not adjust the supply side to react to a lower (higher) cost of imported goods in response to anticipated exchange rate appreciation (depreciation).

In contrast, unanticipated fluctuations of the exchange rate appear more significant in determining output fluctuations in Iran. Consistent with the effects of unanticipated exchange rate appreciation (depreciation) in decreasing (increasing) the cost of production, output expansion (contraction) is evident and significant in Iran. Nonetheless, the effects of demand and supply channels cancel out, rendering the effects of exchange rate fluctuations, both anticipated and unanticipated, insignificant on price inflation in Iran.

The results clearly illustrate the importance of designing exchange rate policy in consistency with agents' forecasts, given underlying macroeconomic fundamentals. Movements in the exchange rate in consistency with agents' expectations have limited effects on the macroeconomy. In contrast, high variability of exchange rate fluctuations around its anticipated value may generate adverse effects in the form of larger output contraction in the face of unanticipated currency depreciation that would raise the cost of production, with limited positive effects to boost net exports, in Iran.

While stimulating net exports through currency depreciation is desirable, it is crucial to ensure a concurrent increase in productive capacity to cope with the increased demand and boost competitiveness, without accelerating price inflation. Relaxing constraints on the supply side are, therefore, necessary to reinforce output growth and stabilize prices in the face of currency fluctuations.

Finally, monetary policy should aim at minimizing extensive fluctuations in the exchange rate that may induce speculative attacks and undermine the stability of the money demand function. Towards this objective, exchange rate policy should aim at striking the right balance between necessary flexibility to ensure competitiveness and desirable stability to increase confidence in domestic currency and underlying fundamentals that provide support to the currency value over time.

APPENDIX A. ECONOMETRIC METHODOLOGY

To account for endogenous variables in the empirical model (1), instrumental variables are used in estimation. The instrument list includes three lags of the growth rate of real government spending, the money supply, energy prices, the nominal exchange rate, FDI, nominal GDP and CPI. In a few cases, the number of lags has been modified until the estimation did converge. The paper's evidence remains robust with respect to modifications that alter variables or the lag length in the instruments list.

Table A1. The KPSS Statistics for Null of Level Stationary (The 5% critical value is 0.463)

	Lag Truncation Parameter				
	0	1	2	3	4
Output	2.02	1.12	0.82	0.68	0.60
Price	2.06	1.14	0.82	0.66	0.56

Test description:

The KPSS (Kwiatowski, Phillips, Schmidt, and Shin) stationarity test procedure examines the null hypothesis of stationarity of a univariate time series. The KPSS test assumes that a time series variable X_t could be decomposed into the sum of a deterministic trend, a random walk, and a stationary error. Then the random walk term is assumed to have two components: an anticipated component and an error term. The stationarity of the error term is established by testing if the variance of the error is zero.

If the calculated lag truncation variable is greater than 0.463, we reject the null hypothesis of stationarity.

Table A2. Cointegration Test Results

ADF test statistics for the null hypothesis of non-stationary residuals. Critical value at 10% = -2.62 Cointegration regression includes energy price, real exchange rate, money supply, and government spending.	
Output	**Price**
-1.17	-2.36

Test Description:

If we have n endogenous variables, each of which is first-order integrated (that is, each has a unit root or stochastic trend or random walk element), there can be from zero to n-1 linearly independent cointegrating vectors. If there is one cointegrating equation, the regression models of the text include a lag of error correction term.

To check for cointegration, we apply the ADF unit root test to the residual from the cointegration regression in which the non-stationary level of output and price are regressed on the level of variables that enter the model.

* The results reject the null hypothesis of non-stationarity at the 10% level.

Table A3. Cointegration Test Results

ADF test statistics for the null hypothesis of non-stationary residuals. Critical value at 10% = -2.62 Cointegration regression includes energy price, real exchange rate, and nominal GDP.	
Output	**Price**
-2.73*	-2.57

Test Description:

If we have n endogenous variables, each of which is first-order integrated (that is, each has a unit root or stochastic trnd or random walk element), there can be from zero to n-1 linearly independent cointegrating vectors. If there is one cointegrating equation, the regression models of the text include a lag of error correction term.

To check for cointegration, we apply the ADF unit root test to the residual from the cointegration regression in which the non-stationary level of output and price are regressed on the level of variables that enter the model.

* The results reject the null hypothesis of non-stationarity at the 10% level.

Table A4. The Results of Endogeneity Tests

	Forecasted Variables				
	Dz	**Ds**	**Dm**	**Dg**	**Dn**
Energy price (Dz)		1.33	0.86	0.21	0.30
Real exchange rate (Ds)	0.81		1.08	0.19	0.10
Money Supply (Dm)	0.23	0.27		1.47	0.72
Government Spending (Dg)	3.41*	1.77	2.51		2.09
Nominal GDP (Dn)	1.50	0.14	0.24	0.82	

* F-value is greater than the critical value of F at 10%.

Following the suggestions of Engle (1982), the results of the test for serial correlation in simultaneous equation models are consistent with the presence of first-order autoregressive errors. To maintain comparability, it is assumed in all models that the error term follows an AR(1) process. The estimated models are transformed, therefore, to eliminate any possibility of serial correlation. The estimated residuals from the transformed models have zero means and are serially independent. Moreover, the residuals are orthogonal to variables in the instruments list and right hand-side variables in the final empirical model.

Econometric Methodology

To account for endogenous variables in the empirical model (1), instrumental variables are used in estimation. The instrument list includes three lags of the growth rate of real government spending, the money supply, energy prices, the nominal exchange rate, FDI, nominal GDP and CPI. In a few cases, the number of lags has been modified until the estimation did converge. The paper's evidence remains robust with respect to modifications that alter variables or the lag length in the instruments list.

Following the suggestions of Engle (1982), the results of the test for serial correlation in simultaneous equation models are consistent with the presence of first-order autoregressive errors. To maintain comparability, it is assumed in all models that the error term follows an AR(1) process. The estimated models are transformed, therefore, to eliminate any possibility of serial correlation. The estimated residuals from the transformed models have zero means and are serially independent. Moreover, the residuals are orthogonal to variables in the instruments list and right hand-side variables in the final empirical model.

Data Sources

The sample period for investigation is 1971-2008. Annual data for the above countries are described as follows:

1. Real Output: Real output of GDP measured in terms of 1997 dollars.
2. The Price Level: The deflator for GDP.
3. The Energy Price: Crude Oil (petroleum), Price index, 2005 = 100, simple average of three spot prices; Dated Brent, West Texas Intermediate, and the Dubai Fateh

4. Government Spending: Nominal values of all payments by the government.
5. Money Supply: the sum of currency plus demand deposits.
6. Real Effective Exchange Rate

Sources: 1 through 6 are taken from the *World Economic Outlook*, data bank available from the International Monetary Fund, Washington, D.C.

REFERENCES

Agenor, Pierre-Richard, (1991)."Output, Devaluation and the Real Exchange Rate in Developing Countries,"*Weltwirtschaftliches Archive*, Band *127*.

Bahmani-Oskooee, Mohsen & Ida Aghdas Mirzaie, (2000)."The Long-Run Effects of Depreciation of the Dollar on Sectoral Output,"*International Economic Journal*, Vol. *14* (Autumn), 51-61.

Bahmani-Oskooee, Mohsen & Ilir Miteza (2003)."Are Devaluations Expansionary or Contractionary? A Survey Article", *Economic Issues*, Vol. *8*, 1-28.

Barbone, Luca & Francisco Rivera-Batiz (1987)."Foreign Capital and the Contractionary Impact of Currency Devaluation, with an Application to Jamaica," *Journal of Development Economics*, Vol. *26*, (June), 1–15.

Bruno, M. (1979)."Stabilization and Stagflation in a Semi-Industrialized Economy," in R. Dornbusch and J. Frankel, eds. *International Economic Policy*, Johns Hopkins University Press, Baltimore, MD.

Cooper, Richard N. (1971)."Currency Devaluation in Developing Countries," *Essays in International Finance*, No. 86, International Finance Section, Princeton University.

Diaz-Alejandro, Carlos F.(1963)."Note on the Impact of Devaluation and Redistributive Effect," *Journal of Political Economy,* Vol. *71*, (August), 577–80.

Edwards, S. (1986)."Are Devaluation Contractionary?," *The Review of Economics and Statistics*, August.

Engle, R. R. (1982)."A General Approach to Lagrange Multiplier Model Diagnostics," *Journal of Econometrics*, Vol. *20*, 83–104.

Gylfason, Thorvaldur & Schmid, Michael (1983)."Does Devaluation Cause Stagflation?"*Canadian Journal of Economics*, Vol. *XVI*, November 1983.

Gylfason, T. & Radetzki (1991)."Does Devaluation Make Sense in Least Developed Countries?"*Economic Development and Cultural Change*, (October).

Guittian, Manuel (1976)."The Effects of Changes in the Exchange Rate on Output, Prices, and the Balance of Payments," *Journal of International Economics*, Vol. *6*, 65–74.

Hanson, James A.(1983)."Contractionary Devaluation, Substitution in Production and Consumption, and the Role of the Labor Market," *Journal of International Economics*, Vol. *14*, 179–89.

Hirschman, Albert O. (1949)."Devaluation and the Trade Balance: A Note," *Review of Economics and Statistics*, Vol. *31*, 50–53.

Kandil, Magda & Ida Mirzaie (2002)."Exchange Rate Fluctuations and Disaggregated Economic Activity in the U.S.: Theory and Evidence," *Journal of International Money and Finance*, No. *1*, (February), 1–31.

Kandil, Magda & Ida Mirzaie (2003). "The Effects of Dollar Appreciation on Sectoral Labor Market Adjustments: Theory and Evidence," *Quarterly Review of Economics and Finance*, Vol. *43*, No. *1*, 89–117.

Kamin& Rogers(2000)."Output and the Real Exchange Rate in Developing Countries: An Application to Mexico," *Journal of Development Economics*, No. *61*.

Krugman & Taylor (1987)."Contractionary Effects of Devaluation,"*Journal of International Economics*, No. *8*, 445–56.

Kwiatkowski, Denis, Phillips, Peter C. B., Peter Schmidt & Yongcheol Shin(1992)."Testing the Null Hypothesis of Stationarity Against the Alternative of a Unit Root: How Sure Are We That Economic Time Series Have a Unit Root?"*Journal of Econometrics*, No. *54*, 159–78.

Lizondo, Saul, J. & Montiel, Peter J.(1989)."Contractionary Devaluation in Developing Countries: An Analytical Overview," *IMF Staff Papers*, *36* (1), (March), 182–227.

Meade, James E.(1951).*The Theory of International Economic Policy, I: The Balance of Payment*, Oxford University Press, Oxford.

Mendoza, E. G.(1992)."The Effect of Macroeconomic Shocks in a Basic Equilibrium Framework," *IMF Staff Papers*, *39*, 4, 855–89.

Pagan, Adrian (1984)."Econometric Issues in the Analysis of Regressions with Generated Regressors," *International Economic Review*, No. *25*, 221–47.

Pagan, Adrian (1986)."Two Stage and Related Estimators and Their Applications," *Review of Economic Studies*, No. *53*, 517–38.

Shone, Ronald(1989)."Open Economy Macroeconomics," Harvester Wheatsheaf.

Wijnbergen, Sweder Van (1989)."Exchange Rate Management and Stabilization Policies in Developing Countries," *Journal of Development Economics*, No. *23*, 227–47.

In: Exchange Rates in Developed and Emerging Markets ISBN: 978-1-62808-164-0
Editor: Mohsen Bahmani-Oskooee

Chapter 11

REMITTANCES AND EQUILIBRIUM REAL EXCHANGE RATES IN EMERGING AND SMALL OPEN COUNTRIES

Serge Rey * ***and Elisa Dienesch***
CATT – University of Pau et Pays de l'Adour, Pau Cedex, France

ABSTRACT

This article proposes a modified version of a small country NATREX model that accounts for the role of remittances in the determination of the real equilibrium exchange rate (REER). To estimate two models—one applied for the REER and another used to find the relative price of non-traded goods—this study considers a group of 24 emerging and small open economies over 1986–2011. Using panel cointegration methods, the authors show that increased absorption, coming from the public sector or private income transfers (remittances), produces a real appreciation of the exchange rate. Although remittances lead to this appreciation, through their impact on the demand of non-traded goods, this result may become questionable, depending on the degree of openness in certain economies. Unlike previous studies, by taking the degree of openness into account, this article shows that remittances associated with greater openness lead to a real depreciation of the exchange rate.

Keywords: Real equilibrium exchange rate, NATREX, remittances, panel cointegration, emerging countries, small open economies

1. INTRODUCTION

Recent approaches to modeling real equilibrium exchange rates assert that it is neither constant nor nonstationary, in contrast with purchasing power parity theory. Rather, its trajectory depends on changes in nonstationary fundamental variables. For the past several decades, three families of models have dominated this literature stream: the FEER

* Corresponding author: E-mail: serge.rey@univ-pau.fr., CATT, University of Pau et Pays de l'Adour, Avenue du Doyen Poplawski - BP1633, 64016 Pau Cedex - France.

(fundamental equilibrium exchange rate) model developed by Williamson (1994); the BEER (behavioral equilibrium exchange rate) model of MacDonald (2000), and Stein's (1994) NATREX (natural real exchange) model. We also add Edwards's (1989) model, focused specifically on developing countries (also see Clark and MacDonald, 1999; Driver and Westaway, 2003; Stein, 2006). These models follow the tradition of Nurkse (1944) and Artus (1977) and ensure that the real equilibrium exchange rate satisfies the macroeconomic equilibrium condition:

$$S - I = CA <==> I - S + CA = 0, \quad (1)$$

where S is the desired savings (public and private), I refers to the desired investment (public and private), and CA denotes the current account, "when the economy is at capacity output and expectations about inflation are met" (Allen, 1995, p. 3). Changes in savings and investments affect the current account, leading to changes in the real exchange rate (R) until it reaches equilibrium. Desired savings and investments usually are considered either independent of R or relatively unresponsive, and saving and investment decisions are made independently. According to these models, S and I depend on different exogenous variables, including productivity rates, social time preferences, terms of trade, net foreign asset positions, and real interest rates—all of which constitute medium- to long-term determinants of the real equilibrium exchange rate. Among these, we can identify variables that affect savings and investments, respectively.

However, models developed in the 1980s and 1990s largely ignored a phenomenon that has become unavoidable in the modern global environment, namely, flows of workers' remittances. Figure 1 depicts these flows, expressed in billion of US dollars for 1970–2011. Clearly, they have increased substantially since the end of the 1990s.

More recent literature on remittances confirms that these flows exert impacts on the consumption exhibited by recipient countries. Chami et al. (2008, p. 28) offer evidence that "the majority of remitted funds are spent on consumption," and other studies confirm this trend, especially for countries such as El Salvador (where 80 percent of funds are allocated to private consumption; Cacerès and Saca, 2006), Pakistan, and Greece. The Multilateral Investment Fund (2004) also reveals that consumption accounted for between 60 and 80 percent of the remittance allocations in Latin American countries, findings confirmed by the World Bank (2006). Research into the motivations to remit often highlights desires for consumption smoothing and investments as two key determinants (Rapoport and Docquier, 2006; Hagen-Zager and Siegel, 2007). Therefore, we seek to reformulate real equilibrium exchange rate models to acknowledge consumption as a fundamental variable.

Barajas et al. (2011) provide a brief review of relevant literature but worry that prior research is largely empirical and tends to favor the estimation of panel models using fixed effects ordinary least squares with instrumental variables (Amuedo-Dorantes and Pozo, 2004; Lopez et al., 2007) or generalized method of moments (Acosta et al., 2009; Lartey et al., 2012).[81] In this sense, prior studies

[81] In a Jordanian study, using a standard Johansen method, Saadi-Sedik and Petri (2006, p.17) conclude: "An increase in workers' remittances of 1 percent will appreciate the equilibrium real exchange rate by 0.4 percent."

> essentially examine the contemporaneous effect of changes in worker remittances on the actual real exchange rate. As such, the effects that they estimate may be purely transitory ones, which leave the equilibrium real exchange rate unchanged. The effects of permanent changes in remittance flows on the equilibrium real exchange rate therefore remain unexamined (Barajas et al., 2011, p. 16).

In our study, we analyze the impact of remittances on the real effective exchange rate (REER) for a group of 24 countries that represent emerging and small open economies (see Appendix 1), from 1986 to 2011, a time period that ensures a balanced sample. We hew close to Barajas et al.'s (2011) recommended approach and apply a cointegration methodology, which enables us to analyze the long-run relationship between the equilibrium exchange rate and remittances. In addition, the methodology is highly relevant, in that the real exchange rate and its fundamentals are nonstationary.

We therefore proceed in three steps. First, we propose a real exchange rate model, which modifies the small open economy NATREX (Stein and Lim, 1995) to account for remittances as a fundamental variable. Second, we apply Pedroni's (1999, 2004) panel cointegration tests to determine if there is a long-run relationship between REER and the fundamentals related to remittances. Third, we use fully modified ordinary least squares (FMOLS) to estimate the long-run cointegration for nonstationary panels. With these steps, we can estimate the long-run macroeconomic impact of remittances on the REER and thereby verify whether increases in workers' remittances catalyze real appreciation of the effective exchange rate, which can produce a Dutch disease phenomenon, as well as compare the role of remittances with other fundamental determinants of the real exchange rate to confirm the need to reformulate standard models.

In Section 2, we thus present stylized facts about remittances flows and REER for each country in our panel. After we detail the theoretical model in Section 3, we present the structural equations with remittance variables. Then in Section 4, we implement several panel unit root tests and test for the existence of panel cointegration relationships. Finally, we present the cointegration relationship estimates in Section 5 and conclude in Section 6.

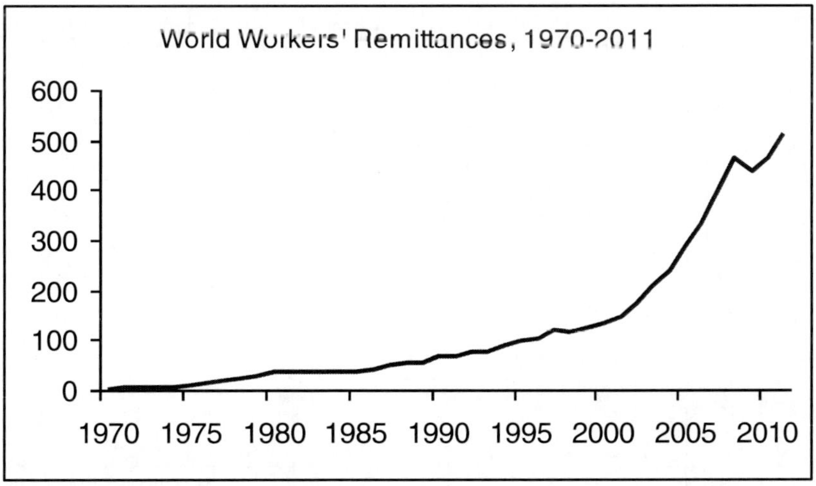

Source: World Bank and IMF Balance of Payments Statistics Yearbook 2012 (calculations by authors)

Figure 1. Worldwide workers' remittances (billions of US dollars).

2. DATA AND DESCRIPTIVE STATISTICS

The real effective exchange rate of a country *i* is the geometric average of bilateral real exchange rates with all trading partners, weighted by their respective trade shares:

$$REER_i = \prod_{j=1}^{N} \left(\frac{N_{ij} \cdot P_i}{P_j} \right)^{\theta_{ij}},$$

where N_{ij} is the bilateral nominal exchange rate between country *i* and its partners *j*, P_i and P_j are the consumer price indexes in each country, and θ_{ij} is the share of country *j* in the total trade of country *i*.

We employ annual data for the nominal exchange rates and consumer prices indexes, which we extracted from an International Financial Statistics (IFS) CD-ROM. To compute trade shares, we used UN COMTRADE data about bilateral exports and imports of goods. To obtain the remittance data, we used World Bank staff calculations, based on data from IMF Balance of Payments Statistics Yearbook 2012 and data releases from central banks, national statistical agencies, and World Bank country desks. These remittances are expressed in millions of US dollars. Gross domestic product (GDP) data come from the World Development Indicators database and IFS CD-ROM. We present the data sources in Appendix 2.

In Table 1 we note some descriptive statistics about remittances in selected countries. This sample of selected countries reveals that remittances do not have the same weight in all economies, even if they exhibit common characteristics. For countries such as Jordan, Morocco, and the Philippines, remittance inflows represent more than 10 percent of GDP; for other emerging countries such as Brazil and China, they represent only 1–2 percent of GDP.

Table 1. Descriptive Statistics: Remittances as a Percentage of GDP

Countries	2011	Mean over Period	Standard Deviation	Minimum	Maximum
Algeria	1.2	1.7	0.78	0.56	3.14
Brazil	0.2	0.2	0.15	0.00	0.53
China	0.8	0.4	0.39	0.00	1.09
Hungary	1.7	0.8	0.61	0.33	1.84
Iceland	0.2	0.6	0.32	0.19	1.02
India	3.4	2.5	1.00	0.73	3.83
Jordan	12	17.9	3.93	10.30	25.10
Morocco	7.2	6.9	1.14	4.87	8.93
Kenya	2.8	1.5	1.31	0.00	4.54
Pakistan	5.8	4.1	1.61	1.50	7.90
Philippines	10.3	7.9	3.58	2.88	13.15
Thailand	1.2	1.0	0.31	0.39	1.84
Tunisia	4.4	4.2	0.55	3.05	5.19

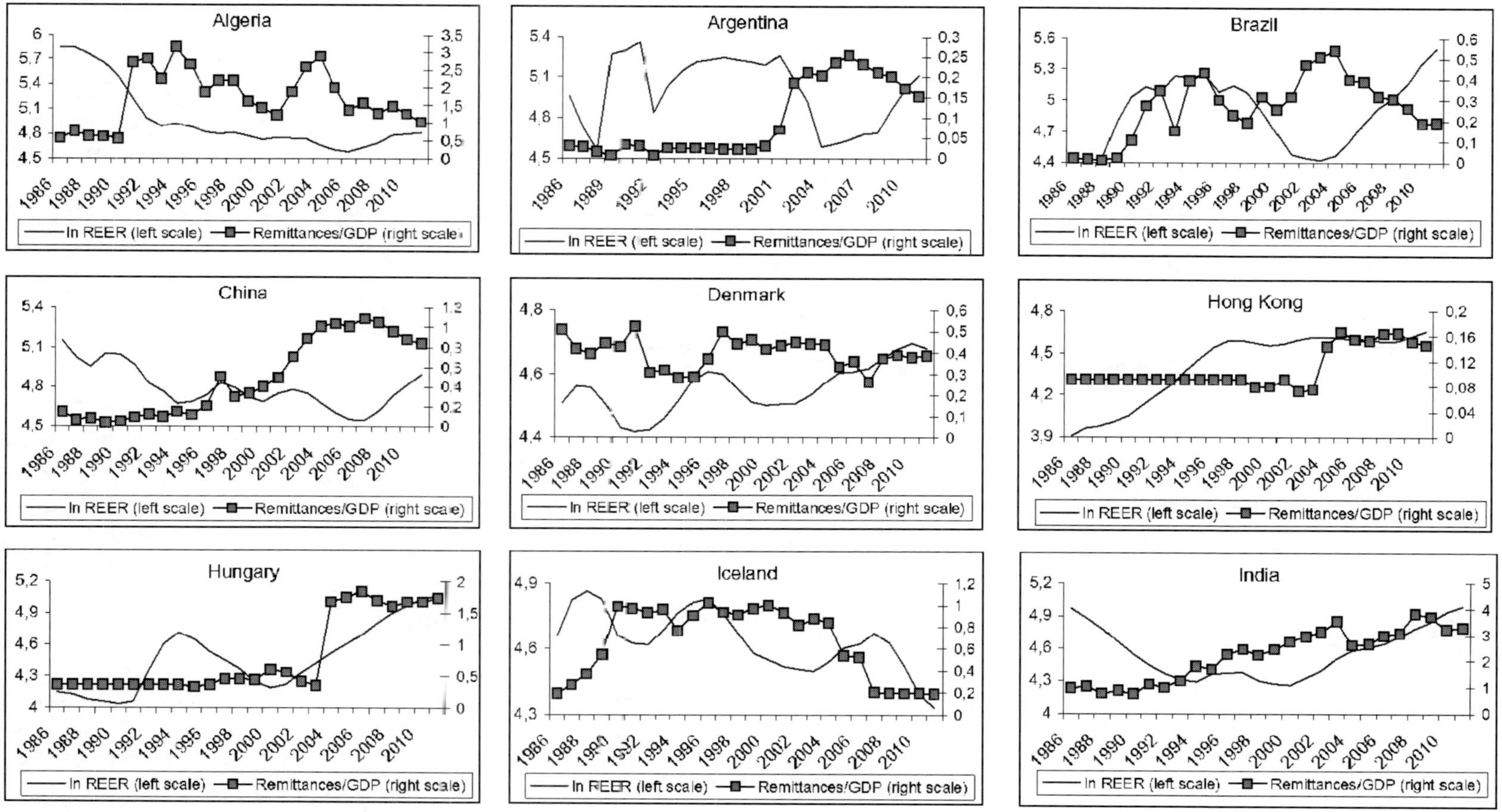

Figure 2. (Continued).

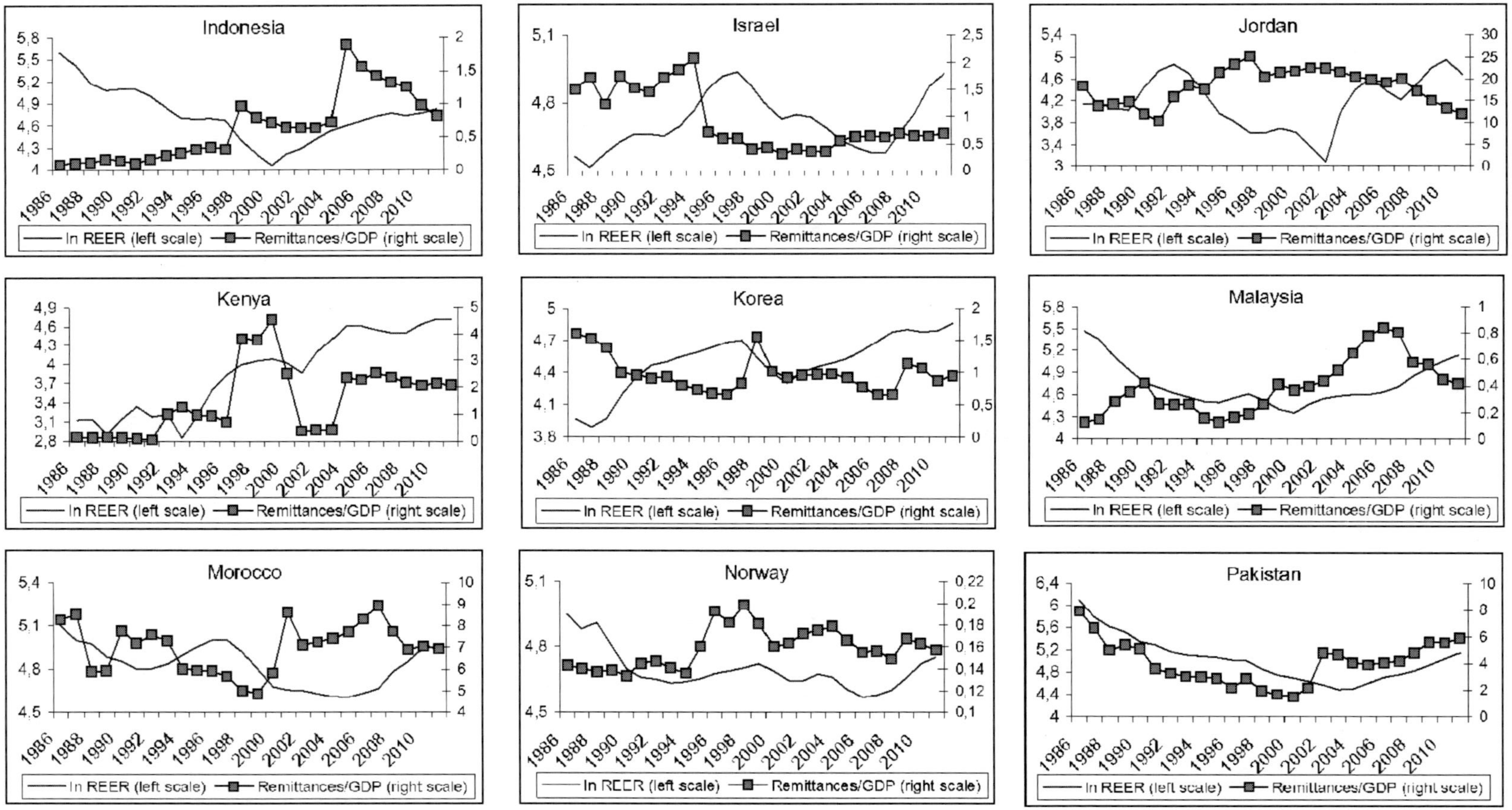

Figure 2. (Continued).

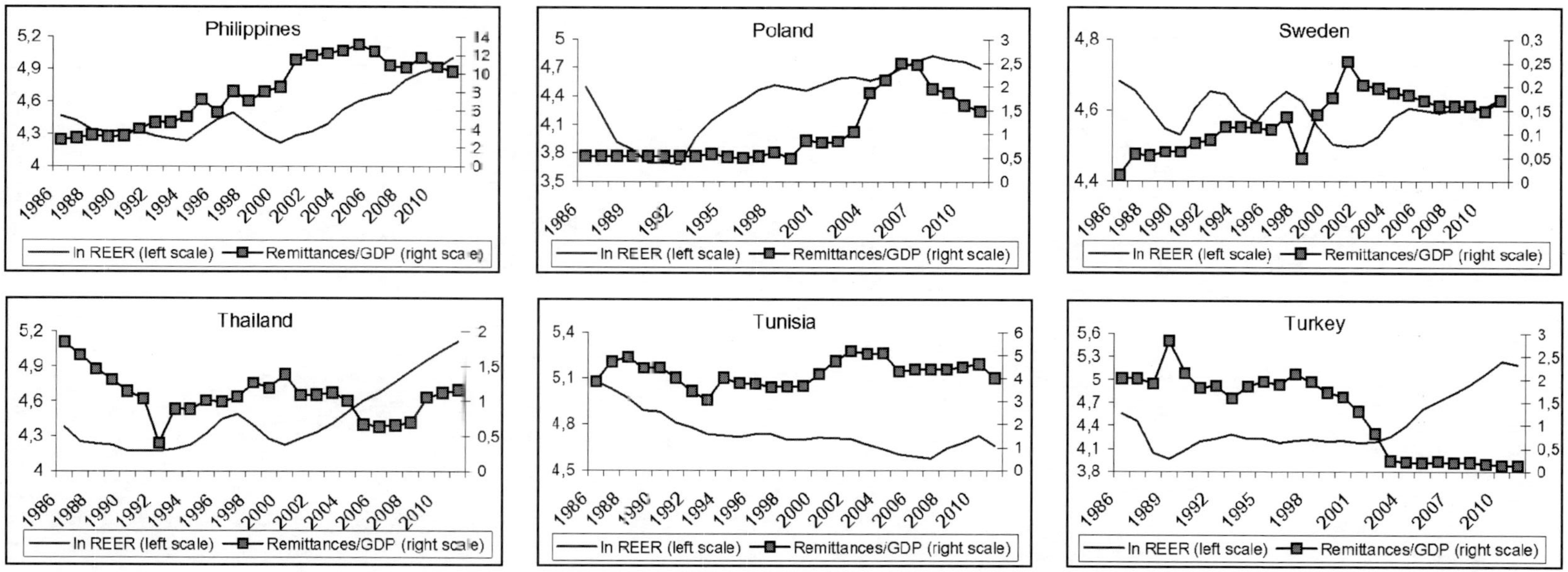

Figure 2. Real effective exchange rate (log) and remittances in terms of GDP (%)

Figure 2 further shows that during the 1990s, remittance inflows rose sharply. Slowdowns in some countries, such as Mediterranean countries, likely reflected political events (e.g., the Arab Spring), which led many migrant workers to return to their countries of origin. For most countries, we also observe a movement of appreciation of the real effective exchange rate in the 2000s, coinciding with a rise in the remittances-to-GDP ratio. For some countries, the subprime crisis might help explain the downturn in this ratio around 2007.

3. MODEL

Following Stein and Lim (1995) and Stein (1994, 2006), we retained a small country version of the NATREX. The equilibrium real exchange rate satisfies the macroeconomic equilibrium condition, $I - S + CA = 0$, where all quantity variables are measured per unit of effective labor in the economy.

3.1. Real Exchange Rate for a Small Country

If R is the bilateral real exchange rate between the domestic currency and a foreign currency,

$$R = N \cdot P/P^{*}, \tag{1}$$

where N is the nominal exchange rate, and P and P^* are the general price levels in the domestic and foreign/partner country, respectively. A rise in N (R) signifies a nominal (real) appreciation of the domestic currency. We distinguish tradable and non-tradable sectors and assume the tradable good produced by the domestic country is the export good, with a price of P_X. Furthermore, a tradable good produced by the foreign/partner country is imported by the domestic country, and its price (in foreign currency) is P^*_M. Therefore, we can decompose:

$$P = (P_X)^{(1-a)} \cdot (P_N)^{a}, \text{ and } P^{*} = (P_M^{*})^{(1-b)} \cdot (P_N^{*})^{b}, \tag{2}$$

where P_N refers to the non-traded goods prices (index N), and a and b are the shares of non-traded goods (with $(1-a)$, $(1-b)$ equal to the shares of traded goods) in these economies. The real exchange rate in Equation (1) thus becomes:

$$R = \left(\frac{N.P_X}{P_M^{*}} \right) . (P_N / P_X)^{a} . \left(P_N^{*} / P_M^{*}\right)^{-b} \tag{3}$$

The first and third term on the right-hand side of this equation represent the terms of trade (*Tot* hereafter) and the relative price of non-tradable to tradable goods in the partner country, respectively. These two variables are exogenous for a small country. That is, the endogenous variations in the real exchange rate correspond to the endogenous variations of the domestic relative price of non-tradable goods (R_N). If we normalize the ultimate term of the equation at unity, we obtain

$$R = Tot.(R_N)^a \quad (4)$$ [82]

In this case, modeling the real exchange rate reduces to modeling the relative price of non-tradable goods. In other words, the goods market clearing condition is equivalent to the non-tradable goods market equilibrium, because the markets for tradable goods always clear at the world prices.

3.2. The Supply of Non-Tradable Goods

We retain a function production of the following form:

$$Q_N = u_N . k_N^{\alpha} . \lambda \quad (5)$$

where Q_N is output per effective worker ($Q_N = Y_N / L$), such that Y_N is the output and L is total labor), u_N refers to the total factor productivity of the non-tradable sector, k_N is the capital intensity of the non-tradable sector (capital/labor ratio), and the λ ratio compares labor in the non-tradable sector to total labor.[83] The capital (K) and labor are allocated between tradable and non-tradable goods sectors. Therefore,

$$\begin{cases} k_N = K_N / L_N \\ k_T = K_T / L_T \\ K = K_T + K_N \\ L = L_T + L_N \\ and\ \lambda = (k - k_N)/(k_N - k_T) \end{cases} \quad (6)$$

where the T and N indices represent the tradable sector and the non-tradable sector, respectively. The value of marginal products from capital and labor is equal in the two sectors, such that we have wage equality and rent equality:

[82] In the case of a REER, this relationship becomes $REER = \frac{N^{eff} \cdot P_x}{P^{eff,}} \cdot (R_N)^a$, where N^{eff} is the nominal effective exchange rate, P^{eff} refers to the effective price, and $\frac{N^{eff} \cdot P_x}{P^{eff,}}$ represents effective terms of trade.

[83] Note that for the tradable sector, $Q_T = u_T . k_T^{\beta} .(1-\lambda)$.

$$MPL_T(k_T;u_T) = R_N.MPL_N(k_N;u_N)$$
$$MPK_T(k_T;u_T) = R_N.MPK_N(k_N;u_N) \tag{7}$$

where *MPK* denotes the physical marginal product of capital, *MPL* is the physical marginal product of labor, and R_N refers to the relative price of non-tradable goods ($R_N = P_N/P_X$). From Equation (6), we obtain:

$$k_T = f_T(R_N, k; u)$$
$$k_N = f_N(R_N, k; u) \tag{8}$$

where $u = (u_T, u_N)$. Then from Equations (6)–(8) we deduce the supply equation:

$$Q_N = Q_N(R_N, k, u), \tag{9}$$

for which $\partial Q_N/\partial R_N > 0$, $\partial Q_N/\partial k > 0$, and $\partial Q_N/\partial u > 0$.

Some literature asserts that remittances may have a positive effect on education and thus on human capital, as well as in some cases a negative effect on the labor supply. However, empirical studies conclude that these effects are unclear and depend on the choice of country (e.g., Rapoport and Docquier, 2006). For this study, we assume the supply of non-tradable goods is not be affected by remittances.[84]

3.3. The Demand for Non-Tradable Goods

The demand for non-traded goods consists of consumption per effective worker C_N and investment per effective worker I_N. Therefore, θ $(1-\theta)$ represents the share of remittances dedicated to consumption (investment), for both traded and non-traded goods.

Consumption of non-tradable goods consists of private consumption C_p and public consumption C_g. Following NATREX, private consumption is proportional to net wealth $k-f$, where *f* represents the external net/foreign debt, measured in terms of effective workers. Thus, $C_p = \delta.(k-f)$, and the coefficient δ is the exogenous discount rate/time preference. Public/government consumption instead is $C_g = g.Y$, where *g* represents an "exogenous fiscal parameter, a political variable" (Stein and Paladino, 2001, p. 118). Aggregate consumption can be decomposed into consumption of non-traded goods and consumption of traded/imported goods. Sharing between non-tradable and tradable/imported

[84] If remittances affect human capital, and therefore factor productivity, positively, we would denote $u(\text{Rem}) = (u_T(\text{Rem}), u_N(\text{Rem}))$, with $u'(\text{Rem}) > 0$, and $Q_N = Q_N(R_N, k, \text{Rem})$ with $\partial Q_N/\partial \text{Rem} > 0$.

goods depends on the price of non-tradable goods relative to tradable/imported goods: $\frac{P_N}{P_M^* / N} = \frac{N.P_X}{P_M^*} . \frac{P_N}{P_X} = Tot.R_N$. An increase in the relative price of non-traded goods decreases demand for these non-traded goods and increases demand for traded/imported goods. Thus the consumption of non-tradable goods can be expressed as $C_N = C_N(R_N, k, f; Tot, \delta, g)$, though contrary to the supply equation, there is no doubt about the impact of remittances on demand for goods. Remittances invariably increase demand for traded and non-traded goods by households. If ψ $(1 - \psi)$ is the share of remittances allotted to non-tradable (tradable) consumption, then the equation for private consumption of non-traded goods becomes $C_p = \delta.[(k - f)] + \theta.\psi.\text{Rem} = C_p.(k - f, \text{Rem})$, where Rem represents remittances, or additions to household incomes (Barajas et al. 2011). Therefore, increased remittances affect private consumption positively. We obtain the following equation for non-tradable goods consumption:

$$C_N = C_N(R_N, k, f; Tot, g, \text{Rem}), \tag{10}$$

where $\partial C_N / \partial R_N < 0$, $\partial C_N / \partial k > 0$, $\partial C_N / \partial f < 0$, $\partial C_N / \partial Tot < 0$, $\partial C_N / \partial g > 0$, and $\partial C_N / \partial \text{Rem} > 0$.

Investment in non-tradable goods includes private and public investments. In the NATREX, private investment I_p depends on the Keynes-Tobin's q ratio, or the present value of expected profits divided by the supply price of investment goods P_K. It "is obtained by capitalizing the current observable value of the marginal product of capital $p.MPK(k;u)$ by the current real rate of interest (r)" (Stein and Lim, 1995, p. 104). Accordingly, $q_t = \int_0^T p.MPK(k;u).\exp(-r.t)dt - p.MPK(k;u)/r$, with p indicating the relative price $p = P_X / P_K$.

If a capital/investment good consists of both traded/imported goods for a share m and non-traded goods for a share $1-m$, then $P_K = (P_M)^m \cdot (P_N)^{1-m}$, and $q = [Tot^m / (R_N)^{1-m}].MPK(k;u)/r = q(R_N, k; Tot, u, r)$. We also assume that a public or government investment I_g is not affected by remittances. But it's possible that some amount of incomes earned abroad could be repatriated and used for investment, not only for consumption. Therefore, [$(1-\theta)\cdot(1-m)$] represents the share of remittances granted to investments in non-tradable goods, which contributes to increasing demand for non-tradable goods. Private investments increase by an exogenous component $(1-\theta).\text{Rem}$, and we have:

$$I_N = (1-m).I = (1-m).(I_p + (1-\theta).\text{Rem} + I_g) = I_N(R_N, k; Tot, \text{Rem}, r), \tag{11}$$

such that $\partial I_N / \partial R_N < 0$, $\partial I_N / \partial k > 0$, $\partial I_N / \partial Tot > 0$, $\partial I_N / \partial r < 0$, and $\partial I_N / \partial \text{Rem} > 0$. Overall, demand for non-tradable goods consists of consumption and investment:

$$Q_N^d = C_N(R_N, k, f; Tot, g, \text{Rem}) + I_N(R_N, k; Tot, \text{Rem}, r) \tag{12}$$

3.4. Remittances and Equilibrium in Non-Tradable Goods Markets

The equilibrium condition for the non-tradable goods market is

$$C_N(R_N,k,f;Tot,g,\text{Rem})+I_N(R_N,k;Tot,\text{Rem},r)-Q_N(R_N,k,u)=0 \tag{13}$$

Because the traded goods market is always in equilibrium, Equation (13) implies that the macroeconomic equilibrium condition is satisfied. By solving Equation (13), we obtain R_N, which depends on the capital stock of external debt and exogenous Z, including remittances,

$$R_N(t)=R_N(k(t),f(t),Z(t)) \text{, with } Z=[Tot,r,u,g,\text{Rem}], \tag{14-1}$$

and therefore,

$$R(t)=Tot.[R_N(k(t),f(t),Z(t))]^a=R(k(t),f(t),Z(t)) \tag{14-2}$$

Figure 3 depicts this equilibrium and supports an analysis of the effects of changes in remittances, such as an increase in the steady state situation, as when $df(t)/dt=0$ and $dk(t)/dt=0$. The initial equilibrium is represented at point A. When remittances rise, which means an increase in private absorption, appreciation occurs in the real equilibrium exchange rate ($R_{N1} > R_{N0}$). This influence is a direct effect. In addition, real appreciation on one side and increased demand for tradable goods generated by remittances on the other side deteriorate the trade balance and current accounts. Conversely, remittance inflows have positive impacts on current accounts, because workers' remittances involve a current transfer between residents of different countries. The equation of current accounts (*CA*) then can be written as:

$$CA=B+Ts-r.f=Q_T^s(R_N,k,u)-Q_T^d(R_N,k-f,g,Tot,\text{Rem})+Ts(\text{Rem})-r.f, \tag{15}$$

where *Ts* indicates the current transfers that depend positively on remittances, *B* the trade balance that is the difference between the supply of traded goods Q_T^s and the demand of traded goods Q_T^d; $B=Q_T^s-Q_T^d$; and $\partial Q_T^s/\partial R_N<0$, $\partial Q_T^d/\partial R_N>0$, and $\partial Q_T^d/\partial\text{Rem}>0$. Globally and in the medium- to long-term, negative effects dominate, and the deterioration of the current account increases external debt (*f*), such that it reduces wealth (*k* – *f*) and consumption of non-tradable goods. The relative price of non-tradable goods thus decreases, through an indirect effect.

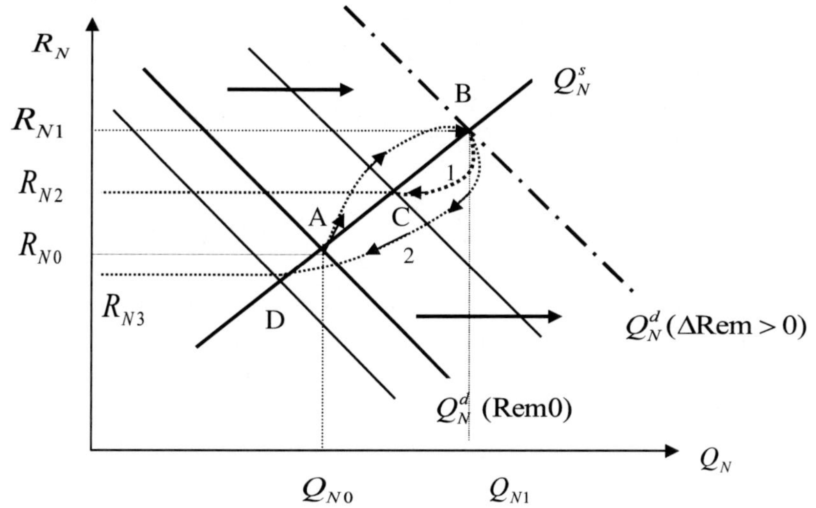

Figure 3. Effects of an increase in remittances on the equilibrium exchange rate.

The final, or long-run, effect depends on whether the direct effect increases R_N by more than the indirect effect depreciates it. In Figure 3, we show that if the direct effect dominates, the equilibrium moves from A to B and finally to C (total effect, trajectory 1). The new equilibrium relative price of non-tradable goods is $R_{N2} > R_{N0}$. If instead the indirect effect dominates, the equilibrium moves from A to D (trajectory 2), as might be observed for a small, very open country. The equilibrium relative price of non-tradable goods becomes $R_{N3} < R_{N0}$.

In the medium-term, we therefore expect a real appreciation of the exchange rate, following a rise of remittances; in the long-term, the effect might be positive or negative, depending on the degree of openness of the economy and the share of remittances dedicated to demand for tradable goods.

4. Panel Evidence

Following Equations 4, 14-1, and 14-2, we can determine the equilibrium real exchange rate in two ways: Estimate the log of R directly or estimate the cointegration relationship for the relative price of non-tradable goods, then deduce the equilibrium value of R (Rey and Bouoiyour, 2005). If $R = Tot.(R_N)^a$, then $(R_N)^a = R/Tot$. That is, we have two possible cointegration vectors, the first for *R* and the second for R_N (or more precisely, $(R_N)^a$, which we denote *Rpn* hereafter). For empirical estimates, *R* is represented by the REER, so to estimate Model 1 for the log of *REER*, we obtain the cointegration vector (x)[85]:

[85] For small open countries in the long-term, we assume the real interest rate is determined by the world real interest rate (real interest rate parity). If this rate is identical for all countries, it cannot be introduced as a determinant of the real exchange rate in the panel cointegration relationship, because this regressor does not vary across individuals or countries.

$$x_{i,t} = \left(\ln REER_{i,t}, \ln Tot_{i,t}, \ln prod_{i,t}, cg\_gdp_{i,t}, rem\_gdp_{i,t}, rem\_gdp * open_{i,t}\right)' \quad (16\text{-}1)$$

In addition, when we consider the equilibrium relative price of non-tradable goods, we note model 2 for the log of *Rpn*. The cointegration vector is

$$x_{i,t} = \left(\ln Rpn_{i,t}, \ln prod_{i,t}, cg\_gdp_{i,t}, rem\_gdp_{i,t}, rem\_gdp * open_{i,t}\right)', \quad (16\text{-}2)$$

where *prod* represents global productivity, *cg_gdp* is the ratio of public consumption to GDP, *rem_gdp* is the remittances-to-GDP ratio, and (*rem_gdp*open*) represents the interaction between the remittances ratio and openness (i.e., the sum of exports and imports divided by GDP). Together, Equations 16-1 and 16-2 reveal that we might retain two alternative measures for remittances. We know that the impact of remittances on the demand for goods depends on whether spending on non-tradable or tradable goods increases. When openness is high, there is a strong probability that remittances increase the demand for tradable goods, deteriorate the trade balance, and negatively affect the real exchange rate, instead of positively, as expected. For each model, we therefore retain three formulations: with only remittances, with remittances and the interaction variable, and with only the interaction variable. With these formulations, we can conduct unit root tests for all the variables.

4.1. Panel Unit Root Tests

We adopt a panel unit root procedure to test the stationarity of the variables. We distinguish two categories of tests in prior literature. The first assumes that cross-sectional errors are independent, whereas the second category accounts for cross-sectional dependence in errors. Because many countries have strong linkages, it may be useful to apply both categories of tests. For the assumption of independence, we apply the tests developed by Levin et al. (2002), Im et al. (2003), and Hadri (2000); for the assumption of dependence, we use the dependent panel unit root tests of Choi (2004), Bai and Ng (2004), Pesaran (2004), and Moon and Perron (2004). Costantini and Lupi (2005) and Hurlin and Mignon (2005) detail most of these tests,[86] so we do not present them here; rather, we focus on an interpretation of their results.

Table 2 contains the results of the panel unit root tests when we assume that the cross-sectional units are independent. The null hypothesis of a unit root is rejected for the REER, the government consumption-to-GDP ratio, and the remittances-to-GDP ratio (10% level); but in all cases, the null hypothesis of stationarity (Hadri's test) is rejected. Therefore, these tests do not recommend rejecting a unit root in the model variables.

However, it may be necessary to relax the independence hypothesis and assume cross-sectional dependence, so we proceeded to test for cross-sectional–correlated panels. As we show in Table 3, for any variable, the null hypothesis of the unit root cannot be rejected for all tests. Some tests do but others do not reject the null hypothesis. Therefore, in line with our

[86] These tests use Matlab software and programs that Hurlin developed (see http://www.univ-orleans.fr/deg/masters/ESA/CH/churlin_E.htm).

previous conclusion, the unit root hypothesis is not rejected, but the stationary hypothesis (Hadri's test) is rejected in all cases. We consider that the variables are not stationary.

Table 2. Independent Panel Unit Root Tests 1986–2011 (individual effects)

	ln REER	**ln Rpn**	**ln Tot**	**ln prod**	**cg_gdp**	**rem_gdp**	**rem*open**
Null: Unit root (assumes common unit-root process)							
Levin, Lin & Chu t*	-3.191** (0.00)	-0.842 (0.20)	0.700 (0.75)	1.158 (0.87)	-3.217** (0.00)	-1.414* (0.08)	-0.881 (0.19)
Null: Unit root (assumes individual unit-root process)							
Im, Pesaran & Shin W-statistic	-3.190** (0.00)	0.028 (0.51)	1.373 (0.91)	5.688 (1.00)	-3.227** (0.00)	-1.376* (0.08)	0.214 (0.58)
ADF - Fisher chi-square	87.48** (0.00)	50.57 (0.37)	43.68 (0.65)	17.39 (0.00)	87.71** (0.00)	57.30 (0.16)	41.44 (0.73)
PP - Fisher chi-square	62.31* (0.08)	39.91 (0.79)	43.34 (0.34)	17.40 (1.00)	97.31** (0.00)	60.09 (0.11)	46.93 (0.52)
Null: No unit root (assumes common unit-root process)							
Hadri Z-statistic	10.22** (0.00)	12.57** (0.00)	14.08** (0.00)	17.76** (0.00)	11.33** (0.00)	8.39** (0.00)	9.86** (0.00)

Notes: The probabilities for the Fisher tests are computed using an asymptotic chi-square distribution. All other tests assume asymptotic normality. Individual effects are the exogenous variables. There were balanced observations for each test. ADF = augmented Dickey–Fuller test; PP = Philipps-Perron. The *p*-values are in parentheses. *Significant at the 10% level. **Significant at the 5% level.

4.2. Panel Cointegration Tests

From Equations 16-1 and 16-2, we determine two expressions for the real exchange rate. Table 3 presents the results when we applied Pedroni's (1999, 2004) panel cointegration test based on pooling, or the "within" dimension (panel tests) for the first four statistics, and the "between" dimension (group tests) for other three statistics. The within-dimension tests take into account common time factors and allow for heterogeneity across countries. The between-dimension tests instead are group mean cointegration tests and allow for heterogeneity in the parameters across countries. The null hypothesis asserts no cointegration. Pedroni's statistics are based on the estimated residuals from the following panel cointegration regressions:

Model 1

$$\ln REER_{i,t} = \alpha_i^1 + \beta_i^1.\ln Tot_{i,t} + \chi_i^1.\ln prod_{i,t} + \delta_i^1.cg\_gdp_{i,t} + \gamma_i^1.rem\_gdp_{i,t} + \ldots$$
$$\ldots + \varphi_i^1.(rem\_gdp * open_{i,t}) + \varepsilon_{i,t}^1 \quad (17\text{-}1)$$

Model 2

$$\ln Rpn_{i,t} = \alpha_i^2 + \chi_i^2.\ln prod_{i,t} + \delta_i^2.cg\_gdp_{i,t} + \gamma_i^2.rem\_gdp_{i,t} + \varphi_i^2.(rem\_gdp * open_{i,t}) + \varepsilon_{i,t}^2 \quad (17\text{-}2)$$

Table 3. Dependent Panel Unit Root Tests: 1986–2011 (individual effects)

Null: Unit root	Statistic	ln REER	ln Rpn	ln Tot	ln prod	cg_gdp	rem_gdp	rem*open
Choi (a)	*Pm*	5.585** (0.00)	2.554** (0.01)	1.594* (0.06)	-1.705 (0.95)	7.828** (0.00)	3.784** (0.00)	2.399** (0.01)
	Z	-4.092** (0.00)	-1.917** (0.03)	0.1756 (0.57)	3.226 (0.99)	-5.651** (0.00)	3.177** (0.00)	-2.012** (0.02)
	L^*	-4.286** (0.00)	-2.030** (0.02)	0.044 (0.52)	3.528 (0.99)	-6.037** (0.00)	-3.281** (0.00)	-2.225** (0.01)
Moon & Perron (b)	t_a^*	-0.007 (0.49)	-4.684** ('0.00)	-0.022 (0.49)	0.1048 (0.54)	-0.072 (0.47)	-0.216 (0.41)	0.195 (0.57)
	t_b^*	-0.321 (0.37)	-18.28** (0.00)	-3.116** (0.00)	19.48 (1.00)	-1.250 (0.12)	-1.332* (0.09)	0.718 (0.76)
Bai & Ng (c)	*PCe_Choi*	-0.258 (0.60)	1.412* (0.08)	0.077 (0.47)	4.451** (0.00)	-1.248 (0.89)	-0.008 (0.50)	0.727 (0.23)
	PCe_MW	45.46 (0.57)	61.83* (0.09)	48.76 (0.44)	91.61** (0.00)	35.76 (0.90)	47.92 (0.48)	55.12 (0.22)
Pesaran (d)	*CIPS p=1*	-2.442** (0.01)	-1.409 (0.88)	-2.221** (0.05)	-2.359** (0.02)	-1.857 (0.35)	-2.119* (0.10)	-2.074 (0.13)
	p=2	-2.046 (0.15)	-1.109 (0.99)	-2.131* (0.09)	-2.149* (0.09)	-1.745 (0.48)	-1.921 (0.27)	-1.960 (0.23)
	p=3	-1.718 (0.53)	-0.677 (0.99)	2.572** (0.02)	-2.331** (0.02)	-1.683 (0.58)	-2.102 (0.11)	-2.034 (0.16)

(a) Lag selection in the augmented Dickey–Fuller/generalized least squares (ADF-GLS) test is determined using the Bayesian information criterion.

(b) t_a^* and t_b^* tests are computed using a quadratic spectral kernel.

(c) *PCe_Choi* is a pooled test standardized statistic on idiosyncratic components (N[0,1] under H0). *PCe_MW* is a pooled tests statistic on idiosyncratic components (x^2 at 2N degrees of freedom under H0).

(d) The *CIPS* test is the mean of individual cross-sectional ADF statistics. The truncated statistics ($CIPS^*$) are not reported because they are always equal to the nontruncated ones. *p* denotes the nearest integer of the mean of the individual lag lengths in ADF tests.

Notes: The *p*-values are in parenthesis. *Significant at the 10% level. **Significant at the 5% level.

In these models, $\hat{\varepsilon}_{it} = \eta_i .\hat{\varepsilon}_{i,t-1} + \mu_{i,t}$ are the residuals from the panel regressions. The null hypothesis (no cointegration) is whether η_i reaches unity. For the six different models, we can reject the no cointegration hypothesis with augmented Dickey-Fuller (ADF) tests but not other tests. The results for the between-dimension statistics (group tests) show that the null hypothesis can always be rejected (at the 1% significance level in three cases, 5% in two cases, and 10% in one case). For the within-dimension statistics (panel tests), the ADF statistics lead to the rejection of no cointegration in five cases. Regardless of the tests, for the model of REER with remittances and the interaction variable, we obtain less conclusive results. However, considering the ADF tests, we admit the existence of a cointegration relationship.

Table 4. Panel Cointegration Test Statistics

		Within-Dimension (panel)				Between-Dimension (group)		
		v	rho	PP	ADF	rho	PP	ADF
Model 1:	(1)	0.31	3.62	1.27	-1.43*	5.74	2.21	-2.06**
Real effective exchange	(2)	0.13	4.41	1.36	-0.69	6.20	2.10	-1.28*
rate	(3)	0.45	3.59	1.27	-1.33*	5.38	2.24	-1.93**
Model 2:	(4)	0.14	1.58	-0.37	-2.25**	3.06	0.34	-2.44***
Relative price of non-	(5)	0.11	3.01	-0.22	-1.82**	4.83	0.38	-2.45***
tradable goods	(6)	0.41	2.03	-0.61	-2.77***	3.83	-0.03	-3.29***

Notes: v is the non-parametric variance ratio statistic; rho is the non-parametric test statistic, analogous to the Phillips and Perron (PP) rho statistic; PP is the non-parametric statistic analogous to the PP t statistic; ADF is the parametric statistic analogous to the augmented Dickey-Fuller statistic. All statistics distributed tend to a standard normal distribution.

***,**, * indicate that the null of no cointegration is rejected at the 1% level, at 5% level and at 10% level. Rejection of the null hypothesis of no cointegration is one-sided. For the variance ratio, at 5% significance, we reject the null hypothesis of no cointegration if $v > 1.645$; for other statistics, at 5% significance, we reject the null hypothesis of no cointegration if statistic < -1.645. For 1% and 10% significance, the critical values are -2.32 and -1.28. Models are with trends; two lags in the ADF tests.

(1) and (4), model with remittances (% GDP).

(2) and (5) model with remittances (% GDP) and interaction variable [remittances (% GDP)*openness].

(3) and (6) model with interaction variable [remittances (% GDP)*openness].

5. Remittances and Real Effective Exchange Rate in the Long-Term

Having established that cointegration relationships exist both for the log of REER and log of *Rpn*, we estimate the parameters among Equations 17-1 and 17-2. The long-term equilibrium relationship can be estimated using panel FMOLS.[87]

The results (see Table 5) are consistent with our theoretical model, insofar as the coefficients of the fundamental variables have the expected signs, except for the terms of trade in column 2.

5.1. Log of REER Estimate

The coefficients of *Tot* are small and insignificant. In contrast, the coefficients obtained for productivity have values between 0.51 and 0.68 and are significant. Thus a 1 percent increase in productivity leads to a long-term increase in the real effective exchange rate of 0.6 percent. This public consumption-to-GDP ratio has the greatest impact on REER, because the coefficients are significant with values between 4.3 and 5.0. Barajas et al. (2011) also obtain relatively high coefficients for this ratio, with values between 2 and 3.6, according to the

[87] "Dynamic least squares has the disadvantage that it requires the inclusion of lead differences and lagged differences in the regression, which further reduces degrees of freedom in estimation and handicaps prediction" (Philipps, 2006, p. 2). Because we have several independent variables and limited time observations, we chose FMOLS estimation.

specifications (fundamentals) of the model. The positive impact of remittances is consistent with the expected direct effect. However, the coefficients of the remittances-to-GDP ratio are not significant, whereas the interaction variable is negative and significant. This latter result might be explained, according to our model, by the recognition that when more economies are open, deterioration in the trade balance will be high, as a result of remittance inflows, which require a long-term, real depreciation of the currency to restore equilibrium to current accounts and stabilize external debt.

Table 5. Panel Cointegration Relationships

Model	Log of Real Effective Exchange Rate			Log of Relative Price of Non-Tradable Goods		
Variables	(1)	(2)	(3)	(4)	(5)	(6)
ln Tot	0.007 (-0.50)	-0.196 (-0.20)	0.088 (1.35)			
ln prod	0.516** (6.08)	0.616** (8.11)	0.680** (8.06)	0.366 (-0.36)	0.307 (0.76)	0.262 (0.96)
Cg_gdp	4.327** (6.05)	5.223** (6.80)	5.084** (6.57)	4.902** (5.61)	3.718** (5.41)	4.933** (6.54)
Rem_gdp	0.035 (-1.50)	1.301 (1.50)		0.292* (-1.89)	1.417* (1.89)	
Rem_gdp * Open		-2.127** (-3.54)	-0.505** (-4.56)		-1.97** (-3.34)	0.040 (-1.55)
Observations	624	624	624	624	624	624

Notes: Common time dummies are included in (1) and (4). The t-statistics are in parentheses. *Significant at the 10% level. **Significant at the 5% level.

5.2. Log of Relative Price of Non-Tradable Goods Estimate

Estimates of the relative price of non-tradable goods confirm the previous results. The impact of productivity is always positive, but the coefficients are smaller than in the REER model, with values around 0.3, and not significant. The public consumption variable has a positive effect with values of coefficients between 3.7 and 4.9. Finally, the coefficients of remittances have the expected signs and are significant. We found, for Model (5), a negative effect of the interaction variable.

CONCLUSION

We propose a modified version of a small country NATREX model that takes into account the role of remittances. If remittance inflows lead to a real appreciation of the exchange rate, through demand of non-traded goods, the degree of openness of economies may have an effect on this link. We estimate two models, one for the REER and the other for the relative price of non-traded goods, for a group of 24 emerging and small open economies over the period from 1986 to 2011. Using panel cointegration methods, we obtained results consistent with the findings of our theoretical predictions. According to the estimates, we can say that, in the long run:

- A rise in productivity leads to an appreciation of the exchange rate.
- A rise of absorption that comes from the public sector or private income transfers (remittances) produces a real appreciation of the exchange rate. These results are coherent with Barajas et al.'s (2011) conclusions for a group of low-income countries and a group of low and lower middle-income countries, and with Combes et al.'s (2011) findings that private capital inflows are associated with REER appreciation.
- When we take the degree of openness of economies into account, remittances associated with higher openness lead to a real depreciation of the exchange rate. We explain this result according to the deterioration of the trade balance and current accounts, which follows from higher demand in tradable goods and necessitates, in the long term, a decrease in the value of the currency to restore the external equilibrium and stabilize the external debt (Rey, 2009).

However, it is not clear whether the Dutch disease phenomenon arises; to prove its presence, we would need to focus, as Lartey et al. (2012) do, on the impact of remittances on resource transfers between the traded goods sector and non-tradable sectors, to measure the effects of these transfers on the relative production of the two sectors. Instead, our results provide a different confirmation. If we are interested in determining the equilibrium real exchange rates for emerging and/or small open economies, it is important to reconsider standard models and integrate remittances among their fundamental determinants.

APPENDIX 1. LIST OF COUNTRIES

Our panel consists of 24 countries over 26 years (1986–2011): Algeria, Argentina, Brazil, China, Denmark, Hong Kong, Hungary, Iceland, Indonesia, Israel, Jordan, Kenya, Korea, Malaysia, Morocco, Norway, Pakistan, Philippines, Poland, India, Sweden, Thailand, Tunisia, and Turkey.

APPENDIX 2. OTHER DATA SOURCES

- Government consumption, expressed as a percentage of GDP, comes from the IFS CD-ROM.
- For productivity, the main data source is the UNIDO World Productivity Database. When data are missing, we used GDP per capita from Penn World Tables to complete the panel.
- We built the terms of trade on the basis of import unit values (total import volume divided by total value) and export unit values, when available in the IFS data. If these data were missing, we built a proxy for terms of trade, as a geometric average of world commodity prices, weighted by commodity trade shares. This proxy is appropriate for our study, because most countries in our panel are emerging and small open countries that can be considered price takers. World commodity prices come from the World Economic Outlook database; trade shares were built from UN COMTRADE data for exports and imports of disaggregated goods.

REFERENCES

Acosta, P., Baerg, N. R. & Mandelman, F. (2009). "Financial Development, Remittances, and Real Exchange Rate Appreciation," *Economic Review, 1*, Federal Reserve Bank of Atlanta, 1-12.

Allen, P. R. (1995). "The Economic and Policy Implications of the NATREX Approach", in *Fundamental Determination of Exchange Rates*, J.L. Stein and P.R. Allen (eds.), Clarendon Press, Oxford.

Amuedo-Dorantes, C. & Pozo, S. (2004). "Workers' Remittances and the Real Exchange Rate: A Paradox of Gifts," *World Development, 32* (8), 1407-17.

Artus, J. (1977). "*Methods of Assessing the Long-Run Equilibrium Value of an Exchange Rate*", IMF Working Paper 77/124.

Bai, J. & Ng, S. (2004). "A PANIC Attack on Unit Roots and Cointegration", *Econometrica, 72*(4), 1127-1177.

Barajas, A., Chami, R., Hakura, D. & Montiel, P. (2011). "Workers' Remittances and the Equilibrium Real Exchange Rate: Theory and Evidence", *Journal of the Latin American and Caribbean Economic Association, 11* (2).

Cacerès, L. R. & Saca, N. N. (2006). "*What Do Remittances Do? Analyzing the Private Remittance Transmission Mechanism in El Salvador*", IMF Working paper WP/06/250

Chami, R., Barajas, A., Cosimano, T., Fullenkamp, C., Gapen, M. & Montiel, P. (2008). "*Macroeconomic Consequences of Remittances*", IMF Occasional Paper.

Choi, I. (2004). "Unit Root Tests Cross-Sectionally Correlated Panels," in Saikkonnen, P. and I. Choi (eds.), *Econometric Theory and Practice: Frontiers of Analysis and Applied Research, Essays in Honor of Peter C.B. Phillips*, Cambridge University Press, Cambridge.

Clark, P. et R. MacDonald, (1999). "Exchange Rates and Economic Fundamentals: A Methodological Comparison of BEERs and FEERs", in R. Mac Donald and J. L. Stein (eds.) *Equilibrium Exchange Rates*, Kluwer Academic.

Combes, J. L., Kinda, T. & Plane, P. (2011). "*Capital Flows, Exchange Rate Flexibility, and the Real Exchange Rate*", IMF Working Paper, *11/9*.

Costantini, M. & Lupi, C. (2005). "Stochastic Convergence among European Economies", *Economics Bulletin, 3*(38), 1-17.

Driver, R. & Westaway, P. (2003). "Concepts of Equilibrium Exchange Rates", *Bank of England*, Working Paper, June.

Edwards, S. (1989). *Real Exchange Rates, Devaluation and Adjustment: Exchange Rate Policy in Developing Countries*, MIT Press, Cambridge, MA.

Hadri, K. (2000). "Testing for Stationarity in Heterogeneous Panel Data," *Econometrics Journal, 3*, 148–161.

Hagen-Zanker, J. & Siegel, M. (2007). "*The Determinants of Remittances: A Review of the Literature*", Working Paper 07/03, Maastricht Graduate School of Governance, Maastricht University.

Hurlin, C. & Mignon, V. (2005). "Une Synthèse des Tests de Racine Unitaire sur Données de Panel", *Economie et Prévision*, 169-171, 251-295.

Im, K. S., Pesaran, M. H. & Shin, Y. (2003). "Testing for Unit Roots in Heterogeneous Panels," *Journal of Econometrics, 115*, 53–74.

Lartey, E., Mandelman, F. S & Acosta, P. A. (2012). "Remittances, Exchange Rate Regimes, and the Dutch Disease: A Panel Data Analysis," *Review of International Economics, 20* (2), 277-395.

Levin, A., Lin, C. F. & Chu, C. (2002). "Unit Root Tests in Panel Data: Asymptotic and Finite-Sample Properties," *Journal of Econometrics, 108*, 1–24.

Lopez, H., Molina, L. & Bussolo, M. (2007), "Remittances and the Real Exchange Rate," World Bank Policy Research Working Paper 4213 (April).

MacDonald, R. (2000). *Concepts to Calculate Equilibrium Exchange Rates: An Overview*, Discussion paper 3/00, Economic Research Group of the Deutsche Bundesbank.

Moon, H. & Perron, B. (2004). "Testing for a Unit Root in Panels with Dynamic Factors", *Journal of Econometrics, 122*, 81-126.

Multilateral Investment Fund (2004). *Sending Money Home: Remittance to Latin America and the Caribbean,* Inter-American Development Bank, Washington, DC.

Nurkse, R. (1944). *International Currency Experience: Lessons of Interwar the Period*, League of Nations, Geneva.

Pedroni, P. (1999). "Critical Values for Cointegration Tests in Heterogeneous Samples with Multiple Regressors," *Oxford Bulletin of Economics and Statistics*, Special Issue, 653-70.

Pedroni, P. (2004). "Panel Cointegration: Asymptotic and Finite Sample Properties of Pooled Time Series Tests with an Application to the PPP Hypothesis", *Econometric Theory, 20*, 597-625.

Pesaran, M. H. (2004). "*General Diagnostic Tests for Cross-Section Dependence in Panels*", Cambridge Working, Papers in Economics No. 435, University of Cambridge, and CESifo Working Paper Series No. 1229.

Phillips, P. C. B. (2006). "Optimal Estimation of Cointegrated Systems with Irrelevant Instruments", Cowles Foundation Discussion Paper n°1547, Yale University.

Rapoport, H. & Docquier, F. (2006). "The Economics of Migrants' Remittances", in *Handbook of the Economics of Giving, Altruism and Reciprocity,* Chapter 17, S.-C. Kolm, and J. Mercier Ythier (eds.), vol. 2, 1135–1198, Elsevier-North Holland.

Rey, S. & Bouoiyour, J. (2005). "Exchange Rate Regime, Real Exchange Rate, Trade Flows and Foreign Direct Investments: Morocco", *African Development Review, 17* (2), 302-334.

Rey, S. (2009). " L'Apport du Natrex à La Modélisation des Taux de Change D'Équilibre : Théorie et Application au Dollar Canadien," *L'Actualité Economique, Revue d'Analyse Economique, 85* (2), 131-181.

Saadi-Sedik, T. & Petri, M. (2006). "*To Smooth or Not to Smooth: The Impact of Grants and Remittances on the Equilibrium Real Exchange Rate in Jordan*," IMF Working paper WP/06/257.

Stein, J. L. (1994). "The Natural Real Exchange Rate of the United States Dollar and Determinants of Capital Flows", in J. Williamson (ed.), *Equilibrium Exchanges Rates*, Institute for International Economics, Washington, DC.

Stein, J. L. (2006). *Stochastic Optimal Control, International Finance, and Debt Crisis*, Oxford University Press, New York.

Stein, J. L. & Lim, G. C. (1995). "The Dynamics of the Real Exchange Rate and Current Account in a Small Open Economy: Australia", in *Fundamental Determination of Exchange Rates*, J.L. Stein and P.R. Allen (eds.), Clarendon Press, Oxford.

Stein, J. L. & Paladino, G. (2001). "Exchange Rate Misalignments and Crisis", *Jahrbusch für Wirstschafts-wissenschaften*, *52*, 111-151.

Williamson, J. (1994). "Estimates of FEERs", in J. Williamson (ed.), *Equilibrium Exchanges Rates*, Institute for International Economics, Washington, DC.

World Bank, (2006). *The Development Impact of Workers' Remittances in Latin America*, Vol. *2*, Detailed Findings, Report No. 37026 (Washington).

In: Exchange Rates in Developed and Emerging Markets
Editor: Mohsen Bahmani-Oskooee
ISBN: 978-1-62808-164-0

Chapter 12

THE RIAL-DOLLAR RATE: DOES IT REVERT TO ITS MEAN?

Mohsen Bahmani-Oskooee[1,*] and Sahar Bahmani[2]
[1]Center for Research on International Economics, Department of Economics, University of Wisconsin-Milwaukee, Milwaukee, WI, US
[2]Department of Economics, University of Wisconsin-Parkside, Kenosha, WI, US

ABSTRACT

Since the Islamic Revolution in 1979, the Iranian rial has depreciated from 70 rials per dollar to as low as almost 12500 rial per dollar before recent sanctions. Since sanctions, the dollar has jumped to almost 30000 rial per dollar. Clearly, dollar appreciation has fueled inflation in Iran where the consumer price index has steadily increased from 0.89 in 1979 to 340.3 in October 2012. The U.S. price index, on the other hand, has increased from 35.00 to only 118.5 during the same period. Have these three variables, i.e., the nominal rial-dollar rate, Iranian CPI and the U.S. CPI followed the path prescribed by the well-known Purchasing Power Parity theory? The main purpose of this chapter is to answer this question.

I. INTRODUCTION

Since its introduction, Iranian rial continuously has lost its value against a reserve currency, the U.S. dollar. On May 1933, the official rate was increased from 11.20 rials to 16.35 rials. The second devaluation took place in October 1941 when the rate was moved to 35.25 rials per dollar and again in January 1, 1942 to 35.50 rials per dollar. Due to political turmoil and ousting of Premier Dr. Mossadegh in 1953, a black market was developed and the exchange rate system went through several changes. Finally, in 1955 Iran introduced eight different exchange rates which ranged from the basic rate of 32.5 to 85.00 rials per dollar. Due to black market

* Corresponding author: Email: bahmani@uwm.edu.

activities, in 1957 Iran decided to abolish the basic rate and introduced a single rate of 75.00 rials per dollar.[88]

The 75.00 rial per dollar with slight variation prevailed during 1960s and 1970s until 1979 when the Islamic Revolution coupled by the Iran-Iraq war caused huge outflow of capital from Iran and again a black market for foreign exchange developed when the black market rate deviated from the official rate and reached 4000 rials per dollar in early 1983. One smart move by the Central Bank of Iran that takes palace once in a while is unification policy. The black market rate in early 1983 was adopted as the official rate. The official rate which was almost the same as the free market rate reached close to 10000 rials per dollar in early 2000 and stayed within 10000-12000 during 2000-2011. However, in July 2012 when economic sanctions led by the U.S. became effective, there was a sharp spark in the rate to close to 38000 rials per dollar. As of writing of this chapter, the free market rate stands at about 30000 rial per dollar.

The first question to answer is why historically rial keeps losing its value over time? The simple answer dictated by economic theory is nothing but high rate of inflation in Iran. The Consumer Price Index that stood at 0.895 in January 1979, took a value of 343.3 in October 2012. The main reason for almost a 384 fold increase in the Iranian CPI must be nothing but abnormal increase in the money supply. Figure 1 which depicts the index of M2 money supply and the CPI supports our conjecture.

The second question to ask is has the movement in the rial-dollar exchange rate followed the path prescribed by the Purchasing Power Theory? This is the question we like to answer in this chapter. To this end, we introduce the theory and the methods of testing it in Section II. We then present the results in Section III with a summary in Section IV.

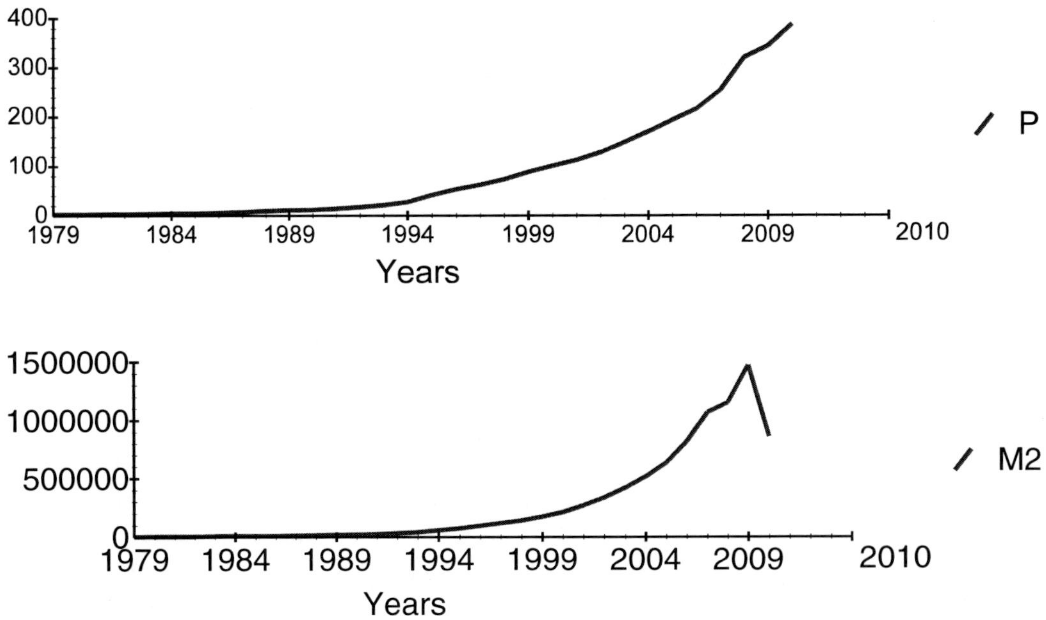

Figure 1. Plot of the Price Level (P) and Money Supply (M2) in Iran.

[88] For more details see Bahmani-Oskooee (2005).

II. THE PURCHASING POWER PARITY (PPP) AND TESTING METHOD

Even though there is neither economic relation nor political relation between Iran and the U.S., still the U.S. dollar is considered the best asset and dominates almost all international transactions between Iran and other countries. Thus, we discuss the PPP using the rial-dollar rate denoted by EX and defined as number of rials per dollar; the price level in Iran (P) and in the U.S. (P*). The PPP theory then asserts that in the long run, converted to the same currency, the two price levels must be equal, i.e., P=EX .P* or

$$EX = \frac{P}{P^*} \tag{1}$$

Or alternatively,

$$\hat{EX} = \hat{P} - \hat{P}^* \tag{2}$$

where a hat above each variable indicates the percentage change in that variable. Intuitively what equation (2) states is that a currency depreciates over time at the rate of inflation differentials. Therefore, if CPI in Iran has moved from 0.895 in January 1979 to 343.3 in October 2012 and the U.S. Consumer Price Index from 35 to 118 during the same period, the exchange rate that stood at 89 rials per dollar should be about 34000 rials per dollar. Indeed the current black market rate has been oscillating in this neighborhood as of writing of this chapter whereas the official free market rate reported by Iran to the International Monetary Fund stands at 12260 rials per dollar in October 2012. Thus, our preliminary inspection of the data reveals that the PPP is supported when we consider the black market exchange rate.[89] This indeed supports Bahmani-Oskooee (1993) who used the official and the black market exchange rate as well as regression analysis to show that the PPP holds only when the black market exchange rate is used. Quarterly data were used over the 1973I-1986II period.[90]

In this chapter we adopt more recent advances in econometrics to test the PPP. Our approach is based on Pesaran *et al.*'s (2001) bounds testing approach to cointegration and error-correction modeling which does not require pre-unit root testing. We write equation (1) in log-linear form as in (3):

$$LnEX_t = a + bLn(\frac{P}{P^*})_t + e_t \tag{3}$$

In testing the PPP we not only must establish that the two variables, i.e., the nominal exchange rate and the relative prices are cointegrated, but also the estimate of long-run coefficient *b* is unity. When Engle-Granger (1987) method was introduced, researchers

[89] For some other studies that have tested the PPP using the black market exchange rate see Phylaktis and Kassimatis (1994), El-Sakka and McNabb (1994), Sanchez-Fung (1999), Kargbo (2003), Chortareas and Kapetanios (2004), and Bahmani-Oskooee and Goswami (2005).

[90] For a review article see Bahmani-Oskooee and Hegerty (2010a).

applied that technique to (3) by showing that while Ln EX and $Ln(\frac{P}{P^*})$ are non-stationary, the residuals in (3) are stationary. Alternatively, (3) is specified in an error-correction format as in equation (4):

$$\Delta LnEX_t = a_i + \sum_{j=1}^{n1} b_j \Delta LnEX_{t-j} + \sum_{j=0}^{n2} c_j \ln \Delta Ln(\frac{P}{P^*})_{t-j} + d\varepsilon_{t-1} + \nu_t \tag{4}$$

and it is shown that if the exchange rate and relative prices are to converge toward their long-run equilibrium values, an estimate of d must be negative and significant. As the two variables adjust, we expect the gap between the left hand-side and the right hand-side of (3) to decline.

One requirement of Engle-Granger (1987) method is that the two variables must be integrated of the same order. In case one variable is integrated of order one, I(1) and the other I(2), the technique couldn't be applied. Pesaran *et al.* (2001) solve this problem by introducing the bounds testing approach. According to their approach we must solve (3) for e_t and lag the solution by one period. We have:

$$e_{t-1} = LnEX_{t-1} - a - bLn(\frac{P}{P^*})_{t-1} \tag{5}$$

We then substitute (5) into (4) and arrive at:

$$\Delta LnEX_t = a_i + \sum_{j=1}^{n1} b_j \Delta LnEX_{t-j} + \sum_{j=0}^{n2} c_j \ln \Delta Ln(\frac{P}{P^*})_{t-j} + \theta_1 LnEX_{t-1} + \theta_2 Ln(\frac{P}{P^*})_{t-1} + \nu_t \tag{6}$$

Equation (6) is an error-correction model in which we have replaced the lagged error term by the linear combination of lagged level variables and is the ultimate model to establish cointegration between the exchange rate and relative prices and test the PPP.

To establish cointegration, Pesaran *et al.* (2001) propose to test joint significance of lagged level variables by using the familiar F test. However, depending on the degree of integration of the variables, they show that the F test has new critical values that they tabulate. By assuming all variables in a given model to be I(1), they provide an upper bound critical value and by assuming all variables to be I(0), they provide a lower bound critical value. They show that the upper bound critical value could still be used even if some variables are I(1) and some I(0), ruling out pre unit-root testing.[91] Once cointegration is established, we derive the long-run effects of relative prices on the exchange rate by normalizing θ_2 on θ_1. For PPP to hold, this normalized coefficient must be equal to one.[92]

Finally, even if we establish joint significance of the two variables in (6), it is not clear if the adjustment will be toward long-run equilibrium values. To establish this, an error-correction term, ECM_{t-1} is constructed using the normalized long-run coefficient estimate and equation (1). Then the linear combination of lagged level variables is replaced by ECM_{t-1} and

[91] On the assumption that macro variables are either I(1) or I(0).

[92] For details of normalization see Bahmani-Oskooee and Tanku (2007).

the model is re-estimated one more time at the same lags. If variables are to adjust toward their long run equilibrium values, ECM_{t-1} must carry a significantly negative coefficient.[93]

III. The Results

We are now in a position to estimate equation (6) and report the results. Concentraing on post-revolutionary period of 1979, monthly black market exchange rate during the period January 1979- December 2003 is available from Bahmani-Oskooee (2005). Thus, we first estimate (6) for this restricted time period. We impose a maximum of 12 lags on each first differenced variable and use Akike's Information Criterion to select the optimum number of lags

We then carry out the F test at optimum lags. The results are as follows:

$$\underset{(60.8)}{LnEX_t = 9.45} + \underset{(13.6)}{0.965}\, Ln(P/P^*)_t \qquad F = 6.7 \qquad \text{Coefficient of } ECM_{t-1} = \underset{(2.86)}{-0.054}$$

Given the upper bound critical value of the F-test at 4.79, clearly our calculated F statistic is highly significant supporting cointegration between the exchange rate and relative prices.[94]

The normalized coefficient of 0.965 is not only close to one but also highly significant, supporting the PPP.[95] Finally, as can be seen, the ECM_{t-1} carries a highly significant coefficient, implying that the two variables do adjust toward their long-run equilibrium value and 5% of the adjustment takes place within one month since data are monthly.

Beyond 2003, although the black market exchange rate has been close to official rate, no data are available. However, we were able to get the free market rate from the International Financial Statistics of the IMF till December 2011. Our initial inspection of the data, especially in 2011 reflects the fact that the free market rate reported by the IMF is not even close to the black market rate. Thus, a priori we suspect some weakness in the PPP if the error-correction model (6) is estimated for the whole period of 1979-2011. The results are as follows

$$\underset{(40.2)}{LnEX_t = 9.05} + \underset{(4.68)}{0.685}\, Ln(P/P^*)_t \qquad F = 5.72 \qquad \text{Coefficient of } ECM_{t-1} = \underset{(2.03)}{-0.02}$$

Although cointegration is supported by the F test, the normalized coefficient of 0.685 is far less than one, implying strong weakness in the PPP. Another implication of these results is that the free market exchange rate that was kept too close to the official rate was not sustainable in the long run. Eventually, the rate had to be allowed to adjust and dollar to move up. Indeed, the coefficient attached to ECM_{t-1} for this period reflects very slow adjustment of the exchange rate to relative prices at 2% per month.

---

[93] Example of others who have applied the bounds testing method to test the PPP includes Coe and Serletis (2002) and Bahmani-Oskooee and Hegerty (2010b).

[94] The critical value is at the 10% level of significance and comes from Pesaran *et al.* (2001, Table C1, Case III, p.300).

[95] Note that the number inside the parenthesis under each coefficient is the absolute value of the t-ratio.

Table 1. The Results of the ADF Test

Sample Period: 1979M1-2003M12			
Variable	**Status of Trend**	**ADF (Lags)**	**Critical Value**
REX	No Trend	ADF(12) = -3.5667	-2.8712
LnREX	No Trend	ADF (1) = -3.7606	-2.8712
REX	With Trend	ADF(12) = -3.4346	-3.4269
LnREX	With Trend	ADF (1) = -3.5266	-3.4269
Sample Period: 1979M1-2011M12			
REX	No Trend	ADF(11) = -2.0859	-2.8693
LnREX	No Trend	ADF (1) = -1.3136	-2.8693
REX	With Trend	ADF(11) = -3.1540	-3.4233
LnREX	With Trend	ADF (1) = -2.8584	-2.4233

An alternative way of testing the PPP is to go back to equation (1) and re-write it as $P^*.EX/P = 1$ which implies that the real exchange rate must be stationary. Thus, we test to see if the real rate has unit root. The common test used here is the ADF test. Again, we minimize the AIC criterion to select the optimum lags in the ADF test. We apply the test to the level as well as the log of the real exchange rate (REX) for the first period as well as for the whole period and summarize the results in Table 1.

It is clear from Table 1 that our calculated ADF statistic during the first period is less than its critical value in all four cases, signifying lack of a unit root in the real exchange rate or support for the PPP. This is not the case in the second period. These findings complement our findings using the bounds testing method.[96]

The standard ADF test that is used to justify mean reverting properties of real exchange rates have been criticized on the ground that it assumes the exchange rate movements is in a linear fashion. Recently, however, Kapetanios, Shin and Snell (2003) have modified the standard ADF test by incorporating non-linearity in movement of a time-series variable. In previous studies when this test (known as KSS test) is applied to test PPP, the mean reverting properties of the real exchange rates are revealed in more countries compared to the standard ADF test. We wonder if the real rial-dollar exchange rate is subject to a non-linear movement too[97]

The non-linear unit-root test introduced by Kapetanios, Shin and Snell (2003) still assumes the null to be the unit root, but the alternative is non-linear stationary smooth transition autoregressive (STAR) process. It is based on the following exponential smooth transition autoregressive (ESTAR) specification:

$$\Delta REX_t = \lambda REX_{t-1}[1 - \exp(-\theta REX_{t-1}^2)] + \mu_t \tag{7}$$

[96] Example of other studies that have used the ADF test to validate the PPP are: Layton and Stark (1990); Corbae and Ouliaris (1988, 1991), Taylor (1988), and Taylor, Peel and Sarno (2001).

[97] Examples of studies that apply non-linear unit root test are: Michael et al. (1997), Baum et al. (2001), Parsley and Popper (2001), Taylor (2001); Taylor, Peel and Sarno (2001), Peel and Venetis (2003), Chortareas and Kapetanios (2004), and Bahmani-Oskooee and Gelan (2006).

where m_t is an error term with usual properties. In this specification, the null of unit root, i.e., $\theta = 0$ is tested against the alternative of $\theta > 0$. Since λ in (7) is not identifiable under the null, Kapetanios, Shin and Snell (2003) use a first-order Taylor series approximation and arrive at :

$$\Delta REX_t = \phi REX_{t-1}^3 + \omega_t \tag{8}$$

Finally, they augment (8) by several lagged value of the dependent variable to make the residuals white noise as in (9):

$$\Delta REX_t = \phi REX_{t-1}^3 + \sum_{k=1}^{n} \rho_k \Delta REX_{t-k} + \omega_t \tag{9}$$

Clearly equation (9) is similar to the standard ADF test with a difference that the lagged level of our variable of concern is raised to power three rather than one. In this set up, the null of unit root, i.e., $\emptyset = 0$ is tested against the alternative of $\emptyset < 0$ by familiar *t* ratio obtained for $\emptyset$. However, the *t* ratio of the new test has a new distribution for which the critical values are tabulated by Kapetanios *et al.* (2003). Since this *t* ratio is for a non-linear model as outlined by (9), we shall denote it by ADF_{NL}. Note that the number of augmentations *n* is selected using the general-to-specific procedure as in Bahmani-Oskooee *et al.* (2007). The maximum number for n was set to be 24, mostly because of the data being monthly, and insignificant augmentation terms were excluded. An ADF_{NL}= 4.4492 statistic was obtained which compared to the critical value of -2.66 from Kapetanios et al. (2003) does not reject the null of non-stationarity which implies failure of the PPP. The result was no different when a trend was included in the regression and when log of the real exchange rate was used.

IV. Summary and Conclusion

Since the Islamic Revolution in 1979, Iranian rial has been under pressure and has lost its value due to capital flight. The free market rial-dollar rate has gradually moved from 70 rials per dollar to 38000 rials per dollar as of writing of this chapter.[98] While most of the pressure in late 2011 and 2012 is attributed to economic sanctions by the U.S. and western countries, inflation in Iran is the main source during last three decades.

The main purpose of this chapter is to establish the link between the rial-dollar rate and inflation differential between Iran and the U.S., following the purchasing power parity theory. The relation was almost exact when the available black market exchange rate was used during 1979-2003. However, when free market exchange rate from the International Monetary Fund was added to extend the sample till October 2011, we noticed some imperfection. This is, perhaps, due to intervention by the Central Bank of Iran to artificially keep the value of the dollar down to control inflation.

[98] February 6, 2013.

REFERENCES

Bahmani-Oskooee, M. (1993). "Black Market Exchange Rates vs. Official Exchange Rates in Testing PPP: An Examination of the Iranian Rial," *Applied Economics*, Vol. *25*, 465-472.

Bahmani-Oskooee, M. (2005). "History of the Rial and Foreign Exchange Policy in Iran", *Iranian Economic Review*, Vol. *10*, 1-20.

Bahmani-Oskooee, M. & Gelan, A. (2006). "Testing the PPP in the STAR Framework: Evidence from Africa", *Economics Bulletin*, Vol. *6*, 1-7.

Bahmani-Oskooee, Mohsen & Goswami, Gour G. (2005b). "Black Market Exchange Rates and Purchasing Power Parity in Emerging Economies," *Emerging Markets Finance and Trade*, *41*(3), 37-52.

Bahmani-Oskooee, M. & Tanku, A. (2008). "The Black Market Exchange Rate vs. the Official Rate in Testing PPP: Which Rate Fosters the Adjustment Process", *Economics Letters*, 40-43.

Bahmani-Oskooee, M. & Hegerty, S. (2010). "Purchasing Power Parity in Less-Developed and Transition Economies: A Review Article", *Journal of Economic Surveys*, Vol. *23* (2009), 617-658.

Bahmani-Oskooee, M. & Hegerty, S. (2010). "Bounds Testing Methods and PPP: Evidence from 123 Countries", *Applied Economics Letters*, Vol. *17*, 1335-1340.

Bahmani-Oskooee, M., Kutan, A. & Zhou, S. (2007). "Testing the PPP in the STAR Framework", *Economcis Letters*, Vol. *94*, 104-110.

Baum, C. F., Barkoulas, J. T. & Caglayan, M. (2001). "Nonlinear Adjustment to Purchasing Power Parity in the Post-Bretton Woods Era", *Journal of International Money and Finance*, Vol. *20*, Issue 3, 379–399.

Chortareas, G. & Kapetanios, G. (2004). "The Yen Real Exchange Rate may be Stationary after all: Evidence from Non-linear Unit-root Tests", *Oxford Bulletin of Economics and Statistics*, Vol. *66*, Issue 1, 113-131.

Coe, Patrick J. & Apostolos Serletis (2002). "Bounds Tests of the Theory of Purchasing Power Parity," *Journal of Banking and Finance*, *26*(1), 179-99.

Corbae, Dean & Sam Ouliaris (1988). "Cointegration and Tests of Purchasing Power Parity", *The Review of Economics and Statistics*, Vol. *70*, 508-511.

Engle, R. F. & Granger, C. W. J. (1987). "Co-integration and Error-Correction: Representation, Estimation and Testing," *Econometrica*, *55*, 1251-1276.

El-Sakka, M. I. T. & McNabb, R. (1994). "Cointegration and Efficiency of the Black Market for Foreign Exchange: A PPP Test for Egypt," *Economic Notes*, *23*(3), 473-80.

Kapetanios, G., Shin, Y. & Snell, A. (2003). Testing for a unit root in the nonlinear STAR framework, *Journal of Econometrics*, *112*, 359-379.

Kargbo, Joseph M. (2003a). "Cointegration Tests of Purchasing Power Parity in Africa," *World Development*, *31*(10), 1673-85.

Layton, Allan P. & Stark, Jonathan P. (1990). "Co-integration as an empirical Test of Purchasing Power Parity", *Journal of Macroeconomics*, Vol. *12*, 125-136.

Michael, P., Nobay, A. R. & Peel, D. A. (1997). "Transaction Costs and Nonlinear Adjustment in Real Exchange Rates: An Empirical Investigation", *Journal of Political Economy*, Vol. *105*, Issue 4, 862–879.

Parsley, D. C. & Popper, H. A. (2001). "Official Exchange Rate Arrangements and Real Exchange Rate Behavior", *Journal of Money, Credit and Banking*, Vol. *33*, Issue 4, 976–993.

Peel, D. A. & Venetis, I. A. (2003). "Purchasing Power Parity over Two Centuries: Trends and Nonlinearity", *Applied Economics*, Vol. *35*, 609-617.

Pesaran, M. H., Shin, Y. & Smith, R. J. (2001). "Bound Testing Approaches to the Analysis of Level Relationship," *Journal of Applied Econometrics*, *16*, 289-326.

Phylaktis, Kate & Yiannis Kassimatis (1994), "Does the Real Exchange Rate Follow a Random Walk? The Pacific Basin Perspective," *Journal of International Money and Finance*, *13*(4), 476-95.

Sanchez-Fung, Jose R. (1999). "Efficiency of the Black Market for Foreign Exchange and PPP: The Case of the Dominican Republic," *Applied Economics Letters*, *6*(3), 173-76.

Taylor, Mark, P. (1988). "An Empirical Examination of Long-Run Purchasing Power Parity Using Cointegration Techniques", *Applied Economics*, Vol. *20*, 1369-1381.

Taylor, A. M. (2001). "Potential pitfalls for the PPP Puzzle? Sampling and specification biases in mean-reversion tests of the Law of One Price", *Econometrica,* Vol. *69*, Issue 2, 473–498.

Taylor, M. P., Peel, D. A. & Sarno, L. (2001). "Nonlinear mean-Reversion in real exchange rates: Toward a solution to the Purchasing Power Parity puzzles", *International Economics Review*, Vol. *42*, Issue 4, 1015–1042.

INDEX

A

B

C

D

G

H

I

J

P

Q

R

S

T